EXAM✓

T0073277

CompTIA®
Data+
DA0-001

Akhil Behl
Siva G. Subramanian

Pearson

CompTIA® Data+ DA0-001 Exam Cram

Copyright © 2023 by Pearson Education, Inc.

ISBN-13: 978-0-13-763729-4

ISBN-10: 0-13-763729-2

Library of Congress Cataloging-in-Publication Data: 2022916122

1 2022

Trademarks

Warning and Disclaimer

Special Sales

For information about buying this title in bulk quantities, or for special sales opportunities (which may include electronic versions; custom cover designs; and content particular to your business, training goals, marketing focus, or branding interests), please contact our corporate sales department at corpsales@pearsoned.com or (800) 382-3419.

For government sales inquiries, please contact governmentsales@pearsoned.com.

For questions about sales outside the U.S., please contact intlcs@pearson.com.

Editor-in-Chief
Mark Taub

Director, ITP Product Management
Brett Bartow

Executive Editor
Nancy Davis

Development Editor
Christopher A. Cleveland

Managing Editor
Sandra Schroeder

Project Editor
Mandie Frank

Copy Editor
Kitty Wilson

Indexer
Erika Millen

Proofreader
Donna Mulder

Technical Editor
Lewis Heuermann

Publishing Coordinator
Cindy Teeters

Designer
Chuti Prasertsith

Compositor
codeMantra

Graphics
Vived Graphics

Pearson's Commitment to Diversity, Equity, and Inclusion

Pearson is dedicated to creating bias-free content that reflects the diversity of all learners. We embrace the many dimensions of diversity, including but not limited to race, ethnicity, gender, socioeconomic status, ability, age, sexual orientation, and religious or political beliefs.

Education is a powerful force for equity and change in our world. It has the potential to deliver opportunities that improve lives and enable economic mobility. As we work with authors to create content for every product and service, we acknowledge our responsibility to demonstrate inclusivity and incorporate diverse scholarship so that everyone can achieve their potential through learning. As the world's leading learning company, we have a duty to help drive change and live up to our purpose to help more people create a better life for themselves and to create a better world.

Our ambition is to purposefully contribute to a world where

- ▶ Everyone has an equitable and lifelong opportunity to succeed through learning

- ▶ Our educational products and services are inclusive and represent the rich diversity of learners

- ▶ Our educational content accurately reflects the histories and experiences of the learners we serve

- ▶ Our educational content prompts deeper discussions with learners and motivates them to expand their own learning (and worldview)

While we work hard to present unbiased content, we want to hear from you about any concerns or needs with this Pearson product so that we can investigate and address them.

Please contact us with concerns about any potential bias at https://www.pearson.com/report-bias.html.

Credits

Figures 3.1, 3.2, 3.7, 3.8, 3.11, 4.3-4.5, 4.9-4.16, 7.3-7.7, 7.9-7.14, 7.16-7.20, 9.1-9.3, 9.6, 12.5-12.7, 13.1, 13.6, 13.8, 14.1-14.15, 16.4, 16.8: Microsoft

Figures 3.9, 3.10, 4.17: Google

Figure 7.1: IBM

Figures 7.15, 7.21-7.23: Oracle

Figures 9.4, 9.5, 12.1-12.3, 12.8, 13.9, 13.12, 13.13, 16.3: TABLEAU

Figure 10.5: DI Management Services Pty Limited

Figures 13.2, 13.3: PowerSlides

Figure 13.4: opicobello/123RF

Figure 13.5: Visme.co

Figure 13.11: Creately

Figure 14.16: Vista.com, Crello Ltd

Figure 14.7: worditout.com

Figures 14.8, 14.9: Piktochart.com

Figure 15.1: Reebok

Figure 15.5: Google Cloud

Figure 18.1: CompTIA

Contents at a Glance

Table of Contents

About the Authors

Akhil Behl is a passionate technologist and business development practitioner. He has more than 20 years of experience in the IT industry, working across several leadership, advisory, consultancy, and business development profiles across OEMs, telcos, and SI organizations. Akhil believes in cultivating an entrepreneurial culture, working across high-performance teams, identifying emerging technology trends, and ongoing innovation. For the last 7+ years, he has been working extensively with hyperscalers across industry verticals. He is employed at Red Hat, leading the Global System Integrator (GSI) partner alliances for the ANZ region.

Akhil is a published author. Over the past decade, he has authored multiple titles on security and business communication technologies. This is his fifth book with Pearson Education. He has contributed as technical editor for over a dozen books on security, networking, and information technology. He has published several research papers in national and international journals, including *IEEE Xplore*, and presented at various IEEE conferences, as well as other prominent ICT, security, and telecom events. Writing and mentoring are his passions.

Akhil holds CCIE 19564 Emeritus (Collaboration and Security), CompTIA Data+, Azure Solutions Architect Expert, Google Professional Cloud Architect, Azure AI Certified Associate, Azure Data Fundamentals, CCSK, CHFI, ITIL, VCP, TOGAF, CEH, ISM, CCDP, and multiple other industry certifications. He has a bachelor's degree in technology and a master's in business administration.

Akhil lives in Melbourne, Australia, with his better half, Kanika, and two sons, Shivansh (11 years) and Shaurya (9 years). Both of them are passionate gamers and are excellent musicians, sporting guitar and keyboard, respectively.

In his spare time, Akhil likes to play cricket, chess, and console games with his sons, watch movies with his family, and write articles or blogs. The family enjoys building LEGO! The family are big *Star Wars* fans and have keen interest in *Star Wars* as well as Technic and Creator LEGOs.

Dr. Siva Ganapathy Subramanian Manoharan is a senior professional with more than 18+ years of expertise in the data, analytics, artificial intelligence, and machine learning arenas, spanning a wide range of data portfolios. He heads the Data & Analytics Business Unit for Searce Inc in his current role as global chief data officer. He is a cloud data and platform architect with a background in data engineering, management, and analytics. He has considerable experience in a variety of enterprises across sectors. He is an ambitious leader with a startup-to-scale growth mindset who has built/ launched new practices and strategic business units for several corporations and scaled them to huge growth.

Siva specializes in the sales, strategic solutions, P&L consulting, pre-sales, delivery of information management advisory, data architecture, and implementation services in the various industry verticals. He has extensive experience serving more than 200 customers globally, with a travel history of more than 25 countries. Over the past 8+ years, he has been living in the United Kingdom.

Siva leads a technology-focused group of individuals and motivates them for professional certifications and knowledge sharing. He has himself attained more than 81 IT certifications. Siva mentors and guides IT professionals and youth across the globe in their journey for a successful future in information technology focused on data analytics and artificial intelligence.

Siva is a technology-integrated author. He has several IT blog posts and book publications to his credit on data and analytics, artificial intelligence, and machine learning technologies. He has contributed as a technical editor for multiple blogs and whitepapers and hosted many events on data and analytics and information technology.

Siva was awarded the International Achievers award in 2022 by IAF India, the Leader of Excellence award in 2022 by BIZEMAG, and the Most Admired Global Indians 2022 with Passion Vista. He completed a bachelor's degree in electronics communication engineering from the University of Madras, an international MBA from Russian Ulyanovsk State University, a Ph.D. from the University of Swahili, and a D.Sc. from Azteca University.

Siva lives in London with Gaurave SGS (10 years) and Thejashvini SGS (5 years). Both of them are innovative artists, passionate gamers, and excellent creators. In his leisure time, Siva likes to watch movies, travel to new locations, play with Gaurave and Thejashvini, and write whitepapers, articles, and blogs.

Dedication

I would like to dedicate this book to my family, parents, and grandparents: You are the source of my inspiration, and without your support, I wouldn't be where I am. I'm forever indebted to you! Thank you from the bottom of my heart! I love you!

My spouse and my kids: Kanika, you're the pillar on which my world rests. Without your sacrifices, I wouldn't have been able to finish writing this book. Without your support, this book would not have been possible. You have my eternal gratitude. Shivansh and Shaurya, my dear sons, you have encouraged me to do more and spend more time on the book than we could amongst ourselves. Thank you, my dear children.

—Akhil Behl

I would like to thank people involved in my personal and professional life; my parents, grandparents, and relatives. I am dedicating this book to them. Thanks for giving me a good education and great ethics and support throughout my life. All the success in my life is completely because of you!

I would like to thank all my mentors, friends, and colleagues throughout my career. Thank you for supporting me and encouraging me to achieve more. Thank you from the bottom of my heart ! I am dedicating this book to you ! I love you!

Gaurave SGS and Thejashvini SGS, you're the pillar of my strength, and everything I do in life is for you. Thanks for motivating me and encouraging me. Without your support, this book would not have been possible. I am dedicating this book to you !!

—Siva G. Subramanian

Acknowledgments

The authors would like to give special recognition to:

Nancy Davis, *Executive Editor.* Thank you so much for giving me the opportunity to write and anchor this book in my core subject area, data and analytics. You were very supportive throughout the journey and process!

Chris Cleveland, *Development Editor.* Thanks for shaping this book to the best version. It was great working with you, and I look forward to more collaborations with you!

Lewis Heuermann, *Technical Editor.* Thanks for your detailed feedback and ideas to make the book's content crisp and clear!

Akhil Behl, *Co-Author and Friend.* Thanks for having confidence in me and asking me to author this excellent book!

Also, I'd like to thank the Pearson Production and Editorial Team. Without you all, this book wouldn't have made it to the printer and gotten published. This is my first experience with Pearson, and *CompTIA Data+ Exam Cram* was a very demanding and challenging project! Thanks to the complete team!

Going beyond the people directly involved in this book, I'd also like to thank:

I'm forever indebited for the support, guidance, and love from my family—my grandfather Shri Madan Mohan Behl, my grandmother Smt Santosh Behl, my father Shri Ravi Kumar Behl, my mother Smt Vijay Behl, my spouse Kanika Behl, and my kids Shivansh and Shaurya Behl. You complete me and are my world!

And a special thank you to the many readers. I hope this book helps you not just ace the exam but gives you a glimpse of the possibilities of the applications of data in real life. My hope is that this book will give you a head start in the world of data!

—Akhil Behl

Going beyond the people directly involved in this book, I'd also like to thank people involved in my personal and professional life:

A very special thank you to the all the book readers in the world. The goal in writing this book was to explain the basics of data and analytics. This book will surely help you to pass your exam and become a data and analytics professional in your career. It will give you an accelerated start to the universe of data and analytics!

—Siva G. Subramanian

About the Technical Reviewer

Lewis Heuermann (CISSP, Data+) is a military veteran, cybersecurity consultant, and professor. He has worked as a systems engineer, network engineer, network defense analyst, and cyber risk management consultant. Lewis has taught and developed curriculum for college-level courses on network defense, information systems management, cyber defense programming using Python, and data analytics courses using SQL and Tableau. He holds several industry certifications, including Tableau Desktop Specialist and CompTIA Data+ certifications.

We Want to Hear from You!

As the reader of this book, *you* are our most important critic and commentator. We value your opinion and want to know what we're doing right, what we could do better, what areas you'd like to see us publish in, and any other words of wisdom you're willing to pass our way.

We welcome your comments. You can email or write to let us know what you did or didn't like about this book—as well as what we can do to make our books better.

Please note that we cannot help you with technical problems related to the topic of this book.

When you write, please be sure to include this book's title and authors as well as your name and email address. We will carefully review your comments and share them with the authors and editors who worked on the book.

Email: community@informit.com

Reader Services

Register your copy of *CompTIA® Data+ DA0-001 Exam Cram* at www.pearsonitcertification.com for convenient access to downloads, updates, and corrections as they become available. To start the registration process, go to www.pearsonitcertification.com/register and log in or create an account*. Enter the product ISBN 9780137637294 and click Submit. When the process is complete, you will find any available bonus content under Registered Products.

*Be sure to check the box that you would like to hear from us to receive exclusive discounts on future editions of this product.

Introduction

Welcome to *CompTIA® Data+ DA0-001 Exam Cram*. This book prepares you for the CompTIA Data+ DA0-001 certification exam. Imagine that you are at a testing center and have just been handed the passing score for this exam. The goal of this book is to make that scenario a reality. Your authors, Akhil and Siva, have been in the information and communications technology industry for about two decades and have shared their experience with you in this book. We are really excited to have the opportunity to serve you in this endeavor. Together, we can accomplish your goal of attaining CompTIA Data+ certification.

What Is Data?

What is data? Can there be a single comprehensive definition for it? Or is there a way that many definitions can possibly be summarized?

In very informal terms, *data* enables a business or an individual to achieve desirable outcomes by *knowing what we know* and *uncovering what we do not know*, yet.

In more formal terms, *data* is known facts that have implicit meaning. In other words, data is a collection of facts, such as:

▶ Numbers or numerical values

▶ Quantities or measurements

▶ Recorded observations about objects

▶ Descriptions of objects

For example, details about employees such as last name, first name, age, number of years of experience, and current pay are data about the employee. For a type a of car produced, quantity, colors, and variations are data about the vehicle.

> **Fun Fact**
>
> The word *data* is related to the word *datum*. *Datum* is singular (a single piece of information), whereas *data* is plural. However, you are likely to hear the term *data* used to describe both discrete and multiple pieces of information.

The Importance of Data

Basically, data is information. Information can be described as everything around us—everything we see, hear, or can sense by way of speech, touch, smell, taste, and so on. When we collect information and record it, it becomes data.

Data is one of the most valuable assets in many facets of life. Data has become the single most precious resource and has been leveraged very well by organizations of all sizes to their advantage—both in terms of monetization and in getting an edge over the competition. Data comes in various formats and forms, and you will get to know more about them in Chapter 3, "Data Types and Types of Data." Moreover, where and how data is stored and utilized are important aspects of the data life cycle, which is covered in Chapter 1, "Understanding Databases and Data Warehouses," and Chapter 2, "Understanding Database Schemas and Dimensions."

Think about medicine, science, engineering, economics, and many streams of our daily life where data is being collected on an ongoing basis. The transactions you make with your bank using their (or a third-party) payment gateway and the purchases you make online reveal a lot about you and your persona to interested parties. Organizations want to know what products you browsed and bought, your spending capacity, what brands you like most, and many other facts that become apparent through the way you go about a purchase. Banks and e-commerce merchants would like to leverage this type of information in order to post advertisements that capture your interest.

In another realm, the information captured by performing medical experiments in a lab is vital to the success of new life-saving vaccines and drugs. Unless researchers know genetic information about a pathogen, they are not adequately empowered to perform research on the pathogen.

In addition, space exploration has given us a lot of data to work with, and today humans understand more than ever before about the vast space, galaxies, stars in our solar system, neighboring solar systems, and much more. Space probes such as *Voyager I* have provided immensely helpful insights about the vast space beyond our reach.

Not all data is created or acquired equally. Data often includes noise (unwanted information), gaps (missing information), and duplication (repeated or redundant information)—in other words, inconsistencies. Further, data can be structured, semi-structured, or unstructured in nature.

What Is the Importance of Data?

If some businesses did not have data at their disposal, they would not be able to function properly. For example, without the right data around demand and supply, a retail organization would not know how much stock to have at each store to meet demand.

For other businesses, data is a way of monetization and without appropriate data, they would be less effective. For example, a Facebook influencer would not be much of an influencer without the right data around the things they want to influence about. Subscribers would only follow and subscribe when they saw value in the information being given.

In some organizations, data actually *is* the business. For example, big entertainment houses run on metrics about what people like to see (drama, action, romance, comedy, and so on). Unless they know what their audience is aching for, they cannot deliver, and if they do not deliver, they lose business. For these organizations, data is essential, and without access to the right data insights, they will crumble.

These examples should give you an idea of the importance of data in today's world. Many case studies and TV series have been created about data, and you can browse Google to find them.

What Are the Sources of Data?

Where is data generated? That is, what are the sources of data? The answer, surprisingly, is very straightforward: Data is generated by almost everything around us. Every single electrical and electronic system is capable of generating data. For example, data is generated by computers, vehicles, household appliances, fitness devices, communication devices, electrical grids, POS machines, cloud instances, RFID systems, and HVAC systems, just to name a few. Any analog or digital system is capable of producing data.

What data is useful to you? Is the data being generated by an electric grid of any use to you, or is the data from your own house's smart power meters more important to you? Is the data being generated by your car's tire pressure sensor more important than the data being transmitted by the radio station about the weather in the upcoming week? Getting to know crucial information by way of data is not just for commercial purposes but can very well be lifesaving.

The following are some of the potential sources of data for individuals and organizations:

▶ Personal electronic gadgets, such as phones, smart devices, and wearables

- ▶ Smart home electrical appliances

- ▶ Smart vehicles

- ▶ Smart meters

- ▶ Health devices

- ▶ E-commerce or banking transactions

- ▶ Website transactions

- ▶ Cloud data storage

- ▶ Clinical research

- ▶ Online and in-person surveys

- ▶ Protected health information (PHI)

- ▶ Personally identifiable information (PII)

- ▶ Data Expansion over the Past Few Decades

The digital footprint of data has grown incredibly in the past couple of decades. Popular search engines have made data much more accessible. Advancements in technology such as mobility and the advent of the cloud have increased the demand for data in individuals' lives and in organizations' decision making.

In the past, data sources were many, data was siloed, and not a lot happened without cooperative efforts of various groups working together. Now, with online and cloud-hosted databases and data warehouses, the availability of meaningful data has increased dramatically. As storage costs have come down over the past few decades—especially with the advent of the cloud in the early 2010s—the amount of data being generated and stored has grown exponentially.

Over the past few years, the flexibility and varied offerings of cloud platform providers have enabled organizations to build and leverage complex databases and data warehouses where data from numerous data sources can coexist. Private and public cloud architectures offer a lot more than could previously be accomplished from both data generation and consumption viewpoints. Your wearables can transmit directly to a cloud server leveraging wireless or mobile connectivity (LTE/4G/5G), and the data from hundreds of thousands of transmissions can be processed in the cloud, leading to insights into health metrics! This is just one application of generating viable data and making sense of it using some form of visualization. We will cover these topics in more detail later in the book.

Data Terminology

This section covers the basic terminology pertinent to data across a vast range of topics, including data analysis, data analytics, data mining, and data warehousing. The purpose is to make you comfortable with some key terms and their meaning in the context of real-life data collection, (pre)processing, storage, analysis, visualization, and many other aspects. Again, the topics covered here are introductory and are covered in more depth throughout this book.

To keep the examples in this section streamlined, we leverage a fictitious mining organization called Mining The World (MTW) to describe these terms:

▶ **Dataset:** A dataset is a group or structured collection of related data that shares the same set of attributes or properties as other data in the same dataset. For example, MTW can leverage geospatial locations stored in a comma-separated values (CSV) file for undersea mining operations.

▶ **Data analysis:** Data analysis is the process of examining available data artifacts (or datasets) to discover facts, relationships, insights, trends, or patterns in order to support better decision making. For example, MTW can leverage data analysis to analyze locations for future mining operations.

▶ **Data analytics:** Data analytics encompasses data life cycle management across different phases, such as data collection, cleansing, normalization, organization, analysis, storage, and governance. For example, MTW can run analytics on datasets available from multiple locations and derive meaningful information about the specific locations for mining the precious gems.

▶ **Data governance:** Data governance includes people, processes, and technologies to ensure the integrity of data and leading practices for data management. For example, MTW can appoint a chief data officer (CDO) to ensure that its data initiatives are driven strategically and that only relevant employees have access to raw or processed data.

▶ **Data mining:** Data mining is the process of analyzing massive volumes of data (or datasets) to detect patterns and relevant points that can be leveraged by organizations to drive unbiased and intelligent decision making. For example, MTW could leverage data mining to focus on proactive maintenance of field machinery based on the number of hours of usage and prevent loss of revenue due to breakdowns.

▶ **Data model:** A data model focuses on the relationships among different data types and the various ways in which data can be grouped and organized as well as its formats and attributes. For example, MTW could process multiple data models across oil and gas mining as well as precious gem mining to ascertain that the geographic areas of maximum impact in terms of mining capacity are explored.

▶ **Data structure:** A data structure is a format for organizing, processing, storing, and retrieving data. A common example is arrays where one or more items that have similar data type are stored.

▶ **Data visualization:** Data visualization is the process whereby data is represented in a graphical format to provide insights about key findings or data points. Common examples are pie charts, graphs, and maps generated based on data analytics. For example, MTW can generate a report summary with pie charts on successful efforts and funding for finding and digging new resources in mountains.

▶ **Data warehouse:** A data warehouse enables organizations to collate data sources and leverage the collected data repository to make informed business decisions by performing data analytics. For example, MTW can leverage an on-premises or cloud-based data warehouse to get insights into areas of investment where technology for mining can be improved with minimal disruption to ongoing mining operations. This would lead to massive savings based on reducing the time to mine and ship products to end consumers.

▶ **Database:** A database is an organized collection of information that can be queried against to yield results. MTW can have one or more (relational or non-relational) databases to store information where the queries can be run to extract relevant information, such as customer or employee records. Databases are an important source of information on customer or employee records and transactions.

Target Audience

The CompTIA Data+ exam assesses whether candidates have the competencies of an entry-level data professional with the knowledge equivalent of at least 18–24 months of experience in a report/business analyst job role, exposure to databases and analytical tools, a basic understanding of statistics, and data visualization experience.

This book is for professionals who have experience working with data across reports, dashboards, and visualizations; data processing; data manipulation; data analysis; databases, data warehouses, and data lakes; and more. This book does not cover everything in the data world, however. How could anyone do so in such a concise package? Despite its brevity, this book offers a lot of insights and a whole lot of test preparation.

Essentially, this book is for three types of people:

▶ Those who have been working with data analytics, visualization, and other aspects and want to achieve a vendor-neutral certification, and validate their knowledge

▶ Those who want to sharpen their understanding of data analytics and are fairly new to the data world

▶ Those who simply want a basic knowledge of what data is all about and how organizations leverage data to create more meaningful offerings for customers

For those of you in the first group, the CompTIA Data+ certification can have a positive career impact, increasing the chances of getting to the next level or securing a higher-paying job. It also acts as a steppingstone to more advanced certifications. For those in the second group, preparing for the exam serves to keep your skills sharp and your knowledge up to date, helping you remain a sought-after technician. For those of you in the third group, the knowledge in this book can be helpful in any career path you decide to take and can be beneficial to just about any organization you might work for—because almost every organization leverages data for driving decision making.

Regardless of your situation, one thing to keep in mind is that this book is written not just to help you pass the CompTIA Data+ exam but to teach you how to be a well-rounded data professional. While the main goal of this book is to help you become Data+ certified, we also want to share our experience with you so that you can grow as an individual.

About the CompTIA Data+ Certification

This book covers the material tested on the CompTIA Data+ DA0-001 exam, which you must pass to obtain the CompTIA Data+ certification. This exam is administered by Pearson Vue and can be taken at a local test center or online.

Passing the certification exam proves that you are an experienced problem solver and can support today's data-first approach to solving some of the most complex analytical problems that organizations face.

Before doing anything else, we recommend that you download the official CompTIA Data+ objectives from CompTIA's website. The objectives are a comprehensive bulleted list of the concepts you should know for the exam.

This book directly aligns with those objectives, and each chapter specifies the objective(s) it covers.

For more information about how the Data+ certification can help you in your career or to download the latest objectives, access CompTIA's Data+ web page at https://www.comptia.org/certifications/data#examdetails.

About This Book

This book covers what you need to know to pass the CompTIA Data+ exam. It does so in a concise way that allows you to learn the facts quickly and efficiently.

The book is composed of 18 chapters, each of which pertains to one or more objectives covered on the exam. At the beginning of each chapter you will find a list of exam topics that the chapter covers so you know what topics to focus on as you prepare for the exams. Chapter 18 discusses how to get ready for the Data+ exam and gives some tips and techniques for passing it.

The organization of this book is based on the order of the official CompTIA Data+ objectives. Typically, you will find one objective covered in each chapter. However, a chapter may cover two objectives, and in a couple of instances, an objective stretches across two chapters. The CompTIA objective or objectives covered are listed verbatim at the beginning of each chapter and in the subsequent major headings. This organization allows you to easily locate whatever objective you want to learn more about. In addition, you can use the index to quickly find the concepts you are after.

Regardless of your experience level, we don't recommend skipping content. This book is designed to be read completely. The best way to study for the Data+ exam is to read the entire book.

Chapter Format and Conventions

Every Exam Cram chapter follows a standard structure and contains graphical clues about important information. The structure of each chapter includes the following:

▶ **Opening topics list:** The chapter begins with the CompTIA Data+ objective(s) covered in the chapter.

▶ **Topical coverage:** Each chapter explains its topics in a hands-on and a theory-based way. The book includes in-depth descriptions, tables, and figures geared toward building your knowledge so that you can pass the exam.

▶ **Cram Quiz questions:** At the end of each topic is a quiz. The quizzes and ensuing explanations are meant to help you gauge your knowledge of the subjects you have just studied. If the answers to the questions don't come readily to you, consider reviewing individual topics or the entire chapter. You can also find the Cram Quiz questions on the book's companion web page at www.pearsonitcertification.com.

▶ **Exam Alerts, Fun Facts, and Notes:** These are interspersed throughout the book. Watch out for them!

ExamAlert

This is what an Exam Alert looks like. An alert stresses concepts, terms, hardware, software, or activities that are likely to relate to one or more questions on the exam.

Fun Fact

This is what a Fun Fact looks like. It emphasizes something interesting about or relevant to the context of Data.

Additional Elements

Beyond the chapters, there are a few more elements that are helpful in your journey preparing for the CompTIA Data+ exam. They include:

▶ **Practice Exams:** Practice Exams are available as part of the custom practice test engine at the companion web page for this book. They are designed to prepare you for the multiple-choice questions that you will find on the real CompTIA Data+ exam.

▶ **Cram Sheet:** The tear-out Cram Sheet is located at the beginning of the book. It is designed to provide some of the most important facts you need to know for the exam onto one small sheet, allowing for easy memorization. It is also available in PDF format on the companion web page. If you have an e-book version, the Cram Sheet might be located elsewhere in the e-book; run a search for the term "cram sheet," and you should be able to find it.

The Hands-on Approach

It is incredibly important that you apply what you are learning to real-world application of data analytics, processes, visualization, and more. This is the leading practice that we have recommended for years. It works! Practice as much as you can on databases, data warehouses, visualization dashboards, and whatever you can get your hands on.

In this book we give as many use cases and actual technology examples as possible, including SQL queries, screenshots of data system/software navigation, and so on. By referencing real-world applications of data processing, visualization, and analytics tools technology in actual scenarios, we infuse some real-world knowledge to solidify the concepts you need to learn for the exam. This hands-on approach can help you to visualize concepts better.

This book frequently refers to various websites that provide sample datasets, tools, and other materials to help you with your exam preparation.

Goals for This Book

We have three main goals in mind for preparing you for the CompTIA Data+ exam.

The first goal is to help you understand Data+ topics and concepts quickly and efficiently. To do this, we have tried getting right to the facts necessary for the exam. To drive these facts home, the book incorporates figures, tables, real-world scenarios, and simple, to-the-point explanations.

The second goal for this book is to provide you with an abundance of *unique* questions to prepare you for the exams. Between the Cram Quizzes and the practice exams, that goal has been met, and we think it will benefit you greatly. Because CompTIA reserves the right to change test questions at any time, it is difficult to foresee exactly what you will be asked on the exams. However, to become a good data-focused professional, you must know the *basics and concepts*; you can't just memorize questions. Therefore, each question has an explanation and maps back to the chapter covered in the text.

The third goal is to give you real-world examples and to ensure that you get a broader understanding of topics than just getting prepared for the exam. This will be immensely useful in activities in your real life at your job.

Good luck in your certification endeavors. We hope you benefit from this book. Enjoy!

Sincerely,

Akhil Behl

Siva G. Subramanian

CHAPTER 1

Understanding Databases and Data Warehouses

This chapter covers portions of Objective 1.1 (Identify basic concepts of data schemas and dimensions) of the CompTIA Data+ exam and includes the following topics:

▶ Databases and database management systems

▶ Relational databases vs. non-relational databases

▶ Data warehouses

▶ Data lakes

For more information on the official CompTIA Data+ exam topics, see the Introduction.

This chapter covers topics related to databases, data warehouses, and data lakes, as well as key topics related to relational and non-relational databases. Databases and database systems are an indispensable component of our life that impact both trivial and very complex transactions online and offline. Data warehouses and data lakes enable modern systems to leverage information—which may be structured or unstructured—for analytics. Understanding the types of databases, data warehouses, and data lakes helps you understand the role they play as well as the key aspects of their existence in organizational constructs.

Databases and Database Management Systems

CramSaver

If you can correctly answer these questions before going through this section, save time by skimming the Exam Alerts in this section and then completing the Cram Quiz at the end of the section.

1. An RDBMS is an example of a(n) _____ database.

   a. structured

   b. unstructured

   c. semi-structured

   d. fluid

2. Cloud providers provide options for both _____ and _____ databases. (Choose two.)

   a. unorganized

   b. structured

   c. unstructured

   d. organized

3. A relational database can be organized into _____.

   a. charts

   b. graphs

   c. histograms

   d. tables

Answers

1. **Answer: a. structured.** A relational database management system (RDBMS) is a program that allows you to create, read, update, and delete data in a relational database. In a relational database, the data is structured in a table that contains rows and columns. An RDBMS typically requires the use of Structured Query Language (SQL) to access the data fields in the structured database.

2. **Answer: b. structured, c. unstructured.** Cloud providers or cloud platform vendors offer both structured and unstructured databases for consumption by their consumers.

3. **Answer: d. tables.** A relational database is structured into tables consisting of rows and columns.

A database can be defined as a collection of related data (or datasets). This data might include names of people, their ages, their addresses, their phone numbers, their Social Security numbers, and so on. While this sort of data can exist in various shapes and forms (for example, in a physical notebook or a file), it is most useful for analysis, storage, and retrieval purposes to store it in a computer system. Computer programs can then access the data as and when required, which in turn allows humans to access and make decisions or carry out pertinent tasks.

Consider a simplified view: A database is a collection of related data that can be stored in a rational and organized manner. For example, an organization's accounting department would need access to details such as the following about every employee:

▶ First and last name

▶ Bank information

▶ Address

▶ Department

▶ Contract rate (for example, permanent or contractual and hourly rate)

All this information is needed in order to keep track of employees' hours worked and issue the appropriate compensation. Without a way to order and access information about employees, trivial tasks such as issuing bank transfers toward the end of month to pay the employees won't be possible.

> **Note**
>
> Data can be documented and indexed using software such as Microsoft Access or Excel on an individual's system. However, approaching data this way is not useful unless the right people have access to the data in order to gain insights and drive the outcomes desired. Storing data in a database makes the data much more usable as it acts as a centralized repository of information for the organization.

Another key example where a database is required is when you make a booking with a hotel and pay for your stay. In the process, you select the room type, the amenities, including breakfast in your room rate, and so on, and your reservation is created in the hotel's database by the database operator. In addition, based on your membership level with that hotel chain (silver, golden, platinum, and so on), you may get additional perks. Because the hotel chain's database holds information on your status, your perks are automatically added for each stay. This is a good example of the importance of databases in our daily lives.

Table 1.1 shows a very simple relational database.

TABLE 1.1 **Employee Database**

Employee_id	Firstname	Lastname	State	Department
L00220	Kate	Mayer	NJ	Sales
L00230	Smith	Yale	TX	HR
L00240	Anna	Shoup	FL	Finance
L00250	Sammy	McDonald	CA	Marketing

Data can be stored in a number of ways, including:

▶ Structured data

▶ Unstructured data

▶ Semi-structured data

> **Note**
>
> To define a database, it is key to define the structure of the records by specifying the different types of data elements to be stored in each record. You can further define the type of database that can be created: relational or non-relational.

It is important to understand why data must be stored in a specific format as well as the advantages and disadvantages of one format over the other. Chapter 4, "Understanding Common Data Structures and File Formats," covers these aspects in more detail.

The next section covers the topic of DBMS.

Database Management System (DBMS)

A database management system (DBMS) is an electronic system that enables users to create and manage a database containing up-to-date and relevant information.

> **Note**
>
> The term *electronic system* has been used to call out that DBMSs are digital systems, as opposed to the physical files or folders that served as organizational data stores a few decades ago.

While users can access data from a database directly, the process is not intuitive. The information may be segregated across multiple fields and structured in a way that forces the user to search through a number of fields—which is tedious and error prone.

A DBMS enables users to run queries to find the data they're after, which facilitates the processes of describing, constructing, operating, and sharing databases among the users in an organization as well as the applications that need access to the data. Examples of commonly used DBMSs include:

▶ Microsoft SQL

▶ Oracle SQL

▶ PostgreSQL

▶ MongoDB

▶ RedShift

Following are the highlights of DBMSs:

▶ A DBMS offers a centralized view of data that can be accessed by multiple users or applications (via connectors or APIs).

▶ A DBMS abstracts the physical and logical construct of data from the users; that is, it allows users to interact with the database without knowing where it is located.

▶ A DBMS acts as a broker between the user and the database. DBMS enables database administrators to implement authentication, authorization, and logging, thereby limiting what each type of user can see and do with the data they have access to.

DBMSs offer the following functionalities for users and administrators, depending on the rights they are assigned:

▶ Create databases

▶ Backup and restore databases

▶ Connect to and manage multiple local and remote databases

▶ Create tables in databases

▶ Create, read, update, and delete (CRUD) data in databases

▶ Query data in databases

▶ Set up multiple user accounts and roles as well as apply permissions to access data objects

A DBMS also stores the database definition in the form of a database catalog or dictionary. This descriptive information, called *metadata*, is data about data. (Refer to Chapter 4 for more information on metadata.) A data catalog is an organized inventory of all data assets, such as structured and unstructured data, data visualizations, and data reports. A data dictionary contains the metadata.

Figure 1.1 illustrates a DBMS, including users, applications, databases, and the flow of information.

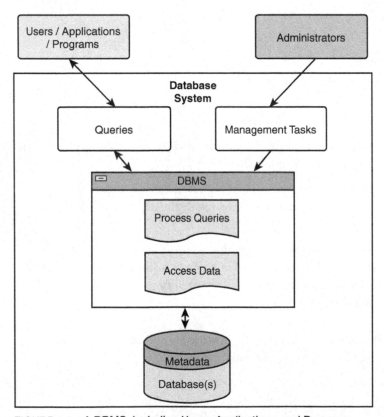

FIGURE 1.1 **A DBMS, Including Users, Applications, and Programs**

As Figure 1.1 illustrates, there are two main types of connectivity to DBMSs:

▶ **User/application/program:** Primarily focused on queries made to the DBMS for extracting and changing/updating data from the underlying databases by the end users and apps

▶ **Administrative:** Primarily focused on management of data as well as databases via DBMS

> **Note**
>
> A DBMS is seen as an abstraction layer between the databases and the consumer, and it offers capabilities that are much more refined than direct access to the databases.

Next, we will discuss relational and non-relational databases and how records may be arranged.

Relational Database

A relational database is quite simply defined as a database in which data is stored in tables. Tables consist of columns and rows. Table 1.2, which expands on Table 1.1, illustrates what a relational database looks like in the real world.

TABLE 1.2 **Employee Relational Database**

Table Employee_Details

Employee_id	Firstname	Lastname	State	Department
L00220	Kate	Mayer	NJ	Sales
L00230	Smith	Yale	TX	HR
L00240	Anna	Shoup	FL	Finance
L00250	Sammy	McDonald	CA	Marketing

Table Salary

Salary_Code	Salary_Weekly	Employee_id
1A220	2000	L00220
2B230	1500	L00230
3C240	1500	L00240
4D250	1000	L00250

In many ways, a relational database might seem similar to an Excel spreadsheet; however, there are some key differences, including the following:

► A relational database breaks data into multiple tables.

► A table consists of rows and columns.

► The data within each row is referred to as a *record*.

► A column defines the data types, such as char, varchar, and integer.

► Each row is uniquely identified by the respective primary key column.

► Rows in one table are related to rows in another table via a foreign key.

In the example shown in Table 1.2, Employee_id is the primary key for the Employee_Details table. As part of the Salary table, Employee_id is the foreign key, and the primary key is Salary_Code. These keys relate the two tables—hence the term *relational database*.

> **Note**
>
> The *relational* part of *relational database* is the feature that allows a connection (that is, relationship) between different tables in a database, as shown in Table 1.2, via primary and foreign keys.

Relational databases can be operated using Structured Query Language (SQL). SQL isn't a database type itself; rather, it is a language that is used to create, modify, and query data in a relational database. SQL is the basic language used in database management systems.

> **Fun Fact**
>
> Authors came across SQL during their university days working with OracleDBMS version 9. SQL is a fairly simple language, and anyone can learn it quickly.

The tables in a relational database can be joined to make it easier for a user to understand the relationships in the data. SQL has the ability to do basic mathematical operations such as counting, adding, grouping, subtotaling functions, and making logical transformations. Data analysts can view a table in different orders, such as by date, name, or any other column name available.

Common examples of relational databases include:

- ▶ Oracle
- ▶ MySQL
- ▶ PostgreSQL
- ▶ Microsoft SQL Server

DBMSs That manage relational databases are known as relational database management systems (RDBMSs).

Some advantages of RDBMSs are as follows:

- ▶ Relational databases work well for structured data and offer quick lookups and query times that are typically very fast.
- ▶ RDBMSs offer flexibility as SQL is a well-known standard language, and almost every RDBMS tool supports SQL queries.
- ▶ There are multiple on-premises and cloud RDBMS solutions available, and making the transition from an on-premises to a cloud-based RDBMS is not very complex.
- ▶ RDBMSs offer reduced redundancy by offering data normalization.
- ▶ RDBMSs offer ease of backup and disaster recovery by automating data backup jobs.

Relational databases are ideal for transactional processing, such as website user authentication or e-commerce transactions. You'll learn more about this later in the chapter, in the section "Online Transactional Processing (OLTP)."

Non-relational Databases

Non-relational databases (also called NoSQL databases) do not use tables to store data. Instead, they employ a different method of storing data.

> **Note**
>
> Non-relational/NoSQL databases are so named because they do not require SQL for managing data.

Because there are no tables in non-relational databases, there is no need to connect tables. The simple design of a non-relational database increases scalability.

Social media, mobile applications, and data analytics are some of the most common examples of where NoSQL databases are often leveraged.

> ## ExamAlert
>
> NoSQL databases are very popular among data scientists and data engineers and are a common offering with most cloud platform providers. Expect to see questions on NoSQL databases on CompTIA Data+ exam.

There are four types of non-relational databases:

▶ **Document data stores:** In a document data store, the data is stored in document format. Usually, the data is stored as Java Script Object Notation (JSON) documents in a semi-structured format. This type of data store keeps the data together and available for developers to access as part of their code (since it's already in JSON or JSON-like format such as YAML or XML), thereby decreasing the processing required to make data insights. The data structures can be changed within a document to offer more flexibility to developers. Common examples of NoSQL document data stores are MongoDB, DocumentDB, and Cosmos DB.

▶ **Columnar data stores:** A columnar data store is a NoSQL database in which the data is stored as columns. The columns are grouped together into column families, each of which consists of a set of columns that are logically related and can be retrieved or manipulated as a unit. Whereas in a relational database the data is optimized across rows, in a columnar data store the data is optimized for fast retrieval of columns. A columnar database can store unstructured or semi-structured data. Figure 1.2 shows a columnar database using the Employee database example from earlier in this chapter. Examples of columnar data stores include MariaDB, RedShift, and Apache HBase.

Employee_id	Firstname
L000220	Kate
L000230	Smith
L000240	Anna
L000250	Sammy

Employee_id	Lastname
L000220	Mayer
L000230	Yale
L000240	Shoup
L000250	McDonald

Employee_id	Department
L000220	Sales
L000230	HR
L000240	Finance
L000250	Marketing

FIGURE 1.2 **Columnar Data Store**

▶ **Key/value data stores:** Key/value data stores are the simplest form of non-relational (or NoSQL) databases. Such a data store is organized as a dictionary with key/value pairs. Each unique record consists of a key and value. A dictionary contains a collection of records, which are stored and retrieved using a unique key.

Figure 1.3 provides an example of a key/value data store in which major Indian cities are listed as keys pointing to specific cities (values) across northern and southern India.

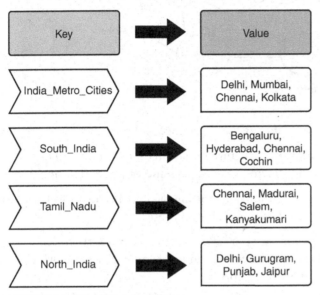

FIGURE 1.3 **Key/Value Data Store**

▶ **Graph data store:** In a graph data store, the data is stored as knowledge graphs. The nodes of a graph can be persons, objects, or places. Graph data stores work by storing data alongside relationships; by retrieving a relationship, you can describe the related data. This may seem quite different from the concept of a relational database, with data stored based on relationships. Graph data is usually used for storing and managing the network of connections between the elements in the graph. Figure 1.4 illustrates a graph database. In this graph, the nodes (colored bubbles) represent people and may contain data about their attributes (such as Employee_id), and the lines connecting the nodes show the relationships.

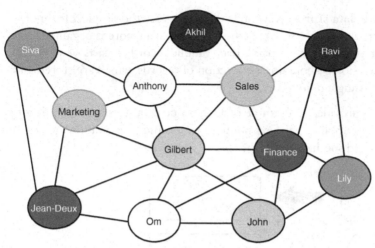

FIGURE 1.4 **Graph Data Store**

The key advantages of non-relational databases are as follows:

▶ They provide a very flexible structure for storing semi-structured or unstructured data as documents, graphs, keys and values, and so on.

▶ NoSQL databases are recommended for big data operations as well as analytics as the speed of data retrieval is very fast.

▶ NoSQL databases can be very cost-effective compared to structured relational databases as not all information needs to be processed, which means data can be stored in raw format.

▶ Non-relational databases are designed to be reliable and continuously available. Many modern cloud first databases are NoSQL.

Note

Many database management systems today are multi-model. For example, relational database systems often include aspects that are typically associated with NoSQL, such as document stores, column stores, and graphs.

Table 1.3 summarizes the differences between relational and non-relational databases.

TABLE 1.3 **Differences Between Relational and Non-Relational Databases**

Chracteristic	Relational Database	Non-Relational Database
Data storage	Data is stored in tables.	Data is stored in non-tabular format as documents, graphs, or key/value pairs.
SQL vs. NoSQL	Relational databases are also called SQL databases.	Non-relational databases are also known as NoSQL databases.
Joining	The tables can be joined together.	There is no joining function.
Data volume	Not suitable for processing large volumes of data.	Can process large volume of data.
Structured, Unstructured vs. semi-structured data	Only structured data can be stored in SQL databases.	Unstructured and semi-structured data types are commonly stored in NoSQL databases.
Examples	MySQL and PostgreSQL are examples.	Cassandra and MongoDB are examples.

Cram Quiz

Answer these questions. The answers follow the last question. If you cannot answer these questions correctly, consider reading this section again until you can.

1. The preferred option for storing unstructured data for data analytics is
   _____.

   ○ **a.** RDBMSs

   ○ **b.** SQL databases

   ○ **c.** NoSQL databases

   ○ **d.** Object Storage

2. A primary key is a(n) _____ for a table.

   ○ **a.** attribute

   ○ **b.** information

   ○ **c.** unique identifier

   ○ **d.** common identifier

3. The unique feature of a non-relational database is the _____.

   ○ **a.** tabular form

   ○ **b.** use of SQL

   ○ **c.** cost-effectiveness

   ○ **d.** non-tabular form

4. In document data stores, data is stored in the form of _____.

   ○ **a.** HTML

   ○ **b.** JSON

   ○ **c.** graphs

   ○ **d.** columns

Cram Quiz Answers

1. **Answer: c. NoSQL databases.** NoSQL or non-relational databases are the preferred option for storing unstructured or semi-structured data. This is primarily because of the speed of access and the relatively low costs for storing datasets.

2. **Answer: c. unique identifier.** A primary key is a unique identifier for the datasets in a table.

3. **Answer: d. non-tabular form.** NoSQL or non-relational databases use alternative data storage mechanisms such as documents and key/value approaches.

4. **Answer: b. JSON.** Document data stores store data in JSON-like formats (such as YAML or XML).

Data Warehouses and Data Lakes

Organizations have evolved over the past years, and their data requirements have evolved as well. While in a traditional manner, data related to employees and customers is still very important, organizations are well on their way to being more competitive by conducting analysis on the voluminous data they have from offline and online transactions. This data is primarily used to drive data-based decision making, whether for IT budgets or for making decisions about investing in lines of business or new products to launch.

Data is not all created equal, and neither are the ways of dealing with data. There are heaps of structured data, and there's even more unstructured data (which is being generated as part of online activities, such as posts, searches, and so on). While data warehouses were created out of the need to structure data in a singular manner to make sense of it, data lakes were conceptualized primarily to cater to modern challenges to dig more deeply into heaps of data.

Again, not all analytics were made the same, and while some leverage real-time (or streaming) data based on a data lake, other analytics may be dependent on piles of data being pushed together to a data warehouse—in other words, batch data.

The following sections explain concepts related to data warehouses and data lakes.

> **ExamAlert**
>
> Data warehouses and data lakes are very commonly used by cloud providers and are likely to be included on the CompTIA Data+ exam.

Data Warehouses

A *data warehouse* is a centralized repository of data that is predominantly used for business analytics and business intelligence. The key purpose of a data warehouse is to offer insights for future decision making based on historical data.

It is key to note that a data warehouse only supports structured data and well-defined schemas. A data warehouse supports a schema-on-write approach that follows a predefined schema for the data.

A data warehouse may contain information from multiple organizational sources. The key functions of a data warehouse are as follows:

▶ Data extraction

▶ Data cleansing

▶ Data transformation

▶ Data loading/refreshing

Figure 1.5 illustrates the concept of a data warehouse.

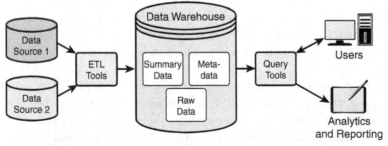

FIGURE 1.5   **Data Warehouse Overview**

> **Note**
>
> The data in a data warehouse is read-only as the CRUD operations are performed at the data source level, typically as part of OLTP systems. Batch data is pushed to data warehouses for point-in-time analytics.

As shown in Figure 1.5, a data warehouse consists of multiple components:

- ► **Data sources:** The source of data to be processed and analyzed; the data is typically online transactional processing (OLTP) data.

- ► **ETL tools:** Extract, transform, and load (ETL) tools are used to extract data from data sources and cleanse the data as well as transform it before loading it in the data warehouse.

- ► **Database:** Data warehouses leverage RDBMSs as data management tools.

- ► **Data:** The data in a data warehouse is the raw data from OLTP systems, and this raw data is used to derive metadata and summary data.

- ► **Query tools:** Tools such as query and reporting tools as well as data mining applications enable users to analyze data and interact with a data warehouse.

- ► **Analytics and reporting:** Users can leverage reports to drive decision making.

The data in data warehouses is structured, processed data that results from ETL processes and can be leveraged by queries and data mining tools.

Data warehouses can be architectured in three ways:

- ► **Single-tier architecture:** A single-tier architecture can store a minimum amount of data and is focused on getting data only from a restricted number of sources as well as data de-duplication. This architecture is not widely used at an enterprise level.

- ► **Two-tier architecture:** A two-tier architecture separates the physically available data source(s) from the data warehouse. Such an architecture is not expandable and hence is not commonly used by large organizations focusing on multiple users and multiple data sources.

▶ **Three-tier architecture:** This architecture consists of three tiers: top, middle, and bottom. The top tier is a front-end client layer that contains tools such as query, reporting, analysis, and data mining tools. The middle tier is an OLAP server that acts as a mediator between an end user and the database. The bottom tier is a relational database system in which data is cleansed, transformed, and loaded using tools from the back end.

Some common examples of data warehouse solutions are:

▶ AWS RedShift

▶ Azure SQL Data Warehouse

▶ Oracle Data Warehouse

The key advantages of leveraging a data warehouse are as follows:

▶ Data warehouses support quick access to critical data and metadata.

▶ Data warehouses integrate data from multiple data sources.

▶ Data warehouses reduce turnaround time in the process of analyzing the information.

▶ Data warehouses enables users to analyze data from different time periods to make future predictions.

▶ Data warehouses provide consistent information by virtue of their dependency on RDBMSs.

Data warehouses also have some key disadvantages:

▶ As data warehouses are based on RDBMSs, unstructured data cannot be stored in them.

▶ It is difficult to alter data types and data source schema, as data warehouses can only ingest structured data that fits predefined schemas.

There is a subset of a data warehouse called a *data mart* that is typically used by a specific set of users in an organization. The core purpose of a data mart is to partition a smaller set of data to provide easier data access for specific targeted groups within an organization. For example, a sales data mart could be used by a sales department to know the details about sales statistics related to a newly launched product. No other department would have access to the sales data mart.

Figure 1.6 illustrates the various data marts that could be created to cater to specific lines of business.

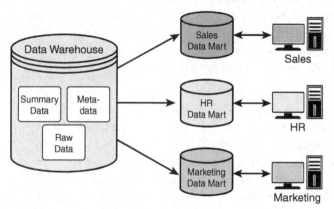

FIGURE 1.6   **Data Mart Overview**

Three types of data marts can be created, depending on an organization's requirements:

▶ **Dependent data mart:** This type of data mart is created from the existing enterprise data warehouse and follows a top-down approach, with all pertinent data extracted according to the analysis requirements. Because it leverages the existing data warehouse and extracts only meaningful data partitions, the only additional work is related to defining the data required by the respective line of business. A dependent data mart can be seen as a subset of a data warehouse.

▶ **Independent data mart:** This type of data mart is a standalone system that is created without the use of the enterprise data warehouse. It follows a bottom-up approach in that it has its own ETL specifics for extracting, processing, and storing or retrieving data as and when needed. An independent data mart can be seen as a much smaller-scale data warehouse.

▶ **Hybrid data mart:** This type of data mart is a combination of a dependent data mart and an independent data mart. It uses both top-down and bottom-up approaches for managing the data, with existing interesting data captured from the data warehouse and new interesting data extracted from source systems directly.

The next section covers the insights to data lakes.

Data Lakes

A *data lake* is a large data storage repository that can store structured, semi-structured, and unstructured data from multiple data sources. It can also contain raw data as well as processed data. Think of a data lake as a data warehouse on steroids. The major advantage of a data lake is that the data need not be processed before it is stored, as it must be with a data warehouse.

However, the data from a data lake cannot be used directly and requires processing on the fly. Data lakes leverage a "schema-on-read" approach, which means the data is transformed at query time. In other words, whereas data warehouses use ETL, data lakes thrive on ELT (extract, load, and transform). Therefore, the resource consumption and extraction of data from data sources (such as blogs, logs, searches, and image and multimedia repositories) is extremely fast compared to consumption and extraction with traditional ETL processes, thereby reducing the cost and complexity associated with the ETL processes.

Figure 1.7 illustrates the typical structure and components of a data lake.

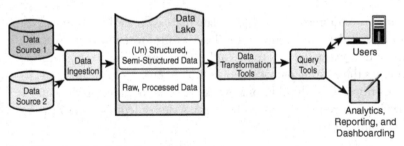

FIGURE 1.7   **Data Lake Overview**

As shown in Figure 1.7, a data lake consists of multiple components:

▶ **Data sources:** Multiple data sources from which data can be loaded to be processed and analyzed.

▶ **Data ingestion layer:** This layer is used to ingest data (in its native format) from multiple data sources. For example, media files can be imported as MP4 or JPEG files, and well-structured data from SQL databases can be imported consequently.

▶ **Data transformation tools:** A variety of tools are used for transform functions to normalize the schema and ready the data for consumption by analysts.

▶ **Query tools:** Tools such as query and reporting tools as well as data mining applications enable users to analyze the data and interact with the data warehouse.

▶ **Analytics and reporting:** Users can leverage reports or dashboards to drive decision making. Reports and dashboards are created based on analysis on the data loaded in the data lake in line with one or more use cases.

Data lake solutions have become increasingly prevalent due to the large volumes of data that need to be analyzed and the many types of people who use them, for example, data engineers, data analysts, data architects, and data scientists. A data lake is often used as part of a cloud service offering or in a hybrid arrangement with a cloud-hosted data lake with on-premises data sources. This combination of downstream analytics and reporting as well as dashboarding tools offers state-of-the-art data-based decision-making ability.

Some of the most common and popular examples of data lakes are:

▶ Google BigQuery

▶ AWS Lake Formation

▶ Azure Synapse

▶ Snowflake

The key advantages of leveraging a data lake are as follows:

▶ Data lakes support raw, processed, structured, semi-structured, and unstructured data from a variety of sources. They eliminate silos by offering a single repository for all data types and types of data. More on data types and types of data in Chapter 3, "Data Types and Types of Data."

▶ Data lakes require no schema lock in and are therefore great for data portability from a variety of data types and types of data.

▶ Data lake solutions enable data analysts to query data in new ways and create new use cases as the business demands.

Data lakes also have some disadvantages, including:

▶ Data lakes are meant primarily for data analysts, data engineers, and data scientists. A much higher-than-average skillset is required to leverage the true potential of data lakes.

▶ Non-selective data storage from multiple data sources may imply higher storage costs.

Table 1.4 summarizes the differences between data warehouses and data lakes.

TABLE 1.4 **Differences Between Data Lakes and Data Warehouses**

Characteristic	Data Lakes	Data Warehouses
Type of data	Data from all type of data sources can be stored, regardless of the data schema.	Data from OLTP systems and data with quality metrics and their attributes are stored.
Storage	Data is typically stored in raw form and processed on the fly when queried.	Data is stored after processing and ready for queries.
Users	Data lakes are ideal for data scientists and data engineers.	Data warehouses are ideal for operational users.
Processing time (ingestion and analytics)	Processing time is faster.	Processing time is slower.
ELT vs. ETL methodology	Uses ELT (extract, load, and transform) processes.	Uses ETL (extract, transform, and load) processes.
Schema	The schema is defined after the data is stored, via a schema-on-read approach.	The schema is well defined before the data is stored, via a schema-on-write approach.
Cost of storage	Data storage is comparatively inexpensive.	Data storage is comparatively expensive.

Cram Quiz

Answer these questions. The answers follow the last question. If you cannot answer these questions correctly, consider reading this section again until you can.

1. Data lakes are primarily used by/for _____ and _____.

   O **a.** data analysts

   O **b.** system updates

   O **c.** data scientists

   O **d.** keeping inventory

2. Which of the following are types of data marts? (Choose three.)

   O **a.** Normal

   O **b.** Dependent

   O **c.** Hybrid

   O **d.** Independent

3. What is represented by the ? in the following figure?

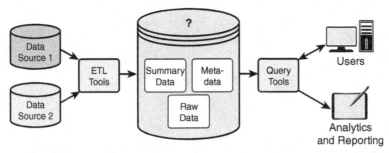

   O **a.** Database

   O **b.** Data lake

   O **c.** Data warehouse

   O **d.** Data mart

Cram Quiz Answers

1. **Answer: a. data analysts, c. data scientists.** Data lakes are primarily meant for use by data analysts and data scientists. A much higher-than-average skillset is required to leverage the true potential of data lakes.

2. **Answer: b. Dependent, c. Hybrid, d. Independent.** The three types of data marts are dependent, hybrid, and independent.

3. **Answer: c. Data warehouse.** In this figure, the ? represents a data warehouse.

OLTP and OLAP

CramSaver

If you can correctly answer these questions before going through this section, save time by skimming the Exam Alerts in this section and then completing the Cram Quiz at the end of the section.

1. OLTP is used by _____.

   a. researchers

   b. business analysts

   c. operations staff

   d. top management

2. OLAP is typically used by _____.

   a. data architects

   b. business analysts

   c. operations staff

   d. data analysts

3. OLTP follows _____ design principles.

   a. ACID

   b. RAIN

   c. MUD

   d. TRY

Answers

1. **Answer: c. operations staff.** OLTP is leveraged for transactional data and is mostly used by operations staff.

2. **Answer: d. data analysts.** OLAP is leveraged for data analytics by data analysts for reporting on findings from historical data.

3. **Answer: a. ACID.** OLTP follows ACID design principles, leveraging atomicity, consistency, isolation, and durability for transactions.

Online Transactional Processing (OLTP)

You have certainly used a point-of-sale (POS) system to make a card transaction using a debit/credit card or reserved a plane ticket to go on a dream vacation. It is possible, however, that you haven't recognized that those systems leverage OLTP. Think about it: You wouldn't wait hours for a merchant to process your transaction; rather, you can complete a purchase by making a payment to a merchant in moments, which implies that these transactions are done in real time. OLTP transactions—including those already mentioned as well as online banking, online shopping, and ATM transactions—typically occur in milliseconds.

> **Note**
>
> OLTP involves real-time or streaming transaction data unlike the batch data that is pushed to a data warehouse.

OLTP is a software system that is specifically built to process transaction-focused data in a database. OLTP data stores enable large numbers of concurrent real-time transactions. It is important to note that OLTP data stores take an all-succeed or all-fail approach; that is, the transactions either succeed or fail and do not remain in an intermediate state. Figure 1.8 provides an overview of an OLTP system.

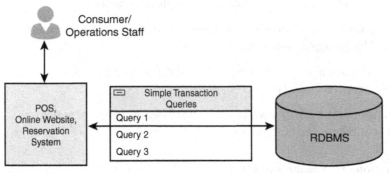

FIGURE 1.8 **OLTP Overview**

With OLTP, it is important that the transactions go as expected and that there are no hiccups because any transactional issues (including data corruption or data inconsistency) can lead to undesirable outcomes. OLTP data stores offer reliability and consistency by implementing the ACID (atomicity, consistency, isolation, and durability) design principle. ACID is a transaction management process that uses concurrency controls to ensure that consistency is maintained.

> **Note**
>
> ACID is not a novel concept and has been used for designing DBMSs with large numbers of concurrent transactions as well as user access to the data.

The ACID design principle has these components:

▶ **Atomicity:** This implies that all transactions always succeed or fail completely. In other words, if there's an incomplete transaction, it is not *valid*.

▶ **Consistency:** This ensures that a database that was in a consistent state remains in a consistent state following a successful transaction.

▶ **Isolation:** This ensures that one transaction does not intervene or disrupt another transaction.

▶ **Durability:** This ensures that the results of a successful transaction are committed and cannot be rolled back.

As with any other database system, there are tools available to manage OLTP systems. End users and applications can manage OLTP systems via Data Manipulation Language (DML) using update, insert, and delete operations on an ongoing basis.

Following are the key tenets of OLTP:

▶ OLTP can process multiple concurrent simple transactions.

▶ OLTP maintains the integrity of the data, even when the same data is accessed by multiple users at the same time.

▶ OLTP provides indexed datasets, and thus, the data can be rapidly searched, retrieved, and queried.

▶ A complete data backup must be maintained because large transactions are processed concurrently by the users.

The next section gives insights to OLAP.

Online Analytical Processing (OLAP)

If your organization launched a new product last year and is about to launch a new version of that product, how do you know if the previous product did well in the market and how it fared against competition? How do you identify the demand patterns? How do you identify the customer sentiments? While you might have all this data available across a range of systems (such as sales records and ERP and CRM systems), there isn't a single source of truth unless you have performed analytics on the historical data and arrived at a conclusion that can drive the success of the new release. This is where you can leverage an online analytical processing (OLAP) system for data analysis. Planning, analyzing, forecasting, and budgeting are some of the common functions that are performed by business analysts using OLAP. OLAP systems process large volumes of data from data warehouses, data marts, or any other centralized data stores and are important in business intelligence and data mining processes.

OLAP systems are used for various analytics, such as diagnostic, predictive, and prescriptive analytics. Unlike with OLTP systems, where the datasets are not so large, OLAP systems execute complex queries against large multidimensional databases and data lakes. Figure 1.9 depicts an OLAP system.

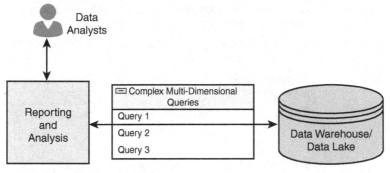

FIGURE 1.9   **OLAP System Overview**

Following are the key tenets of OLAP:

▶ OLAP supports multidimensional conceptual views of datasets.

▶ OLAP acts as a middle layer between a data warehouse and a front end.

▶ Data can be represented in advanced presentations such as 3D cubes, pivot tables, and cross tabs.

▶ OLAP can perform advanced computational functions and advanced data modeling functions.

Table 1.5 lists the key differences between OLTP and OLAP systems.

TABLE 1.5 **Differences Between OLTP and OLAP Systems**

Characteristic	OLTP	OLAP
Use-cases	It is an online transaction system mainly targeted at concurrent transactions.	It is an online analysis and data retrieving process leveraged for data analytics.
Processing capacity	It can process a large number of short online transactions.	It can process a large volume of data.
Types of queries	It deals with standard and straightforward queries such as insert, delete, and update queries.	It deals with complex multi-dimensional queries that involve select functions.
User personas	OLTP is primarily used by operational staff such as clerks and cashiers.	OLAP is primarily used by business analysts and data engineers.
Type of data processed	It addresses current transactional data.	It addresses primarily historical data.
Response time	Response time is milliseconds.	Response time is from a few seconds to minutes.
Backups	Requires complete back-ups of data.	Requires data backups from time to time.

Finally, it is important to know that OLTP and OLAP are not competing systems; rather, they are complementary systems. Typically, an organization has transactional data and batch data undergoing analytics and reporting. While from a business transaction perspective OLTP is key, analyzing the data is an aspect of OLAP, and this is where the two systems come together to give a holistic view into the organizational processes leading to business insights and feeding back into the process for continuous improvement.

To simplify this, let's consider an example of a new product to be launched and look at historical performance of an earlier version of the product. An OLTP system would have the historical data based on consumer transactions and key operational insights (such as inventory management and customer surveys). This data could be leveraged by OLAP and a data warehouse/data lake to get deeper insights into what changes are required from the previous product as well as what will make the new product sell like hotcakes in the market—whether it be a launch campaign or social media publicity/ads. Figure 1.10 depicts this arrangement at a high level and on an architectural level.

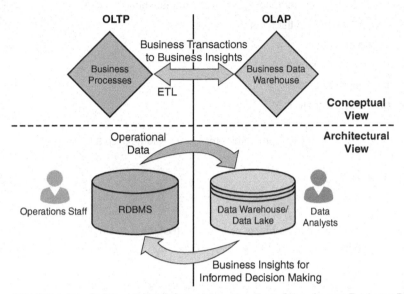

FIGURE 1.10 **OLTP and OLAP Complementing Each Other Across Business Processes and Business Insights**

The integration of OLTP and OLAP includes the following components:

▶ **Business processes:** These are the processes that the business follows to achieve the goals/outcomes set forth by the business owners/leaders.

▶ **Customer transactions:** This is information about the customers, products, and transactions stored in the OLTP database.

▶ **ETL (extract, transform, and load):** The transactional data from various relational database management systems is retrieved, transformed, and loaded in the data warehouse/data lake.

▶ **Data warehouse/data lake:** Data is accessed by the data mart from the data warehouse or from the data lake that is used by OLAP to store processed data.

▶ **Data mining, analytics, and decision making:** The data is extracted from the data warehouse/data lake through data mining, and after analysis, it is used for decision making.

Cram Quiz

Answer these questions. The answers follow the last question. If you cannot answer these questions correctly, consider reading this section again until you can.

1. OLAP is used for which of the following?

   - ○ **a.** Ad hoc data
   - ○ **b.** Transactional data
   - ○ **c.** Analytical data
   - ○ **d.** Heuristic analysis

2. True or false: OLAP and OLTP are complementary systems from a business perspective.

   - ○ **a.** True
   - ○ **b.** False

3. Large volumes of data can be processed by which of the following?

   - ○ **a.** OLTP
   - ○ **b.** SDLC
   - ○ **c.** OWASP
   - ○ **d.** OLAP

Cram Quiz Answers

1. **Answer: c. Analytical data.** Online analytical processing (OLAP) is focused on driving analytics-based insights on data imported from multiple data sources.

2. **Answer: a. True.** OLTP and OLAP are seen as complementary systems rather than as competing systems from a business perspective.

3. **Answer: d. OLAP.** OLAP systems are capable of managing large volumes of data.

What Next?

If you want more practice on this chapter's exam objective before you move on, remember that you can access all of the Cram Quiz questions on the Pearson Test Prep software online. You can also create a custom exam by objective with the Online Practice Test. Note any objective you struggle with and go to that objective's material in this chapter.

CHAPTER 2

Understanding Database Schemas and Dimensions

This chapter covers portions of Objective 1.1 (Identify basic concepts of data schemas and dimensions) of the CompTIA Data+ exam and includes the following topics:

▶ Schema concepts

▶ Snowflake and star schemas

▶ Slowly changing dimensions

▶ Keeping current information

▶ Keeping historical information

For more information on the official CompTIA Data+ exam topics, see the Introduction.

This chapter covers topics related to database schemas, particularly snowflake and star schemas. In addition, it explores the importance of keeping database information in current and historical formats.

Schema Concepts

CramSaver

If you can correctly answer these questions before going through this section, save time by skimming the Exam Alerts in this section and then completing the Cram Quiz at the end of the section.

1. A schema represents the _____ of a database.

   a. structure

   b. function

   c. relationships

   d. dimensions

2. The star schema is characterized by which of the following?

   a. High query complexity

   b. Bottom-up model

   c. Normalized data structure

   d. High level of data redundancy

Answers

1. **Answer: a. structure.** A database schema shows the structure used to store data is saved in a database.

2. **Answer: d. High level of data redundancy.** Because there is no normalization in the star schema, it has a high level of data redundancy.

We have already established the fact that data is a key component for business growth and to accelerate the presence in today's competitive market. Due to the increasing focus on the value of data, organizations are collecting massive volumes of data—running into petabytes—across data warehouses and data lakes.

Data is most useful if it is stored in a structure that is easy to understand and gives logical descriptions of and shows relationships between data objects. A schema represents the structure of the database. It shows how the data is arranged and the relationships among the data objects, such as tables, fields, packages, views, relationships, primary keys, and foreign keys. A schema is not data; rather, it provides information about the structure of data and relationships among tables or models. A database schema specifies which tables or relationships form a database and the fields included in each table.

There are three types of schema:

▶ **Physical schema:** A physical schema represents how data is stored physically in a disk storage or other storage system in the form of files. A database that is designed physically is known as a physical schema.

▶ **Logical schema:** A logical schema specifies the logical constraints that can be applied to the stored data. It shows the integrity constraints, which are rules that are used to maintain quality for insertion and update of data in a database management system. Entity relationship modeling is a process that specifies the relationships between the entities.

▶ **View schema:** A view schema describes the end user's interaction with a database system.

> **Note**
>
> A *view* can be described as a virtual table in the form of a predefined SQL query. A view can contain selected rows and can be created from multiple tables.

Figure 2.1 illustrates the three schemas.

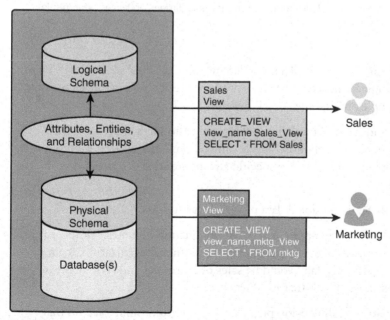

FIGURE 2.1   **Three Types of Database Schemas Logical, Physical, and Views**

> **Note**
>
> The process of creating a database schema is called *data modeling*.

Two data warehouse schemas are very commonly used:

▶ Star schema

▶ Snowflake schema

Before we get into the nuts and bolts of these schemas, let's take a moment to consider the importance of schemas in a data warehouse. As established in Chapter 1, "Understanding Databases and Data Warehouses," a typical data warehouse may store data from multiple data sources. Dimensional modeling provides the support needed for the high volume of queries against the data in a data warehouse. Dimensional modeling optimizes a database for faster retrieval of data.

> **Note**
>
> Ralph Kimball developed the concept of dimensional modeling based on "fact" and "dimension" tables. You'll learn more about fact and dimension tables later in this chapter.

The structure and storage of data in a data warehouse are designed such that the data warehouse can accommodate and decrease the time required for processing of complex multidimensional queries.

Dimensional modeling is implemented by using the star schema and the snowflake schema in data warehouses. These dimensional models have a unique method of data storage and offer specific advantages that are covered in this chapter.

The elements of a dimensional data model are as follows:

▶ **Facts:** As the name implies, facts are the quantified metrics or measurements from a business process perspective. In an organization, from a sales perspective, a fact would be sales of a product and retirement of the quota associated with that product.

▶ **Dimensions:** A dimension provides the context around a fact in that it defines the what, why, when, who, how, and so on. Again, in an organization, from a sales perspective, a dimension could be the type of product, how much of it sold in the last quarter, the profit margins, why it could not do as well as predicted, which salespeople reported an increase in volume sales of the product, and so on.

▶ **Attributes:** The attributes are the characteristics of the dimensions, such as where the product sold well (in which states or cities) or the average age of consumers.

▶ **Fact table:** The fact table is the primary table in dimension modeling, and it contains aggregate measures or data (from facts) as well as the foreign key to the dimension table(s).

▶ **Dimension table:** A dimension table contains the associated dimensions about the fact(s). As described previously, a dimension table is joined to a fact table by a foreign key. There may be one or more dimension tables associated with a fact table.

ExamAlert

Facts and dimensions are an important topic pertinent to database schemas.

Cram Quiz

Answer these questions. If you cannot answer these questions correctly, consider reading this section again until you can.

1. _____ developed the concept of dimensional modeling based on fact and dimension tables.

   ○ **a.** Ralph Kimball

   ○ **b.** Elvis Johnstone

   ○ **c.** Ben Parker

   ○ **d.** Harpreet Singh

2. True or false: A data warehouse is meant to process only single-dimensional queries.

   ○ **a.** True

   ○ **b.** False

3. There can be _____, _____, and _____ database schemas. (Choose three.)

- ○ **a.** relational
- ○ **b.** physical
- ○ **c.** logical
- ○ **d.** view

Cram Quiz Answers

1. **Answer: a. Ralph Kimball.** The concept of dimensional modeling was developed by Ralph Kimball.

2. **Answer: b. False.** Data warehouses contain data that is typically multidimensional; therefore, the queries against such data tend to be multidimensional and complex queries.

3. **Answer: b. physical, c. logical, d. view.** There are three database schemas: physical, logical, and view schemas.

Star and Snowflake Schemas

If you can correctly answer these questions before going through this section, save time by skimming the Exam Alerts in this section and then completing the Cram Quiz at the end of the section.

1. The following figure is an example of what type of schema?

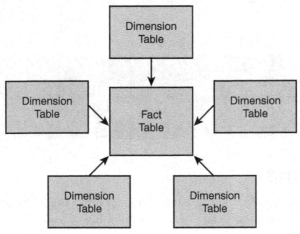

   a. Star schema

   b. Snowflake schema

   c. Dimensional outlook schema

   d. Fact table schema

2. A fact table has which of the following types of columns? (Choose two.)

   a. Column that contains dimension attributes

   b. Column that contains facts

   c. Column that contains foreign keys to the dimension table

   d. Row that contains the substitute keys

3. The _____ schema has multiple dimension and sub-dimension tables.

   a. star

   b. fact

   c. dimension

   d. snowflake

Answers

1. **Answer: a. Star schema.** This figure shows the star schema, with fact table joined to multiple dimension tables.

2. **Answer: b. Column that contains facts, c. Column that contains foreign keys to the dimension table.** A fact table is a collection of quantifiable facts and points to a dimension table or tables for attributes around these facts.

3. **Answer: d. snowflake.** The snowflake schema extends the star schema by adding sub-dimension tables.

ExamAlert

The snowflake schema is becoming increasingly pertinent in data warehousing and has been adopted widely across data warehousing applications. The CompTIA Data+ exam is likely to focus on this schema.

Star Schema

A star schema, as the name implies, is a star-shaped schema that consists of a star structure with one (primary) fact table and a number of associated dimension tables. The star schema supports querying for large datasets.

Figure 2.2 illustrates the star schema.

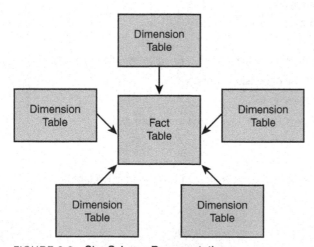

FIGURE 2.2 **Star Schema Representation**

You have already learned a bit about fact tables and dimension tables. In this section, we'll look at them more closely.

You already know that a fact table contains facts, and it is connected to a dimension table via a foreign key. Further, a fact table has two types of columns:

▶ Column that contains facts

▶ Column that contains foreign keys to the dimension table

The fact table consists of a primary key, which is usually a composite key made up of all the foreign keys. The facts in the fact table include either detail-level facts or aggregated facts.

The dimension table is composed of one or more hierarchies that classify the data. If there are no hierarchies in a dimension table, then it is termed a *flat dimension* or a *list*. The primary keys of a dimension table are components of composite primary keys of the fact table. The attributes of a dimension table are descriptive and textual values. A dimension table is smaller in size than a fact table.

To put all this information about fact and dimension tables into context, let's look at an example. Consider the following fact table, called **Sales_Revenue**:

Table Sales_Revenue

Sales Revenue
Product_Number
Region_ID
Customer_ID
Sales_RepID
Target_ID

Now consider the dimension tables **Product_Number**, **Region_ID**, and **Customer_ID** that expand on the **Sales_Revenue** fact table:

Tables Product_Number, Region_ID, Customer_ID, and Sales_RepID

Product_ Number	Region_ID	Customer_ID	Sales_RepID	Target_ID
Product_SaaS_ID	SaaS_Govt	Customer_ Name	Sales_Rep_ Name	Sales_Rep_SFDC
Product_SaaS_ List_Price	SaaS_ Public_Sec	Customer_ SFDC_ID	Sales_Rep_ Product_SaaS	Sales_SaaS_Target
Product_PaaS_ List_Price	PaaS_Govt	Customer_ Industry	Sales_Rep_ Product_PaaS	Sales_PaaS_Target

Product_Number	Region_ID	Customer_ID	Sales_RepID	Target_ID
Product_SaaS_Demographics	PaaS_Public_Sec	Customer_Existing_Assets	Sales_Rep_Govt_Sec	Sales_SaaS_Quota
Product_PaaS_Demographics	SaaS_Others	Customer_Renewals	Sales_Rep_Public_Sec	Sales_PaaS_Quota

Note

This example shows only some of the dimension tables involved in this schema.

Based on this example, Figure 2.3 outlines the way the star schema would look.

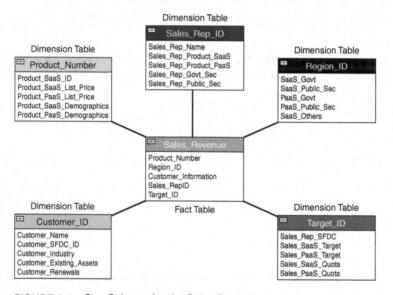

FIGURE 2.3   **Star Schema for the Sales Example**

Following are the key characteristics of the star schema in this example:

▶ Each dimension is represented by only one dimension table.

▶ The fact table consists of a key and a measure.

▶ Each dimension table consist of a set of attributes.

▶ The dimension tables are joined with the fact table via foreign keys.

▶ The dimension tables are not joined to each other directly.

▶ The performance compared to that of the snowflake schema is better as the structure is simpler, and queries are faster.

Next, we will cover the snowflake schema.

Snowflake Schema

The snowflake schema is an expansion or extension of the star schema in that the dimension tables are further connected to sub-dimension tables. The representation of the fact table, dimension tables, and sub-dimension tables resembles the shape of a snowflake—hence the name *snowflake schema*. Figure 2.4 shows the structure of the snowflake schema.

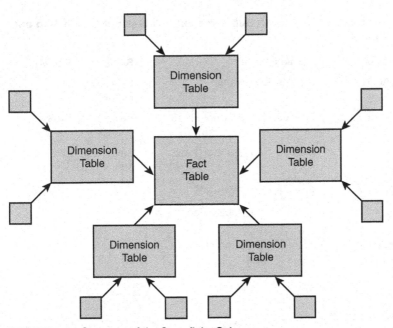

FIGURE 2.4   **Structure of the Snowflake Schema**

As shown in Figure 2.4, the fact table is surrounded by dimension tables; and in addition, sub-dimension tables are associated with dimension tables through a many-to-one relationship. Each dimension table represents one level in the hierarchy that is extended by one or more sub-dimension tables. There is no limit to the sub-dimensions that can be created for a given dimension table.

Consider the sub-dimension tables for the dimension tables Product_ID and Sales_Rep_ID:

Dimension Table Product_Number with Sub-dimension Tables Product_PaaS and Product_SaaS

Product_PaaS	Product_Number	Product_SaaS
Product_PaaS_Cloud	Product_SaaS_ID	Product_SaaS_Cloud
Product_PaaS_Hybrid	Product_SaaS_List_Price	Product_SaaS_Hybrid
	Product_PaaS_List_Price	
	Product_SaaS_Demographics	
	Product_PaaS_Demographics	

Dimension Table Sales_RepID with Sub-dimension Tables Sales_Rep_Info and Sales_Rep_Funnel

Sales_Rep_Info	Sales_RepID	Sales_Rep_Funnel
Sales_Rep_Address	Sales_Rep_Name	Sales_Rep_SaaS_Funnel
Sales_Rep_Education	Sales_Rep_Product_SaaS	Sales_Rep_PaaS_Funnel
Sales_Rep_Age	Sales_Rep_Product_PaaS	Sales_Rep_Total_Funnel
	Sales_Rep_Govt_Sec	
	Sales_Rep_Public_Sec	

Figure 2.5 shows these tables in the snowflake schema.

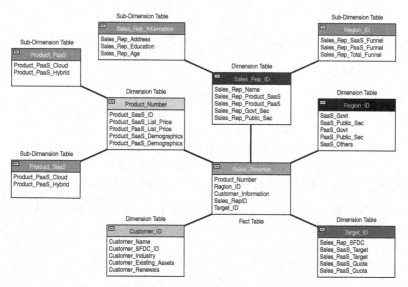

FIGURE 2.5 Snowflake Schema for the Sales Example

The key characteristics of the snowflake schema are as follows:

▶ The performance is slower compared to that of the star schema due to the presence of multiple tables.

▶ The schema is easier to implement than the star schema primarily due to the extensive use of dimension tables.

▶ The snowflake schema normalizes information.

▶ Operational maintenance of the snowflake schema is difficult because there are many tables.

> **Note**
>
> *Normalization* is the process of structuring database tables in order to reduce data redundancy and improve data integrity.

Table 2.1 provides an overview of the differences between the star and snowflake schemas.

TABLE 2.1 **Star Schema vs. Snowflake Schema**

Characteristic	Star Schema	Snowflake Schema
Structure	The star schema contains one fact table that is surrounded by one or more dimension tables.	The snowflake schema is an extension of the star schema in which there are sub-dimension tables that are connected to the dimension tables.
Design complexity	The design of the database is simple because there are no sub-dimension tables.	The presence of sub-dimension tables makes the database design complex.
Data redundancy	There is a high level of data redundancy.	There is a very low level of data redundancy.
Data structure	The data structure is denormalized.	The data structure is normalized.
Foreign keys	The number of foreign keys is low, which means the query time is fast.	There are many foreign keys, which means it takes more time to process the queries.
Suitability and relationships	The star schema is suitable for data marts with simple relationships.	The snowflake schema is suitable for data warehouses with complex relationships.
Use cases	The star schema is recommended for a dimension table that has a small number of rows of records.	The snowflake schema is recommended when there are multiple dimension tables with multiple rows or records because it reduces redundancy.

Cram Quiz

Answer these questions. If you cannot answer these questions correctly, consider reading this section again until you can.

1. The snowflake schema _____ the data stored.

   ○ **a.** reduces

   ○ **b.** normalizes

   ○ **c.** compresses

   ○ **d.** absorbs

2. True or false: The star schema is suitable for a data warehouse with complex relationships.

   ○ **a.** True

   ○ **b.** False

3. In the star schema, dimension tables _____ have sub-dimension tables.

   ○ **a.** may

   ○ **b.** may not

   ○ **c.** definitely

   ○ **d.** do not

Cram Quiz Answers

1. **Answer: b. normalizes.** The snowflake schema stores data in normalized format, with a very low level of redundancy.

2. **Answer: b. False.** Data warehouses with complex relationships should leverage the snowflake schema.

3. **Answer: d. do not.** The star schema boasts dimension tables joined with fact tables, whereas the snowflake schema extends the star schema by adding sub-dimension tables to dimension tables to store complex relationships.

Slowly Changing Dimensions, Keeping Historical Information, and Keeping Current Information

CramSaver

If you can correctly answer these questions before going through this section, save time by skimming the Exam Alerts in this section and then completing the Cram Quiz at the end of the section.

1. SCD type 0 represents which of the following?

   a. Never changing data attributes

   b. Sometimes changing data attributes

   c. Updating from historical to current data attributes

   d. Historical tables created as part of fact tables

2. An organization has data about customers that used to and still have a relationship with the organization. One customer announces that it has a new CIO, and this information is updated in the organization's data warehouse. This is an example of which of the following?

   a. Historical information

   b. Current information

   c. Categorical information

   d. Consistent information

3. True or false: Data dimensions do not necessarily change periodically.

   a. True

   b. False

Answers

1. **Answer: a. Never changing data attributes.** Slowly changing dimension (SCD) type 0 refers to data attributes that never change; these attributes will continue to persist as is and will not be updated in the data warehouse. An example would be the date that an organization was established.

2. **Answer: b. Current information.** As the customer's information changes, the organization updates its data warehouse. This is an example of keeping the information current.

3. **Answer: a. True.** Data dimensions change with time; however, the changes may or may not occur periodically.

Data collected over time can be analyzed to help in guessing what will happen in the near future based on past events. It is important to understand that, as the years go by, the data stored in the past is not current and should be treated as historical data, whereas current data is just that—current information that may be leveraged for real-time decision making.

Data dimensions change gradually over time rather than over predetermined time periods or intervals. Some characteristics continue to evolve, whereas others become irrelevant. You can see this in your own life, where some experiences help you make decisions in the future, whereas others are just experiences at a point in time and have no value in the near or far future.

The following sections cover slowly changing dimensions as well as topics related to keeping current information and keeping historical information.

Keeping Current and Historical Information

Information that is current—or the "now" information in a data warehouse—is typically leveraged for purposes of producing reports, dashboards, and data-driven business metrics, which enable an organization to make informed decisions. For example, the current information about how many employees have achieved their sales targets enables a business to project the near-future sales quota that should be created for the sales reps as well as define the market cap the company should pursue.

On the other hand, keeping historical information implies that an organization has access to historical records and can base future decision making on what happened a while ago. For example, an organization might look at how product A did vs. product B across the last 3 to 5 years to determine whether there's any reason to keep the lower-performing product in the market when investment in R&D of the higher-performing product would yield better results that drive the organizational goals and keep it ahead of competition.

In order for an organization to effectively and efficiently use a data warehouse, the data warehouse must be designed such that users are able to analyze historical and current information and drive decisions based on data points.

Slowly Changing Dimensions

Slowly changing dimensions (SCDs) refers to the concept where data dimensions in a data warehouse contain both current and historical data, and the data dimensions change over time (though not necessarily periodically). SCDs are mostly seen as a progressive factor among data engineers, administrators, architects, and consultants as they have to manage and keep on top of changing attributes.

> **ExamAlert**
>
> Slowly changing dimensions is a key topic and expect to see questions on it in CompTIA Data+ exam.

Why keep both current and historical data in a data warehouse—and why bother keeping historical data at all? The rationale for keeping historical data has already been mentioned: Analyzing historical data can help in making future decisions. Whether to keep historical data is largely a business decision that is likely to be governed by the business needs and goals of an organization. A business may require historical insights to reflect on what is possible tomorrow to drive sales, for example.

To further contextualize SCDs, let's take a look at an example. In an organization, the sales department has to maintain data for its customers as well as sales reps and products. As time progresses, sales representatives may move on from the organization. Moreover, customer accounts may change as the organization acquires new customers and loses old ones. In addition, the organization's products will continue to evolve, with new versions/releases replacing old ones. In this case, keeping track of how many customers have been acquired or lost is an important metric for the business to have and will drive its decisions related to attracting and retaining more customers. The product lines that are no longer relevant may just be archival data; this data would not have any impact on future products. Finally, the data related to sales reps who are no longer with the organization can provide valuable insights on controlling attrition in the workforce.

Let's take a look at the various SCDs and how they can help organizations adopt effective ways to manage the information in their data warehouses.

Slowly Changing Dimension Type 0

SCD type 0 refers to data attributes that never change. These attributes will continue to persist as is and will not be updated in the data warehouse. An example would be the date the organization was established as this is an attribute associated with an immutable fact about the organization. You would not expect this specific dimension to change in the data warehouse. The advantage of SCD type 0 records is that they never require updating and are persistent.

Slowly Changing Dimension Type 1

SCD type 1 data is new information; with this type, the latest snapshot of the record overwrites the earlier data in the data warehouse. In other words, no historical records are kept. An example would be an employee changing their marital status. Because this is an attribute associated with the employee, keeping any historical records would not have any meaningful context or outcomes.

Another example would be the type of customer record. For instance, as shown in the following tables, the customer field Cust_Type changed from Retail to Corporate. However, the business records would not gain much from keeping this historical information.

Before the Change

Cust_ID	Cust_Name	Cust_Type
C001	Alex Murphy	Retail

After the Change

Cust_ID	Cust_Name	Cust_Type
C001	Alex Murphy	Corporate

The key advantage of SCD type 1 is that it offers an easy solution to handle the SCD issues as there is no need to keep track of the historical information. One the other hand, the disadvantage is that all history is lost, and it is not easy to trace back older records.

Slowly Changing Dimension Type 2

SCD type 2 refers to new data that is added in new rows; it does not overwrite the old data. Hence, all the historical data is kept intact for future use. This is a common approach for maintaining and leveraging historical records along with current data. However, a large data warehouse is needed to store all the current and historical data. Hence, the usability of the data should be evaluated to determine whether the data is required for business reports. Here's an example of changing dimensions and leveraging SCD type 2:

Before the Change

Cust_ID	Cust_Name	Cust_Type	Start_Date	End_Date	Current_Customer
C001	Have More	Retail	1.1.2020	31-12-9999	Y

After the Change

Cust_ID	Cust_Name	Cust_Type	Start_Date	End_Date	Current_Customer
C001	Have More	Retail	1.1.2020	31-12-2020	N
C002	Jacky's Spaceships	Corporate	22.2.21	31-12-9999	Y

Slowly Changing Dimension Type 3

SCD type 3 refers to data added in new columns. This is very similar to type 2, but instead of adding rows in type 2, type 3 adds columns for new dimension attributes. When one of the attribute value changes, the old value is moved to a separate column, and the current column is updated with the new value. The following example shows how the rep's department change is reflected.

Before the Change

Rep_ID	Rep_Name	Profile	Salary_Annual	Rep_Dept_Current
R001	Satya Singh	Consultant	$50000	Retail

After the Change

Rep_ID	Rep_Name	Profile	Salary_Annual	Rep_Dept_Current	Rep_Dept_Old
R001	Satya Singh	Consultant	$50000	Corporate	Retail

> **Note**
>
> SCD type 2 is much more commonplace than SCD type 3.

Slowly Changing Dimension Type 4

SCD type 4 refers to the data changes handled by creating and maintaining a new table altogether for historical information and keeping the original table updated with current data. This approach leads to the creation of multiple historical information tables in a data warehouse. Type 4 is not common.

The following example, which builds on the previous one, shows an employee changing roles/profiles within an organization that uses SCD type 4.

Current Table

Rep_ID	Rep_Name	Profile	Salary_Annual	Rep_Dept_Current
R001	Satya Singh	Consultant	$50000	Corporate

Historical Table

Rep_ID	Rep_Name	Profile	Salary_Annual	Rep_Dept_Current
R001	Satya Singh	Graduate Hire	$30000	Corporate

Cram Quiz

Answer these questions. If you cannot answer these questions correctly, consider reading this section again until you can.

1. SCD type 4 relies on creating _____ to reflect historical data.
   - a. new rows
   - b. new columns
   - c. a new table
   - d. a new database

2. Slowly changing dimensions (SCDs) is seen as a(n) _____ by data engineers, administrators, and consultants.
   - a. essential outcome of adopting databases
   - b. new plug-in for data warehouses
   - c. DBMS for data warehouses
   - d. standard in-built feature of data warehouses
   - e. issue

3. SCD type 3 relies on creating _____ to reflect historical data.
   - a. new rows
   - b. new columns
   - c. a new table
   - d. a new database

4. An employee joins the organization and undergoes orientation, where he learns about the organization's past. The date the organization was established would be SCD type _____.

  ○ **a.** 4

  ○ **b.** 1

  ○ **c.** 3

  ○ **d.** 0

Cram Quiz Answers

1. **Answer: c. a new table.** SCD type 4 relies on creating a new table for historical information in the data warehouse and keeping the current table updated with new data.

2. **Answer: e. an issue.** SCDs are seen as an issue as data engineers, consultants, administrators, and so on have to deal on an ongoing basis with data that changes over time.

3. **Answer: b. new columns.** SCD type 3 relies on creating new columns in the same row to reflect historical information.

4. **Answer: d. 0.** Never-changing data attributes are categorized as SCD type 0.

What Next?

If you want more practice on this chapter's exam objective before you move on, remember that you can access all of the Cram Quiz questions on the Pearson Test Prep software online. You can also create a custom exam by objective with the Online Practice Test. Note any objective you struggle with and go to that objective's material in this chapter.

CHAPTER 3

Data Types and Types of Data

This chapter covers Objective 1.2 (Compare and contrast different data types) of the CompTIA Data+ exam and includes the following topics:

▶ Introduction to data types

▶ Different data types compared and contrasted

▶ Discrete vs. continuous data

▶ Categorical vs. dimension data

▶ Types of data audio, video, and images

For more information on the official CompTIA Data+ exam topics, see the Introduction.

This chapter covers topics related to data types and types of data. It is essential to understand the types of data that are available to you as well as what a data type is. This chapter introduces additional types of data, discrete vs. continuous data, and categorial and dimensional data types. Finally, this chapter looks at various types of data, including images, audio, and video.

Introduction to Data Types

CramSaver

If you can correctly answer these questions before going through this section, save time by completing the Cram Quiz at the end of the section

1. What is the minimum length of any data type?

   a. 1 byte

   b. 2 bytes

   c. 4 bytes

   d. 8 bytes

2. Which of the following are defined as reserved locations for memory to store the data values?

   a. Arrays

   b. Variables

   c. Strings

   d. Pointers

3. Which of the following is the storage size of the double data type?

   a. 12 bytes

   b. 8 bytes

   c. 4 bytes

   d. 2 bytes

Answers

1. **Answer: a. 1 byte.** The minimum length of any data type is 1 byte (that is, 8 bits).

2. **Answer: b. Variables.** Variables are reserved locations in memory for storing values; for example, a user who creates a variable allocates certain memory space. Based on the variable type of data, the OS allots memory and determines what can be placed in reserved memory.

3. **Answer: b. 8 bytes.** The storage space required for a double data type is 64 bits (that is, 8 bytes). Such a data type may have between a 1.7 e-038 minimum value and a 1.7 e+038 maximum value.

Think of the beautiful images that you see on your phone or computer or the audio files that contain your favorite music. How is such data interpreted and stored or retrieved by machines? In a computer, even complex data consists of some basic types of data or data types. There are several kinds of data types available for storing and retrieving data. They are the building blocks of modern computing systems and the foundation for data analysis.

> **Note**
>
> Don't forget that the main aim of computer programs is to extract, process, and store data. Therefore, organized data can have a profound impact on the memory needs and running time of a program leveraging the data.

A data type can be defined as:

- ▶ A number of values (or a single finite value) along with rules set for varied operations

- ▶ A data classification that instructs the interpreter or compiler on the use of data

- ▶ What and how the data is inserted into the programming language

- ▶ A system for denoting functions and variables of varied types of data

Data types can be of various lengths. The minimum length of a data type is 1 byte (that is, 8 bits). Every type of data has a default value. The data type determines how you insert data into a database or how it is leveraged in a programming language.

These are the basic data types:

- ▶ Character

- ▶ Float

- ▶ Integer

- ▶ Double

- ▶ String

> **Note**
>
> There are variations to these basic data types, such as long float and short integer.

Storage Sizes of Various Data Types

Different data types tend to have different sizes. The size of a data type depends on the compiler or system architecture (for example, 32-bit or 64-bit architecture). Table 3.1 lists the storage sizes of various data types.

TABLE 3.1 **Storage Sizes of Various Data Types**

Data Type	Storage Size
Character	1 byte
Integer	2 or 4 bytes
Float	4 bytes
Double	8 bytes
String	1 byte per character

The following sections cover these data types in more detail.

Character

The character data type is used for an individual value. It can include numeric digits (that is, 0 through 9), upper- and lowercase letters (that is, a through z or A through Z), and special characters and symbols (such as . , ; and :).

> **Note**
>
> The values of characters are represented as ASCII.

You use the keyword char to denote the character data type. For example, in MySQL, the character data type is defined as CHAR(*value*). For example, CHAR(5) would create a character data type with five characters (for example, ABCDE or 12345 or A1B3C).

There are two types of character data types: signed char and unsigned char. Whereas the signed char type can store zero, positive, and negative integer values, the unsigned char type can store only non-negative integer values.

The next section covers the topic of integer data type.

Integer

Integers are the whole numbers that can have negative, zero, and positive values. An integer cannot include decimal places or fractional parts. Examples of integers are 1, 6, 9, and 99.

> **Note**
>
> An integer is a set of binary bits in a computer program.

The size of an integer data type is usually 4 bytes.

The integer data type is created using the keyword int. For example, in MySQL, the integer data type is defined as INT(*value*).

The next section covers the topic of float and double data types.

Float and Double

A number that includes a fractional and/or decimal portion is known as a floating point number (or a float). A floating point number may include a decimal portion (for example, 0.1, 3.15, 7.3, and 130.5) or may be a fraction (such as 1/10, 7/30, or 9/90).

Usually, the keyword float is used to indicate a floating point number. In MySQL, you create a float by using the syntax FLOAT(*value*).

> **Note**
>
> Floating point numbers are real numbers, but for real-life values, approximations may be used for floats. For example, in discussing distance in meters, whereas a computer will use a precise value such as 1.01 m, humans might round off to 1 m. For computers, every decimal value is important as these values can change outcomes greatly.

There's an alternative to float: the double data type. While a float data type occupies 32 bits, a double data type occupies 64 bits. The major difference between the two is precision; that is, a double has 15 decimal digits of precision, whereas a float has only 7. The digits of precision refer to total number of digits, including the decimal places. For example, a float data type might show the decimal value 1.123456, whereas a double data type can show the same value as 1.12345671234567. As you can see, a double data type gives much more precise results when performing calculations.

With MySQL, a double data type would be created as follows:

DOUBLE(p,s)

where p is the total size, or precision, of the number, and s is the scale, or the number of digits shown after the decimal point. (You'll learn more about precision and scale later in this chapter.)

> **Note**
>
> A double data type has twice the precision of a floating point number and uses double the space in memory.

The next section covers the topic of array data type.

Array

An array is a linear data structure that comprises of a set of data elements of similar data type. An array is stored in a contiguous memory location. For example, in C++ you can define an array as follows:

int array[10] = { 0, 1, 2, 3, 4, 5, 6, 7, 8, 9 };

In this case, the array has been defined as type integer with 10 values, 0 to 9.

The next section covers the topic of string data type.

String

A string data type contains alphanumeric data—that is, letters, numbers, spaces, and other symbols. A real-world example of a string is plaintext. For example, "Data Packet" and "1001 Data packets" are both string data types.

> **Note**
>
> Whereas floating point, double, and integer data types are used for numerals, the string data type is used for text. A number can be set as a string, but if it is, numeric calculations cannot be performed on it as it is treated as text.

Although a string can include numbers as well as letters and special characters, it is handled as text. In SQL, strings can be represented by CHAR, VARCHAR, and TEXT.

The next section contrasts and compares the various data types.

Cram Quiz

Answer these questions. If you cannot answer these questions correctly, consider reading this section again until you can.

1. The word "School" and the phrase "I go to college" are _____ data types.
   - ○ **a.** string
   - ○ **b.** character
   - ○ **c.** integer
   - ○ **d.** char

2. True or false: A number that includes a fractional or decimal portion is a floating point number.
   - ○ **a.** True
   - ○ **b.** False

3. What is the decimal place precision of the float data type?
   - ○ **a.** 7
   - ○ **b.** 10
   - ○ **c.** 13
   - ○ **d.** 14

Cram Quiz Answers

1. **Answer: a. string.** Both the word "School" and the phrase "I go to college" are string data types.
2. **Answer: a. True.** A number that includes a fractional or decimal portion is a floating point number. For example, 3.15 and 130.5 are floating point numbers.
3. **Answer: a. 7.** A float has 7 decimal places of precision, whereas a double has 15 places of precision.

Comparing and Contrasting Different Data Types

CramSaver

If you can correctly answer these questions before going through this section, save time by skimming the Exam Alerts in this section and then completing the Cram Quiz at the end of the section.

1. True or false: VARCHAR and TEXT can both have a maximum of 65,535 characters.

   a. True

   b. False

2. The alphanumeric data type can contain which of the following? (Choose all that apply.)

   a. Letters

   b. Numeric values

   c. Whitespace

   d. Special symbols

3. The _____ data type is used for non-integer constants.

   a. float

   b. numeric

   c. integer

   d. constant

4. What is the result of applying money_used(5,1) to the number 56789 in context to precision value?

   a. 556789

   b. 5678.9

   c. 5.67890

   d. .56789

Answers

1. **Answer: a. True.** Both VARCHAR and TEXT can store a maximum of 65,535 characters.

2. **Answer: a. Letters, b. Numeric values, c. Whitespace, d. Special symbols.** The alphanumeric data type can consist of letters, numeric values, whitespace, and special symbols.

3. **Answer: b. numeric.** The numeric data type is used for non-integer constants.

4. **Answer: b. 5678.9.** Precision is the total number of digits, whereas scale is the number of digits after the decimal place. Therefore, given the number 56789, if the precision value is 5 and the scale value is 1, the result is 5678.9.

ExamAlert

Expect the CompTIA Data+ exam to test you on date, numeric, alphanumeric, currency, and text data types in the context of the exam objectives and in relation to real-world applications.

This section focuses on different data formats and types and covers their features and how they are leveraged. These data formats and types are the basic elements that build a database and that are leveraged as inputs/outputs in computer programs.

We will start by covering the details around date data type.

Date

As its name suggests, the date data type reflects date information. The type of data in this field is formatted in a particular way, and the format depends on the way the computer is set up in terms of region and user preference, as well as the software in use. A date field is used, for example, to capture initiation/termination dates, creation or order dates, and follow-up dates.

The following are some of the examples of date data formats:

mm/dd/yyyy

dd/mm/yyyy

dd/mm/yy

m/d/yy

d/m/yy

As you can see in these examples, date data includes year, month, and day values. A date data type stores a date from a calendar as an integer value.

Figure 3.1 illustrates how date data can be formatted on a Windows PC.

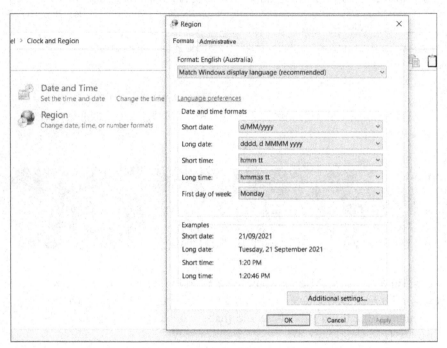

FIGURE 3.1   **Date Formatting on a Windows PC**

Fun Fact

Try to set a date beyond 9999 A.D. on a PC.

Let's consider an example. In the date 10/15/2007, 10 is the month value (which can range from 1 to 12), 15 is the day of the month (which can range from 1 to 31), and 2007 is the year (which can range from 0001 to 9999).

The values of a date data type have independent output and input formats. This means that a user can enter date data values in one style and handle them in a different style.

Note

The date data type manages years from 1 A.D. to 9999 A.D. according to the Gregorian calendar system.

The next section covers the topic of alphanumeric data type.

Alphanumeric

The alphanumeric data type is restricted to numeric and alphabetic characters—that is, letters, numbers, whitespace, and some common symbols. For a database that expects alphanumeric entries, a user can enter any name that includes both letters and numbers (for example, Happy2022, CompTIA Data Exam 2022).

> **Note**
>
> The alphanumeric character set includes punctuation marks in addition to upper- and lowercase letters.

The alphanumeric field type is helpful in describing the input that can be entered in a field (for example, an alphanumeric password).

What happens if non-alphanumeric characters are entered in an alphanumeric field (in the absence of data validation)? Well, in this case, the non-alphanumeric characters are considered symbols, which are handled as whitespace.

The next section covers the topic of numeric data type.

Numeric

Numeric data consists of just numbers. It can be represented using small integer, integer, float, and double data types.

Numeric data is broadly classified into two types: approximate and exact. Approximate numeric data can be stored in the floating point data type, and exact numeric data can be stored in the decimal and integer data types.

> **ExamAlert**
>
> It is important to understand the key difference between exact and approximate. With exact, all the values in the data type range can be represented exactly with adjusting precision and scale. With *approximate*, not all values in the data type range can be represented exactly.

In SQL, exact data types can be represented as NUMERIC(p,s) and DECIMAL(p,s), where p is precision and s is scale.

What are precision and scale? Essentially, precision is the total number of essential digits that the data type stores or the number of digits both before and after the decimal point. Scale is the number of decimal places to the right of the decimal point. The scale must be less than or equal to the precision.

In a real-world application, you would see numeric data leveraged for things like money, so that you could insert a value into a table with a certain precision. For example, say that you use the following notation to set the precision to 9 and the scale to 4:

money_balance numeric(9,4)

This allows numbers such as 11111.1111 and 99999.9999, which both have precision of 9 and scale of 4.

The next section covers the topic of text data type.

Text

The text data type stores any text data. It can include both multibyte and single-byte characters that are defined by the locale. The text type of field is used for alphanumeric data (that is, letters, numerals, symbols, and whitespace). This type of field is the least restrictive type of field in a database.

Text data can be broadly categorized into three categories: TEXT, MEDIUM-TEXT, and LONGTEXT. Whereas TEXT can support up to 65,535 characters, MEDIUMTEXT can store strings up to 16 MB, and LONGTEXT can store strings up to 4 GB.

In addition, you have another option for storing more characters than CHAR supports. For example, in MySQL you can use VARCHAR (which stands for variable CHAR). VARCHAR supports 65,535 characters, but while the text field is fixed at that length, you can actually define a variable field between 0 and 65,535 characters by using VARCHAR. You might, for example, use VAR-CHAR for storing a few strings and use TEXT for storing paragraphs.

The next section covers the topic of currency data type.

Currency

Currency data is numeric monetary data that is formatted using a currency symbol (such as $ or €) and two decimal places. Currency variables are 64-bit numbers in integer format scaled by 10,000 to present a fixed-point number with 15 digits to the left of the decimal point and 4 digits to the right of the decimal point. A currency field permits users to enter the values in the currencies of various countries.

Figure 3.2 shows the currency settings in Windows that you can set for a particular region.

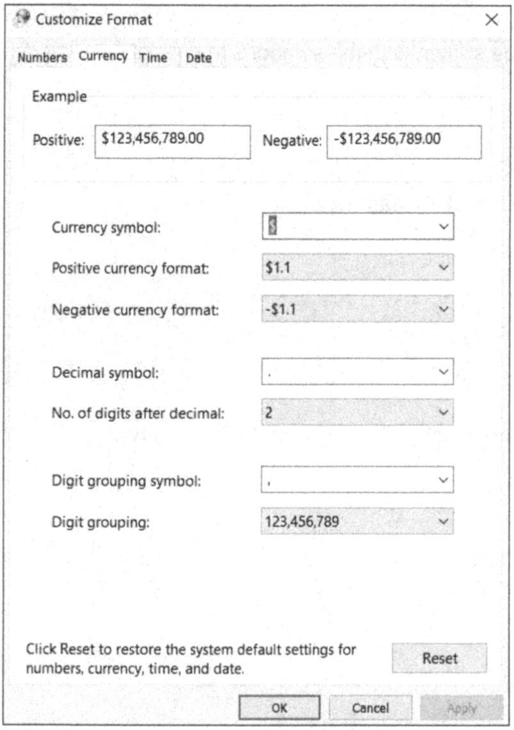

Customize Format ✕

Numbers   Currency   Time   Date

Example

Positive: | $123,456,789.00 | Negative: | -$123,456,789.00 |

Currency symbol: [ ]

Positive currency format: $1.1

Negative currency format: -$1.1

Decimal symbol: .

No. of digits after decimal: 2

Digit grouping symbol: ,

Digit grouping: 123,456,789

Click Reset to restore the system default settings for numbers, currency, time, and date.   [Reset]

[OK]   [Cancel]   [Apply]

FIGURE 3.2   **Currency Settings on a Windows PC**

Microsoft Access has a field called Currency that holds up to 15 digits before the decimal point and 4 digits after. SQL, on the other hand, has functions such as money (8 bytes) or smallmoney (4 bytes).

The next section gives insight to the topics of categorical vs. dimensional and discrete vs. continuous data types.

Cram Quiz

Answer these questions. If you cannot answer these questions correctly, consider reading this section again until you can.

1. True or false: Currency can only be shown with the symbol $ in a database.

   ○ **a.** True

   ○ **b.** False

2. What is the storage size of the LONGTEXT data type?

   ○ **a.** 1 KB

   ○ **b.** 1 MB

   ○ **c.** 16 MB

   ○ **d.** 4 GB

3. Numeric data can be classified into which of the following? (Choose two.)

   ○ **a.** Exact

   ○ **b.** Approximate

   ○ **c.** Continuous

   ○ **d.** Dimensional

Cram Quiz Answers

1. **Answer: b. False.** Currency can be shown in the local currency or in any other currency.

2. **Answer: d. 4 GB.** Text data can be broadly categorized into three categories: TEXT, MEDIUMTEXT, and LONGTEXT. Whereas TEXT can support up to 65,535 characters, MEDIUMTEXT can store strings up to 16 MB, and LONGTEXT can store strings up to 4 GB.

3. **Answer: a. Exact, b. Approximate.** Numeric data can be broadly classified into two types: approximate and exact.

67

Categorical vs. Dimension and Discrete vs. Continuous Data Types

Categorical vs. Dimension and Discrete vs. Continuous Data Types

CramSaver

If you can correctly answer these questions before going through this section, save time by completing the Cram Quiz at the end of the section.

1. Categorical data can be represented using which of the following? (Choose all that apply.)

   a. Bar graph

   b. Pie chart

   c. Bar chart

   d. Line graph

   e. None of these options are correct.

2. Discrete data can be best represented using which of the following?

   a. Bar graph

   b. Plot graph

   c. Line graph

   d. Scatter plot graph

3. Continuous data is best represented using which of the following?

   a. Line graph

   b. Scatter plot graph

   c. Bar graph

   d. All of these answers are correct.

Answers

1. **Answer: a. Bar graph, b. Pie chart.** Categorical data can be represented using bar graphs and pie charts. Bar graphs show categorical data using bars, with gaps between the bars, and pie charts show categorical data in a pie fashion, with each category occupying a piece of pie.

2. **Answer: d. Scatter plot graph.** Discrete data can be represented using a scatter plot graph, which shows the relationship between two or more numeric variables.

3. **Answer: a. Line graph.** Continuous data can be best represented using a line graph, which is estimated on a scale with several possible values.

This section covers the categorical and dimension data types.

Categorical/Dimension Data Types

The categorical data type represents variables with two or more categories or classifications. At times it is also used for data that can be identified by groups of observations that share a similar trait. Figure 3.3 shows categories of sales across infrastructure, server, database, SaaS, and PaaS as a pie chart; the same data could instead be shown using a bar graph or histogram.

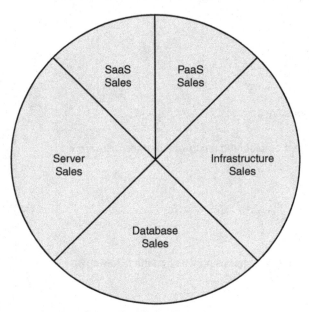

FIGURE 3.3   **Categorical Sales Data**

Another example of categorical data is survey data. Say that a survey is launched to capture responses about shopping experiences. This type of data would not have any numeric values; rather, it would be qualitative in nature (for example, what is working for the customers, what can be done better to create a good customer experience while people shop).

Categorical data can be classified into nominal and ordinal data. Nominal data implies named categories—like SaaS, PaaS, database, servers, and infrastructure in Figure 3.3. Ordinal data is ranked. For example, in the survey example, customers can be asked to provide feedback on a scale of 0 to 5, where 0 is worst service and 5 is best service; these ordinal values from the survey reflect areas of excellence and improvement, without absolute meaning assigned to each value (that is, each value is a label rather than a number that can be used in calculations).

69

Categorical vs. Dimension and Discrete vs. Continuous Data Types

Dimensions (such as names or group names or scale values) can be used with categorical data that contains qualitative values. Dimensions are typically leveraged to appropriately group/segment data as well as to understand details.

The next section gives an overview to the topic of discrete vs. continuous data.

Discrete vs. Continuous Data Types

The discrete data type is a numerical data type that includes numbers with fixed and specific values. Discrete data can comprise the values that are not divisible (absolute values) and that are presented as a set of incremental values. Examples of discrete data are as follows:

▶ The number of students in a class can only be an absolute whole value, such as 20, 25, 30, or 35, and can't be 22.5, 30.5, or 35.1.

▶ Standard shoe sizes can be 7, 7.5, 8, 8.5, 9, and so on but can't be 7.3 or 7.7.

▶ A software program can have 100 or 200 or more lines of code; however, it cannot have 100.85 or 200.90 lines of code.

Figure 3.4 uses a scatter plot to illustrate discrete data regarding software lines of code.

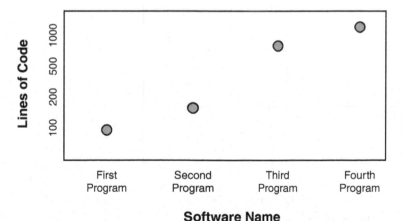

FIGURE 3.4   Discrete Data Scatter Plot Example

As you have seen in earlier examples, discrete values are discontinuous and have definite boundaries. Continuous data, on the other hand, involves different data values that are estimated over a particular interval of time. Continuous data can include any values. These values can be abstract and represent divisible (fractional) values. For example:

▶ The speed of wind measured over a week can be 30.4 km/hr, 50.8 km/hr, or 65 km/hr.

▶ Daily temperature measured in degrees Celsius can be 22, 30, 28.2, 31.4, and so on.

▶ Courier box dimensions can be 10×10×10 cm, 10×10.5×10.8 cm, or 10×10×20.5 cm.

▶ The height of students in a university can be 4′10″, 5′10″, 5′11″, 6′7″, and so on.

Continuous data cannot be counted in absolute terms, however, but can be measured over a period of time. Continuous data is best shown on a line graph or chart, which makes it possible to show how data values change in a given time frame. For example, Figure 3.5 shows a line graph that illustrates the relationship between age and height of children in a school. As you can see, this representation makes it much easier to interpret the data.

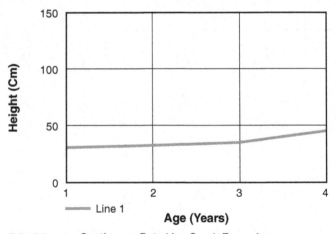

FIGURE 3.5   Continuous Data Line Graph Example

Categorical vs. Dimension and Discrete vs.
Continuous Data Types

CramQuiz

Cram Quiz

Answer these questions. If you cannot answer these questions correctly, consider reading this section again until you can.

1. What type of data does the following graph illustrate?

   ○ **a.** Continuous data

   ○ **b.** Discrete data

   ○ **c.** Noncontinuous data

   ○ **d.** Nominal data

2. The number of students in a class can only be an absolute whole value such as
   20, 25, 30, or 35. What type of data is this?

   ○ **a.** Continuous data

   ○ **b.** Discrete data

   ○ **c.** Cumulative data

   ○ **d.** Nominal data

3. Categorical data can be classified into which two types of data? (Choose two.)

   ○ **a.** Exact

   ○ **b.** Approximate

   ○ **c.** Nominal

   ○ **d.** Ordinal

Cram Quiz Answers

1. **Answer: a. Continuous data.** This figure shows continuous data represented
   using a line chart.

2. **Answer: b. Discrete data.** The discrete data type is a numeric data type that
   includes numbers with fixed and specific values.

3. **Answer: c. Nominal, d. Ordinal.** Categorical data can be classified into nominal
   and ordinal data.

Types of Data: Audio, Video, and Images

CramSaver

If you can correctly answer these questions before going through this section, save time by completing the Cram Quiz at the end of the section.

1. Image, audio, and video signals are candidates for _____.

   a. data cleansing

   b. data compression

   c. data classification

   d. All of these answers are correct.

2. Video data usually exists as what type of analog signals?

   a. Discrete

   b. Continuous

   c. Logarithmic

   d. None of these options are correct.

3. An image is explained in terms of which of the following?

   a. Raster graphics

   b. Vector graphics

   c. Raster graphics and vector graphics

   d. Raster graphics or vector graphics

4. Which of the following file formats is recommended for good-quality sound?

   a. Lossless

   b. Compressed

   c. Lossy

   d. All of these answers are correct.

5. Which of the following is an open source container format used for storing audio and video data?

   a. MP3

   b. OGG

   c. WAV

   d. All of these answers are correct.

Audio, images, and video together are known as *multimedia*. There has been a great transformation in multimedia across the past few decades, from black-and-white TV programs to visually appealing standard definition (SD) graphics to modern ultra-high definition (UHD) and 4K graphics and videos. Let's take a peek into the world of multimedia data, starting with audio.

Audio

The sounds that you hear using your ears as sensory organs occur in the form of analog signals. Early audio systems were analog; for example, conventional tape recorder and gramophone technologies captured sound waves and stored them in analog format on magnetic tapes and vinyl records. Audio data that is being recorded, read, retrieved, interpreted, or compressed has unique requirements.

Note

This section focuses specifically on digital media—that is, digital audio, digital video, and images. This is primarily because, when data is stored in computer systems or storage media, it is stored as digital data rather than as analog data.

Because computers are digital devices, it is necessary to convert analog sound data to a digitized format in order to store it on a computer. A digital recording system works by capturing audio waveforms at specific intervals (known as the sampling rate) and converting those samples (after quantization) to equivalent binary audio signals. Sampling implies the process of observing/recording the values of a composite analog signal during regular intervals of time. Figure 3.6 illustrates this process.

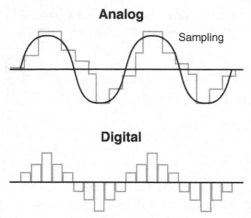

FIGURE 3.6   Analog-to-Digital Conversion Using Sampling

As you can see, the digitized audio is a binary representation of the analog signal.

> **Note**
>
> There is a lot of theory involved in how sound is sampled and converted by leveraging amplitude (that is, the height of curves or crests and troughs), but the details are beyond the scope of this book. If you are keen to study more about this topic, you can start with Nyquist theorem and encoding algorithms such as pulse code modulation (PCM), differential pulse code modulation (DPCM), and adaptive differential pulse code modulation (ADPCM).

Each captured waveform is converted to a binary integer value and is stored on computer storage media. The quality of an audio signal depends on how identical the sample is to the original sound. In other words, the higher the quality of the sample, the higher the quality of the digitized audio format.

The manner in which an audio signal is compressed and stored is called the codec (which stands for "code and decode"), and it determines the file size. For example, files with the .mp3 extension use the MPEG Layer 3 codec, and files with the .wav extension are encoded with the PCM codec. Also, it is important to note that not all audio formats are lossless; some are lossy in nature, due to compression and type of codecs used. While compression makes it possible to save audio files using a reduced amount of space, it can decrease the quality of the audio compared to the original file. On the other hand, a lossless format (such as WAV) preserves the original quality and does not use any compression algorithm.

For this discussion, we can divide audio file formats into two broad categories:

▶ **Open standard:** As the name suggests, an open standard can be used by any vendor to store audio files. For example, Microsoft leverages the open standard WAV format for the Windows sound effects for startup, logon, and so on.

▶ **Proprietary:** A proprietary format is created by an organization for its own use, and any other organization that leverages that format has to pay royalty rights or fees to the organization that developed it. For example, Windows Media Audio (WMA) format was created and licensed by Microsoft.

Note

This section looks at common open standard and proprietary file formats, but it does not provide exhaustive coverage of all file formats.

Now let's look at the formats for audio files. The following standard audio formats are available for digitized media:

▶ **WAV:** Waveform Audio File Format (WAV), the most common audio file format, is typically used for storing uncompressed and PCM-encoded sound files. WAV files tend to be much larger than other file formats; they may be as large as around 10 MB per minute of music at 16 bits and 44.1 kHz. The WAV format was developed by Microsoft and IBM in the early 1990s and continues to be used openly across systems today.

Figure 3.7 shows the various Microsoft Windows audio files that are in WAV format by default. You can find these files under C:\Windows\ Media (though the drive letter and folder may be different, depending on where you installed Windows on your machine).

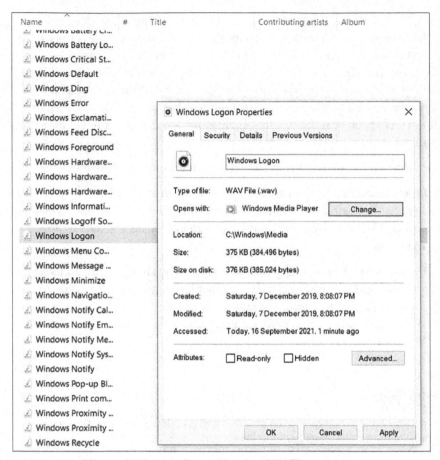

FIGURE 3.7　**Microsoft Windows Sound Files Are WAV Files**

▶ **AIFF:** Apple developed Audio Interchange File Format (AIFF) primarily for its Mac platform—much as Microsoft developed WAV format. AIFF is an open format with file extension .aiff and can be used across platforms.

▶ **MP3:** Since the early 2000s, MPEG Layer 3 (MP3) has been a very popular file format for downloading and storing music.

Fun Fact

We have fond memories of one of the most revered pieces of MP3 software in the early 2000s: Nullsoft Winamp. It was perhaps the most popular program for playing MP3 files back in the day. It could be customized using skins, which was a pretty advanced concept at the time!

An MP3 file leverages MPEG Layer 3 for encoding. MP3 is a compressed file format and takes a fraction of the space required for uncompressed WAV files (which explains why it is a popular format for downloading and storing music). For example, the Windows Logon file is 375 KB in WAV format but only 65 KB in MP3 format (see Figure 3.8). That's a huge savings in terms of space, and the reduction in quality is unnoticeable.

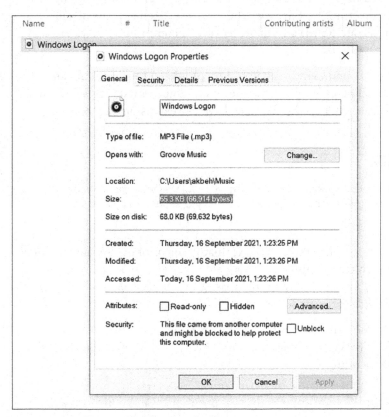

FIGURE 3.8   **Size of MP3 File vs. WAV File**

▶ **AAC:** The Advanced Audio Coding (AAC) audio format is based on the MPEG-4 audio standard defined by AT&T Bell Labs, Dolby, Nokia, and Sony. AAC is an enhanced version of MP3 and is better in multiple aspects, such as support for enhanced compression with better quality and a wider range of sampling rates. Apple leverages the AAC format extensively and has implemented digital rights management (DRM) for music in form of FairPlay.

▶ **FLAC:** Free Lossless Audio Codec (FLAC) offers lossless compression, reducing the size of a music file to half the size of a WAV file—but with the same quality. If you compress a WAV (PCM) file to FLAC and then decompress it again, you end up with a file that is a perfect copy of the original.

▶ **GSM:** This format, which based on Graphic Description Language, is very closely related to Global System for Mobile. This file format, which was created for Internet telephony in Europe, is used for recording mobile conversations. Files with the extension .gsm are encoded using constant bitrate (CBR) encoding and offer a compromise between sound quality and file size.

▶ **OGG:** This open source container format is used to store audio and video data. The OGG file format leverages unpatented Ogg Vorbis audio compression. OGG audio files may have the extension .ogg or .oga.

> **Note**
>
> OGG file format was developed by Xiph.Org. You can visit www.xiph.org to learn more about the projects and file formats created and supported by Xiph.Org.

OGG is often compared to MP3 format in terms of quality and compression, though the quality of an OGG file is better than that of an equivalent MP3 file. This is perhaps the reason that Spotify has chosen to use OGG for its streaming service.

▶ **RAW:** As the name suggests, this file format is for raw uncompressed audio data. RAW audio files typically (though not always) contain audio in PCM encoding.

Now let's look at the most commonly used proprietary audio file formats:

▶ **WMA:** Windows Media Audio (WMA) is a proprietary file format created by Microsoft. It is a compressed audio format, with the file extension .wma, and primarily works with Windows Media Player and Apple iTunes. WMA was designed with DRM incorporated for copy protection.

> **Fun Fact**
>
> WMA was commonly used with Apple iPods in the early 2000s, and it was difficult to get around the DRM protection. Users had to use a DRM-capable audio player to play WMA files.

The idea behind creating the WMA format was to compete with MP3 by offering better compression while keeping an equivalent level of sound quality at low bit rates. Both file formats offer a higher bit rate of 320 Kbps, which was commonly used with iPods and other MP3 players.

▶ **ATRAC:** The Adaptive Transform Acoustic Coding (ATRAC) file format, which was developed by Sony primarily for Windows computers, leverages Sony's SonicStage software. ATRAC was created as another attempt to compete against the popular MP3 format and lock in music to Sony's ecosystem. Playing ATRAC format audio files required either a plug-in with a software application like Nullsoft Winamp or a Sony device such as PlayStation Portable (PSP) or Sony Walkman.

The next section covers the topic of video data.

Video

You probably use video in everyday life, and while you consume it on mobile devices, via on-demand TV, on websites, in news articles, and in many other streams, you might not think about how video files are encoded and saved. Video data usually exists as continuous analog signals, and it must be stored digitally (that is, as sets of bits or in a binary form) in computer memory or on a hard disk.

Interestingly, the video we are used to seeing on big screens is recorded by cameras at a rate of 24 fps (frames per second), but today's modern displays can easily scale from 30 to 60 to 120 on a regular monitor and up to 144 fps on a gaming monitor. The human eye can adjust to and distinguish between lower and higher refresh rates or fps. Technically, 50 fps = 50 Hz.

Without getting into the intricacies of video displays, this section focuses on how video is stored in various formats. This section explores the most commonly used video file formats, which include the following:

▶ **AVI:** Audio Video Interleave (AVI) is an extensively used video file format created by Microsoft in the early 1990s. AVI files, which have the extension .avi, tend to be larger than files in other video formats. It is a lossless video format and is therefore widely used for recording, processing (editing), and storing videos. AVI video files can contain different types of video compression codecs. AVI files are natively supported on the Windows platform and are also playable on other platforms using video players like VLC by VideoLAN.

▶ **WMV:** Windows Media Video (WMV) is a video file format that was created by Microsoft in the late 1990s. WMV files leverage Advanced Systems Format (ASF) for encoding to produce small file sizes—but with poor video quality. While this format can be played cross-platform by leveraging VLC and other open source players, it is not very popular.

▶ **MPEG:** MPEG (or MPG) is a video format that was developed by the Moving Picture Experts Group (MPEG) in the early 1990s. It is one of the most commonly used formats, and MPEG files have the file extension .mpg or .mpeg.

> **Note**
>
> Moving Picture Experts Group created a number of formats under the MPEG umbrella, including MPEG-1, MPEG-2, MPEG-3, MPEG-4, MPEG-7, and MPEG-21.

Both MPEG-1 and MPEG-2 support lossy compression of video and audio.

▶ **MP4:** MPEG-4 (also known as MP4 or MPEG-4 Part 14) format was developed by the Moving Picture Experts Group in 2001. This format can contain audio, video, and subtitle data across multiple tracks.

> **Note**
>
> MP4 is based on the Apple MOV file type and is a container for audio and video content.

MP4 files are commonly used for streaming video via the Internet, for transferring video files over messaging apps, and for posting videos on social media. MP4 files are higher quality, with lower storage footprint due to high compression.

▶ **MOV and QT:** The MOV and QT (QuickTime) file formats developed by Apple are used specifically with Apple's QuickTime player. MOV files, however, use MPEG-4 encoding and are compatible across Mac and Windows. QuickTime uses atoms and QT atoms for storage of the QT file type on the system. MOV and QT files are high quality but have a large storage size.

▶ **WebM:** Google developed the WEBM file format in 2010 specifically for online media exchange. WebM files, which have the .webm extension, are containers for audio and video content, and codecs like Vorbis (OGG) are used for encoding. WebM video files have a relatively small size, and they are not as high quality as MP4 files. You can find more details at https://www.webmproject.org/about/.

Fun Fact

The WebM video format is used for one of the largest video streaming services in the world: YouTube.

▶ **OGG:** Yes, you're reading this correctly: OGG format is not just for audio but works for video files as well. (This makes sense when you think about the fact that it is a container format rather than a type of encoding for a specific audio/video file.) OGG files are used mostly for streaming services and are high quality compared to WebM files. OGG video files have the .ogv extension; however, in HTML source code, the .ogg extension is used within the <video> tag.

Note

WebM, OGG, and MP4 are the three key file formats supported in HTML pages for video files (see https://www.w3schools.com/html/html5_video.asp).

The next section covers the topic of image data.

Images

When you browse the Internet or read a news article or a blog post, you typically come across multiple images. While images make pages interesting to look at (after all, a picture is worth a thousand words!), you aren't likely to think about the details behind what makes an image bright or colorful but probably just consume the information as it is presented.

Graphics are broadly classified into two formats: raster and vector. Table 3.2 differentiates between them.

TABLE 3.2 **Raster vs. Vector Graphics**

Characteristic	Raster Graphics	Vector Graphics
Composition	Composed of pixels	Composed of paths based on mathematic calculations
Common uses	Commonly used across computer systems and the Internet for images	Uncommon outside of 3D animation, computer-aided design (CAD), and other engineering programs
Zoom quality	Become blurry (based on pixels per inch [ppi]) upon zooming the image; that is, doesn't scale optimally	Retains image quality upon zooming without any significant loss; that is, scalable
File size	Images or graphic files are much smaller than vector files	Images or graphic files tend to be much larger than equivalent raster files
Conversion	Conversion from raster to vector is typically time-consuming	Conversion from vector to raster is relatively straightforward

For example, Figure 3.9 shows a comparison between raster and vector images, using the Pearson logo. The image on the left is a raster image (PNG file), and the one on the right is vector image (SVG file). Both images are at original size without any scale-out (zoom in), and they are visually similar.

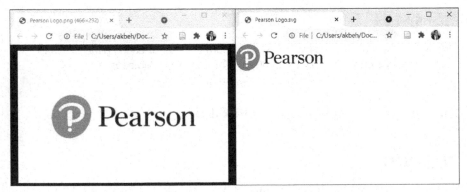

FIGURE 3.9 **Raster vs. Vector Images at Original Size**

Now, as you can see in Figure 3.10, the raster image starts losing clarity when scaled out (that is, zoomed in), whereas the vector image retains clarity and can be scaled without any issues. You can see that the pixels start appearing in the raster image on the left side, whereas there is no distortion in the vector image on the right side.

FIGURE 3.10   **Raster vs. Vector Image Scaling**

Common raster graphic formats include PNG, JPEG, and GIF. Common vector graphic formats include EPS, SVG, and PDF.

Next, we will look at raster images, and then we will look at vector images. The following list discusses the most common raster image formats:

▶ **BMP:** Bitmap (BMP), or "map of bits," is an older raster format that maps individual pixels with almost no compression, resulting in very large image files. A BMP file could be six to eight times larger than an equivalent JPEG file. BMP files are therefore not the best choice for online exchange as they take up a lot of precious storage space and introduce latency in file transfer. Figure 3.11 shows the same image files in BMP and JPEG formats for comparison.

Name	Date	Type	Size	Tags
OEMLOGO	29/04/2015 4:06 AM	BMP File	43 KB	
OEMLOGO	19/09/2021 5:04 PM	JPEG File	5 KB	

FIGURE 3.11   **BMP vs. JPEG Files**

▶ **JPEG:** The Joint Photographic Experts Group (JPEG) helped create the JPEG (or JPG) standard. JPEG is a raster image file format with lossy compression that is suitable for sharing images. JPEGs are lossy in that they reduce file size—but at the cost of reduced image quality. JPEG is one of the image file types most commonly used on the Internet (such as in blogs and online articles).

Fun Fact

When you upload any image from a smartphone or PC to a social media platform like Facebook, the images are automatically put in JPEG file format.

▶ **PNG:** Portable Network Graphics (PNG) is a raster graphics format that is typically used for reproducibility of high-quality graphics to preserve details and the contrast between colors. PNG format supports lossless compression and is usually leveraged for screenshots and infographics. PNG files are larger than equivalent JPEG files.

▶ **GIF:** Graphics Interchange Format (GIF) is a very well-known and commonly used file format for image and graphics on the Internet. Text messages that have moving graphics (animations) are typically GIF images. GIF, which is a raster format and uses lossless compression, constrains images to 8 bits per pixel and a limited palette of 256 colors. Hence, GIF provides a very basic image reproduction capability at a huge size reduction, which is required for the millions of images used on the Internet and in instant messaging.

▶ **WebP:** Google developed this file format along the lines of WebM specifically for web graphics. It is a raster format that supports both lossless and lossy algorithms. WebP images are approximately 30% smaller than JPEG files.

These are the most common vector image formats:

▶ **SVG:** Scalable Vector Graphics (SVG) is a vector graphics file format that leverages XML text to outline shapes and lines using mathematical equations based on vectors (X, Y in 2D) to create graphs. SVG images can scale without any loss of quality. SVG is a great format for high-quality lossless graphics; however, it is not usable across platforms for all graphics because it produces very large files.

Fun Fact

SVG was developed by the World Wide Web Consortium (W3C) as a markup language to render 2D images.

▶ **EPS:** Encapsulated Postscript (EPS) is a vector image file format used as a container for storing depictions across CorelDraw and Adobe Illustrator. EPS is used in text-based documents to outline shapes and lines with code (vectors), and it supports lossless scaling.

▶ **PDF:** Portable Document Format (PDF) is a format that you have certainly come across for documents. However, you might not know that it leverages the same PostScript language as EPS. Just like EPS, it is lossless and can be used to store illustrations and graphics for later printing. PDF format offers much more than SVG and EPS as it provides searchable text fields. It is typically used for reporting and creating dashboards from analytics software.

Cram Quiz

Answer these questions. If you cannot answer these questions correctly, consider reading this section again until you can.

1. The PDF format is which of the following?

   a. Lossy

   b. Linearly lossy

   c. Lossless

   d. Log function lossy

2. Image, audio, and video signals are candidates for which of the following?

   a. Data cleansing

   b. Data compression

   c. Data classification

   d. All of these answers are correct.

3. Which of the following is a vector file format that acts as storage container for text and graphics?

   a. SVG

   b. BMP

   c. GIF

   d. PDF

4. PCM is which of the following?

   a. A codec

   b. An image format

   c. A video format

   d. A graphics format

5. True or false: AVI is a lossless format.

   a. True

   b. False

Cram Quiz Answers

1. **Answer: c. Lossless.** Portable Document Format (PDF) is a format that you have certainly come across for documents. However, you might not know that it leverages the same PostScript language as EPS. Just like EPS, it is lossless and can be used to store illustrations and graphics for later printing.

2. **Answer: b. Data compression**. Image, audio, and video signals are candidates for data compression, which involves modifying data to reduce file size.

3. **Answer: d. PDF**. PDF is a vector file format that offers much more than SVG and EPS as it provides searchable text fields. It is typically used for reporting and creating dashboards from analytics software.

4. **Answer: a. A codec.** Pulse Code Modulation (PCM) is a codec that is used to convert audio from analog format to digital format.

5. **Answer: a. True.** Audio Video Interleave (AVI) is an extensively used video file format created by Microsoft in the early 1990s. It is lossless video format and is used widely for recording, processing (editing), and storing videos.

What Next?

If you want more practice on this chapter's exam objective before you move on, remember that you can access all of the Cram Quiz questions on the Pearson Test Prep software online. You can also create a custom exam by objective with the Online Practice Test. Note any objective you struggle with and go to that objective's material in this chapter.

CHAPTER 4

Understanding Common Data Structures and File Formats

This chapter covers Objective 1.3 (Compare and contrast common data structures and file formats) of the CompTIA Data+ exam and includes the following topics:

▶ Structured vs. unstructured data

▶ Various file formats

For more information on the official CompTIA Data+ exam topics, see the Introduction.

This chapter covers topics related to data structures, structured data, unstructured data, and the file formats encountered in everyday work and personal life. These can be as trivial as rows and columns from a structured database or an Excel sheet or as complex as highly unstructured datasets used for artificial intelligence and machine learning. In addition, there can be multiple (and very familiar) file formats, such as text or flat files, as well as less common formats, such as XML. It is the vividness of data formats across storage, retrieval, and presentation that makes data ever so interesting.

Structured vs. Unstructured Data

If you can correctly answer these questions before going through this section, save time by skimming the Exam Alerts in this section and then completing the Cram Quiz at the end of the section.

1. Data is stored in (pre)defined formats such as _____ and _____ in relational databases. (Choose two.)

   a. columns

   b. relations

   c. rows

   d. overviews

2. What is shown as an abstracted view in the following figure?

   a. Structured data

   b. Unstructured data

   c. Linear data

   d. Growth data

3. Google BigQuery is an example of which of the following?

   a. Structured database

   b. Data lake

   c. Semi-structured database

   d. Fluid database

Data structures have been used since the invention of computers to store, retrieve, and process data. A data structure is a representation of data in a memory space that is used to perform retrieval and storage operations effectively. In simple terms, a data structure provides a way to store and organize data so that it can be used efficiently and effectively. Efficiency or effectiveness implies speedy access to data (timeliness) as well as accuracy of data being structured in a certain format.

While different programming languages have different data structures (for example, a stack, an array, a linked list, queues, or trees), the concept of data structures is relevant across almost all languages. There are some exceptions where one or another data type is not found or is not prevalent; however, without data structures, there is no way a programmer or a data engineer can store data in either a structured or unstructured format, and this renders the usability of data close to meaningless.

Data, whether structured or unstructured, can be acquired from many sources, including social media, emails, photos, instant messages, blogs, and articles. These are all examples of human-generated data sources. In addition, machine-generated data is generated by software applications, IoT sensors, and other hardware devices. Examples include security alerts from a commercial warehouse security system and IoT sensors related to air quality control. All this data, if processed, needs to be stored in a certain format, and this is where the relevance of structured vs. unstructured data comes into the play.

The key types of data in terms of storage, processing, and querying are as follows:

▶ Structured data

▶ Unstructured data

▶ Semi-structured data

> ### ExamAlert
>
> The different types of data structured, unstructured, and semi-structured have their relevant places in terms of data handling and processing. These are a key topic for the CompTIA Data+ exam.

The following sections discuss the differences between structured and unstructured data and briefly touch on semi-structured data and metadata.

Structured vs. Unstructured Data

Data can be broadly classified into structured and unstructured data. Table 4.1 shows the major differences between structured and unstructured data.

TABLE 4.1 **Differences Between Structured and Unstructured Data**

Characteristic	Structured Data	Unstructured Data
Data storage	Data is stored in (pre)defined defined formats, such as columns and rows (in relational databases).	Data is stored in undefined and native (or raw) formats.
Data types	Data types can be dates, strings, and numbers.	Data types can be audio, video, word processing files, images, and emails.
Storage space requirements	Structured data requires less space for storage compared to unstructured data.	Unstructured data needs much more storage space compared to structured data.
Security and legacy compatibility	Structured data is simpler to secure and process/handle with legacy solutions.	Unstructured data is much more difficult to secure and process/handle with legacy and requires modern solutions for management.
Data storage	Structured data is often stored in data warehouses.	Unstructured data is often stored in data lakes.
Volume of data in %	Approximately 20% of organizational data is structured data.	Approximately 80% of organizational data is unstructured data.
Quantitative vs. qualitative	Structured data is quantitative.	Unstructured data is qualitative.
Ease of accessing data	With structured data, it is easy to search and query against the defined fields.	As there is no structure to unstructured data, specialized mechanisms are needed to access it efficiently.

The following sections cover the key aspects of structured and unstructured data and provide real-world examples.

Structured Data

Structured data resides in a fixed field within a record or a file. Structured data may be text, numbers, and any other values that can be stored in a well-defined and linked format (used to capture relationships between different entities) such that a query against the data would yield meaningful results in an expected time frame. Structured data is often stored in tabular form. Figure 4.1 provides an abstract view of structured data.

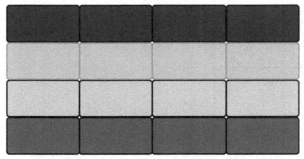

FIGURE 4.1   **An Abstract View of Structured Data**

For example, in a cookbook, a recipe page displays data about the ingredients, cooking time, calories, temperature, and other details. In addition, each recipe may be related to a table of contents (TOC), which makes it easier for readers to locate the information they want. A reader who is looking for a vegetarian curry recipe or a barbecue recipe, for example, can look at the TOC for the page numbers where the recipe can be found and jump straight to the recipe for the delicious dish. Figure 4.2 illustrates this structured relationship.

As another example, structured data makes it simpler for online search engines to understand what data should be displayed as the result of a query. Structured data improves the accuracy and efficiency of the search engine.

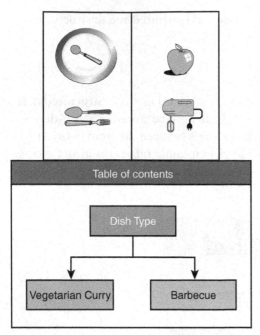

FIGURE 4.2 **TOC of a Book as Structured Data**

> **Note**
>
> With massive data volumes of unstructured data, the speed at which the data can be queried decreases, and alternative algorithms may be needed to search through the unstructured data at unprecedented speeds. This topic and related intricacies are beyond the scope of CompTIA Data+ exam.

Structured data is mostly organized in tables as rows and columns (as well as key/value pairs). In the relational model, a database is represented as a collection of relations, and a relation is defined as a table. Relational database systems such as Microsoft SQL Server and PostgreSQL leverage the relational structure to store and process data. The next section discusses rows and columns in the context of relational databases.

Rows and Columns

A row consists of related cell values that run horizontally across a table. A table can contain one or more rows, and all rows are by default independent of other rows in the table. Figure 4.3 provides an example of rows in an Excel sheet.

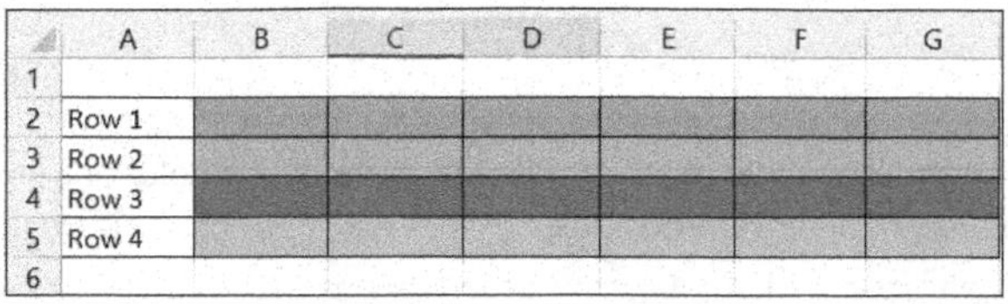

FIGURE 4.3   **Rows in an Excel Sheet**

A column consists of vertically stacked cell values in a table. Like rows, columns are also independent of other columns in a table. A table can contain one or more columns, as shown in Figure 4.4.

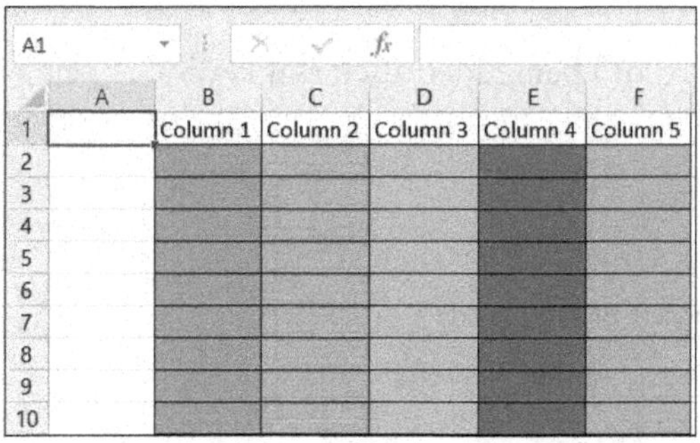

FIGURE 4.4   **Columns in an Excel Sheet**

Now to make things more interesting, while rows and columns by themselves may not be so useful as they do not relate to real-world relationships, when they intersect and create relations (yes—that's why it is called relational database!) they become far more useful. The relationship of rows and columns is known as just that—relation (table)! A column header of a relational database is known as an attribute of a relation. The row is defined as a tuple in a relational table. Figure 4.5 illustrates this arrangement.

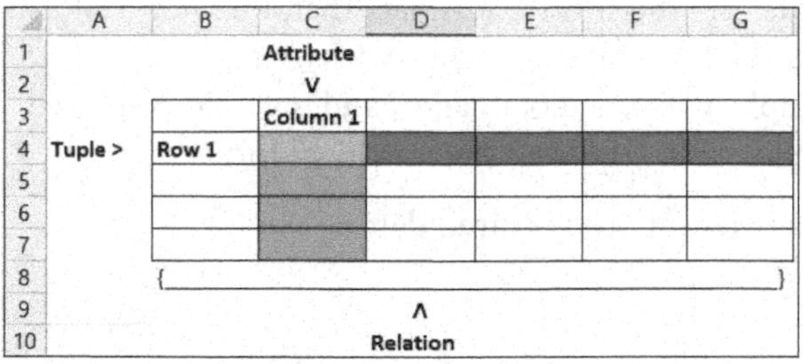

FIGURE 4.5   **Attributes, Tuples, and Relation**

> **Note**
>
> From a big data perspective, structured data is simpler for applications to consume for analytics than unstructured data. However, most modern data analytics solutions are making great strides in the area of unstructured data.

Key/Value Pairs

A key/value pair has two elements (hence the word *pair*): a *key*, which is a unique identifier that refers to the value, and a *value*, which is the data itself and may be based on set of variables.

Consider an example of a customer record being identified as a key/value pair, as shown here:

Key	Value
C899-1	Always Light Technologies
C899-2	Kongrad St, Ethos, EU
C899-3	Antivirus, Anti-malware

Here, the key is a unique identifier that points to the relevant value, which can be customer name, customer address, or a product sold to customers.

The advantage of key/value pairs is that they are very flexible and offer very fast lookups for reads/writes as a single key returns its related value. This can be beneficial when you are not looking to run complex queries against linked tables.

Unstructured Data

Unstructured data is data that is not organized according to a schema or per a defined structure of preset data. In other words, it is data that does not conform to any data model or schemas. The two most relevant types of unstructured data are multimedia (for example, video, audio, images) and text. Unstructured data does not have a predefined framework, and it exists in all forms.

Figure 4.6 provides an abstract view of unstructured data.

FIGURE 4.6   **An Abstract View of Unstructured Data**

Fun Fact

Unstructured data is becoming more plentiful and common compared to structured data due to the spurt in data growth over the past few decades. There has been a proliferation of unstructured data from web searches, online sites, applications, software, email, and social media; in addition, machine data, point-of-sale (PoS) data, Internet of Things (IoT) sensor data, and other automated forms of data are becoming increasingly common. Most such data is left in its raw state—which is unstructured data.

Modern toolsets and software are required to process and analyze unstructured data as traditional tools and methods are not efficient with unstructured data. Specialized data analytics tools may be needed for preprocessing and management before queries can be run. For example, audio, video, text, image, and other unstructured data cannot be segmented into simple row-and-column constructs unless they have been preprocessed with specialized applications. One of the ways to handle unstructured data is to leverage non-RDBMS (relational database management system) or NoSQL tools/applications.

Note

It is common for data lakes such as Google Cloud Platform (GCP) BigQuery and Microsoft Azure Synapse to leverage unstructured data for data analytics as well as machine learning. Raw data tends to be unstructured by default, and instead of structuring it, data lakes use unstructured data with advanced algorithms to reduce analysis time and to increase efficiency in terms of searching and indexing.

Most of the machine-generated data that is created automatically by the operations and activities of networked devices (for example, smartphones, PCs, linked wearable products, IoT sensors, and embedded systems) is by default unstructured and in the raw form (even, in most cases, after processing).

A marketer can, for example, utilize the unstructured data by leveraging reports or dashboards to understand the trends and formulate the content to continue connecting with potential audiences and consumers.

Finally, the fields in a database can be defined as null, or they can be undefined. A *Null* value means an empty (yes, that's right) field or a field with no value. Remember that null is not zero. You can use the SQL statements IS NULL and IS NOT NULL to find out whether a field has a null value. *Undefined* implies that the field might contain a variable for which a value is not yet defined.

Semi-structured Data

Semi-structured data is somewhere between structured and unstructured data. It shares the characteristics of both. Semi-structured data is mostly textual in nature and conforms to some level of structure (though it may not conform to the rigid structure used in relational databases). Semi-structured data follows certain patterns and schemas. Common examples of semi-structured data are JSON, XML, and CSV documents. While structured data is the easiest type of data to process, semi-structured is the next easiest, and it's more straight-forwardly processed than unstructured data. Data analytics tools are required for preprocessing and managing semi-structured data. Figure 4.7 provides an abstract view of semi-structured data.

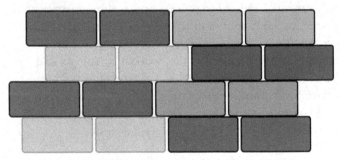

FIGURE 4.7   An Abstract View of Semi-structured Data

Metadata

Data about data is known as *metadata*. It implies a description of and context for data. Metadata is used to find, organize, and analyze data. An example of metadata is the information contained in photographs, such as:

▶ The date and time the photo was taken

▶ The location where the photo was taken

▶ The filename of the photo

While photographers don't typically use photo metadata, search engines and analytical tools can use metadata to sort, organize, analyze, and describe a photo.

Cram Quiz

Answer these questions. The answers follow the last question. If you cannot answer these questions correctly, consider reading this section again until you can.

1. The preferred option for storing unstructured data is _____.

    a. RDBMS

    b. SQL

    c. non-relational databases

    d. DBMS

2. Data about data is known as which of the following?

    a. Metadata

    b. Full data

    c. Unstructured data

    d. Structured data

3. The amount of _____ data collected has grown exponentially in the past few decades, and this type of data plays an important role in data analytics.

    a. any

    b. storing

    c. structured

    d. unstructured

Cram Quiz Answers

1. Answer: **c. non-relational databases.** Unstructured data is best stored in non-relational databases as the data does not conform to any structure.

2. Answer: **a. Metadata**. Data about data is known as metadata. This presents further information about the data such as location and time at which a photo was taken from a smartphone.

3. Answer: **d. Unstructured data.** Unstructured data has grown exponentially as a result of web searches, blogs, articles, social media etc. This contributes to increase in text, audio, video, documents, and other.

Data File Formats

CramSaver

If you can correctly answer these questions before going through this section, save time by skimming the Exam Alerts in this section and then completing the Cram Quiz at the end of the section.

1. Tab-delimited format is also referred to as which of the following?

   a. Comma-separated values

   b. Delimited values

   c. Comma values

   d. Tab-separated values

2. The following figure is an example of which of the following?

	Employee Name	Department	Employee Number
Record 1	Ashley James	Sales	111
Record 2	Jamie Angus	Marketing	222

FIGURE 4.9   **Flat File Structure (Fixed-Width Format)**

   a. Comma-separated values

   b. XML

   c. Flat file

   d. JSON

3. Extensible Markup Language is a subset of _____.

   a. text

   b. SGML

   c. SHTML

   d. HTML

Answers

1. **Answer: d. Tab-separated values.** Tab-delimited format is also referred as tab-separated values, or TSV format. These two terms can be used interchangeably.

2. **Answer: c. Flat file.** This figure shows an example of a flat file, where all numbers and characters are stored in plaintext.

3. **Answer: b. SGML.** XML and HTML are file formats derived from the parent language Standard Generalized Markup Language (SGML).

Data (including numeric, text, video, and audio data as well as images) can be represented in multiple file formats, as shown in Figure 4.8.

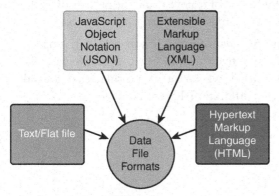

FIGURE 4.8   **Data File Formats**

A data file format may include scripts, text, and documentation. For example, a text file and a web page may be written in a word processor and are both regarded as data files.

ExamAlert

Various data file formats such as flat files, XML files etc. are an important area of focus for CompTIA Data+ exam.

The sections that follow cover the various data file formats.

Text/Flat File

Using a flat file (also known as a *text database*) is the simplest way to store information in plaintext. In this format, all the information (including numeric and alphanumeric values) is stored as text. Each line of the file contains one record of the dataset, as shown in Figure 4.9.

	Employee Name	Department	Employee Number
Record 1	Ashley James	Sales	111
Record 2	Jamie Angus	Marketing	222

FIGURE 4.9   **Flat File Structure (Fixed-Width Format)**

With plaintext, the key benefit is that complex software is not needed to create or process a text file. In addition, it is easy to view and modify plaintext data. Flat files are mostly portable across different systems and require a low-level interface.

The main drawback of plaintext files is their simplicity. This may seem counterintuitive, based on what we just discussed as the benefits of plaintext. However, there are no standards that specify the data format of plaintext, and the process of accessing information in plaintext is inefficient compared to standardized databases.

For each line in a flat file, there are two main approaches to differentiating fields: using delimited format and using fixed-width format. Delimiters (commas, semicolons, braces, etc.) can be used to keep the data formatted at a fixed width, and they make it easier to find different fields within a record. Figure 4.10 shows the delimiter format.

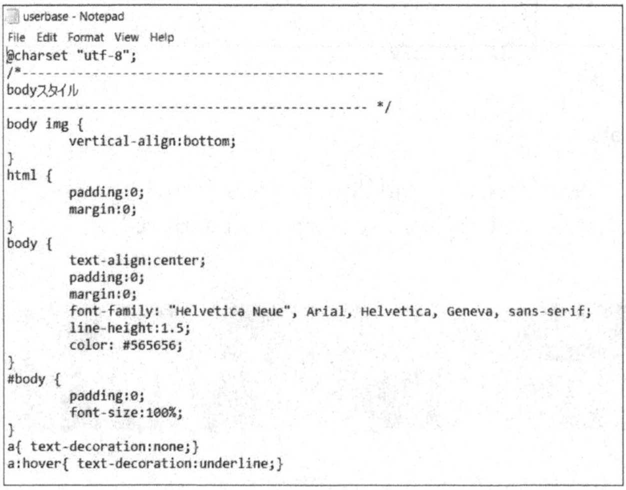

```
userbase - Notepad
File  Edit  Format  View  Help
@charset "utf-8";
/*--------------------------------------------------
bodyスタイル
-------------------------------------------- */
body img {
        vertical-align:bottom;
}
html {
        padding:0;
        margin:0;
}
body {
        text-align:center;
        padding:0;
        margin:0;
        font-family: "Helvetica Neue", Arial, Helvetica, Geneva, sans-serif;
        line-height:1.5;
        color: #565656;
}
#body {
        padding:0;
        font-size:100%;
}
a{ text-decoration:none;}
a:hover{ text-decoration:underline;}
```

FIGURE 4.10   **Flat File Delimiter Format**

With the fixed-width format, each column is allocated a fixed width in number of characters with one entry per row. Refer to Figure 4.9 for an example of fixed-width format.

Tab-Delimited File

A tab-delimited file is composed of records with datasets structured in a row format; as the name implies, the delimiter is a tab character. Every dataset in a row comprises more than one piece of information, and every piece of information is known as a *field*. With tab-delimited file format, the first row consists of headers for the column names; this provides a structured format for tab-delimited files.

> **Note**
>
> Another term for *delimiter* is also *field separator* as delimiters (such as a tab character) separate fields from one another.

Excel sheets can be saved in tab-delimited file format, as shown in Figure 4.11.

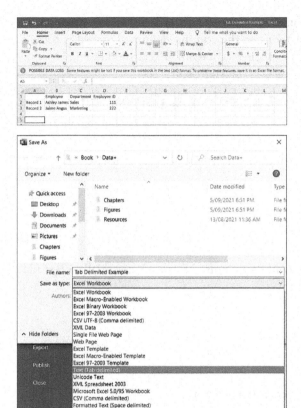

FIGURE 4.11 Saving in Tab-Delimited Format

The tab-delimited file format stores data from a spreadsheet or database in a tabular format. Tab-delimited format is also referred as tab-separated values, or TSV format.

It is important to remember that tab-delimited format and comma-delimited format (discussed in the next section) are text file formats. As you can see in Figure 4.11, Excel warns that saving in tab-delimited or comma-delimited format causes all formatting to be lost. Figure 4.12 shows what this looks like after the data from Figure 4.11 is saved in tab-delimited format.

```
Tab Delimited Example - Notepad
File  Edit  Format  View  Help
       Employee          Department        Employee ID
Record 1       Ashley James    Sales   111
Record 2       Jaime Angus     Marketing       222
```

FIGURE 4.12 Tab-Delimited Format is Plaintext Format

Comma-Delimited File

As you have likely guessed, in the comma-delimited format, the data is separated by commas. This is the one of the most common file formats for exchanging information between applications, and almost all data systems are capable of exporting and importing comma-delimited information. Also known as comma-separated values (CSV) format, the comma-delimited format is commonly used in many applications, such as Microsoft Excel and Google Docs. Figure 4.13 shows the CSV format file in Microsoft Excel.

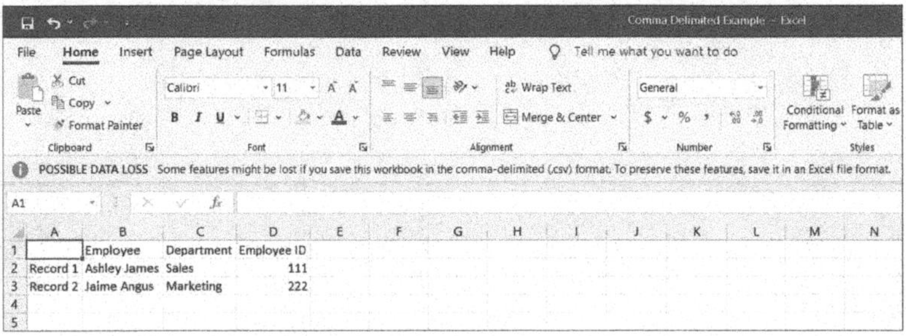

FIGURE 4.13   **Comma-Delimited Format**

As you can see in Figure 4.14, comma-delimited format is essentially a text file with datasets delimited by commas.

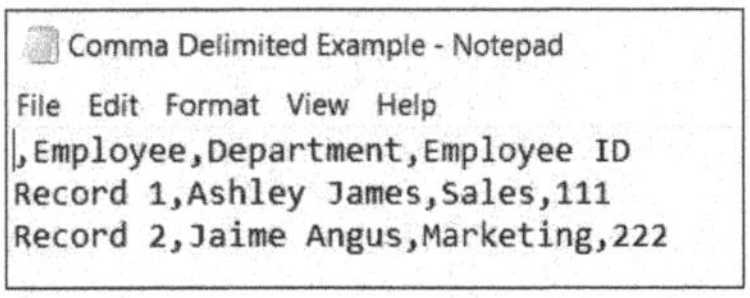

FIGURE 4.14   **Comma-Delimited Format is a Text File**

It is important to note that the delimiter is typically not within a field itself but is used to separate the fields from one another. In order to prevent delimiter mixing with data fields, qualifiers are used. A qualifier would be placed around each field to ensure that delimiters are not included as part of a field. The most common qualifier with CSV files is double quotes (that is, " ").

> **Note**
>
> CSV files are commonly used in data science projects. In some files, semi-colons are used instead of commas to delimit values; in such a case, the file would be called a delimiter-separated values (DSV) file.

JavaScript Object Notation (JSON)

JSON is a lightweight text-based file format for storing and transporting data. It is often used when data is sent from a web server to a client web page. The JSON format was first detailed in March 2001 by Douglas Crockford. RFC 8259 (see https://datatracker.ietf.org/doc/html/rfc8259), which is the main reference for JSON data interchange format, was published in December 2017 by the Internet Engineering Task Force (IETF).

JSON is an open standard format and easy to understand. JSON is self-describing, as it enables the reader to read the actual content in a hierarchical manner. JSON is simple for users to write and read, and it makes it easy for machines to generate and parse the data. Example 4.1 shows an example of JSON syntax.

EXAMPLE 4.1 **JSON Syntax**

```
{
    "EmployeeInfo":[
    {"firstName":"Ashley",
    "lastName":"James",
    "department":"sales",
    "ID":111,
},
    {"firstName":"Jaime",
    "lastName":"Angus",
    "department":"marketing",
    "ID":222,
},
    ]
}
```

JSON syntax follows these rules:

▶ **Data is stored in name/value pairs.** In a JSON file, a name/value pair consists of a field name, followed by a colon, followed by a value (with both field names and values in double quotes). In Example 4.1, "firstname": "Ashley" is a name/value pair. The values can be of the following types:

  ▶ Boolean (true or false)
  ▶ String
  ▶ Object
  ▶ Number
  ▶ Array

▶ **Data fields are delimited by commas.** In Example 4.1, note that there is a comma after each name/value pair.

▶ **Square brackets ([]) are used to hold arrays.** An array in JSON is an ordered collection of values.

▶ **Curly braces ({}) are used to hold objects.** An object in JSON is an unordered set of name/value pairs. An object begins with { and ends with }.

Extensible Markup Language (XML)

XML is a platform-independent (or platform-agnostic) standard markup language that uses the same rules of data formatting and encoding across platforms. The XML file format was created for storing and transporting data without being dependent on the underlying platform. In fact, the *X* in XML stands for *Extensible*, which implies that the format can be extended to any number of symbols, based on the user's requirements.

Moreover, XML is represented as extensible because it is not a fixed format (as Hypertext Markup Language [HTML] is), and it makes it simple to denote metadata in a reusable and portable format. XML enables the use of structured and portable data for display on wireless devices such as smartphones. XML files have the extension .xml.

> **Fun Fact**
>
> Standard Generalized Markup Language (SGML) is an international standard for the definition of markup languages. In other words, it is a metalanguage. Both XML and HTML are document formats derived from SGML.

Like many other web languages, XML is both human and machine comprehensible. XML stores data in plaintext in order to enable data exchange between incompatible systems. XML is widely used for exchanging data over the World Wide Web (WWW) as well as data storage. This is a key difference from HTML, which is used primarily for data representation on the web rather than for data transfer. HTML is covered in detail in the next section.

> **Note**
>
> It is important to remember that XML is not only suited for web use but can be used across multiple platforms to achieve various outcomes. For example, XML can be used for sharing data between Internet of Things (IoT) sensors and IoT platforms.

Example 4.2 shows a standard tab-delimited file structured in XML.

EXAMPLE 4.2   **XML Document on Employee Information**

```
<?xml version="1.0" encoding="UTF-8"?>

<!DOCTYPE article PUBLIC "-//OASIS//DTD DocBook XML V4.1.2//EN"
"http://www.oasis-open.org/docbook/xml/4.1.2/docbookx.dtd">

<article lang="">
```

```
<para>          Employee        Department          Employee ID</para>
<para>Record 1        Ashley James        Sales           111</para>
<para>Record 2        Jaime Angus         Marketing            222</para>
</article>
```

To create this example, authors used an online XML tool to generate XML from the tab-delimited file shown in Figure 4.12, earlier in this chapter.

Let's examine the structure of this file and the syntax of XML in general:

▶ **XML Prolog:** This component added at the beginning of an XML document includes the XML declaration, DOCTYPE, comments, and processing instructions. In Example 4.2, XML Prolog is:

```
<?xml version="1.0" encoding="UTF-8"?>
<!DOCTYPE article PUBLIC "-//OASIS//DTD DocBook XML V4.1.2//EN"
"http://www.oasis-open.org/docbook/xml/4.1.2/docbookx.dtd">
```

▶ **XML declaration:** This line right at the top (in Example 4.2, <?xml version="1.0" encoding="UTF-8"?>) tells the device reading the file that this is an XML document and gives the version of XML (in this case, version 1.0).

▶ **XML tag:** XML tags are used to mark the beginning and end of statements. In Example 4.2, the opening tag is <para>, and the closing tag is </para>.

▶ **XML element:** An XML element consists of an opening tag, attributes, content, and a closing tag. An element can contain:

  ▶ Text
  ▶ Attributes
  ▶ Other elements
  ▶ A mix of the above

In Example 4.2, one of the elements is

```
<para>Record 1        Ashley James        Sales           111</para>
```

Example 4.3 provides another XML document example.

EXAMPLE 4.3 **XML Document on Customer Information**

```
<?xml version="1.0" encoding="UTF-8" standalone="yes" ?>
<?xml-stylesheet type="text/css" href="/style/design"?>
```

```
<!DOCTYPE html PUBLIC "-//W3C//DTD XHTML 1.0
Strict//EN""http://www.w3.org/TR/xhtml1/DTD/xhtml1-strict.dtd">
<customer_list>
        <customer>
                <lastname> Behl </lastname>
                    <firstname> Akhil </firstname>
                <location> AU </location>
        </customer>
        <customer>
                < lastname> G S </lastname>
                    <firstname> Siva </firstname>
                <location> UK </location>
        </customer>
</customer_list>
```

As you can see in Examples 4.2 and 4.3, XML does not have defined tags as HTML does; in fact, tags can vary from one XML document to another. XML tags are used to recognize the data and to arrange and store the data rather than to denote how to show it (whereas HTML tags are used to actually show the data).

Hypertext Markup Language (HTML)

Hypertext refers machine-readable text, and *markup* refers to structuring in a particular format. HTML is code that is used for web page structure and its information. HTML is the basic language of scripting and is used by web browsers to use pages on the WWW. Hypertext permits a user to click a link and be redirected to a new referenced page automatically.

It is important to remember that HTML is a presentation language, whereas XML is a data-description language. Basically, HTML defines the way a user sees a web page, whereas XML defines the way data is stored and transmitted across a server and a client or different systems. HTML is the standard markup language for web pages. HTML files have the extension .html or .htm.

HTML comprises a set of elements that allows a browser to show content. In HTML, the content must be structured within a group of paragraphs, using data tables or multimedia or using a list of bullet points.

Let's take a look at an example of HTML. Example 4.4 shows the structure of a standard HTML document.

EXAMPLE 4.4   **HTML Document Structure**

```
<html>
<head>
<title> Title of the page</title>
</head>
<body>
<h1> My First heading </h1>
<p> My First paragraph. </p>
</body>
</html>
```

In Example 4.4:

▶ <html> indicates the HTML page root element.

▶ <head> indicates the HTML page metadata.

▶ <title> denotes HTML page title.

▶ <body> denotes the body of the document, which is visible content.

▶ <h1> indicates a heading on the web page.

▶ <p> indicates a paragraph.

Much like XML documents, HTML documents include tags, and with each opening tag (for example, <html>), there is a closing tag (for example, </html>). Unlike in XML, however, in HTML tags are well defined.

Figure 4.15 shows the content from Example 4.4, ready to be saved as an HTML file.

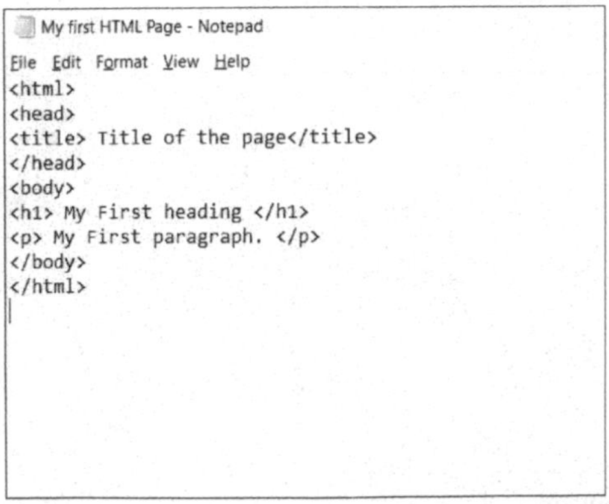

```
My first HTML Page - Notepad
File  Edit  Format  View  Help
<html>
<head>
<title> Title of the page</title>
</head>
<body>
<h1> My First heading </h1>
<p> My First paragraph. </p>
</body>
</html>
```

FIGURE 4.15   **HTML Content in a Text File**

Now you can save this file with the extension .html, as shown in Figure 4.16.

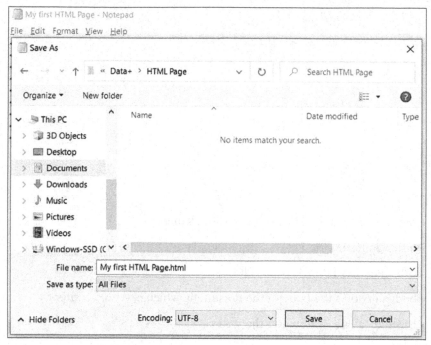

FIGURE 4.16   **Saving the HTML File**

If you now launch this page in a browser, you can see the effect the HTML tags have on the content of the file (see Figure 4.17).

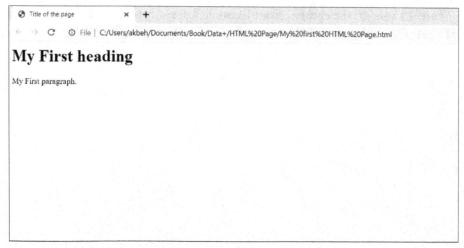

FIGURE 4.17   **HTML Page Viewed in a Browser**

As shown in Figure 4.17, which uses Google Chrome (though you can use any web browser for this code—go ahead try it for yourself!), the browser does not display the HTML tags. Rather, it uses them to determine how to display the document's content.

Table 4.2 compares HTML, XML, and JSON.

TABLE 4.2 **Comparing HTML, XML, and JSON**

Characteristic	HTML	XML	JSON
What markup language it is based on?	HTML is based on SGML.	SML is based on SGML.	JSON is based on the JavaScript programming language.
What it is?	HTML is a markup language.	XML offers a framework to define markup languages.	JSON is a lightweight format that is used for data interchange.
Static vs. dynamic	HTML is static in nature and focused on data presentation.	XML is dynamic in nature and focused on data storage and transfer from databases.	JSON represents objects and is dynamic in nature.
Readability	HTML is relatively easy for humans to read.	XML is difficult for humans to read and interpret.	JSON is easy for humans to read.
Case sensitivity	HTML is not case sensitive.	XML is case sensitive.	JSON is case sensitive.

Cram Quiz

Answer these questions. The answers follow the last question. If you cannot answer these questions correctly, consider reading this section again until you can.

1. A JSON string is enclosed in _____.
    - ○ **a.** curly braces
    - ○ **b.** square brackets
    - ○ **c.** double quotes
    - ○ **d.** single quotes

2. Hypertext Markup Language describes the structure of _____.
    - ○ **a.** an online page
    - ○ **b.** Word
    - ○ **c.** a web page
    - ○ **d.** SQL

3. Data values in a CSV file are separated by _____.

- ○ **a.** letters
- ○ **b.** double quotes
- ○ **c.** tabs
- ○ **d.** commas

Cram Quiz Answers

1. **Answer: b. square brackets.** A string is an ordered set of values in an array, and an array begins with [and ends with].

2. **Answer: c. web page.** HTML is used to describe the structure of a web page (that is, an .htm or .html file).

3. **Answer: d. commas.** CSV stands for comma-separated values and, as the name suggests, a comma is used as a delimiter.

What Next?

If you want more practice on this chapter's exam objective before you move on, remember that you can access all of the Cram Quiz questions on the Pearson Test Prep software online. You can also create a custom exam by objective with the Online Practice Test. Note any objective you struggle with and go to that objective's material in this chapter.

CHAPTER 5

Understanding Data Acquisition and Monetization

This chapter covers Objective 2.1 (Explain data acquisition concepts) of the CompTIA Data+ exam and includes the following topics:

▶ Integration

▶ Data collection methods

For more information on the official CompTIA Data+ exam topics, see the Introduction.

This chapter covers topics related to data acquisition and data monetization. It is important to understand the integration of data from both extract, transform, and load (ETL) and extract, load, and transform (ELT) perspectives. In addition, you need to understand that application programming interfaces (APIs) act as glue between disparate systems. In this chapter you will also learn about data collection, including web scraping, public databases, API/web services, survey, sampling, and observation.

Integration

CramSaver

If you can correctly answer these questions before going through this section, save time by skimming the Exam Alerts in this section and then completing the Cram Quiz at the end of the section.

1. For data integration, organizations mostly prefer which of the following? (Choose two.)

   a. ETL

   b. ELT

   c. XML

   d. APIs

2. The primary function of data mining is _____.

   a. to extract raw data

   b. prediction of data

   c. integration

   d. to identify data

3. Data from which of the following sources can be integrated via ETL or ELT?

   a. SQL or NoSQL databases

   b. Flat or text files

   c. Customer relationship management (CRM) systems

   d. Enterprise relationship management (ERP) systems

   e. All of these

   f. None of these

Answers

1. **Answer: a. ETL, b. ELT.** Organizations leverage ELT or ETL, depending on their resources and needs for data integration from multiple sources in order to perform data analysis.

2. **Answer: a. to extract raw data.** The main goal of data mining is to extract raw data from various sources.

3. **Answer: e. All of these.** ETL and ELT processes can integrate data from multiple sources and can process structured, unstructured, or semi-structured data. These sources include SQL, NoSQL, flat files, CRM, and ERP systems, among many others.

Before we get into the intricacies of data acquisition and monetization, it's important to understand the basics of data mining.

> **Fun Fact**
>
> Yes, data mining is a topic that sounds like mining minerals and ores—and really, it's not very different from real-world mining of rare earth metals or gems. The main difference is that data mining is pertinent to data and happens (mostly) in the virtual world of computing, whereas the mining of metals and compounds is a physical-world process. After all, data is an extremely precious commodity in the virtual world—akin to diamonds and titanium in the physical world.

Data mining is the process of extracting usable information from huge amounts of raw data. Data mining analyzes patterns of data with the help of one or more software tools in order to drive informed decisions based on information mined from seemingly gibberish datasets.

Applications of data mining are diverse and are implemented in various fields, such as:

- ▶ Research and development
- ▶ Mining of rare earth metals
- ▶ Genetics research
- ▶ Cybernetics
- ▶ Marketing

In a business context, data mining allows, for example, salespeople to know about their clients in detail as well as to expand and execute effective sales strategies insightfully and optimally. It helps businesses move from randomly experimenting with sales strategies to establishing structured engagement with clients.

Data mining involves efficient collection of data, data processing, and data warehousing. To segment the data effectively and assess the likelihood of future events, data mining adopts complex mathematical algorithms.

> **Note**
>
> Data mining is also referred as knowledge discovery in databases (KDD).

Now, before we dig deeper into data mining methods and the tools used for it, there's a key term you need to understand: data monetization. Data is mined to help accelerate decision making and to get insights about what might happen and how to benefit from a trend or pattern. It is therefore possible to monetize data and get measurable economical upsides by investing in the process of data mining. Remember that businesses will invest in something if the activity offers return on investment (ROI), and data mining is one of many such activities—and it is an important one.

Some of the key characteritics of data mining processes involved in data mining are as follows:

▶ Predicting probable results

▶ Predicting patterns based on behavior and trend analysis

▶ Finding information to make decisions

▶ Working with very large databases and/or datasets for analysis

▶ Using powerful computing systems and large storage capacity to process and maintain information

Data Integration

Data integration involves combining business and technical processes for collating data from different sources into valuable and meaningful datasets. Data integration does not simply move data from point A to point B; it also makes data usable in the context of moving data from source systems to destination systems and then leveraging the information.

Contemporary data integration solutions integrate on-premises data integration tools with cloud-enabling apps to leverage data across both platforms. It is very common today to see hybrid data platforms with data sources on-premises and data processing happening in the cloud.

Data integration can happen in a number of ways, such as through ETL, ELT, and APIs.

As the times have changed, so have data integration solutions. Interestingly, cloud-based data integration solutions tend to be more user friendly than their on-premises counterparts; business users and IT staff do not need specialized skills to leverage cloud-based data integration solutions. With cloud systems, the configuration is typically straightforward, and the user interface is intuitive.

Extract, Transform, and Load (ETL)

As the name suggests, ETL tools enable data engineers to *extract* data from multiple source systems, *transform* the raw data into a more usable/workable dataset, and *load* the data into a storage system so that the end users can access meaningful data (with minimal noise) and use it to solve business problems. Figure 5.1 illustrates this process.

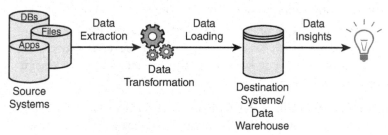

FIGURE 5.1 **The ETL Process**

ETL tools are developed to save money and time as well as to eliminate the need for hand-coding (or other manual efforts) when new data warehouses are developed. For example, in a financial organization that stores and uses data about its clients in different departments and divisions, each department has client data stored and used in a unique way. For example, the accounting department stores the client data by account number, whereas the membership department stores the client data by member number. ETL tools can help the organization collect the data from all the varied sources and combine it into a standardized representation in a database or data warehouse.

> **Note**
>
> ETL processes leverage a schema-on-write approach.

ETL tools extract information from heterogenous data sources (some of which may be legacy sources). They then transform data into a desired schema that is optimized for storing the information and performing analysis. After it is transformed, the data is synchronized and cleansed. Finally, these tools load the information into a data warehouse.

Following are the three stages of ETL:

▶ **Extract:** In this stage, the data is extracted from one or more source systems. This is often a complicated task because the information must be extracted appropriately in order to proceed further. Unless the right source systems are known and data is collated from these systems in a timely way, the outcomes can be underwhelming. These are some possible sources:

- ▶ SQL or NoSQL databases
- ▶ Flat or text files
- ▶ Customer relationship management (CRM) systems
- ▶ Enterprise relationship management (ERP) systems

Extraction includes parsing of extracted information and also verification of whether the extracted information achieves an expected structure or pattern. If data does not meet the expected structure, then it is partly or entirely rejected.

▶ **Transform:** The main aim of this stage is to convert the data into a single format such that it becomes usable by multiple applications. In this stage, data is cleansed and mapped to a specific schema. This process usually involves data staging with monitoring to ensure the quality and integrity of the data. In the event that there are changes or the data quality is not acceptable, the data can be repaired or discarded within the staging database before it goes to the loading stage. A series of business functions or rules are applied in the transform stage to extract the information into the required or desired schema. During the transformation phase, the following may occur:

- ▶ Cleansing and de-duplication of the data
- ▶ Validation and authentication of the data
- ▶ Mapping, translation, and/or summarization
- ▶ Data quality and integrity checks
- ▶ Formatting of data into desired data schema

▶ **Load:** In this stage, data is loaded into the final database or data warehouse from the staging database. This process may differ slightly, depending on the business requirements. During the load stage, the data can be structured according to the limitations, triggers, functions, uniqueness, mandatory fields, and referential integrity of the destination storage. This helps improve the overall data quality and performance in the ETL process.

Note

During the ETL process, metadata is usually stored in a dedicated metadata repository where the users can retrieve, manipulate, or query the metadata.

Figure 5.2 illustrates the ETL process.

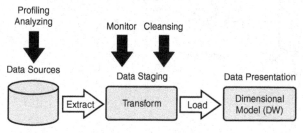

FIGURE 5.2   **The Detailed ETL Process**

The basic steps of a real-life ETL cycle are as follows:

1. Initiate the ETL cycle.

2. Build data for reference.

3. Extract data from sources.

4. Validate the data.

5. Transform the data by performing operations such as cleansing, adopting rules for business, verifying for integration of the data, and creating disaggregates or aggregates.

6. Load data into stage tables, if used.

7. Create audit reports such as for conformity with rules for the business to assist to repair or identify the reason for failure.

8. Publish data to target tables.

9. Archive data.

10. Delete data as per business or regulatory requirements.

Extract, Load, and Transform (ELT)

As the name suggests, ELT is another process involved in data acquisition. While it might sound like ETL, it is a different process with different usage and execution processes. In the ELT process, there is no need for data staging, and most ELT tools leverage cloud-based data lakes or data warehouses for processing raw, unstructured, structured, and semi-structured data. From data sources, the raw data is moved into a destination system, such as a data warehouse or a data lake, as shown in Figure 5.3.

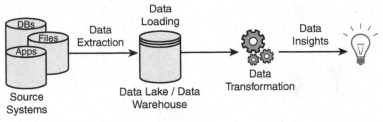

FIGURE 5.3 **The ELT Process**

Finally, the data is transformed at runtime (or on the fly) as required by the business, and data insights are pulled from transformed data on a visualization dashboard or in a report.

> **Note**
>
> ELT processes leverage a schema-on-read approach.

ELT is typically leveraged during business hours, when users run analyses on the data collected from multiple sources in order to gain better insights. This requires the data to be transformed in near real time.

> **ExamAlert**
>
> ELT is increasingly popular among data engineers and data scientists, as well as in context of cloud computing. Be sure to understand ELT for the CompTIA Data+ exam.

The three stages of ELT are as follows:

▶ **Extract:** During this stage, data is exported (or copied) from multiple data sources to a data lake or data warehouse. Data may be raw, semi-structured, unstructured, or structured, and the following types of data can be processed by ELT tools:

  ▶ Document and (flat) text files
  ▶ NoSQL and SQL data
  ▶ Emails
  ▶ Blog posts, articles, or web pages

▶ **Load:** After the extraction stage, the data is stored in a data lake or a data warehouse. It is quite usual for organizations to have a data loading process that is well defined, automated, and continuous. Any required business rules and data integrity checks can be run before the data is loaded into the data lake or warehouse.

▶ **Transform:** In this stage, the schema is applied to data before the analysis occurs. The functions executed in this stage are as follows:

  ▶ The data is cleansed, filtered, authenticated, and validated.

  ▶ Translations, analysis, calculations, or summaries are performed on the raw data. This function involves tasks like modifying column and row headers for consistency, changing units of measurement or currency, averaging or adding values, and editing text.

  ▶ Data is encrypted or masked in line with industry or government regulations.

  ▶ Data is formatted into joined tables or tables on the basis of the schema adopted.

Figure 5.4 details the ELT process.

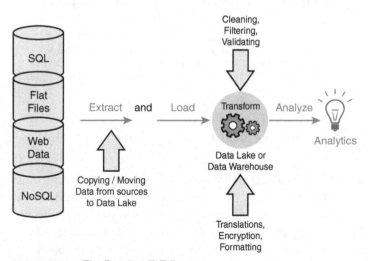

FIGURE 5.4　The Detailed ELT Process

Table 5.1 lists the key differences between ETL and ELT processes.

TABLE 5.1 **Differences Between ETL and ELT Processes**

Characteristic	ETL	ELT
Basic process	ETL extracts data from different data sources into a single consistent data store (that is, a staging database), performs transformations, and then loads the data into the target data store.	ELT extracts (or copies) data from data sources and, rather than moving it to the destination source for transformation, it loads raw data into the target data store(s), and the data is transformed on the fly when the information insights are required.
Target data store	The target data store is usually a data warehouse containing mostly structured data.	The target data store is usually a data lake (and may be a data warehouse) containing structured, semi-structured, or unstructured data.
Tools	ETL tools support artificial intelligence and business intelligence applications.	ELT tools support machine learning, artificial intelligence, real-time data applications, predictive analytics, and event streams.
Data privacy	ETL makes data privacy more systemic and simpler as the data is loaded into the final repository and the structure is well known.	Data privacy with ELT is much more complex as the data is being transformed because there's no set format or structure during this stage.
History and usage	ETL has been around for years, and the key use cases include business transaction processing and data migration from legacy systems.	ELT is a newer process that is extensively used by data scientists and data engineers to crunch data and gather insights.

Now, for the million-dollar question: Should your organization opt for ETL or ELT?

Ultimately, the business requirements and outcomes expected should guide the selection of ETL or ELT. For example, data scientists prefer ELT, as it involves collecting raw data and allows them to customize and transform the data based on their needs on the fly. They don't need to focus on the structure of the data as the focus is on insights. For example, if there is a huge sale, data scientists can predict which items are performing better than others so more similar items can be put on sale.

On the other hand, a business with mostly batch data may use ETL for transactional data loading and analysis. In this case, the structure of data is much more important, and the outcomes do not differ very much over time. For example, at the end of each day, all records from online sales may be processed as a batch, and insights may be driven based on which products sold better than others during the day.

Delta Load

Delta load refers to the process of extracting only the delta—that is, the difference in the data compared to what was previously extracted—as part of the ETL process. It implies that the whole dataset will not be extracted from the table(s) but only the new information will be extracted and loaded to the target data store. In the context of ETL, a full load occurs when you load data for the first time (that is, when you are seeding the destination with initial data). Subsequently, a delta data load occurs when you are either loading changes to already loaded data or adding new transactions. To enable delta loading, it is important to determine which rows (or columns) in the table were already extracted and which dataset(s) is new or should be updated or added to existing datasets.

Application Programming Interfaces (APIs)/Web Services

Application programming interfaces (APIs) have become the new standard for system integration. Think of APIs as a bridge between newer, modern systems and disparate and older (possibly proprietary) systems. An API is collection of well-defined rules that provides details on how applications should interact with other applications.

An API provides a programmable interface for interacting with applications and infrastructure. With APIs you can:

▶ Create custom integrations between applications

▶ Create automation tools to simplify application provisioning

▶ Create a middleware layer to abstract one set of applications from other applications

Hence, APIs enable organizations to selectively share their applications in terms of data and functionality with internal stakeholders (such as developers and users) as well as external stakeholders (such as business partners, third-party developers, and vendors). Consider the example of a transport and logistics organization that has to integrate its order management, tracking, and other systems with vendors and suppliers. Instead of doing this integration on a system-by-system basis and creating dedicated plug-ins, the organization can opt for APIs and offer access based on role-based access control (RBAC) to only parts of the system, as required by the partners.

APIs can be based on multiple frameworks, standards, or protocols, such as representational state transfer (REST), Simple Object Access Protocol (SOAP), and Remote Procedure Call (RPC). Further, APIs can be classified on a systemic or functional basis—that is, based on systems for which they are designed, such as database APIs, web APIs, and remote APIs. APIs can also be classified as follows:

▶ **Private:** Only the organization developing the API has access to it.

▶ **Public:** Anyone has access to the API.

▶ **Partner:** The API is available to only a set of partners.

When working with applications and underlying infrastructure, APIs can be defined as northbound or southbound. A northbound API interacts with applications, and a southbound API interacts with underlying devices/ infrastructure.

Let's look at an example of a user trying to browse a web server and also interacting with rows in a database that is hosted behind the web server as a back end. Figure 5.5 illustrates this API ecosystem.

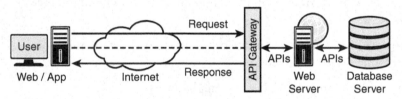

FIGURE 5.5 **An API Ecosystem**

Based on Figure 5.5, the high-level traffic and information flow is as follows:

1. A user web/application starts an API call for retrieving information; this is referred to as a *request*.

2. The request is intercepted by the API gateway, which proxies the API call to the web server. In this case, the web server is communicating with the back-end database using APIs as well.

   The request may consist of the following methods:

   ▶ **Get:** Requests data from the source (for example, browsing web server)

▶ **Put:** Replaces data at the destination (for example, updating a database row)

▶ **Post:** Submits data to the destination (for example, sending login credentials)

▶ **Delete:** Removes data from the destination (for example, removing a row from a database)

3. In response to the request, the web server completes the required operation (according to the method used during the request) and returns a response to the user app via the API gateway.

> **Note**
>
> With REST APIs, results can be published using status codes such as 2XX for success, 4XX for a client error, and 5XX for a server error.

In terms of web services, it is a simpler (and older) model that involves exchanging information between two machines on the Internet. While this process is still largely in use, it is being replaced by APIs as they do not need to broker connections for better control and security. A web service implies that there is a web server that runs on a virtual machine, physical server, or containers and listens for requests from other machines. When a request is received over a network, the web service responds with the requested resources, such as a Hypertext Markup Language (HTML) file, images, audio, or Extensible Markup Language (XML) files. Figure 5.6 provides an overview of the web services process.

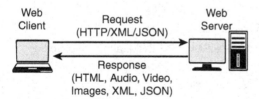

FIGURE 5.6 **Overview of the Web Services Process**

Cram Quiz

Answer these questions. If you cannot answer these questions correctly, consider reading this section again until you can.

1. In the ETL process, a series of business rules or functions can be applied during which stage?

   ○ **a.** Extract

   ○ **b.** Transform

   ○ **c.** Load

   ○ **d.** All of these

2. As which layer do APIs act?

   ○ **a.** Programming layer

   ○ **b.** Execution layer

   ○ **c.** Intermediary layer

   ○ **d.** Functional layer

3. Which of the following can you do with APIs? (Choose two.)

   ○ **a.** Create custom integrations between applications.

   ○ **b.** Create automation tools to simplify application provisioning.

   ○ **c.** Calculate an absolute measure.

   ○ **d.** Calculate a mode.

4. An organization is trying to leverage ETL for pulling data from multiple sources. However, the data administrator isn't sure if ETL can support this. What should you tell the data administrator?

   ○ **a.** ETL can only pull data from one SQL source.

   ○ **b.** ETL can pull data from one or more SQL sources.

   ○ **c.** ETL can pull data from SQL, NoSQL, ERP, CRM, and multiple other sources.

   ○ **d.** ETL can only pull data from data lakes.

Cram Quiz Answers

1. **Answer: b. Transform.** During the transform stage, a series of functions or rules can be applied to extract the information into the required/desired schema.

2. **Answer: c. Intermediary layer.** APIs act as an intermediary layer that transforms data between two or more systems.

3. **Answer: a. Create custom integrations between applications, b. Create automation tools to simplify application provisioning.** With APIs, you cannot just integrate two disparate systems. However, you can automate system interactions and simplify provisioning of applications by leveraging automation.

4. **Answer: c. ETL can pull data from SQL, NoSQL, ERP, CRM, and multiple other sources.** The ETL process is able to integrate data from multiple data sources, such as SQL, NoSQL, and ERP systems. The ETL process can pull data from any data source that holds structured, unstructured, or semi-structured data.

Data Collection Methods

CramSaver

If you can correctly answer these questions before going through this section, save time by skimming the Exam Alerts in this section and then completing the Cram Quiz at the end of the section.

1. What is the purpose of web scraping?

   a. Fetching and extracting structured or unstructured data

   b. Securing data

   c. Identifying data

   d. Loading data

2. Secondary data can be collected from which of the following?

   a. Interviews

   b. Public databases

   c. Surveys

   d. Observation

3. What are the two parts of web scraping applications? (Choose two.)

   a. Scraper

   b. Finder

   c. Pointer

   d. Crawler

4. Why is it import to carry out a survey?

   a. To acquire accurate outcomes

   b. To make a conclusion

   c. To get presentable data

   d. All of these answers are correct.

Answers

1. **Answer: a. Fetching and extracting structured or unstructured data.** Web scraping involves fetching unstructured data and transforming it into structured data.

2. **Answer: b. Public databases.** Secondary data can be gathered from public databases that extract from multiple sources, such as manuals and interviews.

3. **Answer: a. Scraper, d. Crawler.** The scraper and the crawler are two important parts of a web scraping application. The crawler helps find the right URLs to scrape, and the scraper scrapes the required data from the web pages.

4. **Answer: d. All of these answers are correct.** It is important to carry out a survey in order to acquire accurate outcomes, make a conclusion, and get presentable data.

As established earlier in this book, data is an invaluable currency, and organizations are increasingly collecting data for analysis. Data collection and analysis is important in any industry vertical, whether medical, marketing, or sales. For example, using data for accelerating product or service adoption in an organization matters a lot to modern enterprises. What is vital to understand is that data collection is not a random process; data collection occurs in an organized manner to ensure that the quality of data is high and the collection occurs in an ethical manner (as discussed later in this chapter).

There are a number of ways that organizations can collect data, including from primary data sources (that is, direct data collection) and from secondary data sources (that is, indirect collection). With primary data collection, the data is collected firsthand from researcher or surveyor. With secondary data collection, it is the data which was previously gathered, processed, published, or analyzed. This data may be gathered from internal or external sources by investigators, researchers, or surveyors for carrying out statistical analysis and may be referred to as *secondhand data*.

The sections that follow cover the most commonly used data collection methods.

Web Scraping

The World Wide Web (WWW), also commonly known as the Internet, is a huge source of data, and because of the nature of the WWW, the data is mostly unstructured data. Unstructured data is difficult to collect because the file types, sizes, and formats can be varied.

Web scraping—also known as web data extraction or web harvesting—is a method used to extract data from websites and export it into a user-friendly format. While web scraping can be a manual process, more often than not, automated tools known as web scrapers are used for scraping web data; these tools are much more cost-effective and produce results faster than manual efforts. There are sites that offer web scraping as a service. For example, https://webscraper.io/ offers a web scraping tool—that is, an application that's designed specifically to scrape relevant information from websites. A web scraping tool can leverage APIs and other methods to scrape data; in the process, they fetch unstructured data from web pages and change it to structured data as well as store it in data stores.

The web scraping process works as follows:

1. Identify the target websites or web pages and collect their Uniform Resource Locators (URLs) using a crawler.

2. Imitate a user browsing request to get the HTML code from the web pages.

3. Use a web scraper to try to find the interesting data in the HTML code and extract it.

4. Translate unstructured data into structured data (in a JSON or CSV file) for storage and analysis.

Figure 5.7 illustrates the web scraping process.

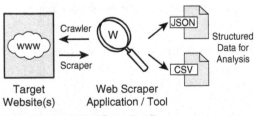

FIGURE 5.7 **Web Scraping Process**

A crawler (also known as a spider) is an automated tool that browses the targeted websites (which could be any website unless crawling parameters are well defined) on the Internet to index and search for content. The crawler goes through one or more specified websites to discover URLs and pass them on to the scraper. The scraper is a specialized application specifically designed to quickly extract data of interest from the crawled web pages. Web scrapers can find interesting data that should be extracted from an HTML file by leveraging HTML parsing libraries, CSS selectors, regular expressions (regex), or other methods. The data is then stored in an unstructured format such as a JavaScript Object Notation (JSON) or structured comma-separated values (CSV) files.

Why perform web scraping? Well, web scraping is seen as fundamental to the way some businesses operate, in that their decisions are based on the data being scraped from other sites. For example, in e-commerce, web scraping can help an organization understand the trends of a competitor and the prices as they're set, in near real time. The most common applications of web scraping results are lead generation, academic research, marketing, and news.

Further, web scraping is an effective technique for collecting big data where collecting huge volumes of data is significant. In addition, search engines use web scraping in combination with web crawling for indexing the WWW in order to create huge volumes of searchable pages. Crawlers grab links so that they can determine where to store data in the record.

Public Databases

A public database is a compilation of data from previously distributed text presented in the public domain. It may contain data from online and offline sources such as literature, reports, textbooks, magazines, newspapers, articles, and published papers.

Surveys

Surveys have been used for many decades to collect data from targeted populations in order to understand patterns, demand, or trends so that businesses can align themselves better to consumers' expectations. Survey data is typically collected from selected participants regarding a particular topic.

Several methods exist for collecting survey data and for performing statistical analysis on the data collected, including:

▶ Online surveys

▶ Paper surveys

▶ Telephone surveys

▶ Face-to-face, or in-person, surveys

Different communication media can be adopted for collecting opinions and feedback from survey respondents. The major factors that influence survey data are:

▶ How the interviewer will communicate with participants (such as offline or online)

▶ How the information on data being collected is presented to the participants

▶ The quality of data and the efficiency of the data collection process

The sections that follow describe the various survey methods.

> **ExamAlert**
>
> Surveys in any form are an important topic as surveys help collate information in various formats. Be sure to understand the various ways in which surveys are useful to collect data.

Online Surveys

Online surveys are the most cost-effective surveys, given that their reachability is greater than can be achieved with other types of surveys, such as face-to-face surveys, telephone surveys, and paper surveys. Following are the highlights of online surveys:

▶ The investment needed for creating surveys and collecting the survey data is minimal compared with other methods. A good example would be a follow-up survey to an e-commerce order you recently placed.

▶ A researcher can ask more questions of the sample population in the same amount of time compared to telephone or face-to-face surveys.

▶ Online surveys are usually simple in their execution and take a small amount of time for participants to answer.

▶ Outcomes can be gathered in real time so that analysts can analyze the data and determine corrective measures.

▶ Online surveys are secure and safe to carry out. No in-person interaction is required, which is especially helpful during a pandemic. For example, during the COVID-19 pandemic, organizations shifted to contactless research and surveys.

Paper Surveys

Paper surveys are commonly used to collate information from respondents by leveraging paper and pen. They are adopted where tablets, computers, and laptops are either not allowed or feasible.

Paper surveys can be more expensive than online surveys as the surveys need to be printed, and someone needs to make the rounds to get respondents to respond to the survey. For example, a restaurant may use paper surveys to gather feedback from customers about the quality and appeal of its food.

Telephone Surveys

Telephone surveys require more investment than online surveys as inbound or outbound phone calls must be handled by real people. The cost of telephone surveys is a little higher than the cost of online surveys. Following are the highlights of telephone surveys:

▶ Communicating with participants via telephone requires less staffing and effort than communicating in person.

▶ The major disadvantage of carrying out telephone surveys is that it takes time to create a friendly environment with the respondent, where it is not possible to put a face to a name. Phone surveys occur in real time, and the respondent may not have time to answer questions.

For example, a research organization might carry out a telephone survey about the buying experience and motivation to invest in different brands.

Face-to-Face Surveys

In-person human interaction has historically been the best way to connect with people and build trust with emotions. Obtaining data from participants through face-to-face surveys has conventionally been much more successful than using the survey methods discussed earlier. When participants trust researchers and give honest feedback regarding the survey subject, the chances of collecting good-quality data increase.

Following are the highlights of face-to-face surveys:

▶ Surveyors can determine whether participants are comfortable with the survey questions and can help clarify if there's any doubt.

▶ With face-to-face surveys, surveyors are likely to be aware of demographics, which gives them an advantage over online surveyors.

Post-Survey Actions

After survey data has been gathered, the information is analyzed to support the original intent of the research. Steps followed in analyzing survey data are as follows:

1. Understand the most common questions and the most common responses to those questions.

2. Filter acquired outcomes (such as by using cross-tabulation).

3. Evaluate the obtained information.

4. Make conclusions based on analysis to inform outcomes.

A number of data analysis techniques can be used to convert information to insights, based on the data obtained in surveys. These are as follows:

▶ Total unduplicated reach and frequency (TURF) analysis

▶ Strength, weakness, opportunity, and threat (SWOT) analysis

▶ MaxDiff analysis

▶ Gap analysis

▶ Cross-tabulation

▶ Conjoint analysis

▶ Trend analysis

Sampling

Sampling is a statistical analysis process that aims to collect data from a subdivision of a given population in order to gain insights about the whole population. For example, if you have been given the task of studying the market to determine the viability of a new product, instead of asking all possible consumers about their preference about the product, you will survey a sample of the population for input purposes, ensuring that the sample represents the whole population in terms of important factors such as age or sex. Their inputs would represent—statistically—the inputs that would have been gathered from a larger population.

> **Note**
>
> Sampling is a complicated process, as the sample population and the inhabitants of the entire population can be very different in their ways of thinking and their responses.

There are various types of sampling methods, including the following:

- ▶ **Random sampling:** As the name suggests, this sampling method involves randomly choosing participants with no order or design—much like randomly selecting a raffle winner from ticket bowl.

- ▶ **Systematic sampling:** This sampling method follows set guidelines for better reliability in sampling. For example, a surveyor might consider only the first 10 out of every 20 respondents until 100 respondents have been selected.

- ▶ **Clustered sampling:** This sampling method looks at clusters, or subgroups, of inhabitants rather than at individuals.

- ▶ **Convenience sampling:** This sampling method leverages a readily available sample (that is, the easiest or closest respondents). For example, a surveyor might stand by a coffee shop, asking all customers about their preferences about a new gadget.

- ▶ **Stratified sampling:** This sampling method classifies individuals into subgroups of people who share similar characteristics or properties. For example, a surveyor may look only at people between 50 and 60 years of age and of either sex for a product that is suitable only for people in that age bracket.

Observation

Observation is one of the oldest methods of data collection, and it is used extensively in scientific research. It enables an observer or investigator to gather data about behavior or surroundings or individuals and then analyze the data in order to reach conclusions. Observation can be categorized based on the environment it is performed in, such as observing participants in a natural environment (participant-based observation), in a controlled environment (structured observation), or spontaneously with a phenomenon (spontaneous observation).

Using observation as a method for collecting data has a number of benefits, including:

▶ The observer does not need to have technical skills for data collection.

▶ Observation offers freedom in terms of describing the respondents' activities and behaviors.

Cram Quiz

Answer these questions. If you cannot answer these questions correctly, consider reading this section again until you can.

1. Data integration requires which of the following?

   ○ **a.** Technical processes

   ○ **b.** Business processes

   ○ **c.** Non-technical processes

   ○ **d.** Both business and technical processes

2. Data lakes are most popular with which type of data integration process?

   ○ **a.** ETL

   ○ **b.** ELT

   ○ **c.** Surveys

   ○ **d.** Observation

3. The importance of delta loading in integration of data is that it allows for which of the following?

   ○ **a.** Appending data

   ○ **b.** Repetition of data

   ○ **c.** Clustering

   ○ **d.** Prediction

4. Web scraping is also referred to as _____.

    ○ **a.** screen scraping

    ○ **b.** web data scraping

    ○ **c.** web harvesting

    ○ **d.** All of these are correct.

    ○ **e.** None of these are correct.

5. REST, SOAP, and RPC are frameworks/protocols used in which of the following?

    ○ **a.** APIs

    ○ **b.** Dispersion

    ○ **c.** Variables

    ○ **d.** Delta loading

Cram Quiz Answers

1. **Answer: d. Both business and technical processes.** Data integration combines both business and technical processes to integrate information from different sources into usable information that can provide insights for decision making.

2. **Answer: b. ELT.** ELT processes can use data lakes or data warehouses for storage. Because of the on-demand transformation often used with ELT, data lakes are the most common storage options.

3. **Answer: a. Appending data.** Delta loading is important because new data can be added after some information is extracted from existing tables. No repetition is allowed.

4. **Answer: d. All of these are correct.** Web scraping is also known as screen scraping, web harvesting, and web data scraping.

5. **Answer: a. APIs.** APIs consist of multiple frameworks and/or protocols, including SOAP, REST, and XML-RPC.

What Next?

If you want more practice on this chapter's exam objective before you move on, remember that you can access all of the Cram Quiz questions on the Pearson Test Prep software online. You can also create a custom exam by objective with the Online Practice Test. Note any objective you struggle with and go to that objective's material in this chapter.

CHAPTER 6

Cleansing and Profiling Data

This chapter covers Objective 2.2 (Identify common reasons for cleansing and profiling datasets) of the CompTIA Data+ exam and includes the following topics:

▶ Duplicate data

▶ Redundant data

▶ Missing values

▶ Invalid data

▶ Non-parametric data

▶ Data outliers

▶ Specification mismatch

▶ Data type validation

For more information on the official CompTIA Data+ exam topics, see the Introduction.

This chapter covers topics related to cleansing and profiling data. Some datasets may include duplicate data or data that's just not worth working with. In this chapter you will learn about redundant data, missing values, invalid data, non-parametric data, and data outliers. This chapter also describes specification mismatches and data type validation.

Profiling and Cleansing Basics

CramSaver

If you can correctly answer these questions before going through this section, save time by skimming the Exam Alerts in this section and then completing the Cram Quiz at the end of the section.

1. Outliers are identified by which of the following?

   a. Inconsistent data

   b. Similar data

   c. Consistent data

   d. Observation

2. Which of the following are examples of errors that can occur while entering data?

   a. Bad entry of data

   b. Mismatch of source and destination

   c. Mismatch of sample rate

   d. All of these answers are correct.

3. Validating data helps to do which of the following?

   a. Detect errors

   b. Correct errors

   c. Remove errors

   d. Identify data inconsistencies

4. Random missing values happen due to which of the following?

   a. Mistakes in data entry

   b. Inadvertently skipping the questions

   c. Not paying close enough attention

   d. All of these answers are correct.

5. Imputation is used for which of the following purposes?

   a. Replacing missing values

   b. Identifying missing values

   c. Deleting missing values

   d. None of these answers are correct.

6. Data cleansing is also known as which of the following?

    a. Data transformation

    b. Data scrubbing

    c. Data loading

    d. Data extraction

Answers

1. **Answer: A. Inconsistent data.** Outliers are anomalous values that deviate from other data points in a dataset. Inconsistent data typically contains outliers.

2. **Answer: D. All of these answers are correct.** Errors can occur while entering data due to bad entry of data, mismatch of source and destination, and mismatch of sample rate.

3. **Answer: D. Identify data inconsistencies.** Validating data helps in identifying data inconsistencies.

4. **Answer: D. All of these answers are correct.** Random missing values happen due to mistakes in data entry, inadvertently skipping the questions, and not paying enough attention.

5. **Answer: A. Replacing missing values.** Imputation is used for replacing missing values.

6. **Answer: B. Data scrubbing.** Data scrubbing, also known as data cleansing, is the process of correcting the errors in a dataset.

It's pretty apparent that data plays a vital role in analysis as well as decision making. In fact, the success of analysis and decision making relies heavily on data quality. For a variety of reasons, the quality of data may be lower than expected. Data may include duplicates or it may be redundant or invalid, as we will discuss in this chapter.

Fun Fact

The phrase "Garbage in, garbage out" applies to data quality. If the data being used for analysis has errors, missing values, and other inconsistencies, working with that data will give you very low-quality or useless outcomes.

Profiling and cleansing the data in a dataset is usually a two-step process involving error detection and correction. Data profiling is carried out in order to identify the records that include corrupted or incomplete data, and verification and validation are conducted to pinpoint missing or incomplete information. The goals of profiling are to spot any errors in a given dataset and recognize any anomalies that could affect the quality of the final analysis.

Data scrubbing, also known as data cleansing, follows the data profiling phase and is aimed at correcting data quality issues before a dataset is leveraged in another system. The goal is to correct data that is incomplete or formatted incorrectly or that includes duplicate records or errors, all of which may reduce its usefulness. During the cleansing phase, data engineers may introduce transformations that clean the data and, hence, enhance the quality. Data cleansing may be performed manually or automatically. Manual cleaning is typically a time-consuming process, whereas automated cleaning is quicker and often more cost-effective.

> **Note**
>
> Once data extraction is complete, data is typically stored in temporary tables, and data cleansing functions are carried out before the data is stored in the target tables.

Duplicate Data

Duplicate data reduces the quality of a given dataset and makes the knowledge acquired from such sources unreliable. Detecting duplicate records requires determining which records refer to the same unique object or entity.

The process of detecting duplicates starts with the preparation stage, in which data entries are stored uniformly in a database that brings some degree of homogeneity to the datasets. The data preparation stage consists of parsing, transforming, and standardizing the data. The processes of extraction, transformation, and loading (ETL) may be used to enhance the quality and usability of data that is collected.

A few steps can be taken to reduce the probability of existing duplicate entities. You may be able to use logic to check that all entered data—such as physical addresses, email addresses, and phone numbers—is entered correctly and to look for duplicate and misspelled entries. It is important to develop a streamlined and standardized process for data input to reduce duplication at the source.

> **Note**
>
> It can be quite difficult to identify similar duplicates in a database. Objects or entities may superficially look alike but differ by only a character or symbol. In the absence of these superficial characters or symbols, they would be precise duplicates.

You can use similarity measurements to look for similar duplicates that are not exact textual duplicates. Based on these similarity measurements, you can decide whether the entries are duplicates. For example, "neighbor" and "neighbour" are similar duplicates: They are not spelled the same but have the same meaning in US and UK English. If you use a string-matching algorithm that estimates the similarity between "neighbor" and "neighbour," you can use the result to determine whether the two terms are the same.

Another option for eliminating duplicate entries is to leverage a knowledge-based approach called IntelliClean. IntelliClean is a proposed framework that provides a methodical way to deal with duplicate entries that involves introducing standardization, detecting anomalies, and removing duplication in databases. The IntelliClean framework involves three stages: preprocessing, processing, and validation and verification. Anomalies in data are identified and cleansed during the preprocessing state. The output of the preprocessing stage is the input to the next stage, processing. In this stage, there are some rules to be followed for identifying duplicates: identification, purge or merge, update, and alert rules. These rules can be executed by the search and comparison engine to compare the rules collection to the objects collection. The actions taken in the preprocessing and processing stages are logged for the verification and validation stage, which may involve human intervention to assure accuracy and consistency.

Redundant Data

> **ExamAlert**
>
> Redundant data is an important aspect pertinent to data cleansing and is an area of focus in the CompTIA Data+ exam.

Removing the noise introduced by redundant data (which might be introduced during the data acquisition or storage phase) is just as important as cleansing data by identifying and eliminating errors. Data redundancy occurs when the same datasets are stored in multiple data sources, such as data warehouses or data lakes. Data redundancy usually starts with poorly designed (relational) databases that are inadequately structured, leading to unnecessary replication of data across the same table. Data redundancy may also be an outcome of backing up data recursively, creating multiple data backups with the same datasets.

For example, say that several business units are collecting customer reviews from the same customer and storing them in different tables. The redundancy can be avoided by leveraging unique IDs or foreign keys to maintain relationships across separate but related tables.

> **Note**
>
> While there are many benefits to reducing data redundancy, one of the key benefits is the reduced storage requirement, which is especially valuable as data volumes grow.

Another common example of data redundancy is repeating a customer's details (such as name, address, and phone number) across columns in a table in a relational database. This duplication can occur as different lines of business (LOBs) work to input data and end up making multiple entries for the same customer. As a result, the same pieces of data end up existing in multiple places.

> **Note**
>
> In the real world, data redundancy can't be eliminated; however, it can be reduced and managed well.

From a data analysis perspective, there are two types of data redundancy:

▶ **Superficial redundancy:** This type of redundancy does not impact analysis as the redundant variables are not considered for future analysis. For example, you might simply ignore repeated values across two tables in a database. Hence, to resolve superficial redundancy, the data engineers can ignore repeated values.

▶ **Deep redundancy:** This type of redundancy exists when you are correlating variables across multiple datasets and/or tables and anything that extends from these redundant values. With deep redundancy, you need to take a more focused approach to ensure that redundant values across a multitude of databases are removed. The data engineers might need to compare the redundant values across multiple tables in multiple databases or data warehouses, which can be done using algorithms.

Before we move on to looking at how to reduce data redundancy, we need to consider the problems that data redundancy can create. Data redundancy can lead to omissions and incorrect measurements, and it can also increase the size of databases and storage requirements. Think about a customer contact database that includes the customer's address as one of the data fields, with multiple entries of the same address across the database columns. Now, if the customer moves to a different location, it will be necessary to update the address across all the columns. Making the needed update in multiple places would be time-consuming, and it would involve the possibility of making typographical errors.

One way to reduce and remove data redundancies is to leverage the process of normalization. *Normalization* allows you to efficiently organize data in a database by eliminating redundant data and ensuring that data dependencies make sense. With data normalization, the attributes and relations of a database are organized such that their dependencies are properly enforced by database integrity limitations. Normalization involves *normal forms* from 1NF through 5NF. Chapter 7, "Understanding and Executing Data Manipulation," covers the concept of normalization and the various normalization forms.

ExamAlert

Data redundancy and normalization are key topics, and you can expect questions along these lines: "What do you need to do to a sample dataset before you can analyze it?" The answer is normalize the data.

To reduce redundancy, organizations often integrate the data from multiple databases into a centralized source, such as a data warehouse or data lake. An organization that does this ends up with less redundancy and also has the opportunity to put limits on data entry and implement validation.

Missing Values

In addition to having duplicate values, a dataset may be missing values. If missing values are not handled properly, researchers or analysts may reach incorrect conclusions about the data, which would impact the analysis and possibly skew outcomes.

Missing values can be broadly categorized as random and non-random:

▶ **Random missing values:** Random missing values result when the respondent or the person entering the data inadvertently fails to provide certain responses, skips some data fields, or makes typographical errors while entering the data. An example is trying to consolidate data from multiple databases and mistakenly skipping one or more entries in tuples.

Random missing values are further classified as missing completely at random (MCAR) and missing at random (MAR). MCAR is a result of absolute missing values in that there is no relationship between a missing data point and any other values in the dataset. For example, while responding to surveys, respondents might miss one or more questions randomly, and it may be impossible to relate these missing values to the type of questions. In case of MAR, the missing values have relationships to the data points; for example, in a survey, a respondent may fail to answer a sex-related question as male, female, or unidentified sex.

▶ **Non-random missing values:** These missing values result when the respondent or the person entering the data intentionally leaves blank fields or incomplete data entries. An example would be if the respondent chooses to leave a field empty in response to a question about sensitive data such as their marital status.

There are multiple approaches for dealing with missing data. While some approaches involve removing variables that have missing values, others include imputation or substituting values. Some of the popular approaches to address missing data are as follows:

▶ **Replace missing values:** One of the ways to deal with missing values is to replace all missing values in a dataset with a unique identifier. For example, blank cells may be filled with five zeros to represent the value "not present" or "N/A."

▶ **Do nothing:** One approach to dealing with missing data is to not do anything about the missing data. However, the data engineers let an algorithm take control over how it responds to the missing data.

> **Note**
>
> The do nothing approach does not imply no imputation. Rather, the imputation method/algorithm will determine the best substitution for the missing data.

Different algorithms react to missing data differently; some algorithms identify the most plausible imputation values for missing data based on training from previous datasets, and others just try to substitute based on prebuilt logic rules.

▶ **Drop if it's not in use:** One way to deal with missing data is to delete all rows that have missing values to get the dataset to the point where there are no missing values. The drawback of this approach is that it can affect the sample representativeness, as the size of population sample might not be sufficient.

▶ **Use imputation with most frequent values:** Missing values, such as numeric or string values, are substituted with the most frequent values. For example, in measuring speed in miles per hour (MPH) most frequent values may be used to replace missing speed values in a dataset.

▶ **Use imputation with mean or median values:** With this method, which works only with numeric data, you start by working out the mean or median of the available values in a column. You then replace the missing values in each column with the calculated values.

▶ **Use extrapolation and interpolation:** This method involves trying to estimate values from other similar observations based on previously known data points. For example, speed of a cruise ship in a certain area of ocean can be determined by previous voyages of other cruise ships in same region.

Invalid Data

Invalid data contains values that were initially generated inaccurately. In most datasets, invalid data values can be difficult to identify; however, they impact the outcomes of analysis and should therefore be removed from a dataset.

Invalid data may be included in a dataset for a number of reasons, including the following:

▶ **Incorrect recording of data:** Someone may have recorded the data values incorrectly, perhaps simply entering incorrect values or putting values in the wrong fields. For example, an office receptionist took the wrong details from a customer for a callback from the marketing team.

▶ **Generation of invalid data:** A tool/software may generate bad or invalid data, or an observer may incorrectly configure the tool. For example, an engineer might calibrate a meter incorrectly, leading to ambiguous readings.

▶ **Measurement of incorrect items:** An observer might need to measure X but instead measure Y. For example, instead of measuring the value of calcium in a blood sample, a clinician might measure zinc and report it as calcium.

Invalid data can be rectified in a few ways. One way is to remove the invalid data from the dataset altogether. Another is to cross-check the data against standard/similar values.

Non-parametric Data

Non-parametric data is data that does not fit a well-defined or well-stated distribution. No fixed parameters are available, and no normal distribution is needed for non-parametric data. *Non-parametric methods* are also known as *distribution-free* or *assumption-free methods*. Because there are no (fixed) parameters available to evaluate the hypotheses, the entire population distribution can be used.

For example, say that in a city, the current population as of 16:00 hours is 1 million. At 17:00 hours, the population becomes 1.1 million. There are no parameters governing this population growth, and so this data is considered non-parametric data. It is important to see here that the data doesn't fit a defined shape (for example, the population grows by x in z time). Also, it is important to know that the data is aligned with time intervals and may contain outliers.

In order to deal with non-parametric data in datasets, it is important to consider the tests that will help deal with this data and associated hypotheses. Non-parametric methods include the sign test, the Spearman correlation test, and the U test. You can use the sign test, for example, to test a null hypothesis and compare two groups for their equality in terms of size. You can use the Spearman correlation test to measure the strength of association between ordinal variables (where a variable is r, and $r = 1$ implies positive correlation and $r = -1$ implies negative correlation). The topic of null hypothesis and hypothesis testing is covered in Chapter 10, "Descriptive and Inferential Statistical Methods."

Data Outliers

An *outlier* in a dataset is an observation that is inconsistent with or that is very dissimilar to the other observations/information. Outliers are anomalous values that deviate from other data points in a dataset. An example of an outlier would be a credit card transaction that's much larger than the user's typical transactions. Some key causes of data outliers are human error, instrument calibration error, and sometimes an environmental change. Outliers may also be present due to the intentional sabotage of data.

> **Note**
>
> Defining an observation as an anomaly depends on what has been defined as normal or baseline. It also depends on how a data analyst defines the baseline compared to anomalies.

Figure 6.1 shows data with outliers that are outside the normal values.

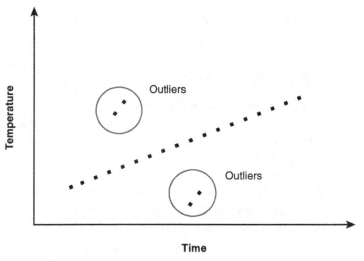

FIGURE 6.1   **Outliers**

There are three types of outliers:

▶ **Type I: Global outliers:** These outliers, also known as point anomalies, have values far outside the rest of the dataset. An example would be lightning striking a building in your community, which is a rare event.

▶ **Type II: Contextual outliers:** The value of this type of outlier, also known as a conditional outlier, deviates significantly from the rest of the data points. Consider a wet summer and the city getting more than 8 inches of rain within a day, causing flooding. It isn't usual to get so much rain in summer; however, getting rains during summer is still a contextual phenomenon.

▶ **Type III: Collective outliers:** As the name suggests, a collective outlier is a subset of anomalous data points within a dataset that collectively diverge from the rest of the dataset. For example, say that almost all homes in a community start replacing their regular Internet cable connection with Internet satellite dish antennas. This isn't a singular event but a collective activity that isn't expected to happen all at once.

Statistical methods can be used to detect outliers. Examples include the standard deviation method, the distance method, the statistical method, and the density method. Some additional ways to detect outliers are as follows:

▶ Visually find outliers by plotting data on histograms for univariate data and scatter plots for multivariate data

▶ Use statistical tests such as Chauvenet's criterion or Grubb's test to compare data within a set to identify outliers

▶ Manually look at data for outliers and remove these anomalies

Specification Mismatches

It is quite common for data from source systems to be incompatible with a destination system. This is sometimes due to specification mismatches, such as unrecognized symbols, mismatches of units/labels, or different data formatting. For example, if the formatting of data isn't the same across two systems, a mismatch may result. Quite commonly, the use of quotes and semicolons in a file causes specification mismatches. Further, specification mismatches may arise due to different terms or abbreviations being used for the same concept (for example, First_Name in one database and F_Name in another or Sex=Male in one database and Sex=M in another). Unless a user curates the data for one-to-one translation or transposition between source and destination systems, specification mismatches may occur among different systems exchanging information.

One of the ways to resolve any data specification mismatches is to have algorithms convert incompatible specifications either during preprocessing or on the fly when the data is being transferred from one to another system. Another way to resolve specification mismatches is to enforce data field types such that any data that is moved or entered has to match with the field type.

Data Type Validation

Data type validation is the process of using one or more checks and/or rules to ensure that the user is only entering a specific data type so that the data is meaningful for later processing.

As discussed in Chapter 3, "Data Types and Types of Data," data types can be any of the following:

▶ Integer (Int)

▶ Character (Char)

▶ String or text

▶ Float

▶ Enum

▶ Boolean

▶ Array

▶ Date

▶ Time

Data type validation ensures that the data entered is of the correct data type to be leveraged at the destination system. For example, a field might accept only string data and reject floating values. This would reject decimal numbers. Similarly, a numeric field should accept any numbers 0 through 9 but should not accept characters or symbols.

> **Note**
>
> In addition to data type validation, there are other data validation mechanisms, such as validation of data range, data consistency, and data format. Multiple data type validation rules can be used to ensure that data being entered meets the minimum standard of the correct data type.

Cram Quiz

Answer these questions. If you cannot answer these questions correctly, consider reading this section again until you can.

1. Why do outliers occur?

   ○ **a.** Human error and malicious activity

   ○ **b.** Environmental change

   ○ **c.** Instrument error

   ○ **d.** All of these answers are correct.

2. Non-random missing values occur due to which of the following?

- ○ **a.** Deleting a question
- ○ **b.** Intentionally skipping a question
- ○ **c.** Formatting a question
- ○ **d.** None of these answers are correct.

3. Deletion of invalid tuples results in which of the following?

- ○ **a.** Missing data
- ○ **b.** Lack of data
- ○ **c.** Loss of information
- ○ **d.** Unusable data

4. Non-parametric methods are also referred as which of the following?

- ○ **a.** Statistical methods
- ○ **b.** Non-statistical methods
- ○ **c.** Distribution-free methods
- ○ **d.** Free methods

5. Data validation ensures which of the following?

- ○ **a.** Accuracy of data
- ○ **b.** Quality of data
- ○ **c.** Quality and accuracy of data
- ○ **d.** Validity of data

Cram Quiz Answers

1. **Answer: D. All of these answers are correct.** Outliers occur due to human error and malicious activity, environmental change, and instrument error.

2. **Answer: B. Intentionally skipping a question.** Non-random missing values occur due to intentionally skipping a question.

3. **Answer: C. Loss of information.** Deletion of invalid tuples results in loss of information.

4. **Answer: C. Distribution-free methods.** Non-parametric methods are also referred to as distribution-free methods.

5. **Answer: C. Quality and accuracy of data.** Data validation ensures quality and accuracy of data.

What Next?

If you want more practice on this chapter's exam objective before you move on, remember that you can access all of the Cram Quiz questions on the Pearson Test Prep software online. You can also create a custom exam by objective with the Online Practice Test. Note any objective you struggle with and go to that objective's material in this chapter.

CHAPTER 7

Understanding and Executing Data Manipulation

This chapter covers Objective 2.3 (Given a scenario, execute data manipulation techniques) of the CompTIA Data+ exam and includes the following topics:

▶ Data manipulation

▶ Recoding data

▶ Derived variables

▶ Data merging

▶ Data blending

▶ Concatenation

▶ Data appending

▶ Imputation

▶ Reduction/aggregation

▶ Transposing

▶ Data normalization

▶ Parsing/string manipulation

For more information on the official CompTIA Data+ exam topics, see the Introduction.

This chapter covers topics related to recoding data, derived variables, data merging, and data blending. It also covers concatenation, data appending, imputation, and reduction/aggregation. Finally, it discusses transposition and normalization of data as well as parsing/string manipulation and data manipulation.

Data Manipulation Techniques

CramSaver

If you can correctly answer these questions before going through this section, save time by skimming the Exam Alerts in this section and then completing the Cram Quiz at the end of the section.

1. Data manipulation is adopted for which of the following?

    a. Acquiring consistent information and project information

    b. Neglecting redundant data

    c. Easily reading and working with data

    d. All of these answers are correct.

2. Data manipulation results in which of the following? (Choose all that apply.)

    a. Semi-structured datasets

    b. Unstructured datasets

    c. Organized and readable datasets

    d. Consistent datasets

3. Concatenation is used for which of the following?

    a. Identifying accurate information

    b. Identifying missing values

    c. Combining two or more datasets

    d. All of these answers are correct.

4. Why should you consider data blending?

    a. To make it easier to recognize useful information

    b. To make better business decisions

    c. To better store data

    d. To combine data

5. Recoding is typically used for _____.

    a. merging categories of variables into fewer groups or different groups

    b. combining attributes of variables into fewer groups or different groups

    c. merging categories of fields into different groups

    d. combining attributes of fields into some groups

6. The NOT logical function _____ values.

   a. adds

   b. combines

   c. merges

   d. groups

   e. reverses

Answers

1. **Answer: d. All of these answers are correct.** Data manipulation can help you get consistency in data, remove redundant data, and easily work with, read, and analyze data.

2. **Answer: c. Organized and readable datasets, d. Consistent datasets.** Data manipulation results in organized and readable data as well as consistent datasets across an organization.

3. **Answer: c. Combining two or more datasets.** Concatenation is used to combine two or more datasets.

4. **Answer: b. To make better business decisions.** Data blending is useful for making better business decisions.

5. **Answer: a. merging categories of variables into fewer groups or different groups.** Recoding is typically used for merging categories of variables into fewer groups or different groups.

6. **Answer: e. reverses.** The NOT function simply reverses a value from True to False or from False to True.

Before we get into the specifics of data manipulation techniques, we need to define a few terms.

For starters, *data manipulation* refers to the process/methodology of modifying or manipulating data to change it to a more readable and organized format such that it becomes easier for users to consume and work with the data. Data manipulation helps standardize datasets across an organization and enables any business unit to access and store data in a common format.

Data manipulation is an important step for business operations and optimization when dealing with data and analysis. For example, for carrying out consumer behavior analysis or trend analysis, you would want data to be structured in an easy-to-understand format. Table 7.1 gives insights into how data can be possibly structured by age to make it easier to read and process. This is just a sample of how age can be related to needs/wants.

TABLE 7.1 **Data Structured on Needs/Wants According to Age**

Age	Category	Needs/Wants
5–12	Very young	Lollies, gum, toys
13–18	Young	Bikes, skates, phones
19–35	Adult	Cars, houses, credit cards
36–55	Middle-aged	Vacations, investments
56 and over	Old-aged	Aged care, well-being

> **Note**
>
> Data Manipulation Language (DML) is a programming language that is used for data manipulation. It helps to amend data, such as by adding, deleting, and changing values in databases, and changes the information so it can be read and understood easily.

Several data manipulation methods are covered in this chapter. Aggregation, sorting, and filtering are the basic functions involved in data manipulation.

Data reconciliation is the verification phase during data migration, in which the destination data is compared with source data to ensure that any issues such as the ones discussed in Chapter 6, "Cleansing and Profiling Data"—for example, missing values, invalid values, and duplicate values—do not impact the data quality.

Recoding Data

Data is comprised of variables. Most of the time, it is necessary to make changes to variables before the data can be analyzed. The process of recoding can be used to transform a current variable into a different one, based on certain criteria and business requirements.

Why should you recode variables rather than use the original variables? It is a best practice to leave the original data unchanged so it can be used again in the future. Instead of changing an original variable, you can recode a variable into a different variable to meet the needs of the organization and maintain the integrity of the original dataset.

Let's look again at the example from Table 7.1. Let's say the data is originally structured as shown in Table 7.2.

TABLE 7.2 **Existing Data**

Age	Needs/Wants
5–12 years old	Lollies, gum, toys
13–18 years old	Bikes, skates, phones
19–35 years old	Cars, houses, credit cards
36–55 years old	Vacations, investments
56 years of age and over	Aged care, well-being

Now, to make sense of the ages expressed in years, this data can be recoded in the format outlined in Table 7.3 (which is very similar to Table 7.1).

TABLE 7.3 **Recoded Data: From Ages in Numbers of Years to Categorical Age Groups**

Age (Years)	New Recoded Category (Age Groups)	Needs/Wants
5–12	Very young	Lollies, gum, toys
13–18	Young	Bikes, skates, phones
19–35	Adult	Cars, houses, credit cards
36–55	Middle-aged	Vacations, investments
56 and over	Old-aged	Aged care, well-being

As you can see, instead of explaining to someone what constitutes young and adult or the age range between middle-aged and old-aged, it is easier to recode from numeric values into categorical strings that clearly segregate one age group from another and their needs/wants. Essentially, if the original data was as expressed in Table 7.2, after recoding it will be as shown in Table 7.3 (almost a replica of Table 7.1) that's easier to comprehend.

Recoding is typically used for merging categories of variables into fewer groups or different groups—as in the previous example, where we recoded data into different (categorical) groups. Recoding can be done with the same or different variables.

Data management and analytics tools such as IBM Statistical Package for the Social Sciences (SPSS) offer solutions to recode data from one variable to another variable (see Figure 7.1).

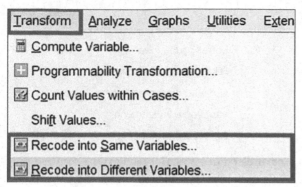

FIGURE 7.1   **Recoding Options in the Transform Menu of IBM SPSS**

There are two main options for recoding data: recoding numeric values or recoding categorical data.

Recoding categorical variables can be useful, for example, if there is a need to use fewer or combined categories than were used in collecting the data. Again using our example of age groups, we could recode categorically as shown in Table 7.4.

TABLE 7.4   **Recoding Categorical Values**

Age (Years)	Age Groups
5–18	Young
19–35	Adult
36–55	Middle-aged
56 and over	Old-aged

Here, we have collapsed the categories very young and young, which are closely aligned, into young by collating the two categories. We have done this because the organization may want to look at this as one broad category.

To see an example of recoding numeric values, consider Table 7.5, which assigns numeric values to sex of an individual.

TABLE 7.5   **Assigning Numerical Values to Sex**

Value	Sex
0	Unidentified
1	Male
2	Female
3	Undisclosed

If the organization does not need to distinguish between the unidentified and undisclosed sex options, we can recode these numeric values as shown in Table 7.6.

TABLE 7.6 **Recoding Numerical Values**

Value	Sex
0	Male
1	Female
2	Other

As you can see, whereas 0 was used for unidentified in Table 7.5, it is used for male in Table 7.6. Similarly, 1 was used for male earlier but is now used for female. The new variable other has been assigned to the number 3.

Derived Variables

As the name suggests, *derived variables* are variables derived from existing variables. In other words, a derived variable is defined by a parameter or an expression related to existing variables in a dataset. For example, if the existing variable is product_manufacture_date, a derived variable could be day_and_time_of_manufacturing or best_before_date.

To put this in context, let's consider an example. Say that every soft drink has a manufacturing or production date, such as:

product_manufacture_date = 24/10/2022

It also has a best before date, as well as an optional time of manufacturing, such as:

best_before_date = 24/10/2023

day_and_time_of_manufacturing = Monday, 11:34 am

It is quite obvious that any derived variables would be used in a similar fashion as any other variable. Because they are dependent on the variables from which they're derived, any change in the value of the original variable will change the values of the derived variable as well. Again, let's look at our previous soft drink example, in this case the variable being changed is the manufacturing date and hence, the best before date also changes accordingly:

product_manufacture_date = 24/11/2022

best_before_date = 24/11/2023

day_and_time_of_manufacturing = Thursday, 11:20 am

Data Merges

A *data merge* (as the name indicates) is a technique for merging two or more similar datasets into one (larger) dataset. Data merge is mostly leveraged for ease of data analysis; if you merge multiple datasets into one larger dataset, you can then run queries on all the data at once. Figure 7.2 shows the data merge process between two datasets (in this case, tables).

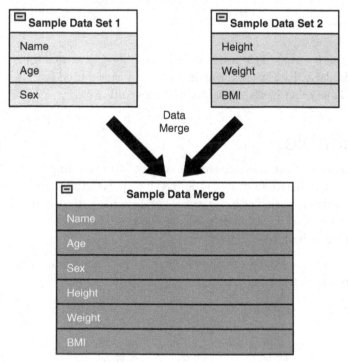

FIGURE 7.2   **Data Merge**

There are two main types of data merge operations:

▶ **Appending data:** This type of merge involves adding rows. For example, Figure 7.2 shows new rows being added to perform a data merge.

▶ **Merging in new variables:** A data merge accomplished by adding new variables implies adding new columns in the table or the new merged dataset.

Data Blending

Data blending is all about combining data from multiple data sources to create a new dataset. Data blending is very similar to data merging, but it brings together data from multiple sources that may be very dissimilar. Data blending allows an organization to bring together data from the Internet, spreadsheets, ERP, CRM, and other applications in order to present the data in a dashboard or another visualization (such as a report) for analysis.

Why not analyze the data separately and then bring together the analysis in one place? The simple answer is that not every organization has the required resources—such as data scientists and advanced analytics tools—at its disposal. In addition, organizations are often looking for rather simple views of data patterns to drive sales or marketing rather than mining deeply.

Blending of data allows a data analyst to incorporate information from almost any data sources for analysis and makes possible deeper and faster business insights. Data blending tools enable faster data-driven decision making by creating a reporting dashboard that automatically populates with real-time data, offering much better and more intuitive insights compared to using multiple reports. With a dashboard, data insights can be focused on a specific problem statement.

The high-level steps in data blending are as follows:

1. **Prepare the data.** This step involves determining pertinent datasets from well-known data sources and transforming different datasets into a general structure that helps form a meaningful blend.

2. **Blend the data.** This step allows blending the data from different data sources and customizing each blend based on the common dimension to ensure that the blending of data is meaningful (that is, the data being blended is in the context of the problem being solved).

3. **Validate outcomes.** As blending from multiple sources can potentially lead to inaccuracies, the data is examined for any inconsistencies as well as any missing information. If required, the data might need to be cleansed and (re)formatted.

4. **Store and visualize the data.** After data blending is completed, the data can be stored in the destination data store. Organizations can leverage business intelligence tools to create dashboards and/or reports. Visualization tools such as Tableau may be used for generating dashboards. The tool chosen depends on the reason data blending was performed and the specific problem being solved.

Concatenation

Concatenation (often shortened to *concat*) is a function or an operation that makes it possible to combine string, text, numeric, or other data from two or more fields in a dataset. Concatenation allows you to merge multiple cells, whether they involve text or numbers, without disturbing the original cells.

Figure 7.3 shows the CONCATENATE function in Microsoft Excel.

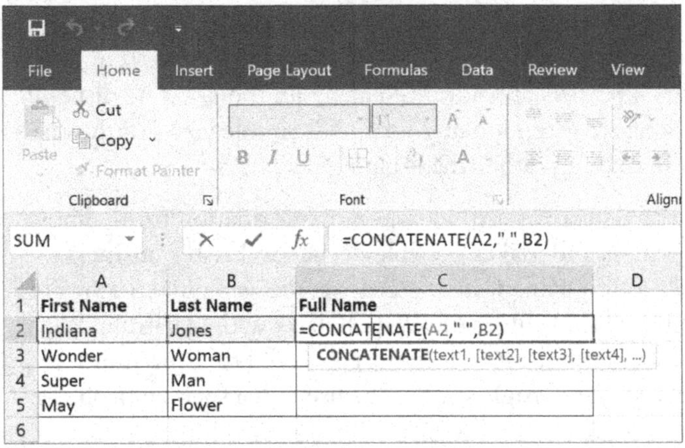

FIGURE 7.3   **Concatenation in Microsoft Excel**

Figure 7.3 shows an example of trying to concatenate the first name and last name, with a space in between. Figure 7.4 shows the outcome of this concatenation.

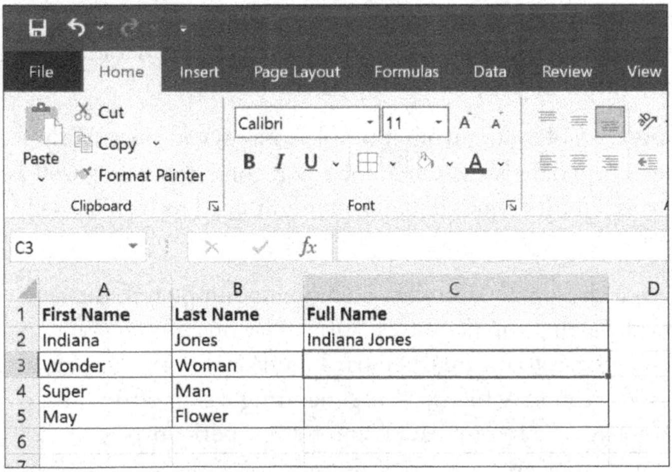

FIGURE 7.4   **Outcome of Concatenation in Microsoft Excel**

Figure 7.5 shows the final outcome when the same function is applied across all fields in the table.

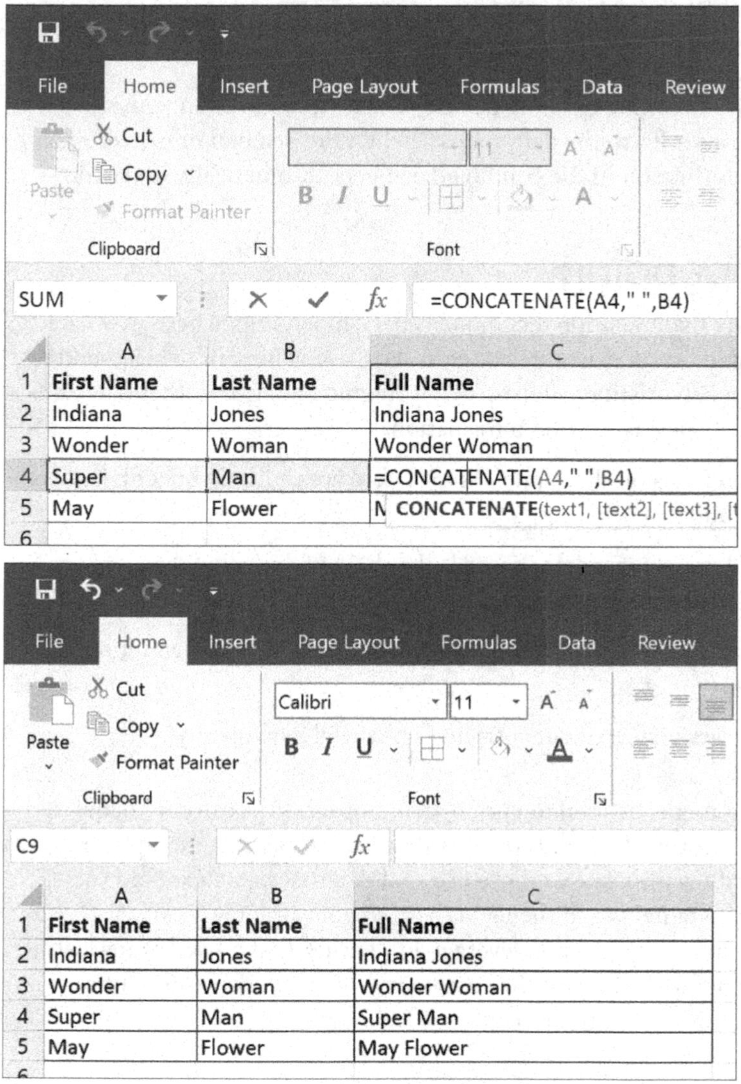

FIGURE 7.5 Concatenation Output Across the Table

> **Note**
>
> Concatenation allows you to combine various data types, like text, strings, and numbers, which is quite difficult to do without a dedicated function.

The key benefit of concatenation is that there is no need to change the data source; rather, you refer to the data source. When the original information is changed, the information in the combined cell gets automatically updated.

Data Appending

Another key data manipulation technique is data appending, where new data elements are added to an existing dataset or database. Think of data appending as supplementing an existing database by leveraging data from other databases to fill in the gaps, such as missing information.

Why should you focus on data appending? There are multiple benefits to data appending, including:

▶ Clean and precise customer records that help with personalized customer approach and interaction

▶ Improved customer acquisition via focused omnichannel marketing campaigns

▶ Reduced data management costs and enhanced data quality

Data appending might be used to enrich an organization's customer database that is missing records like emails or contact information. For example, by matching records against one or more external databases, you can find the desired missing data fields and then add them to your organization's customer database. Data appending is often leveraged to ensure that a sales or marketing strategy is well defined based on the customer data view, such as for running an email campaign for lead generation.

> **Note**
>
> Data appending should be completed to gain the information and insights needed to carry out an organization's overall strategy. However, it does not form part of the strategy itself; instead, it helps identify a baseline to develop a good overall picture of how these efforts can be concentrated.

Figure 7.6 shows the append queries in Microsoft Excel.

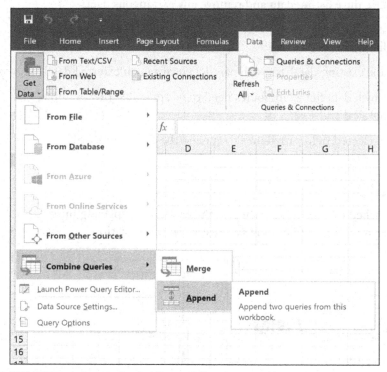

FIGURE 7.6   **Appending in Microsoft Excel**

Figure 7.7 shows the Power Query Editor, where you can append rows into one table. It shows an example of trying to append the sales funnel with tagged deals.

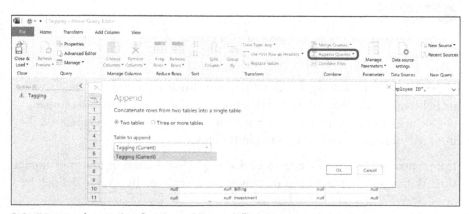

FIGURE 7.7   **Appending Queries in Microsoft Excel**

At a very high level, the following steps are involved in data appending:

1. Normalize the existing data and remove any extraneous data.

2. Set up a validation process to ensure that database fields are correct after appending.

3. Match the existing database with parallel entries in an external database.

4. Select which data fields/attributes need to be appended (for example, email, physical address).

5. Use the selected fields/attributes to append the existing records.

Imputation

We briefly touched on *imputation*, which is the process of replacing missing values, in Chapter 6. Figure 7.8 shows an overview of imputation.

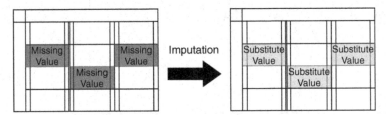

FIGURE 7.8   **Imputation of Missing Values**

Missing data maximizes the probability of making type II and type I errors and reduces the accuracy of statistical outcomes.

> **Note**
>
> Type I and type II errors are discussed in Chapter 10.

Imputation fills in missing values rather than altogether removing the variables or fields that are missing data. While imputation helps keep the full sample size, which can be advantageous for accuracy from a statistical perspective, the imputed values may yield different kinds of bias.

Imputation can be broadly categorized as single imputation or multiple imputation. With single imputation, a missing value is replaced by a value defined by a certain rule or logic. In contrast, with multiple imputation, multiple values are used to substitute missing values.

The various types of imputation that can be used for substituting missing values are as follows:

▶ **Imputation based on related observations:** This is useful when there are large data samples available to substitute similar (though not exact) values. For example, it is possible to use data on weight and height in adults in a certain population to fill in missing values in another population. Such imputations, however, could lead to measurement errors.

▶ **Imputation based on logical rules:** At times it is possible to impute using logical rules, such as the number of hours worked and the cost of labor based on a survey conducted with 10,000 workers. Some respondents might give input on how much they earn per hour for a particular job role; however, 1,000 of the respondents might refuse to answer the earnings question, and thus it is possible to impute zero earnings to these. Logic is important here: If we use 0 as the default filler for nonrespondents, their income is getting recorded as nothing, possibly affecting the sample.

▶ **Imputation based on creating a new variable category:** In some cases, it is useful to use imputation to add a new/extra category or group for the variable(s) that may be missing.

▶ **Imputation based on the last observation carried forward:** With this method, which is typically applicable to time series data, the substitutions are performed by using the pretreated data (that is, using the last observed value of a participant or respondent as a substitute for that individual's missing values).

Data Reduction

Imagine a number of huge datasets coming from different data warehouses for analysis. Data analysts would have a hard time dealing with that volume of data, especially when running complex queries on such a huge amount of data. Complex queries take a long time to execute. *Data reduction*, also known as *data aggregation*, is really useful at reducing complexity.

Data reduction is a data manipulation technique that is used to minimize the size of a dataset by aggregating, clustering, or removing any redundant features. Even though the data size is reduced—which is great for analysis—it yields the same analytical outcomes.

The following are some of the common ways data reduction is achieved:

▶ **Data compression:** Data transformation is applied to the original data to compress the data. You are likely to compress data by zipping up a file or reducing the size of an image on your PC. If the file can be retrieved without any loss, data compression was lossless; however, if the data cannot be retrieved without loss, the compression is considered lossy in nature.

▶ **Dimensionality reduction:** This method leverages encoding to reduce the volume of the original data by removing unwanted attributes. Like data compression, dimensionality reduction can be lossy or lossless. An example of a dimensionality reduction technique is wavelet transformation.

▶ **Numerosity reduction:** This method reduces the volume of the original data to a smaller form of data—such as a data model instead of the actual data. There are two types of numerosity reduction: parametric (for example, log-linear and regression models) and non-parametric (for example, sampling and clustering) numerosity reduction.

Data Transposition

Data transposition involves rotating the data from a column to a row or rotating the data from a row to a column. For example, Figure 7.9 shows an Excel worksheet with the current setup for product sales by region across Q1, Q2, Q3, and Q4. Here the quarters are across rows and regions are across columns.

	A	B	C	D	E
1	Product Sales	Americas	Europe	Asia	EMEA
2	Q1	$21M	$10M	$7M	$5M
3	Q2	$22M	$11M	$9M	$4M
4	Q3	$25M	$13M	$7M	$7M
5	Q4	$20M	$15M	$7M	$6M
6					
7					

FIGURE 7.9 **Original Sales by Region Table**

By using the TRANSPOSE function, you can transpose rows to columns and columns to rows. You do this by copying the existing table, right-clicking anywhere in sheet, and choosing Transpose under the Paste options (see Figure 7.10). Excel swaps the rows and columns.

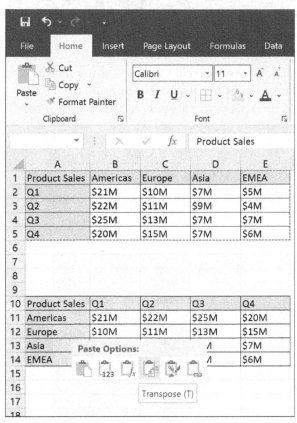

FIGURE 7.10   Transposing Data in Excel

Why would you want to transpose data? Changing the layout of data might make the data simpler to understand and work with. Going by the regions across rows and looking at quarterly sales revenues may be easier to interpret.

Normalizing Data

ExamAlert

Normalization is a fundamental concept used in data redundancy reduction, and you can expect to be tested on this topic on the CompTIA Data+ exam.

The main aim of normalization, as mentioned in Chapter 6, is to remove repetitive (or redundant) information from a database and ensure that information is logically stored (that is, ensure that only related data is stored in a table).

Note

The goal of normalization is to reduce data redundancy by eliminating insertion, updating, and deleting anomalies.

Following are the five normal forms (NF):

▶ First normal form (1NF)

▶ Second normal form (2NF)

▶ Third normal form (3NF)

▶ Boyce–Codd normal form (BCNF), or 3.5 normal form (3.5NF)

▶ Fourth normal form (4NF)

For a table to be in first normal form, it should follow these rules:

▶ It should only have single-valued attributes/columns. In other words, duplicate columns should be eliminated from the table.

▶ Separate tables should be created for each group of related data with their own primary keys.

For a table to be in 2NF, it should follow these rules:

▶ The table should meet the requirements of 1NF.

▶ The table should not have partial dependencies, and you should create relationships between this table and other tables through the use of foreign keys.

For a table to be in 3NF, it should follow these rules:

▶ The table should meet the requirements of 2NF.

▶ The table must not have transitive dependency, so you should remove the columns that are not dependent on the primary key.

For a table to be in 3.5NF, it should follow these rules:

▶ The table should meet the requirements of 3NF.

▶ The table should not have multiple overlapping candidate keys.

For a table to be in 4NF, it should follow these rules:

▶ The table should meet the requirements of 3.5NF.

▶ The table must not have multivalued dependencies.

Parsing/String Manipulation

It is very common to have semi-structured and unstructured data stored in strings. You are therefore likely to be required to deal with string manipulation for data analysis. String manipulation involves handling and analyzing strings and might include operations such as splicing, changing, parsing, pasting, and analyzing strings to be able to use the information stored in the strings.

Filtering

When working with a large amount of data, it can be difficult to explore the key aspects that may be of interest due to the presence of non-required data (or noise). It is very common for data analysts to leverage data filters to better analyze data. As data is filtered, only the rows or columns that meet the filter criteria are displayed, and other (less relevant) rows or columns are hidden.

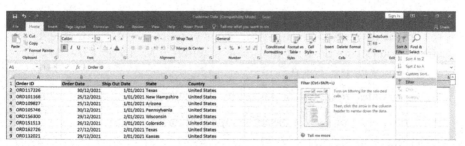

FIGURE 7.11   **Unfiltered Data in Excel**

By applying the filter in Figure 7.11, you can filter the data by state. Figure 7.12, for instance, shows a filter to show all orders for the state of Arizona. This filter helps prune irrelevant orders.

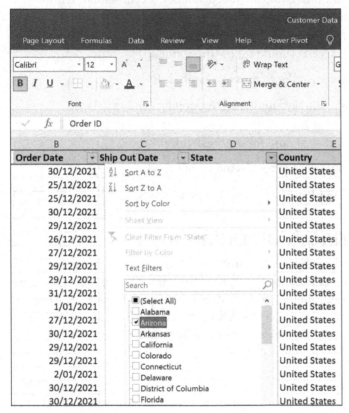

FIGURE 7.12   **Filtering Data in Excel**

Sorting

Data manipulation can be done in various ways, and one of the easiest ways is to sort the data in such a way that it becomes more readable or usable. For example, you can use the built-in sorting function in Microsoft Excel to sort data in a few ways (see Figure 7.13):

▶ From oldest to newest or newest to oldest (based on numerical values)

▶ From A to Z or Z to A (based on alphanumerical values)

▶ Using a custom sort

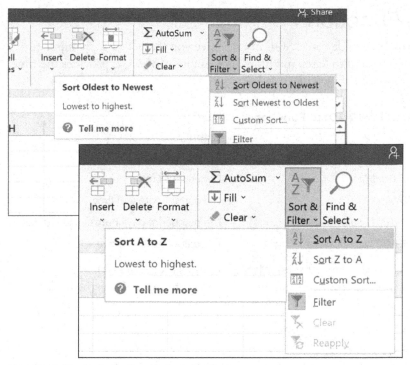

FIGURE 7.13   **Data Sorting Options in Excel**

Sorting is typically applied on a column to sort the data in either ascending or descending order. This gives insight to the applicable data across all rows, as per the chosen sorting option.

When using the custom sort, you can choose the sort value(s) according to the sorting order you want to apply, as shown in Figure 7.14.

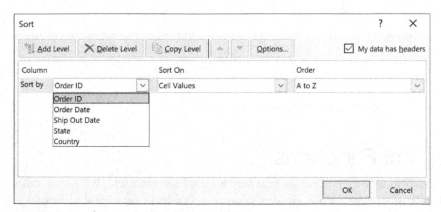

FIGURE 7.14   **Custom Sorting Options in Excel**

Date Functions

Datasets often include dates. SQL queries give you the power to manipulate information related to dates and times. For example, MySQL provides the time and date functions shown in Table 7.7.

TABLE 7.7   **MySQL Date Functions**

Function	Output
Select CURDATE();	The current date
Select CURTIME();	The current time
Select NOW();	The current date and time
DATEDIFF(date1, date2)	The number of days between two dates
DATE_FORMAT(date, format);	The date/time in a different format

Figure 7.15 shows some of these MySQL queries executed using MySQL Workbench as the front end and Azure Database for MySQL as the back end.

FIGURE 7.15   **MySQL Data Function Queries**

Logical Functions

When working with data values, you may want to ascertain whether a condition leads to true or false output. In such a case, you can leverage logical functions to evaluate a given expression against a list of values to get positive (true) or negative (false) output. For example, say that there are two values, A and B, where:

$$A = 200$$

$$B = 100$$

The simplest expressions might be A > B is true while A < B is false. However, when dealing with complex expressions, you need logical functions, including:

► AND

► OR

► NOT

► IF

Let's look at how to leverage the power of Microsoft Excel with logical functions and the two values A and B that we just defined. In Figure 7.16, you can see the expression =AND(A1>50,B1>50). When you press Enter, you should get the answer TRUE.

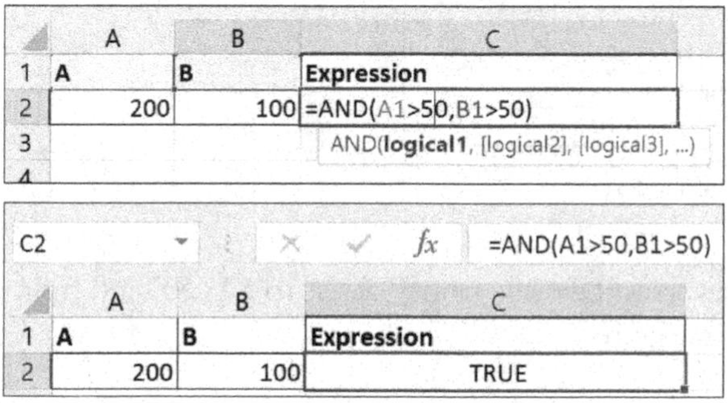

	A	B	C
1	A	B	Expression
2	200	100	=AND(A1>50,B1>50)
3			AND(**logical1**, [logical2], [logical3], ...)
4			

C2			✕ ✓	*fx*	=AND(A1>50,B1>50)

	A	B	C
1	A	B	Expression
2	200	100	TRUE

FIGURE 7.16 **AND Logical Function in Excel**

In this case, the logical operator AND is evaluating all criteria to give the output. In this case, because both values are greater than 50, the answer is TRUE. Now if we set B1<50, we get the outcome shown in Figure 7.17.

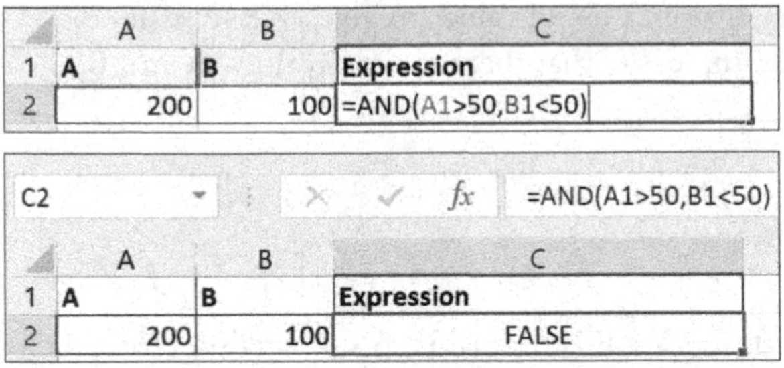

	A	B	C
1	A	B	Expression
2	200	100	=AND(A1>50,B1<50)

C2	▾ ⋮ × ✓ fx	=AND(A1>50,B1<50)

	A	B	C
1	A	B	Expression
2	200	100	FALSE

FIGURE 7.17 **AND Logical Function in Excel, Continued**

Now, because B1 is greater than 50, that part of the expression is false; there-fore, AND leads to the outcome FALSE.

What happens if we keep the expression the same except that we change AND to OR, so that the expression now reads =OR(A1>50,B1<50)? What do you think the output would be? Figure 7.18 shows the answer.

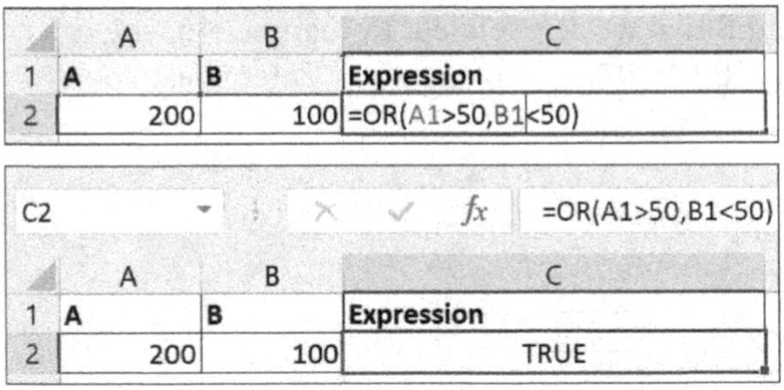

	A	B	C
1	A	B	Expression
2	200	100	=OR(A1>50,B1<50)

C2	▾ ⋮ × ✓ fx	=OR(A1>50,B1<50)

	A	B	C
1	A	B	Expression
2	200	100	TRUE

FIGURE 7.18 **OR Logical Function in Excel**

The NOT function simply reverses the value from TRUE to FALSE and from FALSE to TRUE, as shown in Figure 7.19.

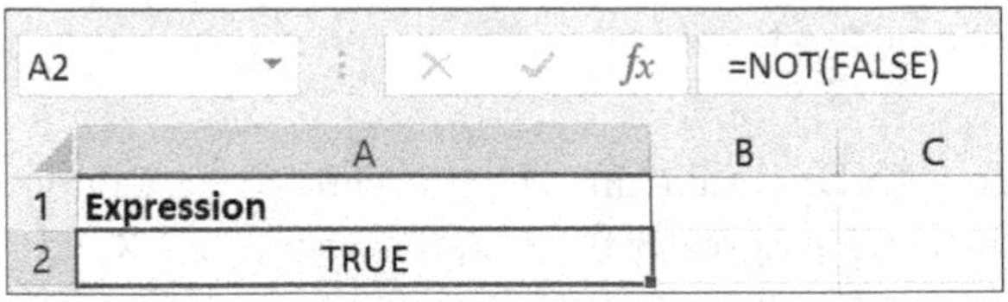

A2	▾ ⋮ × ✓ fx	=NOT(FALSE)

	A	B	C
1	Expression		
2	TRUE		

FIGURE 7.19 **NOT Logical Function in Excel**

The TRUE function (that is, =TRUE()) returns the logical TRUE value, and the FALSE function (that is, =FALSE()) returns the logical FALSE value.

The Excel IF logical function makes it possible to create logical comparisons and has two possible outcomes. That is, if the comparison is TRUE, the first result is returned; if the comparison is FALSE, the second result is returned (see Figure 7.20).

C2			f_x	=IF(A1>50,"THIS IS TRUE","THIS IS NOT TRUE")			
	A	B	C		D	E	F
1	A	B	Expression / Output				
2	200	100	THIS IS TRUE				

FIGURE 7.20 **IF Logical Function in Excel**

> **Note**
>
> For a comprehensive list of all Microsoft Excel logical functions, see https://support.microsoft.com/en-us/office/logical-functions-reference-e093c192-278b-43f6-8c3a-b6ce299931f5.

Aggregate Functions

The word *aggregate* implies bringing together or summarizing. In the context of databases, aggregation implies bringing together/grouping the values of rows. The commonly used SQL aggregate functions are:

▶ **SUM():** This function returns the sum of all values in a particular column.

▶ **AVG():** This function returns the average value of a particular column.

▶ **COUNT():** This function returns the total number of rows matching the query.

▶ **MAX():** This function returns the largest value in a particular column.

▶ **MIN():** This function returns the smallest value in a particular column.

To illustrate a few of the aggregation functions, the following examples run queries in MySQL Workbench against the sample database available at https://github.com/Azure-Samples/mysql-database-samples/blob/main/mysqltutorial.org/mysql-classicmodesl.sql.

Figure 7.21 shows the following COUNT() aggregation query:

> SELECT COUNT(contactFirstName) FROM customers
> WHERE state = "NY";

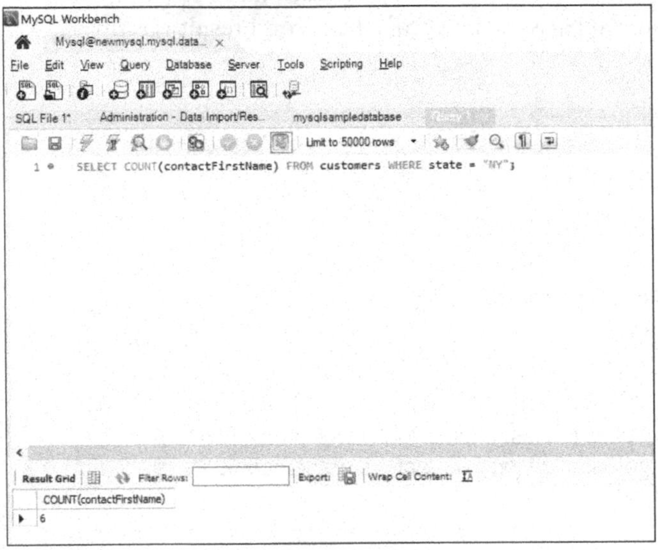

FIGURE 7.21   **COUNT() Query in MySQL**

Figure 7.22 shows the following AVG() aggregation query:

> SELECT avg(creditLimit) FROM customers;

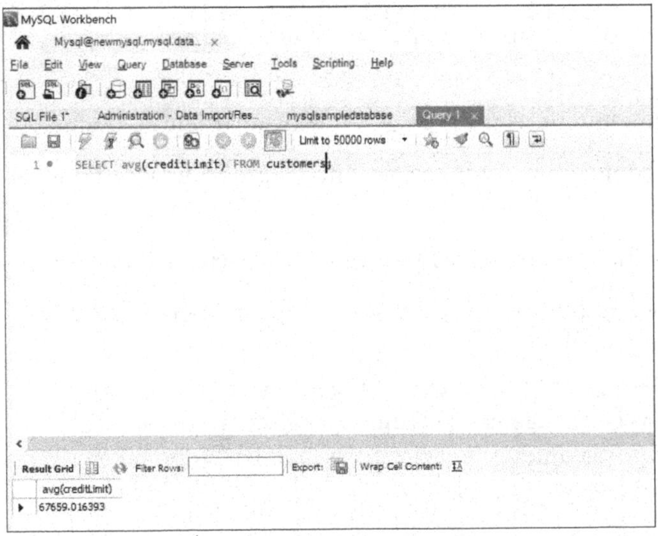

FIGURE 7.22   **AVG() Query in MySQL**

Figure 7.23 shows the following MAX() aggregation query:

SELECT max(creditLimit) FROM customers;

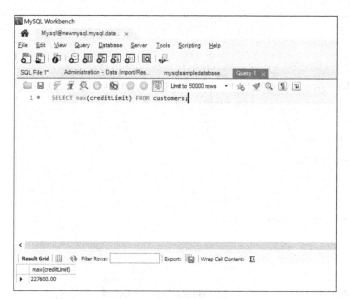

FIGURE 7.23   **MAX() Query in MySQL**

System Functions

System functions are functions that make changes to the database structure or information stored in the database (for example, adding a new row or inputting a new data value in a cell). The key SQL functions that can be used to change the information or structure of a database table are:

▶ **INSERT:** This function enables database administrators/users to add new rows to an existing table.

▶ **UPDATE:** This function enables database administrators/users to update the data of an existing table in a database.

▶ **DELETE:** This function enables database administrators/users to remove existing records from existing tables.

For example, this query inserts values into the sample database:

```
insert into customers values (103,'Atelier,'Schmitt','Carine ',
'40.32.2555','54, rue Royale',NULL,'Nantes',NULL,'44000',
'France',1370,'21000.00');
```

Cram Quiz

Answer these questions. If you cannot answer these questions correctly, consider reading this section again until you can.

1. Imputation is used for _____.

    ○ **a.** replacing missing values

    ○ **b.** identifying missing values

    ○ **c.** deleting missing values

    ○ **d.** None of these answers are correct.

2. Data recoding can be done with _____.

    ○ **a.** the same variables

    ○ **b.** different variables

    ○ **c.** the same and different variables

    ○ **d.** None of these answers are correct.

3. What process is shown in the following figure?

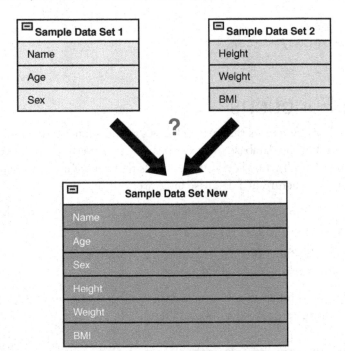

○ **a.** Missing data

○ **b.** Data distribution

○ **c.** Data merge

○ **d.** Data redirect

4. Which of the following allows you to change rows to columns in a database?

○ **a.** Data transposition

○ **b.** Data redirection

○ **c.** Data merging

○ **d.** Data redistribution

○ **e.** Data alignment

5. Which of the following are valid data normal forms? (Choose all that apply.)

○ **a.** First normal form

○ **b.** Second normal form

○ **c.** Third normal form

○ **d.** Boyce–Codd normal form (BCNF) or 3.5 normal form

○ **e.** Fourth normal form

6. Which of the following are logical functions? (Choose all that apply.)

○ **a.** AND

○ **b.** OR

○ **c.** IF

○ **d.** NOT

7. Which of the following date functions outputs the current date and time?

○ **a.** Select CURDATE()

○ **b.** Select CURTIME()

○ **c.** Select DT()

○ **d.** Select NOW()

Cram Quiz Answers

1. **Answer: a. replacing missing values.** Imputation is used for replacing missing values.

2. **Answer: c. the same and different variables.** Recoding can be done with the same and different variables.

3. **Answer: c. Data merge.** This figure shows the data merge process.

4. **Answer: a. Data transposition.** Data transposition involves rotating the data from a column to a row or from a row to a column.

5. **Answer: a. First normal form, b. Second normal form, c. Third normal form, d. Boyce–Codd normal form (BCNF) or 3.5 normal form, e. fourth normal form.** All of these are valid normal forms.

6. **Answer: a. AND, b. OR, c. IF, d. NOT.** All of these are SQL logical functions.

7. **Answer: d. Select NOW().** This function outputs the current date and time.

What Next?

If you want more practice on this chapter's exam objective before you move on, remember that you can access all of the Cram Quiz questions on the Pearson Test Prep software online. You can also create a custom exam by objective with the Online Practice Test. Note any objective you struggle with and go to that objective's material in this chapter.

CHAPTER 8

Understanding Common Techniques for Data Query Optimization and Testing

This chapter covers Objective 2.4 (Explain common techniques for data manipulation and query optimization) of the CompTIA Data+ exam and includes the following topics:

- ▶ Query optimization
- ▶ Execution plan
- ▶ Parametrization
- ▶ Indexing
- ▶ Temporary table in the query set
- ▶ Subset of records

For more information on the official CompTIA Data+ exam topics, see the Introduction.

This chapter covers query optimization and testing. It provides details related to query optimization, parametrization, indexing, temporary tables in a query set, subsets of records, and execution plans.

Query Optimization

CramSaver

If you can correctly answer these questions before going through this section, save time by skimming the Exam Alerts in this section and then completing the Cram Quiz at the end of the section.

1. Every SQL database—including Microsoft SQL Server, MySQL, Oracle, and other SQL databases—has its own _____.

   a. query optimizer

   b. subsetting plan

   c. optimization plan

   d. connection optimizer

2. With MySQL, which statement keyword outlines the query execution plan when executed as part of the query?

   a. INPUT

   b. PREDICTION

   c. INTEGRATION

   d. IDENTIFY

   e. EXPLAIN

3. Which of the following types of temporary tables can be created in Microsoft SQL? (Choose two.)

   a. Permanent

   b. Persistent

   c. Global

   d. Local

   e. All of these

   f. None of these

4. Which structure is shown in the following figure?

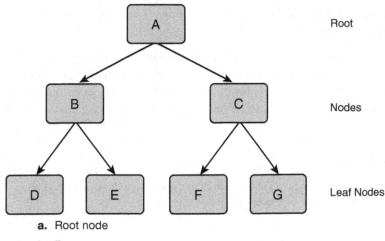

a. Root node

b. B-tree

c. Heap

d. Global tree

e. Local tree

1. **Answer: a. query optimizer.** Each SQL database has its own query optimizer.

2. **Answer: e. Extract.** The EXPLAIN keyword outlines the query execution plan in MySQL.

3. **Answer: c. Global, d. Local.** There are two types of temporary tables that you can create in Microsoft SQL: global and local.

4. **Answer: b. B-tree.** This figure shows the balanced tree, or B-tree, structure. A B-tree is a data structure that offers sorted data for faster searching. A B-tree is formed of nodes, with the tree starting at a root, which has no parent node. Every other node in the tree has one parent node and may or may not have child nodes. A node that does not have any child nodes is called a leaf node.

A computer has computing resources such as a central processing unit (CPU), memory, disk space (storage), an arithmetic logical unit (ALU), optionally a graphics processing unit (GPU), and many more hardware components. When SQL queries are executed against databases, they take up CPU, memory, and other resources. Depending on the complexity of queries, some might take much longer than others to yield results. Performance of queries can be improved in multiple ways—two basic ones being improving or optimizing hardware performance and/or optimizing queries. This chapter is dedicated to query optimization.

Query optimization is an activity that is conducted by a query optimizer in a DBMS to select the best available strategy for executing the query. In other words, query optimization provides a way to get maximum performance for results generated by queries in the minimum amount of time.

> **Note**
>
> Every SQL database—including Microsoft SQL Server, MySQL, Oracle, and other SQL databases—has its own query optimizer.

A query optimizer can leverage a number of methods for optimizing queries. One of the ways a query optimizer works is by leveraging the cost of executing a query.

So, how do you really go about optimizing queries? Well, there are a number of ways; however, they all involve database performance tuning, which is usually the full-time job of database administrators (DBAs). Consider that large databases might have a lot of data that requires tuning; this tuning leads to optimization of queries and much faster results than can be obtained compared to an untuned database. One of the key things to understand is the execution plan. A *query execution plan* or an execution plan is a logical outlay of the resources allocated as well as the operations performed when a query is being executed. The execution plan outlines the logical steps executed in a query. (You will learn more about query execution plans in the next section.)

At a high level, you need to know the following when considering query optimization and database tuning:

▶ Wildcard searches take far more time than more precise searches, and this impacts performance. In many cases, using filters may be a much more appropriate way to manage searches by reducing data set to be searched. For example, this:

```
SELECT * FROM OrgEmployees
```

is going to be far less optimized than this:

```
SELECT EmpFirstName, Location, FROM Employees
```

▶ Indexing (covered later in this chapter) is highly recommended, and having the right indexes in place is an important part of making queries efficient.

▶ A cache should be sized correctly so that it is large enough to hold recurrently accessed data but not so large that it overworks physical memory (random accessible memory or RAM).

▶ Each table added to a query increases the complexity of the query and the time required to traverse the tables. Consider keeping table joins to a minimum where possible.

▶ It is best to leverage correlated subqueries only when you have to. These queries are used for row-by-row processing, and the inner query is run for each row of the outer query that is executed. For example, consider the following query:

```
SELECT EMPLastName, Location
 FROM employees Emp
 WHERE package >
    (SELECT AVG(package)
       FROM employees
         WHERE department =
            Emp.department);
```

In this case, the inner query is driven by the outer query and is executed each time the outer query is executed.

These tweaks can help queries perform better and yield faster outcomes, which is what the users want.

Execution Plans

Everything in life needs a plan. It is often said that "failing to plan is planning to fail." An execution plan works behind the scenes to ensure that a query gets all the right resources and is being executed correctly; the plan outlines the steps for the query execution from start until output.

This section shows examples using MySQL Workbench for database creation and query execution. The database used is Azure Database for MySQL Flexible Server.

> **Note**
>
> You can also work with execution plans in various flavors of SQL software as each piece of SQL software has its own execution plan display/visualization.

In the case of MySQL, the EXPLAIN statement gives insights into how MySQL executes statements; that is, the EXPLAIN keyword outlines the query execution plan. It works with the following SQL statements:

▶ INSERT

▶ SELECT

▶ DELETE

▶ REPLACE

▶ UPDATE

Figure 8.1 shows a query run in MySQL Workbench against the sample database available at https://github.com/Azure-Samples/mysql-database-samples/blob/main/mysqltutorial.org/mysql-classicmodesl.sql.

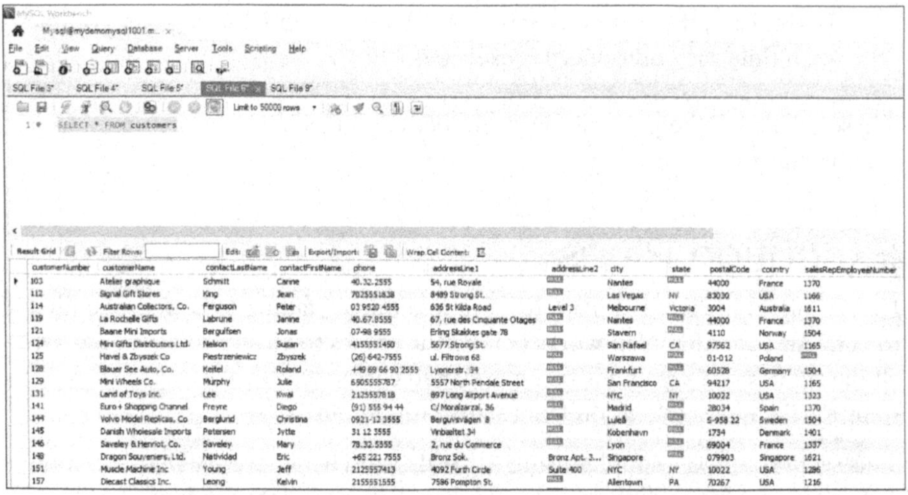

FIGURE 8.1   **MySQL SELECT Statement Output**

Now you can select **Query > Explain Current Statement**, as shown in Figure 8.2.

MySQL Workbench gives you the query execution plan, including the query cost, as shown in Figure 8.3.

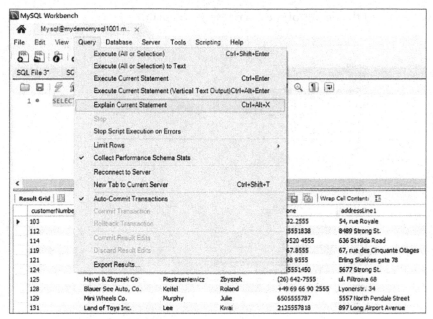

FIGURE 8.2   **MySQL EXPLAIN Statement Output**

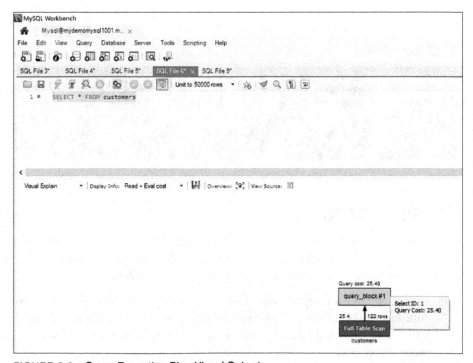

FIGURE 8.3   **Query Execution Plan Visual Output**

Figure 8.4 shows the details of the query execution plan.

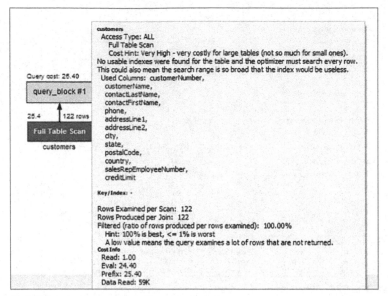

FIGURE 8.4   Query Execution Plan Details

As you can see, an execution plan provides details that can be very helpful for optimizing queries.

ExamAlert

The query execution plan is an important aspect for optimizing queries and for query performance tuning. Ensure that you understand this concept well before you take the CompTIA Data+ exam.

Parametrization

A *parametrized query* enables you to use placeholders for parameters, where the parameter values are supplied at execution time. Why have parametrized queries at all? Well, there are a few benefits to using these queries:

▶ Instead of always using a static input to queries, you can provide inputs at runtime, hence offering flexibility. Essentially, parametrized queries can be used with dynamic data where the values are not known until a statement is executed.

▶ Parametrized SQL queries can be prepared ahead of time and then reused for similar applications. This means you don't have to create distinct queries for each use case.

▶ These queries can be used for improving the performance of a database as you can select specific variables.

▶ As these queries enable the use of runtime inputs, they can be useful for thwarting SQL injection attacks, which may use static inputs.

> **Note**
>
> Parametrized queries are also sometimes known as *prepared statements*.

Next, let's look at an example of a parametrized query, using the database available at https://github.com/Azure-Samples/mysql-database-samples/blob/main/mysqltutorial.org/mysql-classicmodesl.sql.

This is the original (non-parametrized) query:

```
SELECT * FROM customers
```

Figure 8.5 shows the output of this query.

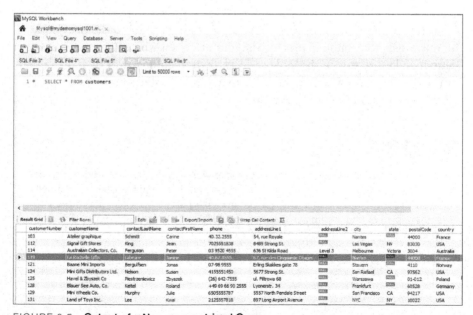

FIGURE 8.5 **Output of a Non-parametrized Query**

Now you can use the following parametrized query:

```
PREPARE stmt FROM 'SELECT * from customers WHERE customerName = ?';
SET @A = 'La Rochelle Gifts';
EXECUTE stmt using @A;
```

Figure 8.6 shows the output of this query.

FIGURE 8.6   **Output of a Parametrized Query**

What is happening in this scenario? A value is being passed to the query, and
the query uses that value to process the output. As shown in Figure 8.5, every
column and every row in the table are returned. In comparison, as shown in
Figure 8.6, for the row where the value matches the value sent in @A, every
column is shown in the query output.

> **Note**
>
> With Microsoft SQL Server, the query optimizer works in the background to param-
> eterize the query plan such that any static values contained in the query are substi-
> tuted with parameters. In this way, the parametrized query plan, which is stored in
> the query plan cache, optimizes the next execution of the same query for different
> values.

Indexing

When you want to find information about a certain topic in a book, what's the easiest way to find it? You could just flip the pages, but it's usually much faster to use the table of contents or the index to pinpoint the page that contains the information you want. Similarly, with databases and queries, to get optimized output when you execute a query, indexes help locate the information quickly, thus improving the user experience.

> **Note**
>
> Index selection is one of the most important and commonly used mechanisms for query optimization. When you leverage the right indexes, the SQL server can improve performance tremendously.

So, how do indexes work? Well, quite simply, indexes help speed up the execution of queries by rapidly finding records and delivering all the columns requested by a query without executing a full table scan. It is helpful to prepare a comprehensive indexing plan that outlines the indexes required for each table, presents the sequence in which the indexes should be created, and outlines the columns to be selected for indexing. Figure 8.7 shows the indexes for the sample database.

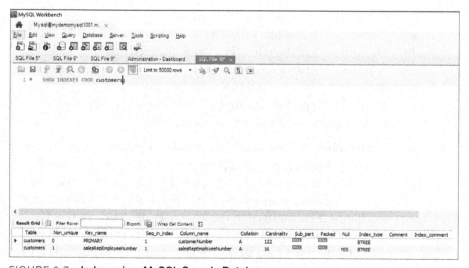

FIGURE 8.7   Indexes in a MySQL Sample Database

In this case, you can see that the index type is BTREE, which stands for *B-tree* (or *balanced tree*).

As illustrated in Figure 8.8, a B-tree is formed of nodes, with the tree starting at a root, which has no *parent node*. Every other node in the tree has one parent node and may or may not have *child nodes*. A node that does not have any child nodes is called a *leaf node*.

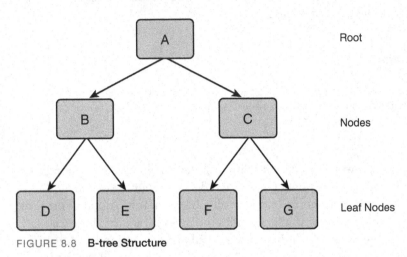

FIGURE 8.8   **B-tree Structure**

Indexes can be classified into two major types:

- ▶ **Clustered index:** This type of index sorts the way records in the table are physically stored. In other words, a clustered index essentially physically orders the rows of the table. Thus, the clustered index contains all of the columns of a row(s). Clustered indexes are stored as trees, and the actual data is stored in the leaf nodes. This helps speed up query processing when a lookup is performed on the index. There can be one clustered index per table that is a primary or clustering index.

- ▶ **Non-clustered index:** This type of index collects data in one place and records in another place, creating a pointer to the data. In other words, the data in a non-clustered index is structured in a logical manner. In a non-clustered index, the rows can be stored physically in a different order than the columns. This means that the leaf nodes of a non-clustered index do not contain the actual data but contain pointers to the data. A *heap* is a collection of unordered rows of data. A table can contain multiple non-clustered indexes.

So you know that creating indexes helps improve the efficiency of read operations by reducing the amount of data that a query needs to process. Are indexes used automatically, or do you need to define an index when running a query? Well, when you execute a query, the query optimizer generates an execution plan—and this execution plan should contain the index or indexes.

> **Note**
>
> One of the key reasons you need to look at execution plans is to determine which columns from what tables should be indexed to optimize performance.

So, when indexes are created, what are some of the things to look for? Generally, you need to consider the following aspects:

▶ Certain indexes may not get used at all. Figure 8.9 shows a performance report from MySQL Workbench that shows the indexes that haven't been used.

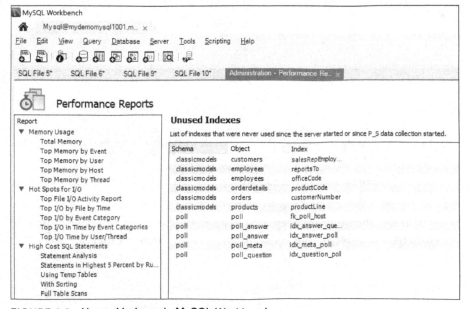

FIGURE 8.9 **Unused Indexes in MySQL Workbench**

▶ As indexes are created around attributes, some indexes might undergo a lot of updates as the attributes undergo changes.

▶ Outside of primary key columns (which are indexed by default), it is recommended to index the columns that are used in the WHERE clauses of SELECT statements. This also applies to foreign keys to speed up JOIN operations.

▶ Once a new index has been created, you should review the execution plan
   to ensure that it is leading to a positive change and evaluate the real application performance.

You can explicitly create indexes when it makes sense to do so. In MySQL, you
can create an index as follows:

```
CREATE [UNIQUE|FULLTEXT|SPATIAL] INDEX index_name USING [BTREE | HASH
| RTREE] ON table_name (column_name [(length)] [ASC | DESC])
```

In this case, you execute a query like this:

```
CREATE UNIQUE INDEX cu_number USING BTREE ON customers(customerNumber)
```

Figure 8.10 shows the outcome of this query.

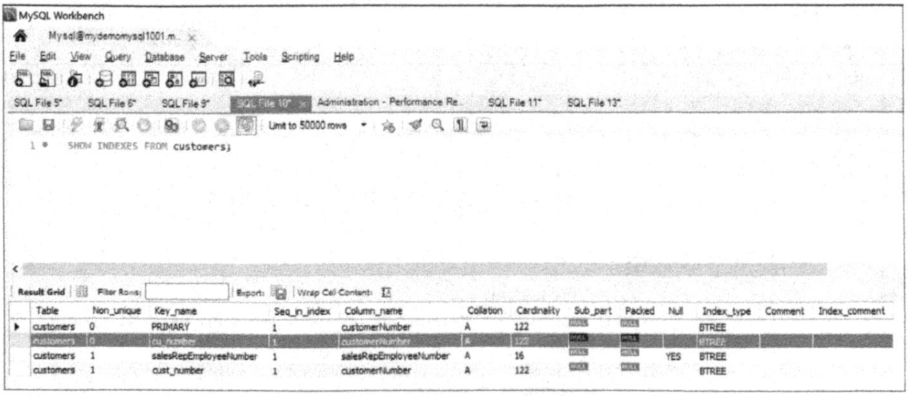

FIGURE 8.10   Creating a New Unique Index

As you can see, the other index created— cust_number—is not unique and
therefore has the Non_unique option set to 1. The statement used for that
index is:

```
CREATE INDEX cust_number ON customers(customerNumber)
```

You can also create an index in Microsoft SQL by using the following
statement:

```
CREATE UNIQUE INDEX index_name ON table_name (column_name1,
column_name2, ...);
```

Temporary Table in a Query Set

At times, you may need to create temporary space for items being moved from one place to another or when sorting out stuff in a database. In SQL, temporary tables are very similar to placeholders and offer workspaces for the transitional results you get when processing data.

To see how temporary tables work, let's consider an example. In this example, you are going to create a temporary table called allcustomers that is based on an original table customers.

Here's the MySQL statement you need to use to create the temporary table:

```
CREATE TEMPORARY TABLE allcustomers SELECT * FROM customers
```

Now, let's compare the results of two queries:

```
select * from customers
```

and:

```
select * from allcustomers
```

Figure 8.11 shows the results of the first query.

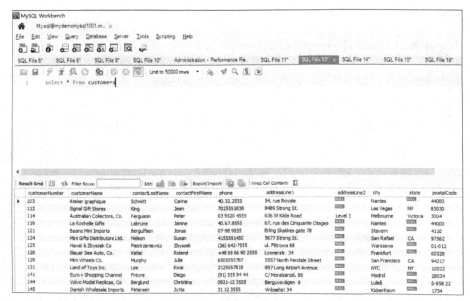

FIGURE 8.11   Results of the Query select * from customers

Figure 8.12 shows the results of the second query.

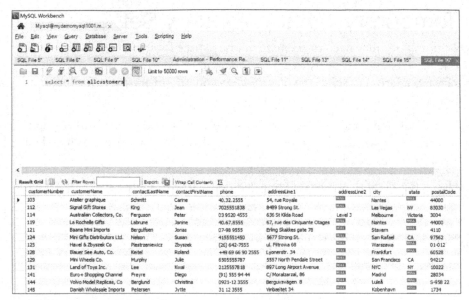

FIGURE 8.12   Results of the Query select * from allcustomers

Now, let's look at all the tables in the database by leveraging the following command:

```
show tables
```

Figure 8.13 shows the output of this command.

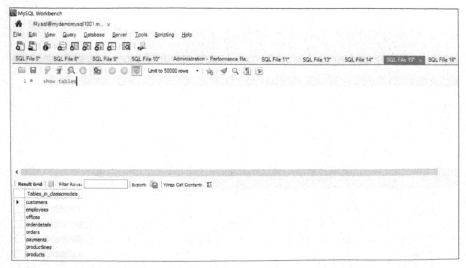

FIGURE 8.13   Results of the show tables Command

As you can see, the customers table shows up, but the temporary table you created (allcustomers) doesn't.

Remember that temporary tables enable you to keep temporary data; in addition, you can reuse these tables several times in a particular session. Like other SQL applications, MySQL deletes temporary tables automatically when the current session is closed or the database connection is terminated.

> **Note**
>
> If you want to delete a temporary table, you can use the DROP TABLE command.

Consider the following points about temporary tables:

▶ Temporary tables allow create, read, update, and delete (CRUD) operations as well as some other operations, just as the actual tables do.

▶ Temporary tables are very valuable when you transform big datasets. You can create stored procedures to run against temporary tables for faster outcomes.

▶ You can insert only the data that is useful for your session so that any unnecessary data does not slow down the query response.

▶ Temporary tables' stores can hold results of individual queries and reports for repeated use.

There are two types of temporary tables that you can create in Microsoft SQL:

▶ **Global:** When you want others to collaborate and perform CRUD and other SQL transactions in the same temporary table, you should use global SQL temporary tables. With these, the result set is visible to all other sessions, and anyone can insert, modify, or retrieve values.

The following is an example of a global temporary table:

```
CREATE TABLE ##CUSTOMERS
( CustomerID INT PRIMARY KEY,
  Customer_last_name VARCHAR(50) NOT NULL,
  Customer_first_name VARCHAR(50) NOT NULL,
);
```

▶ **Local:** Local temporary tables are only available for the local session in which they were created, and no one from outside that session can access them.

The following is an example of a local temporary table:

```
CREATE TABLE #CUSTOMERS
( CustomerID INT PRIMARY KEY,
  Customer_last_name VARCHAR(50) NOT NULL,
  Customer_first_name VARCHAR(50) NOT NULL,
);
```

Notice that for a global temporary table you used ## in front of the table name whereas for a local temporary table you used # in front of the table name.

Subsets of Records

A *subset* is essentially a smaller set of data from a larger database or data warehouse that you can use to focus on only the relevant information. Database subsetting involves creating referentially intact portions of records from larger datasets into a separate database. For example, say that you are working with a database that has hundreds of records on customers from around the globe. If you are interested only in the customers in Europe, you can work with only the subset of data that pertains to the customers based in Europe.

Figure 8.14 illustrates the idea of data subsetting.

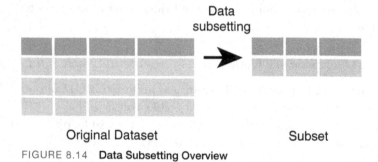

FIGURE 8.14 **Data Subsetting Overview**

> **Note**
>
> Recall from Chapter 1, "Understanding Databases and Data Warehouses," that a data mart represents a subset of the data stored in a data warehouse. A data warehouse can have multiple data marts, with each data mart aligned to a department or business unit.

There are several reasons you might want to work with subsets of data or records:

▶ **Working with non-production data:** You always want to separate production data from non-production, or development, data—and subsets can be really useful for allowing developers to work with data that contains all the necessary links between tables (that is, data that is referentially intact). Using subsets of data allows for parallel testing and deployment of applications (which is an important part of DevOps).

▶ **Reducing the data footprint:** Working with millions of records—as data engineers and data scientists do—is not easy. Creating subsets of only relevant datasets allows data engineers and data scientists to explore meaningful data. For database administrators, it leads to faster query times and higher performance.

▶ **Working with sensitive information:** Your organization might have a dataset that contains sensitive information such as personally identifiable information (PII) or personal health information (PHI), and you probably do not want to give everyone access to all the data. In such a case, you can provide subsets of relevant data to particular departments. (For more on PII and PHI, see Chapter 15, "Data Governance Concepts: Ensuring a Baseline.")

▶ **Ensuring data compliance:** Given that there are mandatory compliance requirements such as the General Data Protection Regulation (GDPR) for European nationals (see Chapter 15), you may want to give access to only necessary information. You can do so with subsetting.

▶ **Dealing with aging data:** As data ages, it might not be relevant for the purposes for which you are trying to leverage it. For example, you may want to remove a certain portion of your data based on criteria such as being older than 5 years. In such a case, you can create a subset of relevant data with age less than 5 years and work with it.

▶ **Avoiding larger storage costs:** Working with copies of a portion of a database rather than the whole database reduces the storage requirements.

As you can see, there are a few really good reasons to leverage data subsetting, including improving performance, allowing parallel tasks at lower infrastructure costs, and taking advantage of abstraction. Moreover, subsetting gives developers and data engineers freedom to do their tests against subsets of data rather than whole databases. Data subsetting is an important aspect that leads to effective data quality management.

How exactly do you perform data subsetting? Well, two of the most famous methods are data sharding and data partitioning. Both allow you to break up data into smaller, more manageable slices, improving the performance of reads.

ExamAlert

Data sharding/partitioning is very commonly used and questions pertinent to the same are likely to be included on the CompTIA Data+ exam.

Data sharding, which is very common in scalable databases, allows shards (that is, logical slices of data) to be stored on multiple compute nodes. In contrast, data partitioning allows you to share shards on one compute node. Data sharding allows you to store new logical slices of data, called *shards*, across multiple nodes to achieve horizontal scalability and improved performance. When creating shards, you are essentially creating schema replicas and dividing the data stored in each shard based on a shard key.

Sharding is done horizontally, and partitioning is done vertically, as shown in Figure 8.15.

Sharding and partitioning of data both enable you to create data subsets. In the example shown in Figure 8.15, partitioning allows you to focus on CustomerID and customer details as well as product relationships, and sharding allows you to segregate customers by number of products.

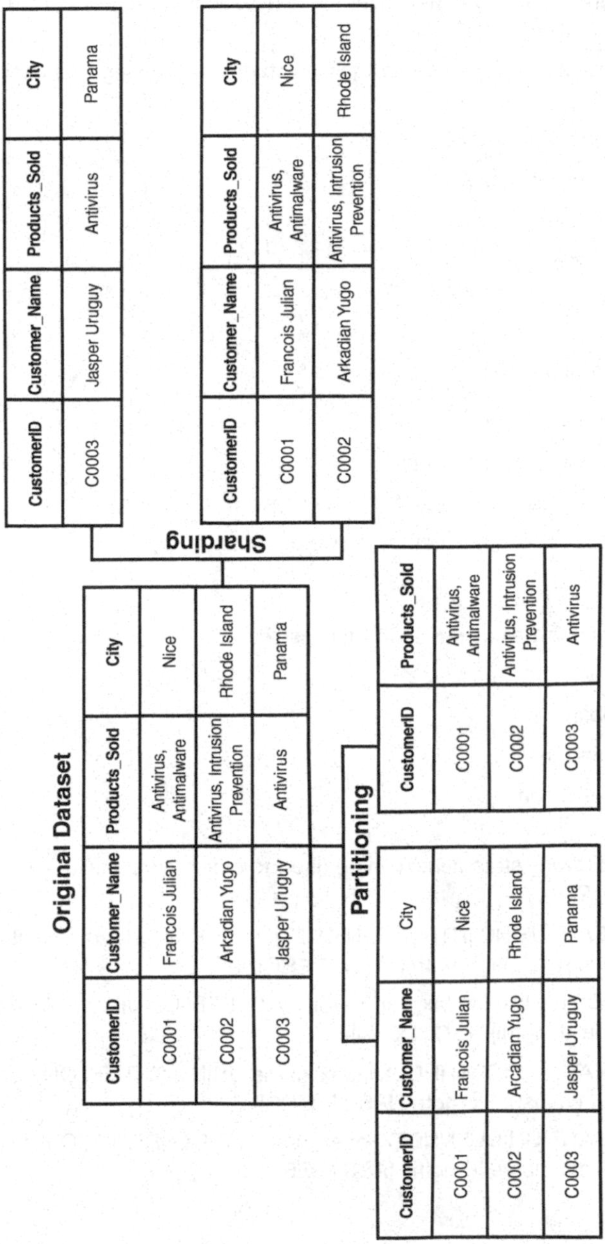

Original Dataset

CustomerID	Customer_Name	Products_Sold	City
C0001	Francois Julian	Antivirus, Antimalware	Nice
C0002	Arkadian Yugo	Antivirus, Intrusion Prevention	Rhode Island
C0003	Jasper Uruguy	Antivirus	Panama

Sharding

CustomerID	Customer_Name	Products_Sold	City
C0003	Jasper Uruguy	Antivirus	Panama

CustomerID	Customer_Name	Products_Sold	City
C0001	Francois Julian	Antivirus, Antimalware	Nice
C0002	Arkadian Yugo	Antivirus, Intrusion Prevention	Rhode Island

Partitioning

CustomerID	Customer_Name	City
C0001	Francois Julian	Nice
C0002	Arkadian Yugo	Rhode Island
C0003	Jasper Uruguy	Panama

CustomerID	Products_Sold
C0001	Antivirus, Antimalware
C0002	Antivirus, Intrusion Prevention
C0003	Antivirus

FIGURE 8.15 Data Sharding and Partitioning

Cram Quiz

Answer these questions. If you cannot answer these questions correctly, consider reading this section again until you can.

1. A query optimizer automatically leverages which of the following for faster query processing?

   ○ **a.** Technical processes

   ○ **b.** Business processes

   ○ **c.** Data shards

   ○ **d.** Data marts

   ○ **e.** Indexes

2. Review the following code:

```
CREATE TABLE ##CUSTOMERS
( CustomerID INT PRIMARY KEY,
   Customer_last_name VARCHAR(50) NOT NULL,
   Customer_first_name VARCHAR(50) NOT NULL,
);
```

   What type of table is being created in this case?

   ○ **a.** Local

   ○ **b.** Global

   ○ **c.** Knowledge

   ○ **d.** Observation

3. Which of the following statements can be used to create a new unique B-tree index in MySQL?

   ○ **a.** CREATE USING [BTREE] [UNIQUE] INDEX index_name ON table_name (column_name [(length)] [ASC | DESC])

   ○ **b.** CREATE INDEX index_name USING [BTREE] ON table_name (column_name [(length)] [ASC | DESC])

   ○ **c.** CREATE [UNIQUE] INDEX index_name USING [BTREE] ON table_name (column_name [(length)] [ASC | DESC])

   ○ **d.** CREATE [UNIQUE] INDEX index_name USING [RTREE] ON table_name (column_name [(length)] [ASC | DESC])

4. Data sharding allows shards to be stored on which of the following?

   ○ **a.** One compute node

   ○ **b.** Web node

   ○ **c.** Multiple compute nodes

   ○ **d.** MySQL nodes

5. What does the following figure show?

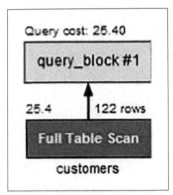

   ○ **a.** API plan

   ○ **b.** Dispersion plan

   ○ **c.** Variable plan

   ○ **d.** Execution plan

Cram Quiz Answers

1. **Answer: e. Indexes.** A query optimizer leverages indexes as part of the execution plan.

2. **Answer: b. Global.** In this example, a global temporary table is being created. For a local table, you would use just one of the # symbols.

3. **Answer: c. CREATE [UNIQUE] INDEX index_name USING [BTREE] ON table_name (column_name [(length)] [ASC | DESC]).** This is the syntax for creating a B-tree in MySQL.

4. **Answer: c. Multiple compute nodes.** Data sharding, which is very common in scalable databases, allows shards (or logical slices of data) to be stored on multiple compute nodes.

5. **Answer: d. Execution plan.** This figure shows the query execution plan in MySQL.

What Next?

If you want more practice on this chapter's exam objective before you move on, remember that you can access all of the Cram Quiz questions on the Pearson Test Prep software online. You can also create a custom exam by objective with the Online Practice Test. Note any objective you struggle with and go to that objective's material in this chapter.

CHAPTER 9

The (Un)Common Data Analytics Tools

This chapter covers Objective 3.4 (Identify common data analytics tools) of the CompTIA Data+ exam and includes the following topics:

- ▶ Structured Query Language (SQL)
- ▶ Python
- ▶ Microsoft Excel
- ▶ R
- ▶ Rapid mining
- ▶ IBM Cognos
- ▶ IBM SPSS Modeler
- ▶ IBM SPSS
- ▶ SAS
- ▶ Tableau
- ▶ Power BI
- ▶ Qlik
- ▶ MicroStrategy
- ▶ BusinessObjects
- ▶ Apex
- ▶ Dataroma
- ▶ Domo
- ▶ AWS QuickSight
- ▶ Stata
- ▶ Minitab

For more information on the official CompTIA Data+ exam topics, see the Introduction.

This chapter covers the most common and not-so-common data analytics tools.

> **ExamAlert**
>
> The intent of this CompTIA Data+ objective is not to test specific vendor feature sets or the purposes of the tools but to ensure that you understand the variety of tools available for data analysts to perform analytics and get insights about their organizations for better decision making.

Data Analytics Tools

> **CramSaver**
>
> If you can correctly answer these questions before going through this section, save time by skimming the Exam Alerts in this section and then completing the Cram Quiz at the end of the section.
>
> 1. SQL is an _____ standard. (Choose all that apply.)
>   - **a.** ANSI
>   - **b.** ISO
>   - **c.** ITU
>   - **d.** IOS
>
> 2. Python was designed as what type of programming language for web development and software?
>   - **a.** Structured
>   - **b.** Query
>   - **c.** Object oriented
>   - **d.** Relational database
>
> 3. Rapid Miner is used as a(n) _____ extension to develop data mining.
>   - **a.** SQL and Python
>   - **b.** R and Python
>   - **c.** Oracle and SQL
>   - **d.** All of these answers are correct.

4. The IBM SPSS software offers advanced _____.

    a. data analysis

    b. predictive analysis

    c. prescriptive analysis

    d. statistical analysis

5. SAS is available only for which OS?

    a. Linux

    b. Android

    c. Windows

    d. macOS

6. Tableau is what kind of tool?

    a. Data sanitization

    b. Data segmentation

    c. Data classification

    d. Data visualization

Answers

1. **Answer: a. ANSI, b. ISO.** Structured Query Language (SQL) is an International Standard Organization (ISO) and American National Standards Institute (ANSI) standard. It is also the de facto standard database query language. SQL is a specialized language for CRUD operations in databases.

2. **Answer: c. Object oriented.** Python was designed as an object-oriented language for web and software development, and it is now also used for data science.

3. **Answer: b. R and Python.** Programmers and data engineers can leverage Rapid Miner to extend the Python and R programming languages for data mining development.

4. **Answer: d. statistical analysis.** IBM SPSS offers advanced statistical analysis and provides a number of ML algorithms, offers open source extensibility, and enables text analysis. It can be used for seamless deployment of big data.

5. **Answer: c. Windows.** Statistical Analytical System (SAS), which is available only for Windows, is one of the most familiar statistical software packages across academia and other industry sectors.

6. **Answer: d. Data visualization.** Tableau is one of the fastest-growing tools for data visualization.

Data analytics tools enhance organizational capability to examine a wide amount of information, enabling better insights and visibility into key processes and leading to data-driven decision making. Data analytics tools make it possible to gain insights ranging from business intelligence to predictive analytics— leveraging unstructured and structured data. The sections that follow briefly describe various data analytics tools.

Structured Query Language (SQL)

Structured Query Language (SQL) is a database query language that was developed for the management and extraction of data in relational database management systems (RDBMSs). SQL has the capability to communicate with several databases at a time and can be used to construct complex queries. SQL operations—including create, read, update, and delete (CRUD) operations— can be used to perform tasks on data in a database.

SQL is an outstanding tool for constructing data warehouses that provide data organization, simple accessibility, and capability to communicate efficiently with business processes and reporting as well as analytics toolsets. Moreover, SQL analytics can be used within languages and/or software platforms such as Hadoop, Python, and Scala.

> **Note**
>
> Chapter 1, "Understanding Databases and Data Warehouses," covers the basics of SQL as a language of choice for relational database and data warehouse solutions.

The following example of a SQL statement allows you to select all values from the specified table:

```
SELECT * FROM <table_name>
```

This example allows you to select all customers with which your organization interacted in the year 2010 and orders them by country names, in ascending order (that is, A–Z):

```
SELECT * FROM Customer
 WHERE year = 2010
 ORDER BY Country
```

It is important to understand that SQL by itself is not an analytics tool; however, analytics tools such as Tableau and Google Looker Studio leverage SQL to interact with data warehouses and data lakes.

Python

Python is a very popular scripting language that is used to automate network operations. It is often used because of its extensive set of libraries by network engineers. It is, however, also very popular among data scientists. Python can manage huge amounts of information and can manage and create data structures rapidly. Python is an open source language, and there is a very strong community around Python-based data analytics. A simple search on Google for "Python data analytics" with "GitHub" would yield multiple results.

For example, Numerical Python, or NumPy, is the fundamental package required for scientific computing and data analysis. With this package, you can run an analysis of variance (ANOVA) test to compare the sample means of multiple groups.

> **Note**
>
> There is a lot more to Python in the context of data analytics and data science; however, the information provided here is all you need to know for the CompTIA Data+ exam.

Microsoft Excel

Microsoft Excel is a very familiar program used primarily for spreadsheets. You can use it to arrange data in rows and columns and leverage formulas that prompt the software to carry out mathematical functions on data. Microsoft Excel is typically used to organize information and perform financial calculations as well as for information technology project management. Its dedicated Data tab offers multiple options for analyzing data (see Figure 9.1) and makes Microsoft Excel a very powerful tool. You can play around with what-if situations and carry out data analysis by leveraging data models and queries from within Microsoft Excel.

FIGURE 9.1 **The Data Tab in Microsoft Excel**

Figure 9.1 shows the default options available on the Data tab. You can add additional options by selecting **File > Options > Add-ins > Analysis Toolpak** (see Figure 9.2).

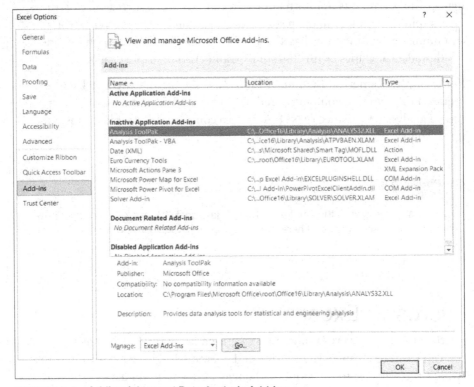

FIGURE 9.2 **Adding Advanced Data Analysis Add-ins**

By selecting the option shown in Figure 9.2, you can add a Data Analysis option to the Data tab that opens the door to many advanced functions, as shown in Figure 9.3.

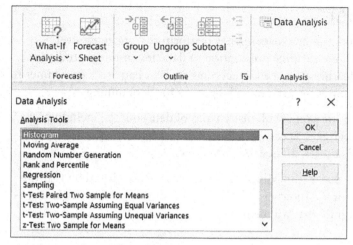

FIGURE 9.3   **Data Analysis Options**

R

R is a data analysis tool that is based on the open source R programming language. R is extensively used for statistics, data visualization, and data science projects. You can use R to manipulate information easily and represent it in various ways. R is very popular for the visualizations it offers, including plots, graphs, and charts.

An R package is a collection of functions and data that extends the capabilities of R. Data analysis in R involves importing data to R and running functions to visualize as well as model the data.

R can be downloaded at https://cloud.r-project.org/index.html. Various R packages are available at this website as well.

You can try https://plotly.com/r/ for creating a variety of graphs using R. And you can find an IDE at https://www.rstudio.com/products/workbench/.

> **Note**
>
> Google uses the R data analytics tool for economic forecasting and determining the effectiveness of ads, Facebook uses it for behavior analysis, Uber uses it for statistical analysis, and Twitter uses it for semantic clustering and data visualization.

Rapid Miner

Rapid Miner is an open source data science platform that includes several algorithms for machine learning, preparation of data, text mining, predictive analysis, and deep learning. Data engineers and analysts can use Rapid Miner to extend the Python and R programming languages for data mining.

Rapid Miner can be combined with many types of data sources, including Microsoft Excel, Microsoft Access, Teradata, Microsoft SQL, Sybase, Oracle, MySQL, IBM DB2, Ingres, dBase, and IBM SPSS.

As an example of its use, Rapid Miner can produce analytics based on real-life data points from multiple Internet of Things (IoT) sensors on livestock to predict the quantity of milk that will be produced.

> **Note**
>
> Rapid Miner offers data mining with a template-based approach that reduces human error and enhances speed of delivery.

To learn more about Rapid Miner, visit https://rapidminer.com/.

IBM Cognos

IBM Cognos is a business intelligence (BI) tool that is used for web-based analytics and reporting. IBM Cognos is primarily used by enterprises to aggregate corporate data and produce user-friendly reports. It can be used to create and view reports, examine data, and supervise metrics and events, for effective decision making.

IBM Cognos analytics combines modeling, reporting, dashboards, analysis, event management, and stories to help organizations understand their information and make decisions efficiently.

IBM Cognos is now being offered as part of the IBM Watson family of solutions. To learn more about IBM Cognos, visit https://www.ibm.com/products/cognos-analytics.

IBM SPSS Modeler

IBM Statistical Package Social Science (SPSS) Modeler is a machine learning (ML) and data mining solution from IBM. It is used to construct a predictive structure and organize data for further analytics. IBM SPSS Modeler is designed to acquire predictive intelligence for driving decision making by enterprises and/or systems. It offers both programming-based and visual approaches to data analytics and can enhance the capabilities of R- and Python-based analytics.

IBM SPSS offers advanced statistical analysis and provides a large number of ML algorithms, open source extensibility, and text analysis. In addition, it can be seamlessly deployed and easily used with big data.

> **Note**
>
> Data analysts use IBM SPSS Modeler to examine information by carrying out data mining and then organizing the information into models.

IBM SPSS Modeler assists in the whole process of data mining. IBM SPSS Modeler can be bought as a standalone product or employed as a client that is integrated with an SPSS Modeler server.

To learn more about IBM SPSS Modeler, visit https://www.ibm.com/products/spss-modeler.

SAS

Statistical Analytical System (SAS) is one of the most commonly used solutions for complex statistical operations and advanced analytics. The main uses of SAS are to analyze, extract, and present statistical data in an easy-to-consume format. SAS provides descriptive visualization in the form of graphs, and various SAS solutions offer reporting of data mining, time series, machine learning, and other data.

SAS is easy to learn and offers simple and intuitive interfaces for data analysts who know SQL already. SAS is much prominent across academia and is commonly used in a number of industry verticals, such as banking, life sciences, and manufacturing. SAS offers several types of analysis:

▶ Mixed model analysis

▶ Regression analysis

▶ Distribution analysis

▶ Descriptive analysis

To learn more about SAS, visit https://www.sas.com/en_us/home.geo.html.

Tableau

Tableau, which is one of the fastest-growing data visualization solutions, has an intuitive interface. Figure 9.4 shows the Tableau dashboard.

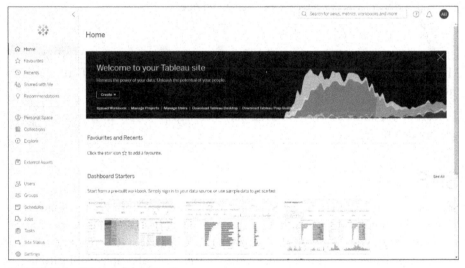

FIGURE 9.4   **Tableau Dashboard**

Figure 9.5 shows a sample Tableau dashboard that illustrates sales progress.

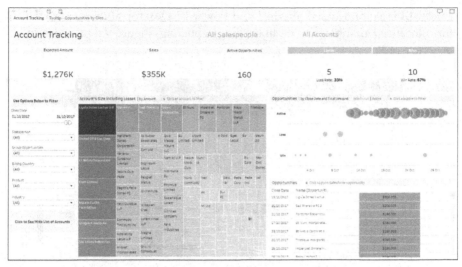

FIGURE 9.5   **Tableau Sample Sales Account Tracking Dashboard**
(Source: https://linpack-for-tableau.com/tableau-dashboard/bank-cash-flow/)

Tableau is a remarkable tool for BI and supports effective decision making.

> **Note**
>
> Tableau uses Visual Query Language (VQL) to transform a SQL into visualizations.
> Moreover, Tableau can handle both continuous and discrete data.

To learn more about Tableau, visit https://www.tableau.com/.

Power BI

Microsoft Power BI is a business analytics solution that enables reporting and visualization—much like Tableau. Power BI is a suite of visualization applications, connectors, and services that can be used together to examine unrelated data sources to form coherent, interactive insights and view immersive visuals.

For example, a sales dashboard might help senior leadership of an organization perceive how the firm is performing in sales compared to the previous year. It may also provide data about the performance of various product segments and what channels are succeeding in acquiring the revenue.

Power BI is a cloud-based offering, and Power BI Desktop allows you to perform localized analytics and dashboarding/reporting. Figure 9.6 provides an overview of Power BI.

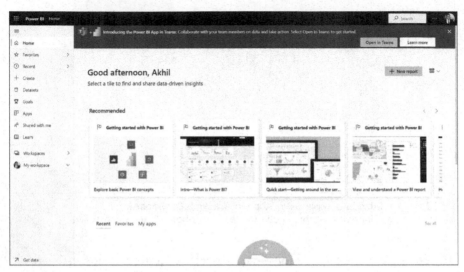

FIGURE 9.6   **Power BI Service (Cloud-Based SaaS)**

By using Power BI, you can import datasets and start creating reports. You can also use Power BI Desktop to connect with data sources.

To learn more about Power BI, visit https://powerbi.microsoft.com/en-us/.

Qlik

Qlik is a self-service tool for data analytics, data visualization, and BI that drives business value. Qlik offers a complete range of creative visualizations and provides artificial intelligence support for creating charts; it suggests relationships, shows the shape of data, and even prepares the data.

Qlik can consume a large number of data rows from a variety of sources, with different schemas, as well as data with multiple dimensions. It provides responses in a fraction of second.

Qlik offers two BI tools:

▶ **QlikView:** QlikView is based on guided data analytics, allowing an end user to work with data models, create diverse visualizations, and deploy their own analytics apps.

► **Qlik Sense:** Qlik Sense is a self-service tool that allows an end user to perform service analytics, create intuitive and interactive dashboards, and perform custom analytics. Qlik Sense is available as a SaaS offering.

If you are a developer and an avid data analyst, you would be likely to work with Qlik Sense. If you are a non-IT user who wants to perform data analytics, you'll leverage QlikView.

Visit https://www.qlik.com/us/ to learn more about Qlik.

MicroStrategy

MicroStrategy is a BI platform that supports data mining, predictive analysis, and visualization. MicroStrategy assists in creating scorecards, interactive dashboards, ad hoc reports, highly formatted reports, and alerts and threshold reports. It also handles automated distribution of reports.

Users can leverage drag-and-drop functionality to generate reports using MicroStrategy cloud-based or on-premises solutions. Users are given a choice of sources to collect data from, such as social media or big data platforms. They can create and modify BI reports or dashboards via the MicroStrategy Desktop. MicroStrategy Cloud offers customers agility, scalability, and performance.

Visit https://www.microstrategy.com/ to learn more about MicroStrategy.

BusinessObjects

SAP owns many software solutions, and BusinessObjects is its core data analytics, reporting, and visualization suite. SAP BusinessObjects can be leveraged to publish, create, store, and share reports. Users can start with discovery of data, perform analysis to attain insights, and ultimately create reports that visualize the insights.

SAP BusinessObjects aims to make reporting and analysis simple enough that users can generate reports and perform predictive analytics without input from data analysts. It is geared toward making reporting and visualization possible from a business user perspective.

Learn more about SAP BusinessObjects at https://www.sap.com/australia/products/bi-platform.html.

Apex

The Apex data analytics tool enhances reference data centralization for reliable reporting and aggregation at the enterprise level.

Apex is a development platform for constructing SaaS applications on top of the CRM functionality of Salesforce.com.

Apex permits software developers to access back-end Salesforce databases and client/server interfaces to create third-party SaaS applications.

Datorama

Datorama is a SaaS solution from Salesforce that is focused on analytics and marketing intelligence. Users can leverage this solution and connectors to acquire data from various marketing tools.

> **Note**
>
> Datorama has artificial intelligence–powered processes that enable users to link multiple marketing tools/sources easily and unify all their marketing information in one place.

Datorama can report on and monitor a variety of marketing information in a unified way. Its dashboards offer stakeholders appropriate KPIs and trends.

> **Note**
>
> While the other tools and solutions described to this point in this chapter are usually industry and line of business neutral, Datorama is very specific to marketing operations. It enables marketing teams to invest valuable time performing marketing work rather than spending resources and time on manual reporting and analytics.

To learn more about Datorama, visit https://datorama.com/.

Domo

Domo is a SaaS platform that offers simplified access to BI for decision makers. Domo Business Cloud offers a self-service approach to performing data analysis, generating reports, and making informed decisions based on key data points. Domo offers prebuilt pages that are assembled based on input data automatically. It also offers automated reporting. Domo provides design flexibility and a user-friendly interface.

Visit https://www.domo.com/ for more information about Domo.

AWS QuickSight

Amazon Web Services (AWS) QuickSight is a machine learning–powered cloud-native BI service. You can use AWS QuickSight to collate data across AWS databases and data warehouse solutions as well as traditional data sources.

Being cloud native gives QuickSight the advantage (as well as other SaaS or cloud-hosted BI and analytic solutions) of being able to scale out without requiring manual provisioning of resources. It offers an intuitive interface for performing data analysis and creating data visualizations and dashboards. AWS QuickSight uses an in-memory engine called Super-fast, Parallel, In-memory Calculation Engine (SPICE)—much like a cache—for quicker data retrieval for visualization in memory.

To learn more about AWS QuickSight, visit https://aws.amazon.com/quicksight/.

Stata

Stata is an integrated package of statistical software that offers everything users need for visualization, data analysis, and data management. It is mostly used in the biomedicine, economics, and political science industry sectors, primarily to investigate patterns of data. Stata offers a graphical user interface (GUI) and can be used from a command-line interface (CLI).

To learn more about Stata, visit https://www.stata.com/.

Minitab

Minitab is statistical software that is primarily used for empowering statistics and visualizing outcomes. It is commonly used in universities and for statistical analysis.

> **Fun Fact**
>
> Almost all major universities around the globe subscribe to Minitab. If you are a university student, it is worthwhile to see if you can get a free student copy of Minitab from your university website. Using Minitab can help you could learn business process improvement via data analysis.

Visit https://www.minitab.com/en-us/ for more information about Minitab.

Cram Quiz

Answer these questions. If you cannot answer these questions correctly, consider reading this section again until you can.

1. Structured Query Language is a standard language for _____.
   - ○ **a.** RDBMS
   - ○ **b.** Oracle
   - ○ **c.** Python
   - ○ **d.** Linux

2. Microsoft Excel is a powerful and helpful program for documentation and _____.
   - ○ **a.** data cleansing
   - ○ **b.** data visualization
   - ○ **c.** data segmentation
   - ○ **d.** data analysis

3. Amazon Web Services (AWS) QuickSight is a machine learning–powered _____ BI service.
   - ○ **a.** on-premises
   - ○ **b.** cloud-native
   - ○ **c.** community
   - ○ **d.** hybrid

4. IBM Cognos exports reports in _____ format.
   - ○ **a.** HTML or XML
   - ○ **b.** Word or PDF
   - ○ **c.** SQL
   - ○ **d.** PDF or XML

5. IBM SPSS Modeler is extensively used as a(n) _____ platform.

   ○ **a.** Rapid Miner

   ○ **b.** Oracle data science

   ○ **c.** predictive analytics

   ○ **d.** SPSS statistics

6. Power BI permits users to share _____ with others.

   ○ **a.** data visualizations

   ○ **b.** data cleansing

   ○ **c.** data segmentation

   ○ **d.** data classification

7. Business objects use _____ language.

   ○ **a.** Linux shell

   ○ **b.** SQL

   ○ **c.** Oracle

   ○ **d.** All of these answers are correct.

Cram Quiz Answers

1. **Answer: a. RDBMS.** Structured Query Language is a language standard for relational database management systems. A number of RDBMS solutions—including Microsoft Access, MySQL, Oracle SQL, Postgres SQL, Sybase, Microsoft SQL Server, and Informix—use Structured Query Language for CRUD operations in a database.

2. **Answer: d. data analysis.** Microsoft Excel is a powerful spreadsheet program that can be used for data analysis.

3. **Answer: b. cloud-native.** Amazon Web Services (AWS) QuickSight is a machine learning–powered cloud-native BI service. You can use AWS QuickSight to collate data across AWS databases and data warehouse solutions as well as traditional data sources.

4. **Answer: d. PDF or XML.** IBM Cognos offers a choice to export reports in PDF or XML format.

5. **Answer: c. predictive analytics.** IBM SPSS Modeler is extensively used as a predictive analytics platform that is designed to apply predictive intelligence to decisions made by groups, individuals, enterprises, and the system.

6. **Answer: a. data visualizations.** Power BI allows users to share their data visualizations with other users.

7. **Answer: b. SQL.** In business objects, database developers use SQL to create new database objects, evolve indexes, manipulate tables, and trigger procedures to materialize views that other report writers can utilize.

What Next?

If you want more practice on this chapter's exam objective before you move on, remember that you can access all of the Cram Quiz questions on the Pearson Test Prep software online. You can also create a custom exam by objective with the Online Practice Test. Note any objective you struggle with and go to that objective's material in this chapter.

CHAPTER 10

Understanding Descriptive and Inferential Statistical Methods

This chapter covers Objective 3.1 (Given a scenario, apply the appropriate descriptive statistical methods) and Objective 3.2 (Explain the purpose of inferential statistical methods) of the CompTIA Data+ exam and includes the following topics:

▶ Measures of central tendency

▶ Measures of dispersion

▶ Frequencies and percentages

▶ Percent change

▶ Percent difference

▶ Confidence intervals

▶ *t*-tests

▶ *Z*-score

▶ *p*-values

▶ Chi-squared

▶ Hypothesis testing

▶ Simple linear regression

▶ Correlation

For more information on the official CompTIA Data+ exam topics, see the Introduction.

This chapter covers topics related to descriptive and inferential statistical methods. It is important to understand the measures of central tendency and measures of dispersion. This chapter also covers frequencies, percent change, percent difference, and confidence intervals, as well as *t*-tests, *Z*-scores, *p*-values, and chi-squared.

Introduction to Descriptive and Inferential Analysis

CramSaver

If you can correctly answer these questions before going through this section, save time by skimming the Exam Alerts in this section and then completing the Cram Quiz at the end of the section.

1. Measures of central tendency are characterized by _____.

   a. nonstatistical measures

   b. dataset summaries

   c. information about individual data

   d. multiple values of a dataset

2. What is the calculated mode in the following table?

Mode
5
5
5
4
3
2
2
1

   a. 2

   b. 1

   c. 5

   d. 20

3. Percent change can be measured by which of the following?

   a. Quality

   b. Quantity

   c. Old value

   d. Final value

4. Absolute measures of dispersion are measured by which of the following?

   a. Observation of data scattering

   b. Observation of normal data

   c. Observation of distributed data

   d. Summary of data

Answers

1. **Answer: b. dataset summaries.** Measures of central tendency reveal the center in a distribution of data and provide dataset summaries.

2. **Answer: c. 5.** *Mode* refers to the most repeated or common value. The most recurrently repeated value in the table is 5, so 5 is the mode.

3. **Answer: b. Quantity.** Percent change is a measure of the variance between new and old values of quantity, stated in percentages.

4. **Answer: a. Observation of data scattering.** Absolute measures of dispersion are measured by the observation of scattered data.

Before we get into the specifics of how descriptive and inferential statistics are carried out, it is important to discuss some basics about statistical methods.

The study of statistics can be categorized into two major categories: descriptive statistics and inferential statistics. Performing a statistical study requires identifying a population, group, or collection of target entities nominated for gathering data. The population, group, or collection of entities could be a group of cattle for a livestock study, a group of human beings for a study of DNA trait statistics, or a collection of data around sea level in an area across a number of days.

Descriptive statistics helps summarize data in a meaningful way such that statisticians can realize any patterns that emerge from the data collected. In other words, descriptive statistics is simply a way to describe data and does not aim to make conclusions or formulate any hypothesis about the data being analyzed.

Inferential statistics, on the other hand, is all about making inferences based on the data samples collected from a population. In other words, inferential statistics allows you to leverage data samples to hypothesize generalities about the populations from which the samples were drawn and arrive at a conclusion.

The following sections explore descriptive statistics methods such as central tendency, measures of dispersion, and more.

Measures of Central Tendency

In statistics, the *central tendency* refers to a single value of a dataset or a whole distribution. The central tendency is a typical value of the dataset. Central tendency of a dataset can be identified using measures such as mode, median, and mean (see Figure 10.1).

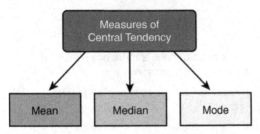

FIGURE 10.1 **Measures of Central Tendency**

Mean

The *mean* is a dataset's average value. It can be estimated as the total of each value in set of data divided by total quantity of values. It is also known as the arithmetic mean and indicated with the symbol μ.

Estimating the mean value is fairly straightforward. The formula for calculating the mean value is as follows:

$$\mu = (X_1 + X_2 + X_3 + \ldots + X_n) / n,$$

where:

X is a value

n is the number of values

For example, the mean for the numbers 2, 4, 6, and 8 can be calculated as follows:

$$\mu = (2 + 4 + 6 + 8) / 4$$

$$= 20 / 4$$

$$= 5$$

Median

The *median* is the middle value in a set of data, where the dataset might be arranged in descending or ascending order.

Let us consider a dataset with an odd number of values arranged in ascending order (see Table 10.1).

> **Note**
>
> This implies not the data values within the fields, but the number of fields in the dataset that are odd.

TABLE 10.1 **Median with Odd Number of Data Fields**

5
6
7
9
10
11
13
14
15
16
18
21
23

You can easily calculate the median value for this dataset because it has an odd number of data fields: It is simply the middle value, in this case 13. Six values are presented above 13, and six values are presented below 13.

Now let's consider the median for an even number of fields that are arranged in an ascending order (see Table 10.2).

TABLE 10.2 **Median with an Even Number of Data Fields**

17
19
22
23
24
26
27
29
30
32
33
35
38
40

In the dataset in Table 10.2, the two middle values are 29 and 27. In this case, the median value is calculated by finding the mean value for the two middle numbers:

$(29 + 27) / 2 = 56/2 = 28$

Thus, the median value for the distribution in Table 10.2 is 28.

Mode

The *mode* is the value that occurs the most frequently in a dataset. Consider the given dataset in Table 10.3.

TABLE 10.3 **Sample Dataset for Mode Calculation**

5
5
5
4
3
2
2
1

The most repeated value in this dataset is 5.

> ## Note
>
> When is each measure of central tendency most useful? It depends on the data properties. For example:
>
> ▶ If you have continuous data with a symmetrical distribution, then all three measures of central tendency—mode, median, and mean—are useful. Many times, analysts use the mean since it applies to all the values in a dataset or distribution.
>
> ▶ In a skewed distribution, the best choice for measuring central tendency is the median.
>
> ▶ With categorical data, the best choice for finding central tendency is the mode.
>
> ▶ With original data, the mode and median are the best measures of central tendency.

Measures of Dispersion

The measure of dispersion, as the name indicates, describes the scattering of data. It explains the variation in data points and gives a clear view of the data distribution. It indicates the heterogeneity or homogeneity of distributed data observations, which are categorized as the absolute measure and relative measure of dispersion:

▶ The absolute measure of dispersion is used for observation scattering in distances such as quartile deviation and range. It denotes differences in observations for the average number of deviations such as standard and mean deviations.

▶ A relative measure of dispersion compares the distributed data with two or more data points.

These include the coefficient of mean deviation, coefficient of range, coefficient of variation, coefficient of quartile deviation, and coefficient of standard deviation.

> ## ExamAlert
>
> Measures of dispersion are most commonly used by statisticians and analysts and are a focus of the CompTIA Data+ exam.

Range

Range is an easily understandable measure of dispersion. Range is the difference between the maximum value and the minimum value of a dataset. If Xi_{min} and Xi_{max} are these two values, the range can be identified using this formula:

$$Range = Xi_{max} - Xi_{min}$$

Quartile Deviation

Quartiles divide a set of data into quarters. Following are the specifics:

▶ The middle number between the median of the dataset and the smallest number is the first quartile (Qu_1).

▶ The dataset median is the second quartile (Qu_2).

▶ The middle number between the largest number and the median is the third quartile (Qu_3).

The formula for quartile deviation is as follows:

$$Quartile\ deviation = (Qu_3 - Qu_1)/2$$

Quartile deviation is the best dispersion measure for open-ended classification. It is independent of origin change and dependent on scale change.

Mean Deviation

Mean deviation denotes the arithmetic mean of observation from absolute deviations. If $x_1, x_2, x_3, x_4, x_5, x_6, \ldots, x_n$ are the observation set, then the deviation of mean of x about average A (mode, median, or mean) is:

$$Deviation\ of\ mean\ from\ average\ Av = 1/n\ [\Sigma_i |x_i - Av|]$$

Deviation of mean from average A for grouped frequency is estimated as follows:

$$Deviation\ of\ mean\ from\ average\ Av = 1/N\ [\Sigma_i fr_i\ |x_i - Av|], N = \Sigma fr_i$$

Here fr_i and x_i are the frequency and middle values of the ith class interval.

Mean deviation gives a minimum value when observations are taken from the measure of the median. It is independent of origin change and dependent on scale change.

Standard Deviation

Standard deviation is the square root of mean of deviation squares of provided values from their mean. Standard deviation is represented by sigma (σ). At the same time, it is also denoted as the deviation of root mean square. Standard deviation can be calculated as follows:

$$\sigma = \sqrt{\frac{\sum |x - \mu|^2}{N}}$$

The square of standard deviation is known as *variance* and is also a dispersion measure. Variance can be represented as σ^2.

Let's consider an example to calculate standard deviation. Say that you have the data points 2, 4, 6, and 8, and you need to calculate standard deviation.

First, you need to find the mean:

$\mu = (2 + 4 + 6 + 8) / 4 = 5$

Next, you need to find the square of the distance from each data point to the mean:

$|x - \mu|^2$

where x is the number, and μ is the mean:

$|2 - 5|^2 = 9$

$|4 - 5|^2 = 1$

$|6 - 5|^2 = 1$

$|8 - 5|^2 = 9$

> **Note**
>
> The brackets in |x| represent the absolute value and non-negative value of x.

Now, you can calculate σ:

$$\sigma = \sqrt{(9 + 1 + 1 + 9) / 4}$$

$$= \sqrt{5}$$

$$= 2.237 \text{ (rounded off)}$$

The variance is σ^2—that is, $(2.237)^2 = 5.0$.

Relative Measure of Dispersion

Relative measures of dispersion are used for comparing the distributed data of two or more datasets. Relative measures compare observations without units. The most commonly used methods for relative measures of dispersion are as follows:

▶ Coefficient of range

▶ Coefficient of quartile deviation

▶ Coefficient of mean deviation

▶ Coefficient of standard deviation

▶ Coefficient of variation

Frequencies

Frequency (*f*) refers to the number of times an observation of a specific value occurs in data. For example, frequency is the number of times that each variable occurs, such as the number of male athletes and the number of female athletes within a sample population.

A *distribution* represents frequency pattern of a variable. A distribution is a set of probable values as well as their frequencies. In other words, a *frequency distribution* represents values and their frequency—that is, how often each value occurs in a sample dataset.

Let's consider an example of a frequency distribution of magazines sold at a retail outlet. The data includes the numbers of magazines sold at a local retail outlet over the past 7 days:

10, 11, 12, 13, 14, 15, 16

Table 10.4 shows how many times each number occurs in this dataset.

TABLE 10.4 **Frequency Distribution of Magazines Sold**

Magazines Sold	Frequency
10	3
11	1
12	0
13	10
14	10
15	9
16	11

As you can see, the frequency tells how often there were 10, 11, 12, 13, 14, 15, or 16 magazines sold over the past 7 days.

A distribution of frequency could indicate either a real number of values falling in observation percentage or a range. In the observation percentage, the distribution of frequency is referred to as a *relative distribution of frequency*. Distributions of frequency tables are leveraged for numeric variables and categorical variables. Continuous variables in a frequency distribution are used only with class intervals.

Percent Change and Percent Difference

Percent change can be used to compare old values with new values. Estimating the percent change between two provided quantities is an effortless process. When an old or initial value and a new or final value of quantity are identified, the percent change formula is applied to identify the percent change. The formula is as follows:

$$\text{Percent change} = \frac{(V_2 - V_1)}{|V_1|} \times 100$$

where:

V_2 denotes the new value

V_1 denotes the old value

If the percent change value is positive, this indicates that the percentage has increased; if the percent change value is negative, this indicates that the percentage has decreased.

For example, if $V_1 = 100$ and $V_2 = 200$, the percent change would be:

Percent change $= [(200 - 100) / 100] \times 100$

$$= [100 / 100] \times 100$$

$$= 100\%$$

Percent difference is a measure of the absolute value of variance among the two numbers, divided by the average of the two values and then multiplied by 100%:

$$\text{Percent difference} = \frac{|V_1 - V_2|}{\left[\dfrac{(V_2 - V_1)}{2}\right]} \times 100$$

Again using the example of $V_1 = 100$ and $V_2 = 200$:

Percent difference $= |100 - 200|/[(100 + 200) / 2] \times 100$

$$= |-100| / [150] \times 100$$

$$= 0.66667 \times 100$$

$$= 66.667$$

Cram Quiz

Answer these questions. If you cannot answer these questions correctly, consider reading this section again until you can.

1. Quartile deviation can be calculated using which of these formulas?
   - a. $Qu = 1/2 \times (Qu_3 - Qu_1)$
   - b. $Qu = 1/2 \times (Qu_1 - Qu_3)$
   - c. $Qu = 1/16 \times (Qu_0 - Qu_1)$
   - d. $Qu = 1/16 \times (Qu_3 - Qu_1)$

2. A relative measure of dispersion compares _____.
   - a. common data
   - b. original data
   - c. multiple sets of data
   - d. a distribution of data

3. Measures of dispersion compare _____.
   - ○ **a.** dispersion
   - ○ **b.** relative measures
   - ○ **c.** absolute measures
   - ○ **d.** absolute measures and relative measures

4. Measures of dispersion denote _____.
   - ○ **a.** homogeneity observations
   - ○ **b.** heterogeneity observations
   - ○ **c.** data scatterings
   - ○ **d.** original data

5. Distributions of frequency are represented as _____.
   - ○ **a.** charts or frequency tables
   - ○ **b.** tables
   - ○ **c.** figures
   - ○ **d.** histograms

6. Percentage differences are measures of _____.
   - ○ **a.** absolute value
   - ○ **b.** average value
   - ○ **c.** maximum value
   - ○ **d.** minimum value

Cram Quiz Answers

1. **Answer: a. Qu = 1/2 × (Qu$_3$ – Qu$_1$).** Quartile deviation can be calculated by using the formula Qu = $1/2 \times (Qu_3 - Qu_1)$.

2. **Answer: d. a distribution of data.** A relative measure of dispersion compares distributed data in two or more datasets.

3. **Answer: d. absolute measures and relative measures.** Measures of dispersion compare absolute measures and relative measures of dispersion.

4. **Answer: c. data scatterings.** Measures of dispersion denote data scatterings.

5. **Answer: a. charts or frequency tables.** Distributions of frequency are represented as charts or frequency tables.

6. **Answer: a. absolute value.** Percent difference is a measure of absolute value of variance between two numbers.

Inferential Statistical Methods

CramSaver

If you can correctly answer these questions before going through this section, save time by skimming the Exam Alerts in this section and then completing the Cram Quiz at the end of the section.

1. What data values are needed for measuring a *t*-test?

   a. Mean values

   b. Standard deviations

   c. Data values

   d. Mean difference, quantity of data values, and standard deviation

2. The basic formula for the *Z*-score of a sample is _____.

   a. $Z = (x - \mu)\, \sigma$

   b. $Z = (x - \mu) + \sigma$

   c. $Z = (x - \mu) / \sigma$

   d. $Z = (x - \mu)(x + \sigma)$

3. Hypothesis testing is determined by _____.

   a. parameters

   b. measured means

   c. deviation

   d. probability of data

4. A *p*-value > 0.05 implies that the value _____.

   a. is not statistically significant, and thus the null hypothesis should be rejected

   b. is not statistically significant, and thus the null hypothesis should be rejected and the alternative hypothesis accepted

   c. is statistically and highly significant, and thus the null hypothesis should be rejected and the alternative hypothesis accepted

   d. is statistically significant, and thus the alternative hypothesis should be accepted and the null hypothesis rejected

Answers

1. **Answer: d. Mean difference, quantity of data values, and standard deviation.** Data values needed for estimating a t-test include the variance between values of the mean from every set of data—that is, the mean difference, each group's standard deviation, and each group's quantities of data values.

2. **Answer: c. $Z = (x - \mu) / \sigma$.** This is the formula for determining the Z-score.

3. **Answer: a. parameters.** Hypothesis testing is determined by parameters of data in a population.

4. **Answer: a. is not statistically significant, and thus the null hypothesis should be rejected.** Refer to the following table for the p-values.

Interpretations of p-values

p-value	Interpretations
$p < 0.01$	p is statistically and highly significant. Therefore, reject the null hypothesis and accept the alternative hypothesis.
$p > 0.05$	p is not statistically significant. Therefore, reject the null hypothesis.
$p < 0.05$	p is statistically significant. Therefore, accept the alternative hypothesis and reject the null hypothesis.

Inferential analysis is all about making inferences and predictions by performing analysis on sample population data from an original or larger dataset(s). As you can appreciate, a data engineer or a data scientist cannot possibly look at an entire volume of data; it is just too difficult to collect data from a whole population. Instead, they need to work with samples from data stores.

Inferential analysis makes it possible to derive trends by leveraging probability to reach conclusions and by testing hypotheses as well as samples from the population.

Before we get into the specifics of methods to perform inferential analysis, it is vital that you understand the term *hypothesis*. A hypothesis is simply a perception or an idea about a value that can be tested given sample data from a population under study. A hypothesis is very important in the context of inferential statistics as all conclusions about a given population are based on a representative sample. Hence, you need to understand two important terms in the context of inferential analysis: null hypothesis and alternative hypothesis. The *null hypothesis* assumes that there is no association between the two (categorical) variables, whereas the alternative hypothesis does assume that there is an association between the two (categorical) variables. (You'll learn more about hypotheses later in this chapter.)

ExamAlert

Hypothesis testing is an important concept, and it is good to know about type I and type II errors for the CompTIA Data+ exam.

The following sections cover the various inferential statistics methods, starting with confidence intervals.

Confidence Intervals

The *confidence level* is the range of values that are likely to contain plausible population values. Confidence intervals are used to measure the degree of uncertainty in a sampling method. Typically, the most common confidence interval is 95% or 99%; however, it is possible to have other values, such as 85% or 90%.

Note

It is key to understand that it is close to impossible to study a whole dataset, given that terabytes of data are being generated every day. Hence, researchers select a sample or subgroup of a population and work with confidence intervals as a way to measure how well the sample represents the population.

For example, if a data analyst constructs a confidence interval with a 95% confidence level, that analyst is confident that 95 out of 100 times, the estimate will fall between the upper and lower values specified by the confidence interval (see Figure 10.2).

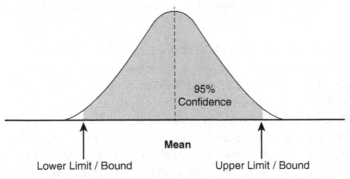

FIGURE 10.2　**Confidence Interval Graph**

Let's consider another example. Say that a device manufacturer wants to ensure that the weight of the devices that will be carried on a military convoy is in line with specifications. A data analyst has measured the average weight of a sample of 100 devices to be 10 kg. He has also found the 95% confidence interval to be between 9.6 kg and 10.30 kg. This means the data analyst can be 95% sure that the average weight of all the devices manufactured will be between 9.6 kg and 10.30 kg.

> **Note**
>
> This calculation was performed using the Omni calculator, at https://www.omnical-culator.com/statistics/confidence-interval.

The formula for the confidence interval is:

$$CI = \overline{X} \pm Z \times \frac{\sigma}{\sqrt{n}}$$

where:

X is the sample mean

Z is the confidence coefficient (Z-score), which is 1.960 for 95% and 2.576 for 99%

σ is the standard deviation

n is the sample size

Z-score

A Z-score, also referred to as a standard score, describes how distant from the mean a data point is. It is also an estimation of how many standard deviations above or below the mean of a population a raw score is.

The basic formula for the Z-score is:

$Z = (x - \mu) / \sigma$

where:

x denotes the observed value

σ denotes the standard deviation of the sample

μ denotes the mean of the sample

If the x value is 1350, the mean value is 1000, and the standard deviation value is 200, then the Z-value is found as follows:

$$Z = (1350 - 1000) / 200$$

$$= 1.750$$

In this case, the Z-score is 1.750 standard deviations above the mean.

Figure 10.3 illustrates a sample Z-score value.

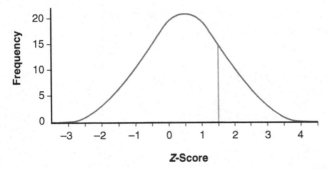

FIGURE 10.3   Z-score Representation

How is a Z-score helpful? A Z-score gives you an idea about how an individual value compares to the rest of the distribution. For example, a Z-score can tell you if devices being produced for military vehicles are being actively used or not, depending upon the weight specifications on the vehicles they are supposed to be used with.

In the previous example, we have a positive Z-score (that is, the individual value is greater than the mean, as shown in Figure 10.3). A negative Z-score indicates a value less than the mean. Finally, a Z-score of 0 means that the individual value is equal to the mean.

t-tests

The t-test, which originated in inferential statistics, is used to identify the main variance between mean values from two groups. In other words, it is used to compare the mean values from two samples and evaluate whether the means of the two groups are statistically dissimilar. t-tests are based on hypotheses.

There are three categories of *t*-tests:

▶ **One-sample *t*-test:** This type of *t*-test compares the average or mean of one group against the set average or population mean. For example, it can be used to compare the sales of a product across a set of new stores against sales in one of the established stores.

▶ **Two-sample *t*-test:** This type of *t*-test is used to compare the means of two different samples and implies that the two mean groups are different from the hypothesized population mean. For example, it might be used to compare the performance of salespeople across two different states for the same product.

▶ **Paired *t*-test:** This type of *t*-test is used to compare separate means for a group at two different times or under two different conditions. For example, it might be used to compare the effect of training of salespeople on selling a sophisticated product before and after training.

Figure 10.4 shows the distribution of *t*-values when the null hypothesis is true.

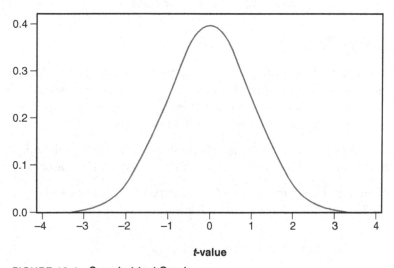

t-value

FIGURE 10.4   **Sample t-test Graph**

p-values

A *p*-value, or probability value, is leveraged as part of hypothesis testing to help accept or reject the null hypothesis. The *p*-value is a number that explains the

244

CHAPTER 10: Understanding Descriptive and Inferential Statistical Methods

probability that a data point happened by chance (that is, randomly). The statistical significance level is denoted as a p-value between 0 and 1.

p-values are usually expressed as decimal figures and can be expressed as percentages. For example, a p-value of 0.054 is 5.40% and implies that there is a 5.40% chance that the results could be random (or happened by chance). In comparison, a p-value of 0.99 translates to 99.00% and implies that the results have a 99% probability of being completely random. Hence, with p-values, a smaller value reflects more significant results. Table 10.5 explains how to interpret p-values.

TABLE 10.5 **Interpretations of p-value**

p-value	Interpretations
$p < 0.01$	p is statistically and highly significant. Therefore, reject the null hypothesis and accept the alternative hypothesis.
$p > 0.05$	p is not statistically significant. Therefore, reject the null hypothesis.
$p < 0.05$	p is statistically significant. Therefore, accept the alternative hypothesis and reject the null hypothesis.

Chi-Square Test

The chi-square test is used for testing hypotheses about observed distributions in various categories. In other words, a chi-square test compares the observed values in a dataset to the expected values that you would see if the null hypothesis were true. A chi-square test can be used to infer information such as:

▶ Whether two categorical variables are independent and have no relationship with one another. This is known as a *chi-square test of independence*.

▶ Whether one variable follows a given hypothesized distribution or not. This is known as a *chi-square goodness-of-fit test*.

Chi-square can be calculated using the following formula:

$$X_c^2 = \Sigma\, (Ob_i - E_i)^2 / E_i$$

where:

c denotes the degrees of freedom

E represents the expected value

Ob represents the observed value

A chi-square test provides the *p*-value, which indicates whether the results of the test are significant (as discussed in the previous section).

Let's consider an example. An organization is conducting research and trying to relate the different levels of education of people to whether those people work in IT or non-IT jobs. Table 10.6 shows the simple random sample the organization is working with.

TABLE 10.6 Sample Data on Education Level Related to IT vs. Non-IT Jobs

	No Bachelor's Degree	Bachelor's Degree	Master's Degree or Higher	Row Total
IT Job	30	80	45	155
Non-IT Job	50	55	15	120
Column Total	80	135	60	275

> **Note**
>
> The authors used the calculator available at https://www.socscistatistics.com/tests/chisquare2/default2.aspx for calculating chi-square in this example. This site provides multiple statistics calculators that you can leverage and walks you through the calculation process step by step. The authors assumed 2 degrees of freedom for this calculation.

The organization can use a chi-square test of independence to determine whether there is a statistically significant association between the two variables (education and working in IT jobs).

In this case, the chi-square (X^2) test gives the number 20.507268, with a *p*-value of 0.000035. Now, given that the *p*-value is less than 0.05, we know that result of the chi-square test is statistically significant. Thus, the alternative hypothesis is acceptable (and rejects the null hypothesis), and there is sufficient evidence to state that there is an association between education level and holding an IT job.

The graph in Figure 10.5 shows the chi-squared distribution graph for this example.

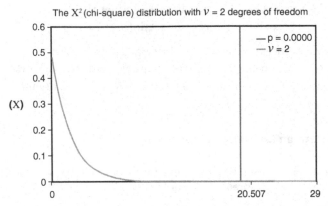

FIGURE 10.5 **Chi-squared Graph (Generated Using the Free Chi-square Calculator at https://www.di-mgt.com.au/chisquare-calculator.html)**

Hypothesis Testing

We began looking at hypothesis testing earlier in this section, when we looked at null and alternative hypotheses. *Hypothesis testing* is a method for testing a hypothesis or claim about a parameter value, based on data from a sample, that helps in drawing conclusions about a population. The first (tentative) assumption is known as the *null hypothesis*. Then, an *alternative hypothesis*, which is the opposite of the null hypothesis, is defined.

To put these hypotheses into context, let's consider an example. Say that an organization is performing an analysis of salaries of salespeople. It takes a sample of 100 salaries from a population of 10,000. The null hypothesis is that the mean salary of a salesperson is less than or equal to $85,000, and the alternative hypothesis is that the mean salary of a salesperson is more than $85,000.

The null hypothesis is usually represented as H_0, and the alternative hypothesis is usually represented as H_a. H_0 (the null hypothesis) is where things are happening as expected, and there is no difference from the expected outcome. H_a (the alternative hypothesis) is where things change from expected, and you have not just rejected H_0 but made a discovery.

Figure 10.6 gives an overview of the test statistic locations and their results.

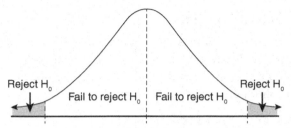

FIGURE 10.6 **Hypothesis Testing Overview**

In the context of our example of salesperson salaries, the sample mean (μ) is:

H_0: $\mu \le \$85,000$

H_a: $\mu > \$85,000$

There are various methods to perform hypothesis testing, such as by using Z-scores, t-tests, and p-values, as discussed earlier in this chapter.

Because hypothesis tests are based on sample information from a larger population, there is always a possibility of errors. To determine if the null hypothesis should be rejected, the hypothesis test should consider the level of significance for the test. The level of significance is represented as α and is commonly set as $\alpha = 0.05$, $\alpha = 0.01$, or $\alpha = 0.1$. When working with hypotheses, errors are broadly classified as two types:

▶ **Type I error:** A type I error occurs when the null hypothesis is incorrectly rejected when, in fact, it is true. This is also known as a *false positive*.

▶ **Type II error:** A type II error occurs when the null hypothesis is not rejected (fail to reject) when, in fact, it is false. This is also referred to as a *false negative*.

> **Note**
>
> Lower values of α make it difficult to reject the null hypothesis, which can lead to type II errors. Higher values of α make it convenient to reject the null hypothesis but can lead to type I errors.

Simple Linear Regression

Simple linear regression helps describe a relationship between two variables through a straight-line equation that closely models the relationship between these variables. This line, which is sometimes called the *line of best fit*, is plotted as a scatter graph between two continuous variables X and Y, where:

> X is regarded as the explanatory, or independent, variable
>
> Y is regarded as the response, or dependent, variable

Note

Simple linear regression is used to determine a trend by observing the relationship between X and Y variables.

For example, variable X could represent sales for a product Y (another variable), and as time passes, sales may go up or down, depending on how popular the product is (that is, the trend). Another example could be the speed (variable X) that the car would go and the miles (variable Y) per gallon (mpg) that the car owner expects. The mileage may vary depending on the speed of the vehicle and show a trend.

The formula to calculate simple linear regression is:

> $y = mx + b$

where:

> m is the slope
>
> x is the mean
>
> b is the intercept

Consider an example with the following sample values across the X and Y axes:

> $X = 100, 200, 300, 400, 500, 600$
>
> $Y = 200, 300, 400, 500, 600, 700$

In this case:

Mean X (MX) = (100+200+300+400+500+600) / 6 = 2100 / 6 = 350

Mean Y (MY) = (200+300+400+500+600+700)/6 = 2700 / 6 = 450

Sum of squares (SSq) = 175,000

Sum of products (Sp) = 175,000

The regression equation is:

$y = bX + a$

where:

b = Sp / SSq = 175,000 / 175,000 = 1

a = (MY) – b(MX) = 450 – (1 × 350) = 100

$y = 1x + 100$

Note

Authors have used the calculator available at https://www.socscistatistics.com/tests/regression/default.aspx for calculating simple linear regression.

The linear regression in this case can be represented as a scatter plot, with the values along the X and Y axes (see Figure 10.7).

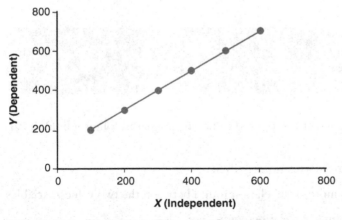

FIGURE 10.7   Simple Linear Regression Scatter Plot

Correlation

Correlation is a statistical measure that denotes the degree to which two values or variables are associated or related. It is used to describe a relationship without indicating cause and effect. Correlation coefficients are used to measure the (linear) relationship between two variables. When both values increase together, the linear correlation coefficient is positive. When one value increases and the other value decreases, the correlation coefficient is negative.

An example of correlation would be fuel prices and inflation in the cost of groceries. An increase in fuel prices impacts grocery prices as it costs more to transport food from farms to retail shops; therefore, as fuel prices rise, grocery prices also rise. This is a good example of positive correlation. On the other hand, as inflation rises, the general spending on items of want (not need) decreases. For example, with rising fuel prices, spending on cosmetics tends to decrease. This is a good example of negative correlation.

If X and Y are the two variables, the correlation coefficient can be represented by the following equation:

$$\rho = cov(X,Y) / \sigma X \sigma Y$$

where:

ρ is the linear correlation coefficient

σ is the standard deviation

cov is covariance, a measure of how the two variables change together

---

ExamAlert

Positive/negative correlation is a common topic of discussion in statistics, and the CompTIA Data+ exam may test you on these concepts.

The correlation coefficient is supposed to be linear (that is, follow a line). It can have several different values:

▶ $\rho = 1$ is a positive correlation coefficient

▶ $\rho = 0$ indicates null/no correlation found between the two values/variables

▶ $\rho = -1$ is a negative correlation coefficient

Figure 10.8 illustrates correlation relationships, including the (perfect) negative, null/no, and (perfect) positive correlations.

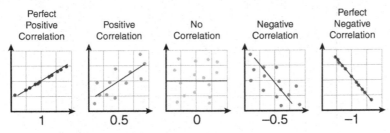

FIGURE 10.8   Correlation Relationship Overview

Cram Quiz

Answer these questions. If you cannot answer these questions correctly, consider reading this section again until you can.

1. The *t*-test is mainly adopted for which of the following?

   ○ **a.** Hypothesis testing

   ○ **b.** Differences of data

   ○ **c.** Mean value

   ○ **d.** Dispersion

2. When working with hypotheses, errors are broadly classified as _____.

   ○ **a.** true positives

   ○ **b.** false positives

   ○ **c.** false negatives

   ○ **d.** false positives and false negatives

3. $p < 0.05$ implies that p is _____.

   ○ **a.** not statistically significant, and the null hypothesis should therefore be rejected

   ○ **b.** not statistically significant, and the null hypothesis should therefore be rejected and the alternative hypothesis accepted

    ○ **c.** statistically and highly significant, and the null hypothesis should there-
fore be rejected and the alternative hypothesis accepted

    ○ **d.** statistically significant and the alternative hypothesis should therefore
be accepted and the null hypothesis rejected

4. What does the following graph represent?

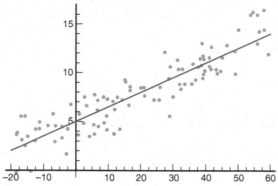

    ○ **a.** A model for a simple linear regression test

    ○ **b.** A model for a *p*-test

    ○ **c.** A model for a *t*-test

    ○ **d.** A model for a frequency distribution

5. The square of the standard deviation is also known as what?

    ○ **a.** Variance

    ○ **b.** Dispersion

    ○ **c.** Variable

    ○ **d.** Delta

Cram Quiz Answers

1. **Answer: a. Hypothesis testing.** *t*-tests are mainly used for hypothesis testing.

2. **Answer: d. False positives and false negatives.** When working with hypotheses, errors are broadly classified as two types: type I (false positive) and type II (false negative).

3. **Answer: d. statistically significant and the alternative hypothesis should therefore be accepted and the null hypothesis rejected.** Refer to the following table for the *p*-values.

Interpretations of p-values

p-value	Interpretations
$p < 0.01$	p is statistically and highly significant. Therefore, reject the null hypothesis and accept the alternative hypothesis.
$p > 0.05$	p is not statistically significant. Therefore, reject the null hypothesis.
$p < 0.05$	p is statistically significant. Therefore, accept the alternative hypothesis and reject the null hypothesis.

4. **Answer: a. A model for a simple linear regression test.** This graph shows a sample model for a simple linear regression test.

5. **Answer: a. Variance.** The square of the standard deviation is known as the variance, and it is also a dispersion measure. It can be measured from the following formula for standard deviation and calculating the square of σ i.e.

$$\sigma = \sqrt{\frac{\Sigma|x-\mu|^2}{N}}$$

What Next?

If you want more practice on this chapter's exam objectives before you move on, remember that you can access all of the Cram Quiz questions on the Pearson Test Prep software online. You can also create a custom exam by objective with the Online Practice Test. Note any objective you struggle with and go to that objective's material in this chapter.

CHAPTER 11

Exploring Data Analysis and Key Analysis Techniques

> **This chapter covers Objective 3.3 (Summarize types of analysis and key analysis techniques) of the CompTIA Data+ exam and includes the following topics:**
>
> ▶ Process to determine type of analysis
>
> ▶ Type of analysis
>
> For more information on the official CompTIA Data+ exam topics, see the Introduction.

This chapter covers topics related to data analysis techniques. It is important to explore the processes used to determine the appropriate type of analysis. This chapter also focuses on reviewing and refining business questions, determining data needs and sources to perform analysis, and scoping/gap analysis. It covers the key aspects of types of analysis, including trend analysis (comparing data over time), performance analysis (tracking measurements against defined goals), exploratory data analysis (basic projections for achieving goals), use of descriptive statistics in determining observations, and link analysis (connections of pathway or data points).

Process to Determine Type of Analysis

CramSaver

If you can correctly answer these questions before going through this section, save time by skimming the Exam Alerts in this section and then completing the Cram Quiz at the end of the section.

1. Data analysis tools enable data analysts to _____.

   a. identify patterns in data

   b. understand the performance of an organization

   c. explore the data

   d. All of these answers are correct.

2. What is the main step before data collection?

   a. Preparation

   b. Analysis

   c. Gathering

   d. Cleansing

3. What are the two types of data collection sources? (Choose two.)

   a. Middle data sources

   b. Generic data sources

   c. Internal data sources

   d. External data sources

4. Why do organizations use gap analysis?

   a. To bridge gaps

   b. To clean data

   c. To identify needs

   d. For visualization and representation

Answers

1. **Answer: d. All of these answers are correct.** Data analysis tools enable analysts to identify patterns in data, understand the performance of an organization, and explore data.

2. **Answer: a. Preparation.** Before collecting data, the main step/phase is to prepare the data from which you can derive insights.

3. **Answer: c. Internal data sources, d. External data sources.** Data collection sources can be classified as internal or external as well as primary or secondary.

4. **Answer: a. To bridge gaps.** Gap analysis is used to bridge gaps between the current or present state and the future or desired state.

Data analysis plays an important role in running a successful business. When data is adopted efficiently, it helps an organization understand its previous performance and make good decisions for future needs. Analysis of data is a process of transforming, cleaning, and modeling data in order to discover the information needed to make better decisions related to the business.

For example, when you want to make a decision in your daily life, you would probably base your decision on what occurred during a past time. You would analyze your past decisions and the outcomes of those decisions, and based on that information, you would make a decision now and in future, expecting a favorable outcome. For example, when buying a loaf of bread, if your experience with a brand has been positive, you would likely prefer that brand over other brands. Likewise, data analysts perform data analysis to help in making business decisions that lead to growth and expansion of the business through acquiring more customers or expanding the service/product footprint.

Determining Data Needs

It is important to understand the basics of data analysis and why an organization would invest in the process of analyzing data. The data analysis process involves collecting data by using an appropriate tool or an application that permits exploration of the data as well as possibly identifying trends or patterns in the data. With the help of such information, conscious decisions can be made.

Data analysis involves the following phases or steps:

1. **Requirements gathering for data:** It is a good idea to consider the need to perform data analysis and the outcomes that may be achieved by analyzing the data collected. That is, it is a good idea to identify the reason for performing data analysis. During the requirements gathering phase,

also known as the preparation phase, you need to decide what to examine, the data structure, and the volume of data. In addition, it is important to understand what/why you are examining and what evaluation methodologies you expect to leverage to perform your analysis.

2. **Collection of data:** Once you have an understanding of what you need to evaluate and what the outcomes/results will be, the next phase is data collection. As data is collected, it needs to be organized or processed for analysis. Because data might be collected from multiple sources, it is a good practice to keep a log of data sources and collection dates/times.

3. **Cleansing of data:** Any kind of data gathered for analysis purposes has to be cleaned so there is minimal noise, redundancy, and duplication in the data and so pertinent information can be extracted as a result of analysis. Data gathered may include white spaces, duplicate records, and errors. Data should ideally be error free and cleansed. The cleansing phase is completed prior to the analysis phase because, after cleansing the data, the results of analysis will be closer to the expected results.

> **Note**
>
> Noise in the context of data refers to unwanted data.

4. **Analysis of data:** After data is gathered, processed, and cleansed, it is ready for analysis. As you analyze/manipulate data, you can identify whether you have all the data required for successful analysis and outcomes or whether you need to gather more data for effective decision making. At this stage, the tools and software for data analysis help you interpret, understand, and make conclusions based on well-defined needs.

5. **Interpretation of data:** After data is analyzed, results have to be interpreted. Data interpretation involves assigning meaning to data such that it can be leveraged for driving/discussing outcomes. Interpretation can be done leveraging the qualitative or quantitative methods.

6. **Visualization of data:** It is common to leverage visualizations to show the analysis and conclusions in the form of graphs and charts. Illustrating data graphically helps make it easy to understand and process. Visualizations may be used for discovering unknown trends and facts. By

comparing datasets and relationships, you can identify a way to discover meaningful outcomes. The most common way to visualize data is via reports and dashboards. Reports can be in simple English or may include charts or tables for brevity.

Review/Refine Business Questions

In order to transform data into business insights and drive decisions, it is important to prepare and follow a set of questions that provides a direction for the analysis performed. These questions will form the basis from which you would acquire answers prior to starting the process of data gathering. These questions can be based on an organization's goals, strategy, budget, addressable market, and target clientele. Some of the questions to be reviewed are as follows:

▶ What is the problem we are trying to solve or outcome we are trying to achieve?

▶ Who is the sponsor for this activity?

▶ What are the resources (people, time, budget) that we should think about?

▶ What are the different sources from which pertinent data can be collected?

▶ How can we assure quality of data?

▶ Which techniques can possibly be applied for data analysis?

▶ What end users or stakeholders might benefit from the analysis?

▶ What type of visualizations might help articulate the findings effectively?

▶ What type of software would help with collection, analysis, and visualization?

▶ Are there other things we should consider to ensure that the outcomes are in line with the business goals?

▶ What are the standard/key performance indicators that may define success criteria?

Data Collection Sources

At the heart of data analysis is data collection. Data may be well organized (for example, in SQL tables) or unorganized (for example, in figures or files), and it may consist of facts.

Broadly, there are two types of data: statistical and nonstatistical data. Statistical sources include official surveys and the census. Nonstatistical sources include administrative records, particularly in the private sector. Additional data sources are categorized on the basis of the methods for collection:

▶ Primary or secondary

▶ Internal or external sources

Figure 11.1 illustrates sources for collection of data, which include the following:

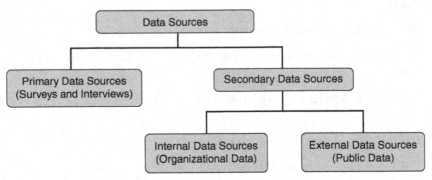

FIGURE 11.1   **Data Collection Sources**

▶ **Primary data sources:** Data collected firsthand from a researcher or surveyor is known as *primary data*. This kind of data is gathered for the first time and may be from internal or external sources.

▶ **Secondary data sources:** Data that was previously gathered, processed, published, or analyzed is known as *secondary data*. This data may be gathered from internal or external sources by investigators, researchers, or surveyors for carrying out statistical analysis and may be referred to as *secondhand data*.

▶ **Internal data sources:** *Internal data sources*, as the name suggests, are internal to an organization (for example, archives, records, and other sources within the organization). The organization (in most cases) has direct control over these data sources.

▶ **External data sources:** *External data sources* are outside the organization, sometimes also referred to as public sources (for example, census data). The organization may not have direct control over or access to them.

Gap Analysis

A gap analysis is typically performed to compare the current state to a future state, and an action plan is created to get from the current state to the desired state. Organizations perform gap analysis to enhance their competence and competitive advantage in terms of their products, services, or processes. Gap analysis enables business leaders to make conscious decisions to optimize the ways in which money, human, and time resources are spent.

> **Note**
>
> Gap analysis is also known as need analysis or need-gap analysis.

Gap analysis yields insights into the following aspects:

▶ Current/present state

▶ Desired/future state

▶ What needs to be done (action plan) to bridge the gap

These aspects can be leveraged to drive performance improvements. Figure 11.2 illustrates the basics of gap analysis.

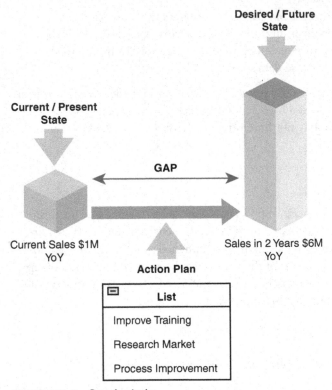

FIGURE 11.2 Gap Analysis

As Figure 11.2 illustrates, the gap separates the present or current condition/ state from the desired or future condition/state. In this example, an organization wishes to bridge the gap between the current state of $1 million in sales year on year (YoY) and the desired state of $6 million in sales YoY by the end of the next 2 years.

Gap analysis can assist in identifying specific areas for enhancement, whether related to optimization of the workforce, efficiency, strategy, or performance.

The following steps are involved in gap analysis:

1. Understand or determine the current or present state.

2. Determine the future or desired state.

3. Understand the gap between the current/present state and the future/ desired state.

4. Implement a plan of action or required steps (also known as *remedies*) to reduce or eliminate the gap and improve performance, productivity, efficiency, and so on.

Several types of gaps exist, and how they are analyzed differs:

▶ **Strategy or performance gap:** This type of gap is analyzed in terms of actual performance vs. expected performance.

▶ **Market or product gap:** This type of gap is analyzed in terms of actual sales vs. budgeted sales for a product or service. It may also be analyzed from a competitive perspective to improve a product/service to compete and increase its market share.

▶ **Manpower gap:** This type of gap is analyzed based on the actual number of work hours vs. a projected number of work hours.

▶ **Profit gap:** This type of gap is analyzed in terms of actual profit vs. target profit.

The gap analysis involves the following steps:

1. Determine what data to analyze.

2. Identify the methods to use to assess the present state.

3. Identify the future state and create an action plan to move from the current state to the future state.

4. Record the attributes that may influence the success or failure from a gap perspective.

Let's consider an example of improving sales figures for a product that your organization wishes to release a new version of. In this scenario, you would need to use gap analysis and develop a plan of action (or action plan).

The current state is the number of products being sold, and the data sources that can be taken into consideration to carry out gap analysis are the historical and current sales figures as well as customer feedback. This information acts as a baseline for the future state or the number of products your organization would like to sell. Based on current sales numbers, you can get an idea of the gap between what is currently being done (for example, sales training, product enhancements, market demand) and create a plan to attain the future-state sales numbers. You should document this plan and ensure that all attributes that influence sales (such as training, market demand, and product features) are communicated effectively within the organization.

Cram Quiz

Answer these questions. If you cannot answer these questions correctly, consider reading this section again until you can.

1. Gap analysis acts as a(n) _____ for performance analysis.

   ○ **a.** guide

   ○ **b.** tool

   ○ **c.** element

   ○ **d.** blueprint

2. Gap analysis can be carried out in the context of which of the following? (Choose all that apply.)

   ○ **a.** Strategy or performance gap

   ○ **b.** Market or product gap

   ○ **c.** Profit gap

   ○ **d.** Time gap

3. Which of the following are valid business questions related to data analysis?

   ○ **a.** What are the different sources from which pertinent data can be collected?

   ○ **b.** How can I assure quality of data?

   ○ **c.** Which techniques can possibly be applied for data analysis?

   ○ **d.** All of these answers are correct.

Cram Quiz Answers

1. **Answer: b. tool.** Gap analysis is a tool for enhancing performance and decisions in a future state.

2. **Answer: a. Strategy or performance gap, b. Market or product gap, c. Profit gap.** Time gap is not a valid measure for which gap analysis may be leveraged.

3. **Answer: d. All of these answers are correct.** All of these are valid business questions related to data analysis.

Types of Analysis

If you can correctly answer these questions before going through this section, save time by skimming the Exam Alerts in this section and then completing the Cram Quiz at the end of the section.

1. What is the basic outcome expected from data analysis?

   a. Transformation of data

   b. Representation of data

   c. Illustration of data

   d. Strategic decisions

2. Which of the following leverages information gathered for analysis from different diverse periods?

   a. Text analysis

   b. Descriptive analysis

   c. Trend analysis

   d. Prescriptive analysis

3. What type of analysis is also known as text mining?

   a. Prescriptive analysis

   b. Descriptive analysis

   c. Insight analysis

   d. Text analysis

Answers

1. **Answer: a. Transformation of data.** Data analysis enables analysts to transform raw information into intelligible data.

2. **Answer: c. Trend analysis.** With the help of trend analysis, information can be gathered from different diverse periods.

3. **Answer: d. Text analysis.** Text analysis is also known as text mining. The core purpose of text analysis is to enable extraction and examination of data.

A number of analysis techniques can be leveraged—including text analysis, statistical analysis, predictive analysis, diagnostic analysis, and prescriptive analysis—and the ones chosen depend on the business needs.

ExamAlert

CompTIA Data+ exam will focus on different analysis techniques.

This list gives you a better understanding of these techniques so that you can better learn the intricacies of trend analysis, performance analysis, and exploratory analysis:

▶ **Text analysis:** Text analysis, also known as *text mining*, involves identifying patterns in large sets of data with the help of data mining tools. The core purposes of text analysis are to enable extraction and examination of data as well as drive data interpretation and patterns. It is primarily adopted for transforming raw data into business-pertinent information.

▶ **Statistical analysis:** Statistical analysis offers insights into the trends and patterns in the data by leveraging existing information and by examining data samples or datasets. It encompasses interpretation, analysis, collection, data modeling, and presentation. Statistical analysis is categorized into two types: inferential analysis and descriptive analysis. These methods are covered in Chapter 10, "Understanding Descriptive and Inferential Statistical Methods."

▶ **Diagnostic analysis:** This type of analysis explains why something happened by determining the root causes, based on insights identified in statistical analysis. Diagnostic analysis is helpful for identifying behavioral patterns. For example, if a new issue is noticed in the business process, you can observe and use diagnostic analysis to find answers to problems with similar patterns. For example, an organization can leverage diagnostic analysis to understand why its marketing campaign was not as effective as expected.

▶ **Predictive analysis:** This type of analysis explores what will happen, based on available information from the past. For example, predictive analysis can be used to forecast future results on the basis of past or current data. A very common example of predictive analysis is the use of existing information to forecast weather patterns up to a month in advance. These analyses provide the best possible approximations, given data on atmospheric pressure, sun, rain, and other factors, and more often than not, the weather forecast on your smartphone is very close to the weather you actually experience.

▶ **Prescriptive analysis:** Prescriptive analysis describes how something will happen and integrates perceptions from prior analysis to determine which actions can be taken for a current decision or problem. Most organizations adopt prescriptive analysis for analyzing data based on current problems and in certain circumstances to make decisions in the future. For example, an organization might leverage past data and prescribe the way its platform should be used by customers to drive better profits.

Trend Analysis

Trend analysis is the process of gathering information from diverse periods (via time series data analysis) to drive insights about trends or patterns. Trend analysis is based on comparisons of data over specific time periods in order to spot patterns or trends.

Note

Time series analysis, or trend analysis, is typically plotted with information on the *X*-axis, or horizontal line, for review.

In a business context, trend analysis can be leveraged for a number of purposes:

▶ **Facilitating comparison:** Based on market trend data, analysts can compare two or more organizations in terms of their sales performance.

▶ **Investment analysis:** Analysts can conduct a comparative study of the financial performance of an organization over a period of time.

▶ **Cost and revenue analysis:** Analysts can measure the profitability of an organization over a period of time.

Figure 11.3 gives an overview of trend analysis in which the analyst studies trends of sales of a product over different periods to determine future demand.

Trend analysis is used across industries, typically to ensure that an organization stays ahead of competition by understanding consumer buying and spending trends as well as trends related to products and features.

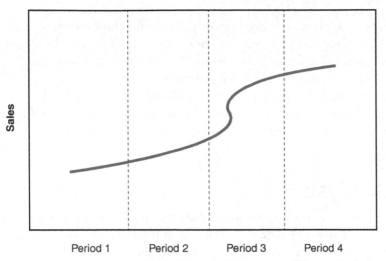

FIGURE 11.3   **Trend Analysis for Sales of a Product over Different Periods**

Comparison of Data over Time

Often organizations have to compare data over different time periods to understand what happened, what is happening, and what may happen. There are four basic factors involved in analyzing data that can assist in transforming raw numbers into information:

▶ **Relationship:** Relationship indicates the connection or correlation of two or more variables and their properties. It shows how the data does or does not influence other variables, negatively or positively. For example, with increasing age in a young human being, height also increases. Age and height are two variables that are related.

Figure 11.4 gives an overview of the relationship factor.

Charts and graphs typically adopted for illustrating relationship include:

▶ Table charts

▶ Line charts

▶ Bubble charts

▶ Scatter plots

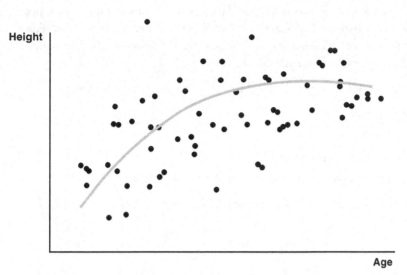

FIGURE 11.4 **Data Relationship Between Height and Age**

► **Composition:** Composition refers to how one or more variables can be integrated to offer better insights. It is used for showing how a total value can be categorized into parts or focus on the importance of every part within the total value. For example, with food items, the amounts of sugars, grains, and other elements constitute the composition.

Composition can be depicted by using the following:

► Waterfall charts

► Stacked area charts

► Donut or pie charts

► Columns or stacked bar charts

Figure 11.5 illustrates composition of data.

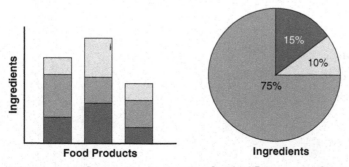

FIGURE 11.5 **Composition Leveraging Stacked Bars and Pie Charts**

▶ **Comparison:** Comparison is used for evaluating and comparing values between two or more variables or data points. Comparison makes it possible to identify the highest and lowest values in a chart. For example, a comparison of revenue for one or more products across different countries gives insights into sales performance.

The types of charts/graphs used to compare data points include:

▶ Bar charts

▶ Column charts

▶ Timeline or line charts

Figure 11.6 provides an overview of data comparison:

▶ The annual salaries of scientists and of engineers using a bar chart

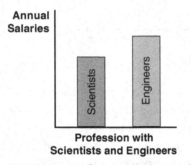

FIGURE 11.6   Comparison Leveraging Bar Charts

▶ **Distribution:** Distribution integrates the functionality and merits of both composition and comparison. It assists in viewing the complete spectrum of a variable or data point and seeing related or unrelated data points. With the help of distribution, you can observe shapes, patterns, averages, correlations, outliers, and clusters.

Charts/graphs adopted for distribution include:

▶ Map charts

▶ Data tables

▶ Area and line charts

▶ Bar and column histogram charts

▶ Scatter plots

Distribution is illustrated in Figure 11.7, using data about the heights of students in a class as a histogram.

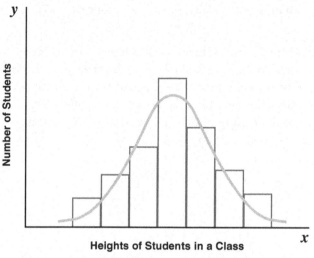

FIGURE 11.7   **Distribution Illustration Using a Histogram**

Performance Analysis

Performance analysis involves studying or comparing the performance of a particular activity or process in order to identify strengths and weaknesses. Performance analysis from a human resources point of view can assist in reviewing the contribution of employees toward a given assignment. It could be used to analyze business performance or sports performance, for example. In either case, an individual's performance is analyzed, and their strengths and weaknesses are noted to improve performance (in terms of sales or race times) in the near or far future.

Performance analysis can be used to improve profitability, increase employee engagement by ensuring that employees' efforts are valued and rewarded, and set a baseline to drive performance measurements across organizations.

Tracking Measurements Against Defined Goals

Goals measure how we meet the target objectives pertinent to activities we set out to do. In the context of data analysis and measuring success, goals are the main element of a digital analytics plan. But how are goals related to performance? Well, they might not be directly related; however, in order to measure performance, you need to track relevant metrics, or key performance indicators (KPIs). KPIs are tangible and measurable values and show progress toward goals.

Now let's put all these pieces together. Say, for example, that an organization wants to increase its sales as well as increase the revenue per employee. In this case, the right KPIs need to be selected; these KPIs need to be relevant to the organization and must be measurable and provide outcomes to achieve the stated goals. Then the goals of increasing sales and revenue should be measured and tracked against these KPIs. The KPIs could be:

▶ Operating margin

▶ Net profit margin

▶ Total cost of operations

> **Note**
>
> Setting KPIs and goals involves setting up milestones, timelines, and more, but these topics are beyond the scope of the CompTIA Data+ exam.

Basic Projections to Achieve Goals

Projections to achieve goals are made in order to observe what the results will be if the present state of a program proceeds as usual and no modifications are made to the program. There are a few ways of making projections, including:

▶ Looking at a trend line and expanding it forward

▶ Adjusting for a number of internally and externally influenced factors

Exploratory Data Analysis

Data scientists and statisticians use exploratory data analysis for analyzing and investigating sets of data and summarizing their major characteristics. In the process, they leverage various methods of data visualization. In a nutshell, this type of data analysis allows data scientists and statisticians to uncover patterns as well as insights, often with the aid of visual methods. It also assists in testing a hypothesis, spotting anomalies, and checking assumptions. Some of the key aspects of exploratory analysis can be categorized based on the outcomes expected, such as:

▶ **Hypothesis:** What patterns are emerging, and how can I explain them?

▶ **Graphs and charts:** What can I see here?

▶ **Grouping (or ungrouping) data:** How can the data be sliced and diced as well as clustered?

▶ **Model building:** What patterns/trends/shapes can be observed, and why?

Use of Descriptive Statistics to Determine Observations

Descriptive statistics involves describing the characteristics of a dataset or sample data and often leverages graphical methods to illustrate data characteristics. Descriptive statistics is usually used for the following purposes:

▶ To offer characteristics of the variables in a dataset

▶ To highlight the potential relationships between two or more variables

The most common measures of descriptive statistics are central tendency, dispersion, and frequency, which are discussed in Chapter 10. Additional methods are shown in Figure 11.8.

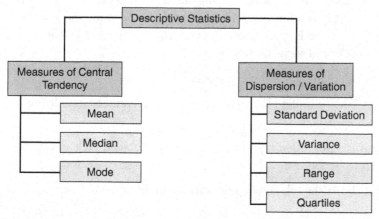

FIGURE 11.8 **Descriptive Statistics Methods**

Descriptive analysis methods can be described or depicted using:

▶ **Measures of position:** A measure of position makes it possible to determine the position of a particular data value within a given dataset. Common measures include standard scores, quartiles, and percentiles.

▶ **Contingency tables:** These tables describe relationships between two or more categorical values in a tabular matrix arrangement.

▶ **Scatter plots:** Also known as scatter charts, scatter plots illustrate relationships between two values across X- and Y-axis plots.

▶ **Histograms:** A histogram is used to graphically illustrate the distribution of numeric values as a series of bars.

▶ **Sociograms:** A sociogram is a graphic representation for finding relationships within a group of people.

Advantages of adopting descriptive statistics are as follows:

▶ It provides a high level of neutrality and objectivity.

▶ It provides a wide representation of an event leveraging the variable characteristics.

Link Analysis

Link analysis is a data mining mechanism that can help structure data as a network of unified nodes and links for identifying and analyzing connections and relationships. Link analysis allows analysts to identify connections and association patterns within the nodes and links of a network. Examples of link analysis are semantic networks and social networks.

Link analysis considers the following key aspects:

▶ **Network:** This is a unified body consisting of interconnected nodes and links.

▶ **Node:** This is a point that represents a real-world object, such as a person or place.

▶ **Link:** This shows the relationship or connection between nodes.

> **Note**
>
> Each node and link may have properties that further define the relationship.

For example, a crime investigator would use clues and evidence to set up a network of suspects and link them to the victim via their relationships, as shown in Figure 11.9. As you can see, for each object/node, there is additional information.

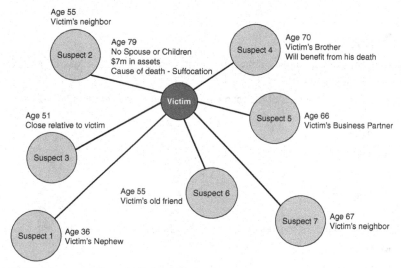

FIGURE 11.9   **A Sample Crime Link Analysis**

Link analysis can be useful for:

▶ Analytical applications that leverage network graphs for drawing conclusions

▶ Assessing the influence of individuals in a social network

▶ Process or path optimization (such as an airline carrier optimizing flight routes for better fuel efficiency)

Connection of Data Points or Pathway

When conducting link analysis, illustrating data with a visual (such as a network graph) requires unraveling the data into individual displays or data points. For example, data on media influencers can be presented in graphs that become unintelligible displays of lines and numbers showing followers and subscribers. It is best to create visualizations that easily represent the association of data points that establish correct associations/relationships and make the network graph usable. Moreover, the pathways created to each node can be meaningful if there's context around why a data point was chosen to create a relationship to a node.

Essentially, the main benefits of a visualization using link analysis data points and pathways are helping determine who the key contacts are, how often they are in contact and for how long, and their long- or short-term relationships.

Cram Quiz

Answer these questions. If you cannot answer these questions correctly, consider reading this section again until you can.

1. Link analysis considers which of the following key aspects or elements? (Choose three.)

   - a. Pattern
   - b. Node
   - c. Link
   - d. Network

2. Which of the following are measures of central tendency? (Choose all that apply.)

   - a. Mean
   - b. Median
   - c. Mode
   - d. Quartile
   - e. Range

3. An organization is trying to determine the best path for deliveries in order to conserve time and fuel. Which type of analysis would be recommended?

   - a. Null hypothesis
   - b. Alternative hypothesis
   - c. Descriptive analysis
   - d. Link analysis

4. In link analysis, nodes and links may have additional_____.
   ○ **a.** properties
   ○ **b.** samples
   ○ **c.** models
   ○ **d.** frequencies

5. Which is the best factor to adopt for analyzing data?
   ○ **a.** Relationship
   ○ **b.** Comparison
   ○ **c.** Distribution
   ○ **d.** Composition

6. Descriptive analysis ensures which of the following?
   ○ **a.** A high level of neutrality and objectivity
   ○ **b.** A wide representation of an event
   ○ **c.** A good method for collecting data
   ○ **d.** All of these answers are correct.

Cram Quiz Answers

1. **Answer: b. Node, c. Link, d. Network.** A network, nodes, and links are the essential elements of link analysis.

2. **Answer: a. Mean, b. Median, c. Mode, d. Quartiles.** All these are measures of central tendency.

3. **Answer: d. Link analysis.** Link analysis can be useful in process or path optimization, such as an airline carrier optimizing flight routes for better fuel efficiency.

4. **Answer: a. properties.** Each node and link may have properties that further define the relationship.

5. **Answer: b. Comparison.** Comparison is the best factor to adopt in representing analyzed data.

6. **Answer: d. All of these answers are correct.** Descriptive analysis provides a high level of neutrality and objectivity and gives a wide representation of an event with the variable characteristics.

What Next?

If you want more practice on this chapter's exam objective before you move on, remember that you can access all of the Cram Quiz questions on the Pearson Test Prep software online. You can also create a custom exam by objective with the Online Practice Test. Note any objective you struggle with and go to that objective's material in this chapter.

CHAPTER 12

Approaching Data Visualization

This chapter covers Objective 4.1 (Given a scenario, translate business requirements to form a report) of the CompTIA Data+ exam and includes the following topics:

► Data content

► Filtering

► Views

► Date range

► Frequency

► Audience to report

For more information on the official CompTIA Data+ exam topics, see the Introduction.

This chapter explores business reports and looks at report data content, filtering content according to the audience or persona, report views, the data range for a report, frequency of report generation/delivery, and the audiences for different reports.

Business Reports

CramSaver

If you can correctly answer these questions before going through this section, save time by skimming the Exam Alerts in this section and then completing the Cram Quiz at the end of the section.

1. Reports and dashboards are usually generated based on data from which of the following?

   a. Various data sources

   b. Other reports

   c. One data source

   d. An organization's website feed

2. A report view usually leverages which of the following?

   a. Full data tables

   b. A subset of the data

   c. Methods of analysis

   d. Manual inputs

3. Which of the following can be useful in a report to show only the data of interest?

   a. Categories

   b. One-page summary

   c. Filter

   d. Overview

4. Which of these are the categories of report audiences? (Choose all that apply.)

   a. Technical

   b. Primary

   c. Secondary

   d. Tertiary

   e. Nontechnical

Answers

1. **Answer: a. Various data sources.** The data in a report may be from various sources of information and typically is used for strategic decision-making, operational, or information purposes.

2. **Answer: b. A subset of the data.** A view may contain only a subset of the data that is relevant to the audience. Different views allow the stakeholders to understand the data and derive conclusions faster.

3. **Answer: c. Filters.** Filters in a report can be very useful for showing only the data of interest and filtering out the irrelevant information.

4. **Answer: b. Primary, c. Secondary, d. Tertiary.** You can possibly categorize an audience in three major categories: primary, secondary, and tertiary.

In the past few years, business stakeholder insights have been driven primarily by PowerPoint presentations or PDF files. These were helpful as the right metrics could be visualized in very sophisticated PowerPoint presentations and later shared as PDF files. As data today is increasingly growing in volume, static reporting, such as presenting metrics in a PowerPoint, is no longer the best option as the stakeholders want to get the latest and greatest insights into business activities—sales, marketing, IT, supply chain, and more.

Business reports and dashboards can visualize data in real time, and specific metrics can be visualized to match the interest of the audience. The high-level objectives of data visualization are as follows:

▶ Data visualization makes it possible to show meaningful insights in a graphical way.

▶ Data visualization is an effective tool for communicating relevant, measurable information across an organization.

▶ Visualizations can be modified based on the business requirements (such as using line charts instead of bar charts).

Data visualization involves design, development, and application of information in a graphical manner. Data visualization makes it simpler to understand business events, trends, patterns, and insights into key decisions. Visualizations in reports and dashboards move away from the noise generated by gigabytes of data and make it simple to understand information using charts, graphs, and pictures.

Chapter 13, "Exploring the Different Types of Reports and Dashboards," as well as Chapter 14, "Data-Driven Decision Making: Leveraging Charts, Graphs, and Reports," build on this chapter and further explore how reports and dashboards ensure that stakeholders are getting the insights they want in an easy-to-consume and intuitive manner.

> **Note**
>
> This chapter is contextualized to an organization driving business insights based on sales reporting and dashboards. All the examples in this chapter refer to a sales context.

Report Content

A business report can be broadly categorized as a formal report or an informal report, depending on the content as well as the audience. A formal report contains far more detail on findings and observations than an informal report, which might just summarize the findings for an at-a-glance read.

Let's consider an example of a formal report. Say that you have a quarterly sales forecast report that looks at the performance of the sales team and provides insights into how the products or solutions are doing in the market. Figure 12.1 gives insights about this report.

> **Note**
>
> The report shown in Figure 12.1 is available at https://public.tableau.com/app/profile/tableau.for.sales.analytics/viz/SalesForecastDashboard_2/Quarterly ForecastDashboard.

As you can see, this dashboard has various textual and graphical sections that give insights about:

▶ The current state of the business

▶ Business forecasts based on prior results

▶ The existing transactional or nontransactional pipeline

▶ Deals that will grow in size

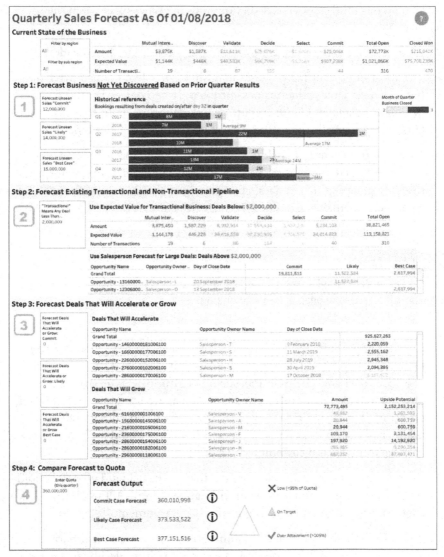

FIGURE 12.1   Quarterly Sales Forecast Formal Report

A report can be broadly categorized as an analytical report or an informational report, based on the content. An analytical report offers analysis on a topic and may also offer recommendations. An informational report provides factual information.

Figure 12.1 shows an analytical report for a sales leader that acts as an analytical tool displaying past, present, and future data to efficiently track and optimize the sales performance of the organization. An example of an informational report would be an IT asset report that outlines the types of assets in the inventory.

For the content of a report, the following key aspects should be considered:

▶ The most important factors are the business problem being solved and the audience. Unless the business problem is well defined and the type of audience (such as CXO, executives, IT managers, or engineers) is well known, the report is not going to be useful to any stakeholders.

▶ Next, it's important to consider the sources of data that will be leveraged to generate the report. Some sources might be flat files, enterprise resource planning (ERP) data, customer relationship management (CRM) data, social media data, and marketing campaigns.

> **Note**
>
> The data in a report could be from various sources and would be used for strategic decision-making, operational, or information purposes.

▶ Another important aspect of reports is to visualize the right key performance indicators (KPIs). Choosing KPIs that align well with specific organizational goals helps in measuring organizational progress accurately, and it also helps in spotting trends that are useful for streamlining processes. For example, sales reports would focus on sales volume and number of new sales as KPIs, whereas IT reports would focus on number of cases resolved and customer satisfaction as KPIs.

▶ Report contents should be actionable; that is, they should give stakeholders greater insights and lead them to clear next steps. Actionable reports enable a progressive data-driven business environment.

▶ A good report should have a clear and crisp story with a clear narrative for stakeholders to drive decision making. Creating a dashboard makes more sense than generating a static report as all the pertinent information is presented on a single screen. Moreover, a dashboard allows stakeholders to interact with graphs and charts. (Chapter 13 provides more information about dashboards.)

> **Note**
>
> There's much more to a report than just its content. It is important to consider colors, fonts, styles, placement of graphs, and other factors that are discussed in Chapter 13.

Filters

The word *filter* typically implies something that isolates unwanted information (or noise) from desired information. This also applies to filters in a report (or dashboard). Filters in a report can be very useful for showing only the data of interest and filtering out the irrelevant information. They can be used to ensure that stakeholders are looking at data that's relevant to them rather than looking at things that might be irrelevant and distracting.

> **Note**
>
> Remember that reports and dashboards are useful only when the audience derives value—that is, facts, analytics, next steps, and recommendations—from them.

Let's consider an example. Figure 12.2 shows a sales pipeline dashboard that includes the various sales stages, deal sizes, and representative progress, among other data. Let's focus on the filters available in the top right and the stage data per the representative.

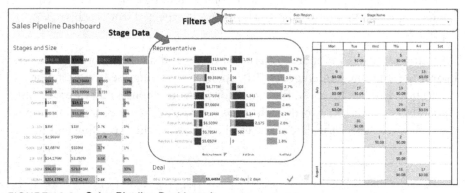

FIGURE 12.2   **Sales Pipeline Dashboard**

Note

The sales dashboard example shown in Figure 12.2 was taken from https://public.tableau.com/app/profile/tableau.for.sales.analytics/viz/SalesPipeline Dashbaord/PipelineDash.

Given that the sales manager is only keen to look at the deal data by representative, where the stage is either select or commit, let's choose those filters. After selecting these filters, the dashboard looks as shown in Figure 12.3.

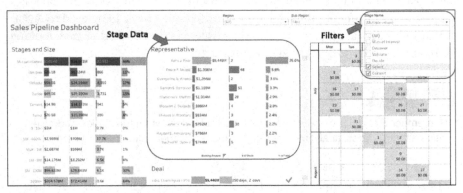

FIGURE 12.3   Sales Pipeline Dashboard: Filters and Focus Insights

As you can see, the filters enable the sales manager to focus only on the data of interest. This helps the manager focus on key findings and on what's happening right now as well as what performance is expected from each sales representative.

The filters available in reports or dashboards depend on the reporting or dashboarding (or business intelligence [BI]) applications being used. Most applications allow basic or advanced filtering—for example, choosing all filters or just some filters or using keywords such as *contains*, *starts with*, or *is*. It is common to use date filters where the date range can be defined as the preceding and next dates within which values can be filtered. For example, in Salesforce reports, you can set relative date values by using the following filters:

Date equal to THIS YEAR

Date less or equal to TODAY

In addition, range filters can be used to filter attached values, such as to filter deals between a value of $10,000 and a value of $50,000.

Views

When you're out in nature, traveling places with family, views are what you're looking for. However, your definition of a view that's beautiful might differ from your family members' definitions, depending on their interest. Everyone may have a unique perspective on what they want to see and explore. This is similar to how different people feel about views in reports.

> ## ExamAlert
> Views are an important topic and CompTIA Data+ may have questions on views.

In the context of a report or a dashboard, a *view* is something that you create to show data aspects pertinent to a topic of interest that you or your audience are keen to explore. A database view is a stored query that can help pull in data from tables as well as other views. A database view represents part of the database but does not actually store any data.

Views can be helpful in the following ways:

▶ A view can contain only a subset of the data that is of relevance to the audience to prevent users from having them mine through tons of information. Different views allow stakeholders to understand the data and derive conclusions faster. For example, a sales manager view may contain more high-level information than a sales person view that contains detailed information.

▶ Views are helpful for abstracting information that it is not to be shared. For example, a sales manager might not want to distribute all information to everyone and can create views that limit access to the information for different teams. You can also create views by geography, and you can allow or disallow specific roles to specific views.

In Tableau, for example, you can create views as custom private or public, and the custom private views are hidden from everyone except the people they are shared with. When using an online report or dashboard, a sales manager can create multiple custom views and share only the relevant views with her team. As an example, Figure 12.4 shows a variety of views and the type of data the sales manager is abstracting vs. sharing with others.

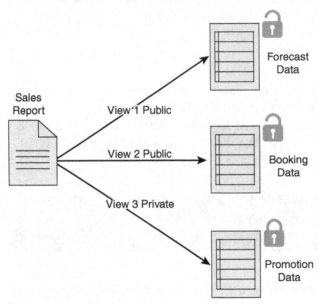

FIGURE 12.4   **Sales Report: Views**

Date Range

Say that it's the end of the quarter, and you are a sales manager, trying to put together information on the performance of your team for the quarter. You have the data from the past few quarters and would like to work with data across just last quarter. To get the relevant information, you need to filter the data by date range or specified time frame, as was discussed earlier in this chapter.

> **Note**
>
> If a report was generated some time ago, the data shown in the report may be out of date. It is ideal to refresh such reports.

When working with dates, you can work with the following elements:

▶ **Calendar year:** You can get information on the whole year, January to December.

▶ **Month:** You can get insights for a whole month.

▶ **Week:** You can get insights for a whole week.

▶ **Day:** You can get insights on per-day basis.

All BI platforms make it possible to show data by date ranges to get pertinent insights. For example, as shown in Figure 12.5, you can set up date ranges by using filters in Power BI.

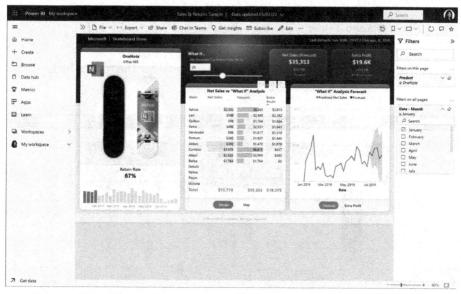

FIGURE 12.5 **Date Range Filter in Power BI**

> **Note**
>
> The sample dashboard shown in Figure 12.5 is available at https://docs.microsoft.com/en-us/power-bi/create-reports/sample-datasets#sales--returns-sample-pbix-file.

You can apply a much more granular filter by editing the report and adding a calendar filter for better insights by quarter and month, as shown in Figure 12.6.

FIGURE 12.6   Calendar Filter

By applying the calendar filter, the sales manager can see the results by quarter and month, as shown in Figure 12.7.

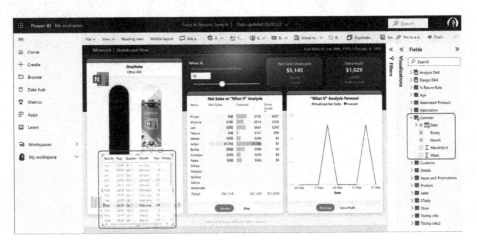

FIGURE 12.7   Insights for Sales Across Date Ranges

Frequency

Frequency can be categorized in two ways:

- ▶ Reporting frequency (or frequency of report generation/delivery)
- ▶ Frequency of data updates in reports

These two categories, while independent, are related. Let's look more closely.

It is crucial that reports be delivered to the intended audience within a certain timeframe so that the end users can make informed decisions. For example, a sales report that doesn't reach management by the time their review meeting occurs is not useful as it does not serve the intended purpose. Hence, the timing of a report as well as the frequency at which it should be generated is important. Understanding when the audience requires a report and how often it needs the report would help remove any ambiguity from the report generation process.

It is also important to consider the channel(s) via which the report will be delivered, such as by email, IM, Slack, or any other medium that your organization may use (see Chapter 13). You can have the recipients subscribe to reports or create an email alias for all recipients and mail them the reports every day or week, as appropriate.

How do you know how often a report should be refreshed? The simple answer is to match the refresh frequency of the data source(s) so that as soon as the data is refreshed at the source, you refresh the report with updated data. It's a good idea to send out updated reports to the intended recipients right away so the users don't rely on obsolete reports.

You can set the refresh frequency to hourly (which is recommended for sales data), daily (which is recommended for transactional data), weekly, or monthly. Figure 12.8 shows the refresh frequency settings in Tableau.

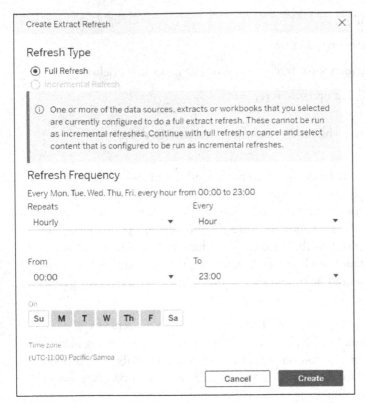

FIGURE 12.8   Tableau Refresh Frequency

Audience for Reports

Reports can be brief or verbose, depending on the audience. It is important to think about who your audience is and focus on how to cater to the target audience. Here are some questions that might be helpful:

▶ Who is the key audience that you would want to read the report?

▶ What might be the key reasons users would have for reading the report?

▶ What topics and key findings would be of interest to the audience?

▶ Will the audience be able to understand all sections in the report or key findings in the dashboard?

▶ What are the key takeaways from the report for the audience?

Once the basics are out of the way, you can start looking at audience types. You can possibly categorize audiences in three major categories:

▶ **Primary audience:** Also known as the *target audience*, the *primary audience* consists of people who would want to read the report. Your primary audience should ideally understand everything that the report articulates about the subject matter. For example, for sales leaders, the report would revolve around targets, quotas, achievement, performance, new business, growth business, and so on. However, for IT leadership, the report would be focused on current software and hardware management, issue resolution, new deployments, workload migration activities, and so on.

▶ **Secondary audience:** The *secondary audience* consists of people who would want to read the report but who might not have direct alignment with the report and may work in a different line of business than the primary audience. For example, marketing might be the secondary audience for a sales report because they would not have a direct connection with sales data but would be expected to work with sales teams on lead generation and marketing campaigns.

▶ **Tertiary audience:** The *tertiary audience* consists of people who do not have any direct relationship with a report but who are indirectly impacted or benefitted by the report content. They might not even read the report and may be informed by the primary or secondary audience about decisions based on findings in the report. For example, administrative staff might be asked to set up meetings or arrange events based on instructions from the primary (sales management) or secondary (marketing team) audience.

Various audience personas fit into these audience categories and are benefitted by a report. Here are the key audience personas:

> **Note**
>
> Many of these audience personas and their reporting requirements are described in detail in Chapter 13.

▶ **Executives:** Executives are primary audience members, and a report for them should focus on high-level information rather than drilling down into details. Executives appreciate summary information about the organization's performance and what actions help uplift growth or customer base. An executive report can just be a one-pager with all facts and recommendations in a minimal space.

▶ **Leadership:** Leadership is part of the primary audience. Leadership reports are meant for directors, vice presidents, CIOs, and anyone else who is a layer between executives and managers. These leaders need more detailed insights into organizational activities than do executives. They need insights into what will help with growth in acquiring new customers and the projection of business performance.

▶ **Managers:** Managers are the people who are managing lines of business; they look at business performance and need much more detailed insights than do executives and leadership; they need details, for example, on employee productivity, customer satisfaction, and inventory. Managers are usually part of the primary audience in an organization.

▶ **IT/operations:** These are the folks who manage the information technology (IT) systems and operations. They are very hands-on, interacting with systems and internal employees of the organization who use these systems. For reporting, they are good candidates for very detailed reporting that outlines the issues, new technology being deployed, new software, licenses, cloud consumption, and so on. IT/operations teams are part of the primary audience.

▶ **Developers:** Developers are an interesting audience as they are only interested in details pertinent to the applications they have launched or are going to launch. These details might focus on the number of connections, scaling out/in, resource consumption, customer profiles leveraging the application, and so on. Developers can be part of the primary or secondary audience, depending on the type of organization.

▶ **Data engineers/scientists:** Data engineers and data scientists are very keen on looking at results from data crunching and making sense of what is working well for their analysis, charts and graphs, and equations. Data engineers/scientists are usually the primary audience in a data-driven organization.

▶ **Marketing:** The marketing team is usually a secondary audience that uses organizational reports to direct the marketing function in driving sales or business generation activities.

▶ **Administrative:** The administrative teams are typically part of the tertiary audience and may be engaged, for example, to set up follow-ups to meetings or to arrange meetings with key organizational leaders to drive initiatives.

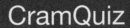

More details on report content and presentation of the content to various audiences are provided in Chapters 13 and 14.

A report can be shared with distribution lists across an organization for maximum reach. If there are existing distribution lists, a link to a dashboard or report can be shared on these lists; alternatively, a report summary (such as for executives) can be shared directly as a PDF over a distribution list. If a distribution list does not exist, the IT team can create one specifically either for the audience persona (executives, marketing, administration, and so on) or for business units, as needed.

Cram Quiz

Answer these questions. If you cannot answer these questions correctly, consider reading this section again until you can.

1. You are working with a report and need to filter information by date range. Which of the following can you work with? (Choose all that apply.)

   ○ **a.** Calendar year

   ○ **b.** Month

   ○ **c.** Week

   ○ **d.** Day

   ○ **e.** Hour

2. What is the ideal frequency for refreshing a report?

   ○ **a.** According to the needs of business leadership

   ○ **b.** Every week

   ○ **c.** According to the data source refresh frequency

   ○ **d.** Every hour

3. Which of the following may be categorized as primary audience? (Choose all that apply.)

   ○ **a.** Executives

   ○ **b.** Managers

   ○ **c.** IT

   ○ **d.** Leadership

   ○ **e.** Administration

4. Which of the following can you use to enable role-based access to report or dashboard content?
   - ○ **a.** Views
   - ○ **b.** Filters
   - ○ **c.** Layouts
   - ○ **d.** Frameworks

5. What type of audience consists of people who do not have a direct relationship with a report but are indirectly impacted or benefitted by the report content?
   - ○ **a.** Technical
   - ○ **b.** Nontechnical
   - ○ **c.** Primary
   - ○ **d.** Secondary
   - ○ **e.** Tertiary

Cram Quiz Answers

1. **Answer: a. Calendar year, b. Month, c. Week, d. Day.** When working with dates, you can work with the following elements:

   Calendar year: You can get information on the whole year, January to December.

   Month: You can get insights for a whole month.

   Week: You can get insights for a whole week.

   Day: You can get insights on per-day basis.

2. **Answer: c. According to the data source refresh frequency.** It is ideal to match the data source refresh frequency; that is, as soon as the data is refreshed at the source, consider refreshing the report with updated data as well.

3. **Answer: a. Executives, b. Managers, c. IT, d. Leadership.** These personas are the primary audience as they are the users driving business/technical decisions based on insights.

4. **Answer: a. Views.** Views are helpful for abstracting information that it is not to be shared. For example, a sales manager who does not want to distribute all information to everyone can create views that limit access to the information based on team membership.

5. **Answer: e. Tertiary.** The tertiary audience consists of people who do not have a direct relationship with a report but are indirectly impacted or benefitted by the report content (for example, administrative staff).

What Next?

If you want more practice on this chapter's exam objective before you move on, remember that you can access all of the Cram Quiz questions on the Pearson Test Prep software online. You can also create a custom exam by objective with the Online Practice Test. Note any objective you struggle with and go to that objective's material in this chapter.

CHAPTER 13

Exploring the Different Types of Reports and Dashboards

> **This chapter covers Objective 4.2 (Given a scenario, use appropriate design components for reports and dashboards) and Objective 4.3 (Given a scenario, use appropriate methods for dashboard development) of the CompTIA Data+ exam and includes the following topics:**
>
> ▶ Report cover page
> ▶ Design elements
> ▶ Documentation elements
> ▶ Dashboard considerations
> ▶ Development process
> ▶ Delivery considerations
>
> For more information on the official CompTIA Data+ exam topics, see the Introduction.

This chapter explores different types of reports and dashboards. It provides details about the report cover page, design elements, and documentation elements. This chapter also focuses on dashboard considerations and the development process, and it highlights delivery considerations in a corporate environment.

Report Cover Page and Design Elements

CramSaver

If you can correctly answer these questions before going through this section, save time by skimming the Exam Alerts in this section and then completing the Cram Quiz at the end of the section.

1. Conclusions in a report are based on which of the following?

   a. Insights

   b. Instructions

   c. Format

   d. Sources

2. Which of the following are the key components of a report? (Choose all that apply.)

   a. Subject matter or topic of the report

   b. Problem statement

   c. Methods of analysis

   d. Findings

   e. General discussions

3. What type of report would be expected to be presented for C-level executives?

   a. A five-page report with details on specific topics

   b. A one-page summary

   c. A 10-page report with detailed findings

   d. A full detailed report

4. Which of these are primary colors?

   a. Red, blue, and green

   b. Red, green, and yellow

   c. Red, blue, and yellow

   d. Orange, pink, and blue

1. **Answer: a. Insights.** Conclusions in a report are based on insights driven by data analytics.

2. **Answer: a. Subject matter or topic of the report, b. Problem statement, c. Methods of analysis, d. Findings.** A report would have the one or more of the following headings, depending on the type of report (for example, corporate, marketing, sales, research):

   ▶ Subject matter or topic of the report

   ▶ Problem statement

   ▶ Methods of analysis

   ▶ Findings

   ▶ Conclusions

   ▶ Recommendations

   ▶ Limitations of the report

   ▶ Summary of key findings, solutions to the problem, and recommendations

3. **Answer: b. A one-page summary.** C-level executives tend to have very short attention spans, and to get your findings through to them, you should present a one-page (executive) summary that captures, at a glance, everything that is important for these executives to know.

4. **Answer: c. Red, blue, and yellow.** Red, blue, and yellow are primary colors.

You have likely seen many reports—from corporate reports to reports on population analysis or reports that talk about increases in the cost of living (yes, we're talking about dreaded inflation). Reports can be very exciting and informative, or they can be very dull, depending on many factors such as color schemes, fonts used to highlight text, and insights presented and how they are presented.

Report Cover Page

A report's cover can be exciting even if the content is not so exciting, however, and if it is, chances are you will read the report or pay attention to someone who's presenting its content. If the cover catches your eye and is welcoming, it has done about half the job of the report—being interesting to read. A good cover can prompt a reader to turn pages, and that's exactly what the report was put together for in the first place: to deliver key information.

Let's consider an example of quarterly sales reports. While these reports aren't usually anything fancy, making the cover interesting—with a storyline or an interesting graphic—can kindle audience interest.

Microsoft PowerPoint gives a good starting point for creating visually appealing reports. In addition, online reporting tools such as Visme and tools like Tableau and Power BI can be used to make reports interesting—with captivating covers and other elements that are covered later in this chapter. Figure 13.1 gives an overview of the types of reports you can create with PowerPoint.

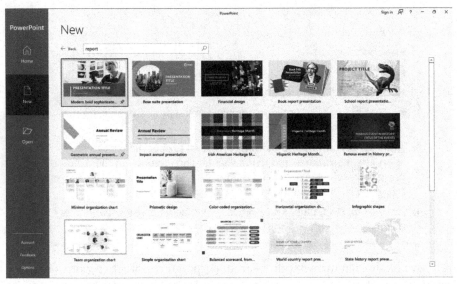

FIGURE 13.1 **Report Options in Microsoft PowerPoint**

Note

Figure 13.1 shows some of the default templates provided in PowerPoint. However, a content creator can customize many different styles of reports by leveraging these templates.

While these templates may not be suitable in certain corporate environments, they can still serve as starting points for creating reports, which is especially helpful for those who haven't ever worked with reports. Templates can help you create reports that fit with the rest of the reports used in your organization.

Instructions

At times, it is necessary to give instructions that provide information to assist a project and/or research team/staff in the completion and submission of reports. The reports may need to be standardized across the organization, or the reporting team may need to have data in a certain format such that all reports look and feel the same (regardless of the content).

Instructions may address how to populate different sections of the report, such as the following:

- Whether to enter data manually or leverage data from another system

- What questions need to be answered (if conducting a study)

- The required steps to be considered, from acquisition to cleansing of data for use in the report

- The way the data should be interpreted while creating the report

- The templates, font, and visualizations to be used in the report

- Any logos that may be used for reports

- Any references and how they should be used

Good instructions help create useful and meaningful reports, especially when report generation is handled by multiple people. Good instructions also lead to homogeneity in the way a set of reporting parameters can be enforced and help standardize corporate reporting.

In general, a report has the one or more of the following headings, depending on what type of report it is (for example, corporate, marketing, sales, research):

- Subject matter or topic of the report

- Problem statement

- Methods of analysis

- Findings

- Conclusions

- Recommendations

- Limitations of the report

- Summary of key findings, solutions to the problem, and recommendations

Summary

A report and its content mean different things to different audiences, and the type of summary used should reflect the content and consider the audience. For example, a report's summary may be an executive summary if the report is being presented to leadership or the board. The audience may only read the executive summary if they're short on time, or they may prefer to read some or all sections of the report.

An executive summary in a report should have the following content:

- ▶ Summary of key findings
- ▶ Summary of the solutions to the problem
- ▶ Summary of recommendations

For example, in a sales presentation to a CEO, you would want to focus on key aspects that led to better sales this month and how your team achieved their goals. This information needs to be crisp as the C-level executives have little time to spend deciphering cryptic phrasing or incomplete thoughts in a dashboard or report. To get your findings through to them, you should present a one-page (executive) summary that captures all the important information at a glance.

> **Note**
>
> The summary of findings should be provided to a C-level audience in the form of a "BLUF" statement—that is, a "Bottom Line Up Front" statement that summarizes the key point of the report.

Figure 13.2 shows an executive summary report template. (This template is from www.powerslides.com.)

Now think about a report for the IT group. If you show this audience only a summary, they will scratch their heads and ask for details. This is quite the opposite of a report for C-level executives, as the IT group folks need details such as what caused the downtime, what vendor or supplier issues occurred, which systems need upgrades, and what activities are being planned for next month. The summary for such a report would be very different from an executive report and would likely span more than a page.

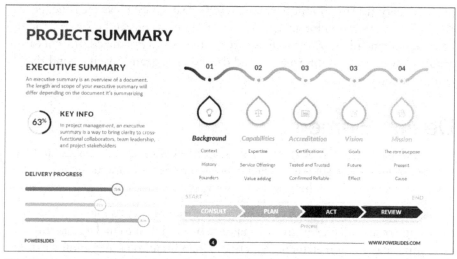

FIGURE 13.2   A Sample Executive Summary Template

Figure 13.3 shows an IT report summary template. (This template was also sourced from www.powerslides.com.) You can appreciate that this summary is very different from—and much busier than—the executive summary shown in Figure 13.2.

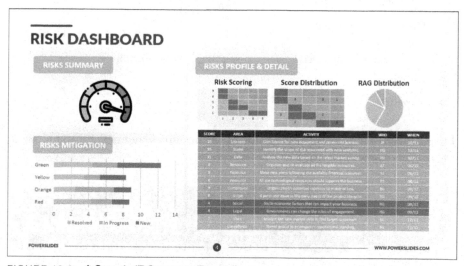

FIGURE 13.3   A Sample IT Summary Template

As you have seen, when preparing a report's summary, it is important to understand your audience in order to get their attention.

In a summary, it is important to summarize factual data such as the time, place, and date of observation for an activity. These observations and insights should be clear and unambiguous as well as easy to follow and organized. Insights are acquired by examining information and data to understand specific conditions and make conclusions.

Design Elements

Design elements are the heart and soul of a report. As you will discover in this section, picking the right color scheme and the right fonts and using other design elements well can help spark your target audience's interest.

When you think of aesthetics or an immersive experience, you might think of the design of an object; design elements can be used well to make something very appealing. Design elements lead the human brain to perceive information much faster than just raw text. A report cover page as well as the report contents (including the summary) can be made much more intuitive using the right design elements, such as:

▶ Color schemes

▶ Layout

▶ Font sizes and styles

▶ Key chart elements

▶ Titles

▶ Labels

▶ Legends

The following sections highlight some of the design elements that can help you create and present an engaging report.

> **ExamAlert**
>
> Report design is an important topic that is often ignored. Expect a few questions on report design elements on the CompTIA Data+ exam.

Color Schemes

Colors are all around us and make things interesting or dull, depending on how we feel about colors and the color themes/schemes used. Color is an important communication tool that can provoke various emotional responses. Reactions to color can be positive or not so positive, depending on what colors are used and whether they work in harmonious or dissenting ways.

While there are millions of colors, they all fall into three major categories:

▶ **Primary colors:** Red, blue, and yellow

▶ **Secondary colors:** Orange, green, and violet

▶ **Tertiary colors:** Red–violet, yellow–orange, blue–green, blue–violet, yellow–green, and red–orange

A *color wheel* shows many colors and helps a user choose which ones to use together. It can be very helpful in choosing a color scheme for a document or report. Figure 13.4 shows a color wheel.

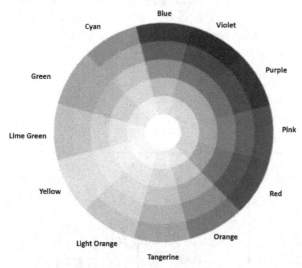

FIGURE 13.4   **Color Wheel**

There are a few basic types of color schemes:

▶ **Monochromatic:** Uses a single color from the color wheel (such as blue) and can present a very consistent look with varying shades and tints of that color

- ▶ **Complementary:** Uses two colors that are directly opposite each other on the color wheel (such as blue and tangerine)

- ▶ **Split complementary:** Uses colors on either side of the complementary color (such as blue with orange and light orange)

- ▶ **Analogous:** Uses one main color from the color wheel and two colors that appear right next to it (such as yellow with light orange and lime green)

- ▶ **Triadic:** Uses a palette of three colors that appear at equidistant points on the color wheel (such as blue, red, and yellow)

- ▶ **Tetradic:** Uses four colors that appear on the color wheel in a rectangular pattern (such as purple, red, yellow, and green)

To choose a good color scheme for a report, it is important to gauge your audience and their liking, the environment, and the purpose of the report. Let's consider an example. Observe the report covers shown in Figure 13.5.

> **Note**
>
> The report covers in Figure 13.5 were created at www.visme.co.

FIGURE 13.5   **Color Schemes for Sales and Art Reports**

The sales report cover uses a very natural and subtle color scheme that goes well with the report's messaging and is not overbearing. In contrast, the art report cover is much more colorful and bright. This color scheme might not invoke the best reactions in a corporate sales presentation, but an arts audience would appreciate the thought behind the color scheme.

The following are a few color scheme considerations that you may find helpful:

- ▶ Choose appropriate colors—solids or shades—for a report based on the topic, the audience, the environment in which the report will be presented, and its message.

- ▶ Pastel colors are usually considered calming; they might not be suitable in a high-energy presentation.

- ▶ Bright colors can reflect happiness and are great for non-corporate presentations; however, they may appear cheap in certain situations or if used poorly.

- ▶ Darker colors denote professionalism and can be useful for executive presentation; however, they might appear too somber in certain situations.

Report Layout

Reports can be very simple or more complicated. A report may be one page, or it may be multiple pages, depending on the audience and topic. Before designing the report cover and report body, it is a good idea to consider the layout that will be used for the body of the report. Consider the following questions when writing a report:

- ▶ Is this a simple one-page report, or will it have multiple pages?

- ▶ Can text convey the message of the report, or would infographics work better?

- ▶ Is the report going to show many data points, and if so, are they graphs or charts?

- ▶ Is the report going to be around for some time (as for a research topic, an annual report, or a report that discusses outcomes of a survey)?

- ▶ What are the main sections in the report?

In general, a report should have one or more of the following pages or sections:

▶ Cover page

▶ Introduction

▶ Executive summary

▶ Overview

▶ Methodology adopted for report findings

▶ Findings and/or analysis

▶ Results and/or recommendations

▶ Summary or conclusion

Another important factor in a report layout is the placement of figures and charts, which can add a lot of visual impact to a report. You might want to experiment and see what works best in the layout of a particular report (such as positioning images or charts across pages alongside text or combining them in some places).

It is crucial to have a well-defined layout for the type of report you want to present as different reports have different sections, and some may be more suitable for one type of report or another. For example, sections such as methodology and recommendations may not be applicable to sales reports, whereas a research report would need these sections.

Font Size and Style

As you have already gathered, a report needs to be presented in a suitable way for the intended audience. As long as the audience can read and understand the various sections of a report, the report can serve its purpose. Ideally, a report should bring out the key data insights in a simple way, and the audience should find the report easy to read and self-navigate. To make a report easy for the audience to use, you can use simple formatting styles—such as easy-to-read fonts and easy-to-spot headings—throughout the report. Good use of typography—font sizes and styles—can make the contents of a report easy to understand and visually pleasing, helping the report deliver maximum impact.

To get an idea of the impact of typography, take a look at Figure 13.6, which shows the font size 18 across a few well-known fonts. You could use any of these fonts to create a very neutral-looking report—which is often what you want for organizational reports. When you use fonts that your audience is used to, users perceive it as a good, clear report to read.

1. This is Calibri in font size 18

2. This is Arial in font size 18

3. This is Verdana font size 18

4. This is Times New Roman font size 18

5. This is Microsoft Sans Serif font size 18

FIGURE 13.6 **Well-Known Fonts**

Following are some formatting-related tips for making reports easy to read and presentable:

▶ Use a font that is compatible with web pages as most reports today are digital reports.

▶ Where possible, use one font for all the text in a report to make it consistent. You may use a different font for the headings.

▶ Use headings and subheadings to differentiate the content in various sections of a report. Headings and subheadings can be the same font as body text but in different sizes, or they can be in a different font.

▶ Use italics or bold in a report to emphasize various topics.

▶ Keep in mind that each font has its own characteristics. Either stick with a standard font that is used in your organization or get creative and see what works best.

Key Chart Elements

A report may contain charts or other graphics that make it easier and intuitive for the audience to take in information. Figure 13.7 shows a sales revenue chart of results from SaaS software across quarter 1—January, February, and March—for forecasts and closed deals.

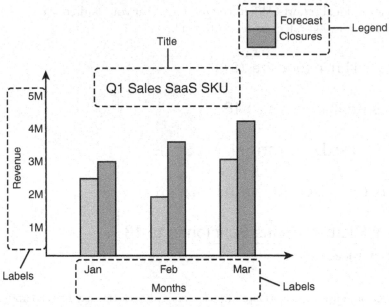

FIGURE 13.7 **Sales Revenue Chart**

Notice the following elements in the chart in Figure 13.7 (some of which are marked with dotted squares):

▶ The title indicates the purpose of the chart.

▶ Legends describe the meanings of colors and shapes used in the chart.

▶ Labels on the X-axis and Y-axis describe the related information.

Using elements like these across charts can make them intuitive for readers to consume.

Corporate Reporting Standards/Style Guide

As discussed previously in this chapter, report cover pages and content can be very different for different audiences. This section provides an overview of the key elements that should be considered for corporate reports (such as branding, color codes, logos/trademarks, and watermarks).

As you have seen throughout this chapter, there can be multiple types of corporate reports, such as:

▶ Annual reports

▶ IT inventory reports

- ▶ Marketing reports
- ▶ Sales and revenue reports

A good and well-thought-out corporate report portrays professionalism, trust-worthiness, and clarity in thought process.

A corporate report cover page should include the following:

- ▶ Report title/subtitle
- ▶ Author's name and job title
- ▶ Organization's name and logo
- ▶ Date of report generation

In addition to formatting, layout, fonts, and colors, there are some other important elements of a corporate report:

- ▶ **Branding:** The branding should be clear and concise, and it should portray the organization correctly. Keep in mind that when you are presenting a report, you are the organization's spokesperson to the customers.

- ▶ **Logos:** A logo may stand alone or may appear with the name of the organization. A logo is seen as an extension of a brand. A logo is created and used to imply the message of the organization and to provide a pictorial representation of the brand.

- ▶ **Watermark:** Some pages in a report may be watermarked with a logo or with "Confidential" or "Secret" text to prevent the intended audience from sharing the information in the report with others.

A corporate report is a package that delivers a corporate message beyond the content. It is a good idea to leverage a data visualization style guide to standardize corporate reports. A data visualization style guide offers increased impact by ensuring consistent adoption of fonts (style and size), colors, types of charts, and formatting organization wide. It saves time as a reporting team does not have to spend hours trying to decide which colors, fonts, or styles should be used. A data visualization style guide helps use the brand logos and other aspects cohesively to help communicate the corporate message in a powerful way.

Cram Quiz

Answer these questions. If you cannot answer these questions correctly, consider reading this section again until you can.

1. What is represented by the ? in the following figure?

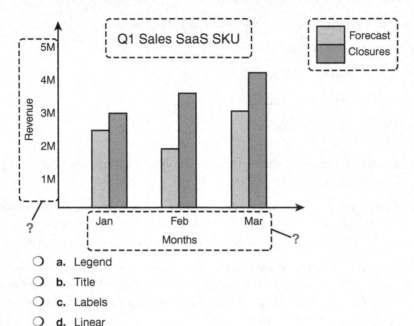

○ **a.** Legend

○ **b.** Title

○ **c.** Labels

○ **d.** Linear

2. Which of the following are secondary colors?

○ **a.** Red, yellow, and blue

○ **b.** Orange, green, and yellow

○ **c.** Blue, green, and yellow

○ **d.** Orange, green, and violet

3. What is the term for the art of arranging and presenting text in order to make the content easy to understand and visually pleasing?

○ **a.** Match making

○ **b.** Typography

○ **c.** Cryptography

○ **d.** Kipography

4. Which of the following describes a triadic color scheme?

◯ **a.** Uses two colors that are directly opposite each other on the color wheel

◯ **b.** Uses a single color from the color wheel and can present a very consistent look with varying shades and tints of that color

◯ **c.** Uses one main color from the color wheel and two colors that appear right next to it

◯ **d.** Uses four colors that appear on the color wheel in a rectangular pattern

◯ **e.** Uses a palette of three colors that appear at equidistant points on the color wheel

Cram Quiz Answers

1. **Answer: c. Labels.** The ? shows labels—specifically axis labels—on the chart.

2. **Answer: d. Orange, green, and violet.** Orange, green, and violet are secondary colors.

3. **Answer: b. Typography.** Typography is the art of arranging and presenting text in order to make the content easy to understand and visually pleasing.

4. **Answer: e. Uses a palette of three colors that appear at equidistant points on the color wheel.** A triadic color scheme uses a palette of three colors that appear at equidistant points on the color wheel (for example, blue, red, and yellow).

Documentation Elements

CramSaver

If you can correctly answer these questions before going through this section, save time by skimming the Exam Alerts in this section and then completing the Cram Quiz at the end of the section.

1. Which of the following ensures that everyone is looking at the latest release of a report?

   a. Statistical measure

   b. Version number

   c. Draft number

   d. Value of dataset

2. Which of the following does the report run date indicate?

   a. What the report represents

   b. How the report was generated

   c. When the report was generated

   d. Which people are the key audience for the report

3. Which of the following can be expected in the appendix section of a report? (Choose all that apply.)

   a. Calculations

   b. Algorithms

   c. Drawings

   d. Formulas

   e. Citations

Answers

1. **Answer: b. Version number.** A report should have a version number to ensure that readers are looking at most recent/updated report.

2. **Answer: c. When the report was generated.** The report run date indicates when a report was generated.

3. **Answer: a. Calculations, b. Algorithms, c. Drawings, d. Formulas.** All of these are common in an appendix; citations appear in the references section.

Gone are the days when documents were all physically handled. Documentation today is almost all digital. Receipts, pay slips, reports, and anything else that needs to be recognized as a document can exist in a digital format. Documentation involves a lot of elements, including digital signing, versioning, and much more. This section discusses these elements.

Version Number

Every document that is digitally created may possibly be modified by authorized users. If the original document had four sections and a revised version of the document has five sections, which one should you work with? How do you know if a document's contents have been changed? Versioning helps with these issues. Every document should have a version number; using versioning is also known as version control. Versioning is important because it helps everyone know which is the latest version of a document and whether any changes can be made to it.

> **ExamAlert**
>
> Versioning is a very important concept in context to documentation and this would one of the focus topics in CompTIA Data+ exam.

A report should have a version number to help readers determine whether they are looking at the most recent/updated report. For example, if a sales team is looking at a sales forecast report, they need to be sure they're using this month's report and not last month's because a recent report will give better insights for better decision making; a date of generation or, better yet, a version number, will help the team ensure that they're using the most current report.

> **Note**
>
> Popular document editing tools like Microsoft PowerPoint and Word have built-in tools to help with versioning.

Typically, version numbers are assigned by the document author, but they can also be system generated. A report may be released as version 1.0, and the next release may be 1.1, then 1.2, and so on. Any changes in the report—manual or system generated—should be reflected in the version number. A revamped report should be considered a major release, and the main version should be updated from 1.x to 2.x and so on.

Reference Data Sources and Dates

Data may be referenced or reused both internally and externally by authorized users. It is a good practice to reference the source(s) of the data used in your report, especially when you leverage an external document or article for text, figures, articles, findings, diagrams, maps, and so on. Ideally you should cite such material within the report. If someone else is using information from a report that you generated, that person should cite your report as the source of the information.

Citations can include the following:

▶ Authors of the original document/article/research report

▶ Publication date of the document/article/research report

▶ Title of the document/article/research report

▶ Persistent identifier/locator (for example, DOI or URL) of the document/article/research report

▶ Version and accessed date of the document/article/research report

▶ Publisher and year of publication of the document/article/research report, if available

Figure 13.8 shows the citation options in Microsoft Word.

FIGURE 13.8 **Microsoft Word Citation Options**

The tool Zotero (see https://www.zotero.org/) allows you to reference almost anything across your documents and lets you keep adding links, research papers, and articles to your collection and then reference them easily.

Every report should be labeled with a report run date. When a newer version is generated or even if the same report is generated on a different day/time, the run date should reflect when the report was generated. This helps viewers determine whether they're looking at the current report.

An important aspect to be aware of regarding data updates is the refresh rate at which data is updated in a report. This is the rate at which data is pulled (or uploaded) from the data sources, goes through analysis, and is reflected in the report. A report administrator can set up a refresh schedule. For example, sales reports from Salesforce can be refreshed as required, but a decent refresh rate would be every hour or every couple hours. Frequent refreshes can help a report reflect new opportunities as well as any movement on opportunities in the system, for example, a sales report.

FAQs and Appendix

An FAQ (frequently asked questions) is a list of commonly asked questions and answers, presented in order to anticipate queries related to a report. The viewers or users of a report may not be familiar with certain sections or how to interpret data across those sections. Hence, it's a good idea to build an FAQ section that describes how the data points were calculated or what certain sections imply.

A good FAQ aims to do the following:

▶ Act as a virtual guide, reflecting on the needs of readers and helping them understand the content of the report

▶ Be frequently updated based on new data insights and as the report evolves

▶ Help readers browse to additional information pertinent to the report

▶ Increase the use of the report and encourage constructive feedback

▶ Answer questions from readers

▶ Offer concise and to-the-point explanations of key facts or subjects

Report appendixes (also sometimes spelled *appendices*) sometimes contain content that is referenced earlier in the report (typically in academic or research reports) and sometimes present calculations, algorithms, drawings, and insights about raw data to bolster the information in the body of the report. For example, you may want to display detailed equations and calculations in an appendix and only the results in main body. A report might have one or more appendixes, depending on the content and length of the report and the type of information included. Each appendix is denoted by a letter or a number in the body of the report. The content in an appendix—references, diagrams, or titles, for example—may be listed as a numbered or unnumbered list.

Cram Quiz

Answer these questions. If you cannot answer these questions correctly, consider reading this section again until you can.

1. Which of the following is not a useful feature of FAQs?
   - ○ **a.** Helping readers browse to additional information
   - ○ **b.** Increasing the use of the report and encouraging constructive feedback
   - ○ **c.** Answering questions from readers
   - ○ **d.** Offering concise and to-the-point explanations
   - ○ **e.** Asking readers to fill out a survey

2. Which of the following is used for referencing information in a report?
   - ○ **a.** Survey
   - ○ **b.** Dashboard
   - ○ **c.** Appendix
   - ○ **d.** Citation

3. If any changes are made to a report, they should be reflected in _____.
   - ○ **a.** version 1.x
   - ○ **b.** version 2.x
   - ○ **c.** the latest release
   - ○ **d.** a complementary report
   - ○ **e.** citations

Cram Quiz Answers

1. **Answer: e. Asking readers to fill out a survey.** Except for asking readers to fill out a survey, all of these are the reasons FAQs should be incorporated in a report.

2. **Answer: d. Citations.** Citations should be used to reference content taken from another source of information.

3. **Answer: c. the latest release.** Any changes should be reflected in the latest release of a report.

Dashboard Considerations, Development, and Delivery Process

CramSaver

If you can correctly answer these questions before going through this section, save time by skimming the Exam Alerts in this section and then completing the Cram Quiz at the end of the section.

1. Which of these is a single-screen construct that gives insights about various metrics?

   a. Dashboard

   b. Dataset

   c. Qualitative value

   d. Hypothetical value

2. A management dashboard is considered a(n) _____ for presenting all significant management KPIs in one place to drive decisions.

   a. source

   b. element

   c. entity

   d. tool

3. In terms of how often the content is updated, what are the major types of dashboards? (Choose two.)

   a. Updating

   b. Lagging

   c. Static

   d. Live

4. What are the two types of data attributes? (Choose two.)

   a. Qualitative

   b. Live

   c. Ongoing

   d. Quantitative

Answers

1. **Answer: a. Dashboard.** A dashboard is a single-screen construct (typically live and on demand) that gives insights about the key performance indicators (KPIs) across a number of functions or a specific business function within an organization.

2. **Answer: d. Tool.** A management dashboard is a tool adopted for presenting all significant management KPIs in one place to drive decisions.

3. **Answer: c. Static, d. Live.** There are two major types of dashboards in terms of how often the content is updated: static and live. A static dashboard presents information that is not updated often. A live dashboard is similar to a streaming video channel, with updated data shown immediately.

4. **Answer: a. Qualitative, d. Quantitative.** The following figure shows the two data attributes—qualitative and quantitative—as well as their subcategories.

Data Attributes

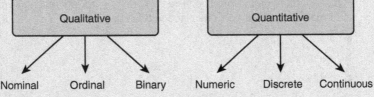

This section is dedicated to dashboards. Before we get into the specifics of how dashboards are developed and delivered, it is good to understand what dashboards are all about and how they are similar to and differ from reports. Dashboards enable near-real-time insights with charts and data points that track performance, and they make it possible to analyze trends by interacting with data.

ExamAlert

Dashboards are a hot topic in the data analytics world, and almost every organization out there is using different dashboards. Be sure to read through the development process and how dashboards are deployed and delivered as there would likely be questions on this topic in the CompTIA Data+ exam.

A *dashboard* is a single screen (typically live and on demand) that gives insights about the key performance indicators (KPIs) across a number of functions or a specific business function within an organization.

A simple real-world example is the dashboard of your car, which tells you about important functions, such as the fuel level, your speed, engine RPM, drive mode, and much more. By using certain functions on the dashboard, you can monitor fuel consumption, fuel economy, and the length of a trip. Much like a car dashboard, a digital dashboard used by an organization makes it possible to see important information, such as KPIs or highlights within the organization. For example, an IT operations dashboard might show the number of tickets being generated in an hour, how many issues have been reported and rectified, any outages, and so on.

Information in a dashboard is available at a glance; in contrast, in a report you can drill down to examine the specifics of an incident. A dashboard is basically a summarized report—a single screen that provides insights in real time, without requiring you to scroll through multiple pages. When you use a dashboard, you probably still want to generate reports; dashboards are not meant to replace reports but to augment them. Dashboard reporting helps users visualize events across the IT landscape. Figure 13.9 shows a sales commission dashboard created with Tableau. This dashboard captures the relationships between compensation type, commissions, and quota attainment for a set of salespeople in an organization.

> **Note**
>
> The dashboard in Figure 13.9 is from https://public.tableau.com/app/profile/ technical.product.marketing/viz/SalesCommissionModel_10_0/CommissionModel.

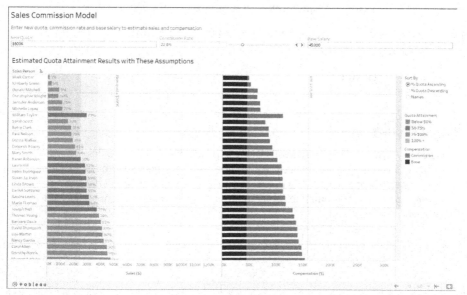

FIGURE 13.9   Sales Commission Dashboard in Tableau

Dashboard Considerations

Dashboards, which can be quite interactive, offer a 10,000-foot to 1000-foot view of information. It is important to consider a few key details when putting together dashboards:

- ▶ What are the sources of the information?
- ▶ What attributes would be useful for viewers?
- ▶ What important aspects are being measured?
- ▶ Who are the users of the dashboard?
- ▶ What type of dashboard is it going to be—static or live?
- ▶ What important insights are being derived from the dashboard?

The next few sections go over these concepts and help you understand the mechanics behind each of these considerations.

Data Sources and Attributes

Dashboards give an organization many ways to view and filter information in the form of charts or graphs. For building dashboards, you need to define the sources from which information is collected, which may include the following:

- ▶ SQL databases (for example, Microsoft SQL, Oracle, MySQL)
- ▶ Data lakes (for example, Azure Synapse, GCP BigQuery)
- ▶ Data from master data management (MDM) platforms (for example, Informatica, Oracle)
- ▶ CSV or flat files

> **Note**
>
> Use of the terms *master* and *slave* is ONLY in association with the official terminology used in industry specifications and standards and in no way diminishes Pearson's commitment to promoting diversity, equity, and inclusion and challenging, countering, and/or combating bias and stereotyping in the global population of the learners we serve.

Data attributes are properties or characteristics that explain the data objects in a dataset. For example, a sales dataset may be defined using attributes such as Customer_ID, Customer_Address, and Products_Services.

Figure 13.10 illustrates the types of data attributes, which are as follows:

▶ **Nominal:** This type of data attribute distinguishes between one data object and others by using name, age, sex, colors, and so on.

▶ **Ordinal:** This type of data attribute shows a meaningful sequence between values, without the magnitude of values being known (for example, grades A through F, without defining what scores constitute A vs. F).

▶ **Binary:** This type of data attribute uses 0 or 1, which may describe false or true, not included or included, and so on.

▶ **Numeric:** This type of data attribute is quantitative and measurable in value (for example, kilometers). Numeric attributes can be further classified as interval or ratio:

   ▶ **Interval:** Measured on an equal scale of units (for example, degree of hot vs. cold in Celsius or Fahrenheit)

   ▶ **Ratio:** Measured in comparative values (for example, a mathematical ratio)

▶ **Discrete:** This type of data attribute is used for data with finite values and whole numbers (for example, number of students in a class, number of employees in an organization).

▶ **Continuous:** This type of data attribute is used for data with non-finite values and continuing numbers (for example, time, amount of rain).

Data Attributes

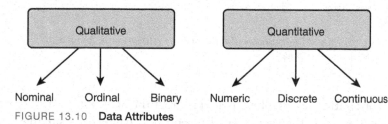

FIGURE 13.10   **Data Attributes**

A dashboard can be prepared with one or more of these data attributes, depending on the requirements of the viewers. For example, if there's a need to categorize data and show a chart about the number of students in a school and their ages, both discrete and continuous data can be pulled from the identified data sources to create the appropriate charts.

It is important to be aware of the way that quantitative and qualitative values are represented in a dashboard. Dashboard dimensions contain qualitative (representative) values, whereas measures contain quantitative (numeric) values. You can use dimension values—such as names, colors, and languages—to categorize and reveal the required details in a dashboard. You can use measures to aggregate age, weight, size, and so on and reveal the relationships between the values being measured.

When using a dashboard, you may want to filter information or set up custom sections. Dashboard fields help map required information across a dashboard as well as filter various elements in the dashboard. Each field has a data type that is automatically applied (for example, integer, string). For example, in Salesforce, you can manage information across fields such as ID, Description, CreatedDate, ChartTheme, and Title.

Continuous/Live Data Feed vs. Static Data

Sometimes viewers are okay with point-in-time data, but at other times, they are more interested in live updates. For example, a dashboard created for asset inventory can be updated once a day because there are not a lot of inventory changes happening every minute. However, with a share price dashboard, viewers don't want to look at share prices from an hour ago; they need this information in near real time.

> **Note**
>
> It is important to understand the purpose of a dashboard and whether its users require a live view or a static view.

Live data feed, or continuous, dashboards are just what the names suggest. Much like streaming video, they get updated as soon as a change occurs in the data source. Live feed dashboards have live inputs that influence the visuals and can be used for making decisions in near real time.

Static dashboards are for viewing information from a particular time in the past. For example, results from reported data could provide insights about how to enhance a process and what might be considered for enhancement.

Consumer Types

If you are developing a dashboard, what should matter most beyond the *how* and the *what* is the *who*. A detailed dashboard with 10 different charts may be popular with an IT team, but executives need only 2 to 4 charts. Different consumers need different metrics, and it is important to know which ones a dashboard audience needs.

Before we get into specific consumer personas, let's talk about the broad categories of consumers: internal and external. It is important that any dashboard that is published is accessible only by internal or external consumers, according to their authorization level and their roles in the organization. Internal and sensitive dashboards should not be published externally. For example, a software solutions organization might want to share quarterly sales results with consumers. In this case, a publicly available dashboard should be published that's accessible by anyone over the Internet. However, the firm may also want to publish for employees details on products by market and profit as well as other details. In this case, an internal private dashboard should be published that's available only to employees.

A C-level executive dashboard should provide very high-level insights to viewers. It should be geared toward KPIs impacting business growth and suggestions on how to grow revenue while minimizing risk and driving productivity. C-level executives would not be interested in aspects such as average reply time or resolution rate but would want to know the impact of these things on customer satisfaction (CSAT).

> **Note**
>
> A C-level audience typically has an attention span of only 15 to 20 minutes. If you provide anything more than higher-level details and suggestions/insights, you risk losing their attention and wasting their time.

For a management or leadership audience, a dashboard is a tool for presenting KPIs as well as improvement suggestions across various verticals within the organization, using tables, graphs, and links to case study data. Leadership needs the information shown for a C-level audience as well as key metrics such as conversion rate, net promoter score, and customer retention rate. Leadership appreciates insights into what is working well and what opportunities for improvement exist.

For an IT team, metrics such as first-contact resolution, volume of tickets, average resolution/reply time, and asset management are most important. Information from various sources of data should be integrated for unified reporting such that the IT team gets a single pane of glass to look at.

For external stakeholder/vendors, such as shareholders and investors, customers, and suppliers, different levels of information and metrics may be required, depending on the external customer. For example, for vendors and suppliers, information like inventory levels, logistics details, and goods ordered may be useful; for investors and shareholders, key information about how the organization is performing overall and net revenue or sales figures may be required.

For the general public, you might want to publish a public dashboard on the latest activities related to consumer focus or products as well as any environmental efforts by the organization.

Development Process

A dashboard needs to tell viewers a story that they are interested in. Dashboards are not just pieces of information presented in one place; they are vehicles used for storytelling. When you are looking at a dashboard, it should seem like you are looking at a larger and coherent picture of events of interest.

Making a dashboard that tells a good story requires a lot of work, including brainstorming ideas, getting those ideas into a storyboard, doing mockups, building layouts, getting the right set of approvals to deploy the dashboard, and deploying the dashboard for the authorized consumers. This section describes these steps and shows how dashboards come to life.

These are the high-level steps of the dashboard development process:

1. **Requirements gathering:** Gather the requirements for this dashboard in order to solve a business problem.

2. **Ideation:** Record ideas about what should be in the dashboard, such as charts or pictorial representations. The result of this stage is known as a *wireframe*.

3. **Storyboard creation:** Get the dashboard story sorted by figuring out which elements are needed to ensure that the dashboard delivers what it is supposed to deliver.

4. **Design layout:** Get the layout approved and place the widgets in the right places to enable consumers to look at the right information. The result of this stage is known as a *mockup*.

5. **Testing:** Have the dashboard tested by using a pilot group, canary, blue-green, or any other deployment mechanism.

6. **Deployment:** Get the dashboard rolled out in production.

7. **Feedback and maintenance:** Gather feedback from consumers to enable development of more widgets or features.

Mockup/Wireframe

Once the business requirements have been well defined and the need for a dashboard has been established, the ideation phase kicks in, and the dashboard outlook/layout is determined. When developing a new dashboard, it is important to make prototypes or drafts (also known as mockups) in order to ensure that the dashboard captures all the required information and allows consumers to look at the KPIs they are interested in. A mockup is essentially a replica of a final dashboard that can be used to demonstrate the look and feel of the dashboard before the development work begins. A wireframe, on the other hand, is a very basic rendering of a dashboard that does not offer an intuitive layout, as a mockup does.

> **Note**
>
> An organization may have standard templates that can be used for mockups or may require designers to build new templates, as per the business requirements.

You can create dashboard wireframes or mockups in your favorite BI tool, such as Power BI or Tableau. Figure 13.11 shows a sample mockup created at https://app.creately.com/. As you can see, this mockup is a work in progress (WIP) and can be changed in terms of outlook, headings, charts, and so on, based on the requirements.

FIGURE 13.11   **Dashboard Mockup Template**

Fun Fact

You can pick up a pen and create a wireframe on a sheet of paper. Even though there are a lot of tools available for creating dashboards, sometimes pen and paper are the perfect tools for getting your ideas about a dashboard jotted down while you still have them fresh in your mind.

It is important to look at multiple layouts and determine which one should make the cut. It's a good idea to work with a design team and stakeholders to ensure that they are on same page and they give you the required approvals before moving from draft to final layout version. Layouts can make or break a dashboard as the way content is presented is often as important as the content itself. For example, whether you should use a line graph or histograms or pie charts would depend on the details you want to show in your layout and the audience. A more technical audience would appreciate more details, and executives would want only important insights.

In terms of flow and navigation, it is a good idea to keep the dashboard layout simple, so that it can explore and capture the most relevant information only. A simple click-and-explore interface allows users to navigate a dashboard effortlessly, and usability increases adoption.

While you might want to group all the metrics onto a single page, it is good to balance graphs and text with suitable whitespace to draw users' attention to details. It's a good idea to get feedback on how the layout and navigation are working for users and then improve the layout and navigation accordingly.

Approvals

It is important to get approval from stakeholders about what needs to be shown on a dashboard and to whom it is shown. In other words, the KPIs and any metrics that are to be shown on a dashboard should be approved by the relevant business stakeholders. For example, dashboards published externally should not show customer purchase details. It is possible to make a dashboard available to many users from multiple groups (such as sales, IT, and marketing) and give access to customer details only to some of these users by applying role-based access control (RBAC).

Approvals may also be related to the events across a dashboard. For example, think about a process flow where approvals are required by relevant stakeholders. With an IT ticket, for instance, the user raising the ticket needs to get approvals upon resolution before closing the ticket. Or with a procurement ticket, approval from the procurement team is required before an order can be placed. These types of approvals would be in effect only when the dashboard is live.

Develop Dashboard

Once approvals are in place, the next step is to develop the dashboards. This is typically done by designers, who work closely with the business intelligence (BI) team. The designers are responsible for deploying and maintaining the dashboard. They take the inputs from the BI team on metrics and post charts and graphics based on mockups or wireframes. Once a dashboard is ready to be deployed in production, the designers ensure that the dashboard is distributed or shared with relevant users, and they get feedback on design elements and keep improving the dashboard as it matures.

Deployment to Production

Finally, a dashboard needs to be deployed in production. During this phase, users get access to relevant information for insights and decision making. This phase occurs both for new deployments and for upgrades of dashboards with new charts or widgets (as in the case of a new release).

With either a new deployment or an upgrade, it is important to have the dashboard rolled out in a phased manner, using one or more deployment methodologies, such as the canary approach or piloting with a subset of users. When the testing feedback is positive and all approvals are in place, you can deploy the dashboard in production. It is also a good idea to incrementally increase user adoption of a dashboard because the dashboard can fulfill its purpose only when the users it was developed for are actively leveraging it. Once a dashboard is deployed, the maintenance and continuous improvement process kicks in.

Delivery Considerations

Once you have developed a dashboard, it is time for users to use it to actively look at the data they want. This can be easier said than done, though. Just developing a dashboard is like developing a product; without any marketing or making noise (in a good way), consumers aren't going to be aware of or actively choose your product (in this case, your dashboard) over other similar products. This section covers topics related to dashboard delivery, including subscriptions, scheduled delivery, and making dashboards interactive.

Subscription

When a dashboard is developed, the hope is that all consumers or users will be able to look at the dashboard for insights. However, when users are on the move or aren't able to sit in front of the dashboard, they can be subscribed to the dashboard feed. Dashboard subscriptions are a great way to keep consumers up to date on the data that matters most to them. Dashboard administrators can use subscriptions to send updates (that is, refreshed dashboards) via email. Such an email typically contains a snapshot of the refreshed dashboard as well as a link to the dashboard. For a team that is using Slack, Microsoft Teams, or some other communication channel, a refreshed dashboard can be delivered via that channel as well.

Scheduled Delivery

Upon activating a subscription for a set of dashboards related to your role, you can set up the subscriptions to deliver refreshed dashboards at regular intervals. You can schedule delivery of dashboards to your email on a periodic basis or get ad hoc delivery. Then recurring deliveries will be made according to the schedules created in the dashboard platform by end users or by dashboard administrators.

Popular BI platforms such as Power BI, Looker, Tableau, Qlik, and Oracle make it possible to easily schedule delivery of dashboards via email in PDF, CSV, and other formats.

Interactive Dashboards

This section describes the different dashboard usage mechanisms—primarily drill-down and roll-up. It also covers other aspects related to the way users consume dashboards.

Drill-down involves double-clicking or zooming into insights. It allows users to move from an overview of data to a more granular view within the same dataset. A user can simply click an interactive section of a dashboard for a metric, and instead of looking at information from a 10,000-foot view, the user can peel the data "onion" to get better insights into the metric. For example, take a look at the two dashboards shown in Figures 13.12 and 13.13. The dashboard in Figure 13.12 shows sales performance data across the United States, and Figure 13.13 shows a drill-down into the Pennsylvania data for much more detailed insights.

> **Note**
>
> The dashboard examples in Figures 13.12 and 13.13 are from https://www.tableau.com/solutions/gallery/superstore.

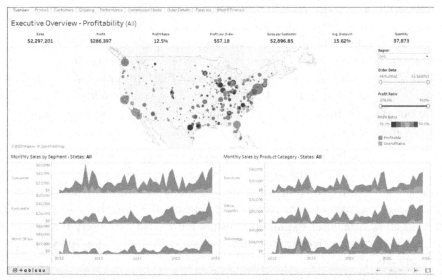

FIGURE 13.12   **Drill-Down Example: Sales Performance Data Across the United States**

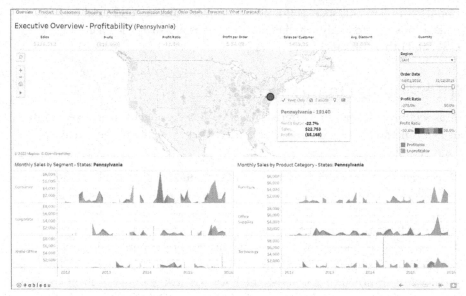

FIGURE 13.13   **Drill-Down into the Pennsylvania Results**

Dashboards are often interactive and allow you to easily perform drill-downs into metrics you're interested in.

A *roll-up* enables you to aggregate or collate data from multiple sources into one place. Specifically, it allows you to get real-time insights from multiple sources of information in one place and take action on those insights. For example, your organization might have multiple websites selling different products, and your teams may be doing search engine optimization (SEO), doing Google and Facebook ad integration, and allowing people to interact across blogs. If you want to see how you can engage better across one or more of these or see where the users are spending most of their time, instead of going across all sites and looking at all the data individually, you can collate all the data in one place by rolling up the data to determine where to focus and how to prioritize the budget.

In addition to allowing drill-down and roll-out, you allow users to add their saved searches to a dashboard so it becomes easier to perform these searches on preselected metrics and pull out data as required. In addition, you can allow users to save their own custom views of a dashboard after they have applied filters. This allows each user to pull up a custom dashboard view every time they want to look for data-driven inputs without needing to spend time applying filters repeatedly.

Earlier in this chapter, we talked about how dashboards are delivered. While dashboards are mostly web based, they can also be delivered via email as snapshots in PDF or CSV format to users who subscribe and set delivery preferences. Dashboards can also be delivered over an app, but in this case, the back-end server is web based.

> **Note**
>
> It is unreasonable to expect C-level executives or members of the board of directors to go to a website to view a dashboard. Instead, you probably want to present them with one or two KPIs from a larger dataset delivered via a presentation; you can deliver dashboards via presentation software such as Microsoft PowerPoint or as PDFs.

Dashboards are naturally always evolving. Users might make requests to change features or the way they interact with dashboard charts, graphs, widgets, and so on. Optimization based on user feedback as well as business requirements is an ongoing phenomenon and takes the same route as any other corporate application: concept formation, development, deployment, and optimization. These are a few ideas about optimizing dashboards in an organization:

▶ Use filters and remove any fields that are not actively used (even after applying filters). Doing so improves the speed of loading and is easy on the eyes.

▶ Where possible, use preprocessed data rather than processing data on the fly when producing or refreshing a dashboard. Doing so helps reduce latency in producing required insights.

▶ Keep narrowing down metrics that become outdated or irrelevant.

▶ Query optimization helps reduce the time to results.

Finally, security is crucial in any organization, and dashboards need to be kept secure. Any dashboards delivered to an internal audience (that is, private dashboards) should be limited to the right audience using access permissions. For example, managers may not be given permission to view a dashboard for directors, and directors may not be given permissions for dashboards meant for executives. Any public dashboards ideally should allow everyone to view the published data insights.

> **Note**
>
> RBAC should be deployed appropriately to give the right permission to the right audience for any privately published dashboards.

Cram Quiz

Answer these questions. If you cannot answer these questions correctly, consider reading this section again until you can.

1. Dashboards can be used to zoom into the details of a specific metric. What is the term for this?
   - ○ **a.** Zoom-out
   - ○ **b.** Pull-up
   - ○ **c.** Roll-up
   - ○ **d.** Zoom-in
   - ○ **e.** Drill-down

2. Users can subscribe to dashboards and reports and have them delivered as which of the following? (Choose all that apply.)
   - ○ **a.** Dashboard snapshots in an email
   - ○ **b.** Dashboard links in an email
   - ○ **c.** Dashboard snapshots over Slack or Teams
   - ○ **d.** Dashboard links over Slack or Teams

3. What type of audience would benefit most from reporting on metrics such as first-contact resolution, volume of tickets, average resolution/reply time, and asset management?
   - ○ **a.** Management
   - ○ **b.** Vendors
   - ○ **c.** IT
   - ○ **d.** Leadership

4. Which of the following is essentially a replica of a final dashboard?
   - ○ **a.** Mockup
   - ○ **b.** Wireframe
   - ○ **c.** Layout
   - ○ **d.** Design outlook

Cram Quiz Answers

1. **Answer: e. Drill-down.** Drill-down involves double-clicking or zooming into insights. It allows users to move from an overview of data to a more granular view within the same dataset.

2. **Answer: a. Dashboard snapshots in an email, b. Dashboard links in an email, c. Dashboard snapshots over Slack or Teams, d. Dashboard links over Slack or Teams.** Dashboards can be delivered as snapshots of a refreshed dashboard or as links or both, and they can be sent via email or Slack or Teams or any other communication software.

3. **Answer: c. IT.** The IT team would use metrics such as first-contact resolution, volume of tickets, average resolution/reply time, and asset management.

4. **Answer: a. Mockup.** A mockup is essentially a replica of a final dashboard that can be used to demonstrate the look and feel before the development work begins.

What Next?

If you want more practice on this chapter's exam objectives before you move on, remember that you can access all of the Cram Quiz questions on the Pearson Test Prep software online. You can also create a custom exam by objective with the Online Practice Test. Note any objective you struggle with and go to that objective's material in this chapter.

CHAPTER 14

Data-Driven Decision Making: Leveraging Charts, Graphs, and Reports

This chapter covers Objective 4.4 (Given a scenario, apply the appropriate type of visualization) and Objective 4.5 (Compare and contrast types of reports) of the CompTIA Data+ exam and includes the following topics:

▶ Types of data visualizations

▶ Types of reports

For more information on the official CompTIA Data+ exam topics, see the Introduction.

This chapter discusses data visualization techniques. It also discusses topics such as static vs. dynamic reports, ad hoc/one-time reports, self-service/on-demand reports, and recurring reports.

Types of Data Visualizations

CramSaver

If you can correctly answer these questions before going through this section, save time by skimming the Exam Alerts in this section and then completing the Cram Quiz at the end of the section.

1. Which of the following charts or graphs leverages geographic data to show values across states, countries, or regions?

   a. Choropleth map

   b. Word map

   c. Word cloud

   d. All of these answers are correct.

2. A histogram represents the data distribution over a(n) _____.

   a. semi-structured period

   b. unstructured period

   c. organized period

   d. continuous interval period

3. Review the following image:

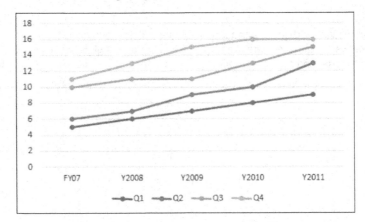

The dots connecting the lines in the line chart are known as _____.

   a. data points

   b. data values

   c. markers

   d. connectors

4. What type of visualization is shown in the following figure?

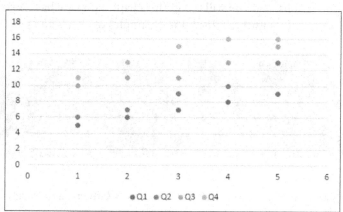

$$\text{Q1} \quad \text{Q2} \quad \text{Q3} \quad \text{Q4}$$

    a. Bubble chart

    b. Scatter plot

    c. Line chart

    d. Waterfall chart

Answers

1. Answer: a. Choropleth map. Geographic map data visualizations, also known as choropleth maps or thematic maps, are a novel way to show comparative values across states, countries, or regions.

2. Answer: d. continuous interval period. A histogram represents the data distribution over a defined period or a continuous interval period. This type of visualization is useful for presenting a particular occurrence frequency; in other words, it shows how many times a specific value occurs.

3. Answer: c. markers. The dots connecting the lines in the line chart are known as markers.

4. Answer: b. Scatter plot. This figure shows a scatter plot.

Data-enabled decision making is vital—particularly in the business world. Businesses run for profit, and insights about what activities will yield maximum profit are essential to business stakeholders. Different parties might be involved in gathering and synthesizing data, making sense of data being collected (via business intelligence), and identifying actionable steps on the basis of insights.

Efficient ways of interacting with information are crucial to the success of any business or organization. Hence, it is vital that information be gathered and synthesized with the help of suitable processes. It is important that outcomes be understood and presented in accessible way.

Many techniques can be used for visualizing data, as discussed in the following sections. Microsoft Excel is one of the most popular tools for generating business charts and graphs, and you will see in this chapter that we have leveraged Microsoft Excel as the software to generate examples of charts and graphs.

ExamAlert

CompTIA Data+ exam focuses on various data visualizations. It is useful to experiment with your own data set and leverage Microsoft Excel to visualize data in various charts and formats and understand how they differ from each other as well as, when one is more useful than other.

To create a graph or a chart in Excel, go to **Insert > Charts**, as shown in Figure 14.1.

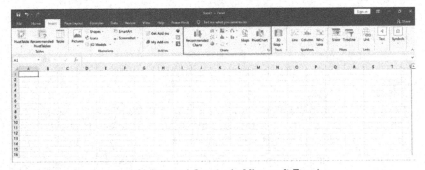

FIGURE 14.1   Creating Charts and Graphs in Microsoft Excel

Line Charts

A line chart (also known as a line graph) shows a set of points (of information) connected by a continuous segment of line. Line charts are usually used to show how information varies over a time period.

Note

Line charts are mostly used to depict trends.

Figure 14.2 shows an example of a line chart.

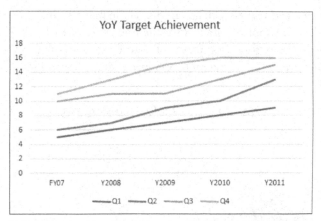

FIGURE 14.2   Line Chart Showing YoY Target Achievement

This chart is built on the data shown in Table 14.1.

TABLE 14.1   **Sales Data by Quarter, Y2007–Y2011 (in $M)**

Quarter	Y2007	Y2008	Y2009	Y2010	Y2011
Q1	5	6	7	8	9
Q2	6	7	9	10	13
Q3	10	11	11	13	15
Q4	11	13	15	16	16

In this line chart, the x-axis shows quarters (that is, Q1, Q2, Q3, and Q4) in a financial year, and the y-axis displays the target achieved during each of these quarters. The individual data points that are connected by the line are known as *markers*. The line connects the markers in a dot-to-dot fashion.

> **Fun Fact**
>
> You can create your very own line charts in Microsoft Excel. All you need to do is create a table with values in it and then go to **Insert > Charts** and select the type of chart you want to make. It's as easy as a few clicks.

Pie Charts

The pie chart is one of the oldest and most basic chart types used for data visualization. A pie chart, also known as a circle chart, resembles a pie with slices that represent data categories and together make up the whole pie, totaling 100%. The size of each slice is proportionate to its value. Pie charts are ideal for making comparisons and visualizing proportions. Because pie charts tend to be very basic, they are appropriate for giving an overview of data splits and for key takeaways.

Figure 14.3 shows a pie chart based on Table 14.1 for Q1 across all years.

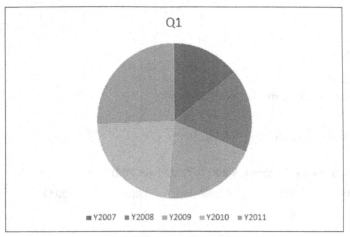

FIGURE 14.3   **Pie Chart in Microsoft Excel**

Bubble Charts

A bubble chart is an extension of a scatter plot graph (discussed in the next section). In a bubble chart, each dot represents a single data point, and the value of the variable for every point is indicated by the size of the dot. The bubble chart in Figure 14.4 shows sales revenue across Q1 and Q3 for the sample data from Table 14.1.

Figure 14.5 shows the selections you use to draw scatter charts (discussed in the next section) and bubble charts in Microsoft Excel. As mentioned earlier, you can draw multiple other charts as well by selecting **Insert > Charts**.

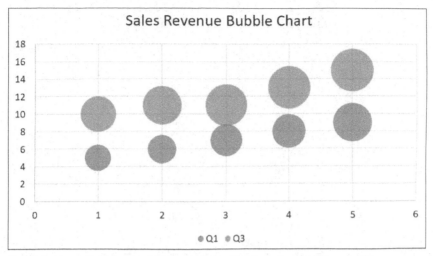

FIGURE 14.4 **Bubble Chart Showing Sales Numbers Across Q1 and Q3**

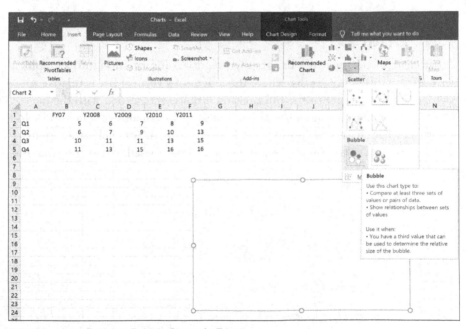

FIGURE 14.5 **Drawing Bubble Charts in Excel**

Scatter Plots

A scatter plot, which is very similar to a bubble chart, represents information for two variables, displayed using points plotted against vertical and horizontal axes. A scatter plot is usually used to determine the relationship between two variables. Figure 14.6 shows a scatter plot for the data from Table 14.1.

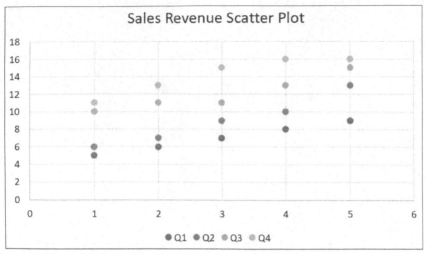

FIGURE 14.6   **Scatter Plot**

Bar Charts

A bar chart, also known as a bar graph, categorizes information into a graphic with bars of different lengths, where the length of a vertical bar is relative to the quantity or amount of the information it represents. Along with the pie chart, the bar chart is one of the oldest and simplest visualization methods. To interpret a bar chart, you consider the length of the bar for each category in order to find its value. Figure 14.7 shows a bar chart based on the information from Table 14.1.

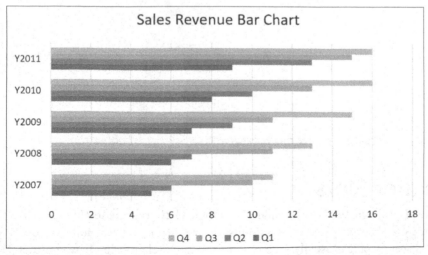

FIGURE 14.7   **Bar Chart**

Bar charts can be oriented both horizontally and vertically. Figure 14.7 shows an example of a horizontal bar chart.

Histograms

A histogram represents the data distribution over a defined period or a continuous interval period. This type of visualization is useful for presenting a particular occurrence frequency; in other words, it shows how many times a specific value occurs.

Figure 14.8 shows a histogram based on the data from Table 14.1.

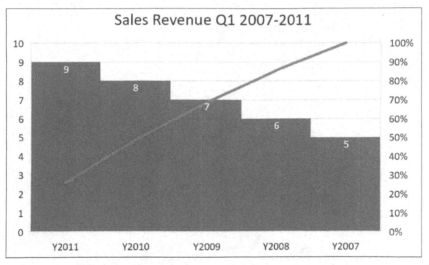

FIGURE 14.8   **Histogram**

What's the difference between a bar chart and a histogram? Well, a bar chart and a histogram are very similar except that a histogram groups numbers into ranges, and there are no gaps between the bars in a histogram.

Histograms are typically used to show results of continuous data, such as:

▶ The number of students in an educational institution

▶ Sales numbers over quarters

▶ Heights

▶ Weights

▶ BMIs

A histogram always looks "backward" in time and never projects forward.

Waterfall Charts

A waterfall chart visualizes data by denoting how a value is modified as it moves between two points and is impacted by various factors, such as time. Such a chart helps identify the net change in a specific value between two points. A waterfall chart is different from a bar chart as it depicts all of the unique elements that lead to that net change and visualizes them individually. This helps the observer understand how a value has declined or grown over a specific period.

Figure 14.9 shows a waterfall chart depicting sales revenue, based on the data from Table 14.1.

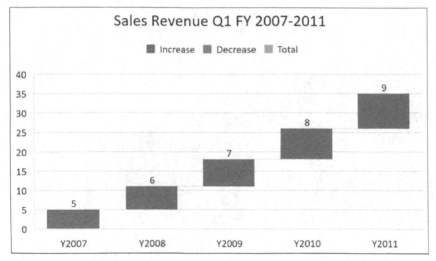

FIGURE 14.9 **Waterfall Chart**

In Figure 14.9, you can see that, from right to left, the values form a waterfall shape—hence the name of the visual. A key element of a waterfall chart is that the beginning point of each bar is the ending point of the previous bar.

Heat Maps

A heat map is a visualization that uses color to show differences in information. Heat maps use colors to communicate values and make it simple for observers to determine trends quickly and get a comparative view of a dataset.

> **Note**
>
> In Microsoft Excel, a heat map is generated based on values in cells, and minimal values are assigned closer to red, whereas maximum values are closer to green. Figure 14.10 shows a heat map in Microsoft Excel based on the data from Table 14.1.

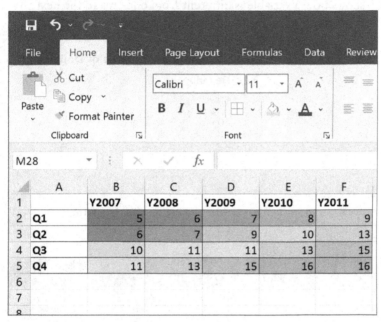

FIGURE 14.10 **Heat Map**

If you're keen to generate your own heat map, you can go to **Home > Conditional Formatting > Color Scales** in Excel (see Figure 14.11).

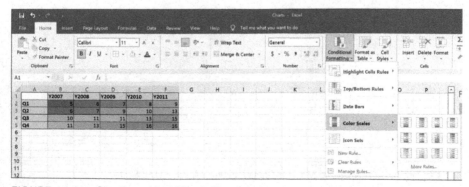

FIGURE 14.11 **Creating a Heat Map in Excel**

Geographic Maps

Geographic map data visualizations, also known as choropleth maps or thematic maps, provide a novel way to show comparative values across states, countries, or regions. A geographic map uses shading, color, and other patterns to visualize the relevant mathematical values across geographic areas. The color of each location on the map is in proportion to its corresponding data values. A geographic map shows how a variable is different from one area to the next. To see an example of this type of visualization, consider the data in Table 14.2.

TABLE 14.2 **U.S. State Data for Sales Revenue (in Millions of Dollars)**

State	Revenue
California	50
Hawaii	10
Indiana	20
Virginia	40

Figure 14.12 shows a geographic map created based on the data from Table 14.2.

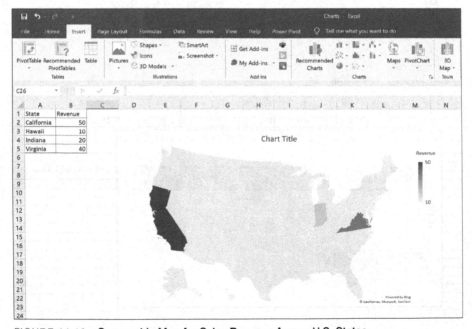

FIGURE 14.12 **Geographic Map for Sales Revenue Across U.S. States**

In this case, the geographic map was generated using the built-in function Maps under **Insert > Maps > Filled Map**, as shown in Figure 14.13.

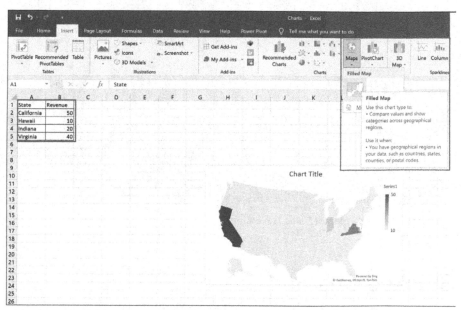

FIGURE 14.13   **Generating a Geographic Map in Excel**

Tree Maps

Tree maps are used to capture data values in a hierarchical structure and present the information visually. A tree map is a series of rectangles, with the tree's branches represented by rectangles and any sub-branches represented by smaller rectangles, each of which represents a proportionate data value.

A larger rectangle shows the division of information in the tree and can be broken into smaller rectangles so that, when a quantitative value is assigned to a field, its size is displayed in proportion to that quantity and to the other quantities (in a part-to-whole relationship) within the parent category.

Figure 14.14 shows a tree map for sales revenue across the years 2007 through 2011, based on the data from Table 14.1.

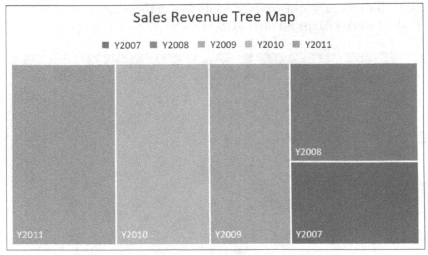

FIGURE 14.14 **Tree Map of Sales Revenue**

Stacked Charts

A stacked chart, also known as a stacked bar graph, is an extension of a bar chart in which each bar is divided into a number of sub-bars stacked together. A bar is drawn for each level of the categorical variable, and the bar's length indicates the numeric value of the variable. Figure 14.15 shows an example of a stacked chart.

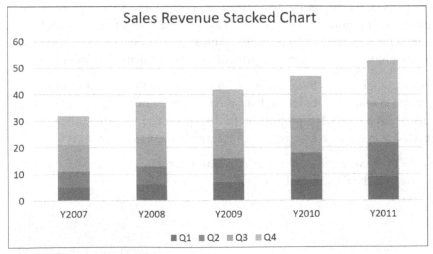

FIGURE 14.15 **Stacked Chart**

This chart is based on the data from Table 14.1. As you can see, the quarterly achievements for each year are stacked together and shown as a categorical representation with clear demarcations across Q1–Q4. This visualization provides an easier-to-read and easier-to-understand view of information than would a bar chart with four bars for each year.

> **Note**
>
> While stacked bar charts look great, they can be hard for audiences to interpret. A stacked bar chart provides a good first look at data, giving a basic idea of year-over-year performance. To get a more granular view of the same data, you can break down each year separately and use a regular bar chart to compare quarters across each year.

Infographics

An infographic, or information graphic, is a visual illustration of data that makes it easier to understand information, often in a fun way. Infographics tend to combine otherwise disparate images, data, and text to tell a compelling story that is easy for stakeholders to understand. Infographics provide a very user-friendly way to view trends and patterns. Figure 14.16 shows an example of an infographic about smart home features.

Many online services can create infographics for you, such as:

▶ **Canva:** https://www.canva.com/create/infographics/

▶ **Visme:** https://visme.co/make-infographics/

▶ **Vista:** https://create.vista.com/create/infographics/ (which was used to create Figure 14.16)

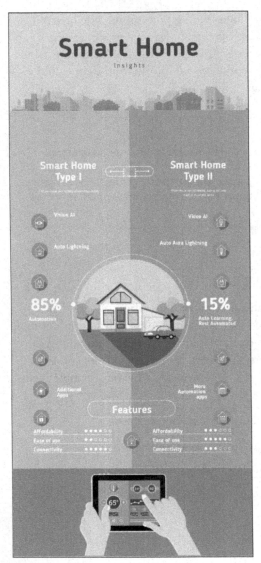

FIGURE 14.16 **Smart Home Infographic**

Word Clouds

A word cloud, also known as a tag cloud, is a visual in which text content is shown in a random graphic manner. As a general rule, the more frequently a specific word is mentioned in a dataset, the larger it appears in the word cloud.

Word clouds are frequently used as eye-catching graphics. In addition to being larger than other words in a word cloud, key words may look bolder and may leverage a color scheme that indicates their frequency. Figure 14.17 shows a word cloud based on sales key words.

FIGURE 14.17 **Word Cloud Based on Frequently Used Sales Terms**

Cram Quiz

Answer these questions. The answers follow the last question. If you cannot answer these questions correctly, consider reading this section again until you can.

1. Which of the following is the most intuitive method for interacting and understanding data insights or trends?

   ○ **a.** Reading processed data tables

   ○ **b.** Visualizing data

   ○ **c.** Reading metadata

   ○ **d.** Extracting data from various sources

2. Which of the following visualizations uses multiple words to visually illustrate outcomes based on the frequency of words?

   ○ **a.** Bar chart

   ○ **b.** Histogram

   ○ **c.** Word cloud

   ○ **d.** Line chart

   ○ **e.** All of these answers are correct.

3. What is shown in the following figure?

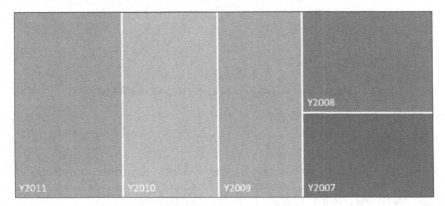

   ○ **a.** Line chart

   ○ **b.** Bar chart

   ○ **c.** Word cloud

   ○ **d.** Tree map

4. Which of the following combines text, images, and other data to tell a compelling story to the audience?

    ○ **a.** Word cloud

    ○ **b.** Metadata

    ○ **c.** Infographic

    ○ **d.** Stacked chart

Cram Quiz Answers

1. **Answer: b. Visualizing data.** Visualizing data or data visualization is one of the most effective ways to help users understand data insights or trends.

2. **Answer: c. Word cloud.** A word cloud is a visualization in which text content is shown in a graphic manner that emphasizes the frequency of the words.

3. **Answer: d. Tree map.** A tree map is a series of rectangles that are used to capture data values in a hierarchical structure to present information visually.

4. **Answer: c. Infographic.** Infographics tend to combine otherwise disparate images, data, and text to tell a compelling story.

Reports

CramSaver

If you can correctly answer these questions before going through this section, save time by skimming the Exam Alerts in this section and then completing the Cram Quiz at the end of the section.

1. Which of the following reports give a clear representation of organizational performance levels?

   a. KPI report

   b. Tactical report

   c. Risk and regulatory report

   d. Compliance report

2. On-demand or self-service reports are beneficial to which of the following? (Choose all that apply.)

   a. Customers

   b. Service providers

   c. External vendors

   d. Non-stakeholders

3. Ad hoc reporting is characterized by which of the following?

   a. It is easy to adopt and follow.

   b. It is web based.

   c. It is robust.

   d. All of these answers are correct.

4. Static reporting is useful for depicting data related to which of the following?

   a. An ongoing time series

   b. Continuous values

   c. A preset period

   d. Metadata

Reports in the context of decision making should be viewed through the lens of analytics as a tool for getting better insights about past, present, and future data to drive decisions as well as optimize the performance of an organization. Reports usually bring together various sources of information that can be used across strategic and operations decision making.

Following are some of the key aspects of creating reports:

▶ It is important to know your target audience. If you don't, your reports may not be as relevant as you think they are.

▶ It is important to consider defining the key performance indicators (KPIs) and key data points used in the report.

▶ It is important to leverage pertinent data sources.

▶ It is important to create reports that are easy to understand and that clearly communicate key highlights.

▶ A report should show clear outcomes and related actionable objectives.

The sections that follow describe the various reports that you can leverage for data-driven decision making.

Static Reporting

As the name suggests, static reports are static in nature and offer insights about data or trends at a point in time or during a specific time period. With static reports, decisions can be made based on data from a particular day, month, or year. Essentially, static reports help examine data points and key information from the past to drive future decision making. For example, during a sales campaign, the number of respondents who responded to the campaign and the features they liked most in a newly launched product could be presented in a static report that would help guide the product owners and other stakeholders to ensure that they incorporate the in-demand features in the upcoming release of the product. In simpler words, static reports help examine the data points and key information in the past to drive future decision making.

Static reports can be saved in many formats, including PDF, Excel, and Word files. Figure 14.18 shows a static report that details sales achievements for fiscal year 2021.

FIGURE 14.18   Static Report Showing Sales Revenue

Note

This static report was created using https://create.piktochart.com/.

Static reports are typically archived after their initial use. However, they can be used later to analyze trends such as sales trends across previous years and to provide direction for things that can be improved in the upcoming year.

Dynamic Reports

In contrast to a static report, a live report portrays information about events as they happen (similar to streaming movie). For example, your personal wearable health device shows you real-time data such as your heartbeat and calories burned during your daily run; this is a form of live reporting. While live reporting is useful at an individual level or perhaps even at a team level, not all live reporting is useful at corporate and leadership levels.

ExamAlert

Static, dynamic, ad-hoc, and self-service, and other reports are a key topic in CompTIA Data+ exam. Be sure to understand the use cases of such reports.

Dynamic reporting is a mashup of static reporting with elements of live reporting. Dynamic reports are usually graphical outlays that combine live and static reporting elements so that an observer can click through links to the different types of data needed—on demand. For example, the dynamic report in Figure 14.19 shows a Q1 sales performance report with live data on projections for the upcoming week.

FIGURE 14.19 Dynamic Report for Sales Performance

> **Note**
>
> This dynamic report was created using https://create.piktochart.com/.

Table 14.3 describes the key differences between static and dynamic reports.

TABLE 14.3 **Static vs. Dynamic Reports**

Characteristic	Static Reports	Dynamic Reports
Key purpose	A static report presents data at a point in time for future decision making.	A dynamic report offers both data at a point in time and real-time insights.
Usability and intuitiveness	Information is mostly text based, and a lack of interactive functions makes deriving insights slower. Moreover, static reports are useful for a shorter period due to the content being relevant for a particular period.	A dynamic report is created using static information as well as stimulating visuals based on KPIs to improve storytelling. It is possible to reuse dynamic reports by updating live content and customizing the content and functionality.
Accessibility	Static reports are generally delivered via emails or distribution lists, and users need access to their corporate email address to get the insights.	Users can log in to the relevant dashboard from anywhere, across their corporate devices or their own devices, to immediately get insights.

Ad Hoc/One-Time Reports

Ad hoc reporting, sometimes also called one-time reporting, helps users generate reports on the fly such that they don't have to wait for reports to be generated to answer business questions immediately. For example, if you're about to walk into a leadership meeting and want to be equipped with updated sales revenue or performance data for the past 2 weeks, you won't want to wait for a standard quarterly analysis report but would want to generate a one-time report to augment the discussion.

Some of the professions/industries where ad hoc reporting is commonly used are:

▶ Sales

▶ Recruitment

- ▶ Retail
- ▶ Education
- ▶ Healthcare

Ad hoc reports are not a substitute for other reports; rather, they should be seen as augmenting to the recurring (static or dynamic) daily, weekly, or monthly reports. Business users should be able to use ad hoc reports to improve the data-driven decision-making process.

Self-Service/On-Demand Reports

As the name suggests, self-service, or on-demand, reports can be generated by end users without any intervention from IT or analysts. Ad hoc reporting is a very good example of self-service reporting.

Users can leverage business intelligence tools to generate self-service reports, which reduce the workload for IT, provide cost savings, save time, and empower users to create their own reports rather than chase down someone to generate reports for them. End users (including executives) can customize reports as they like in order to tell a particular story and put things into perspective. Now, this is user empowerment!

Recurring Reports

Recurring reports are reports that are scheduled and generated based on predetermined KPIs. These reports are useful in that they save time and cost because they are run at known intervals, such as weekly, fortnightly, or monthly, and users can rely on these reports to come in so they can go about getting insights from these reports. Recurring reports may be either sent to specific email addresses or distribution lists, depending on the report content and at the report owner's discretion. For example, whereas a sales revenue report might be sent to all VPs and executives, a performance report might be shared with all sales staff.

There are three categories of recurring reports—compliance, risk and regulatory, and operational reports—as detailed in Table 14.4.

TABLE 14.4 **Compliance, Risk and Regulatory, and Operational Reports**

Characteristic	Compliance Reports	Risk and Regulatory Reports	Operational Reports
Function	These reports help ensure that all required steps are being taken to be fully compliant with local standards.	Regulatory reports are used to share data with local/relevant authorities to showcase that everything is in order as per the required regulatory provisions.	These reports enable insights to processes and efficiencies that can be looked into for optimizing ongoing operations. Operational reports are also known as key performance indicator (KPI) reports.
What they offer	These reports enable risk management based on the extra measures required for compliance.	These reports enable the various departments in an organization to share their insights on various regulatory aspects and to reduce risk by following guidance from previous findings.	These reports help line-of-business stakeholders get better insights into their daily operations and what can be done to increase performance and optimize processes for maximum output.

Tactical/Research Reporting

In a research report, a researcher reports findings on a topic of interest such that readers of the report can understand the outcomes in a straightforward manner. These reports are commonly used in science, medicine, education, and other fields.

Tactical reporting is focused on more immediate goals related to improving operational metrics. These reports focus on associations with operational tasks that are performed in groups or individually to realize strategic outcomes.

When you combine tactical and research reporting, you get tactical research. For example, an organization may have data analysts compare products from competitors, including pricing and the sales figures a class of products is achieving as compared to the parent company. In this case, the analysts may be conducting a tactical pricing comparison while researching key factors for increased sales of competitive products.

Cram Quiz

Answer these questions. If you cannot answer these questions correctly, consider reading this section again until you can.

1. On-demand, or self-service, reporting does not require which of the following?
   - ○ **a.** IT involvement
   - ○ **b.** Vendor support
   - ○ **c.** Cloud resources
   - ○ **d.** All of these answers are correct.

2. What is one of many positive reasons for adopting ad hoc reporting?
   - ○ **a.** It removes duplicate entries.
   - ○ **b.** It ensures data filtering.
   - ○ **c.** It enables access to an external organization's data.
   - ○ **d.** It reduces the workload on the IT department.

3. Dynamic reporting is a mix of which of the following? (Choose two.)
   - ○ **a.** Real reports
   - ○ **b.** Recurring reports
   - ○ **c.** Static reports
   - ○ **d.** Live reports

4. Which type of report is generated based on predetermined KPIs on a regular schedule?
   - ○ **a.** Static report
   - ○ **b.** Live report
   - ○ **c.** Dynamic report
   - ○ **d.** Recurring report

Cram Quiz Answers

1. **Answer: a. IT involvement.** On-demand, or self-service, reporting does not require IT involvement.

2. **Answer: d. It reduces the workload on the IT department.** Adopting ad hoc reporting reduces the workload on the IT department as users have direct access to reports that they can generate from a dashboard.

3. **Answer: c. Static reports, d. Live reports.** Dynamic reporting is based on static and live report content.

4. **Answer: d. Recurring report.** Recurring reports are reports that are scheduled and generated based on predetermined KPIs.

What Next?

If you want more practice on this chapter's exam objectives before you move on, remember that you can access all of the Cram Quiz questions on the Pearson Test Prep software online. You can also create a custom exam by objective with the Online Practice Test. Note any objective you struggle with and go to that objective's material in this chapter.

CHAPTER 15

Data Governance Concepts: Ensuring a Baseline

This chapter covers Objective 5.1 (Summarize important data governance concepts) of the CompTIA Data+ exam and includes the following topics:

▶ Data governance concepts

▶ Access requirements

▶ Security requirements

▶ Storage environment requirements

▶ Use requirements

▶ Entity relationship requirements

▶ Data classification

▶ Jurisdiction requirements

▶ Data breach reporting

For more information on the official CompTIA Data+ exam topics, see the Introduction.

This chapter focuses on data governance concepts. Data governance ensures that there is an established baseline that covers multiple aspects, such as data security requirements, storage requirements, data classification, and more. This chapter covers specifics related to data access, data security, data use, and data storage environment requirements. It also describes entity relationship requirements such as record link restrictions, data constraints, and cardinality. This chapter also covers data classification, which forms the basis for classifying and segregating different types of data, such as personally identifiable information (PII), personal health information (PHI), and Payment Card Industry (PCI) information. The impacts of industry and government regulations are discussed, as are jurisdiction requirements. In addition, this chapter covers data breach reporting.

Data governance is all about ensuring that there is a baseline to uphold the quality, security, accessibility, availability, integrity, and usefulness of data—throughout the data life cycle. Data governance offers bases to define:

▶ Who is allowed to access data within or from outside an organization

▶ Who has control to update data assets within the organization

▶ What sort of reporting mechanisms must be in place to ensure appropriate regulatory and compliance reporting

Data governance is not a solo effort by one body within an organization; rather, it is a cumulative effort by the whole organization. While there are well-defined roles such as data custodian, data owner, and data steward that empower data governance, within an organization, ensuring data governance requires participation from all lines of business and from all stakeholders. Following is a summary of these three key roles:

▶ **Data owner:** Usually represented by a stakeholder in higher leadership, this role looks into the data classification, data protection, data quality, and data use in an organization. This role is responsible for maintaining data quality.

▶ **Data custodian:** As the name implies, a data custodian is responsible for enforcement of security controls based on an organization's data governance standards. Sometimes data custodians are also known as data operators.

▶ **Data steward:** Sometimes also known as data architects, data stewards are responsible for day-to-day data management. They are the subject matter experts for different data domains (for example, supply chain management, business processes).

Data governance ensures that quality data is available at all times for organizational use and that all the right users of data can make decisions based on quality data. Following are a few merits of implementing proper data governance:

▶ **Better and faster decision making for the organization:** When quality data is available throughout the organization, better data-driven insights can be derived, which leads to faster decision making.

▶ **Compliance adherence:** Good data governance automatically leads to better reporting for both internal and external bodies and ensures compliance at all levels.

▶ **Better customer service:** Good quality data implies that customer records are updated and customers can get more personalized service.

▶ **Regulated data management:** Using data governance frameworks, an organization can decide between regulated and unregulated data, and it can classify and manage the data that is subject to various regulations.

Figure 15.1 provides insight into how seriously organizations are taking data governance and consent to use data.

FIGURE 15.1 **Data Consent Request**

Access and Security Requirements

CramSaver

If you can correctly answer these questions before going through this section, save time by skimming the Exam Alerts in this section and then completing the Cram Quiz at the end of the section.

1. Which of the following can be used to limit an employee's access to data?

   a. Contextualization

   b. Traffic updating

   c. RBAC

   d. Software updates

2. Which of the following data types may require that a data use agreement be set up between two or more parties? (Choose all that apply.)

   a. PII

   b. Public

   c. PHI

   d. External

3. Which encryption scheme is shown in the following figure?

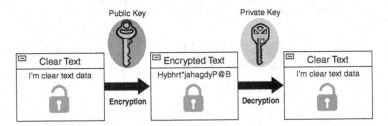

   a. ECC

   b. Symmetric encryption

   c. Public key encryption

   d. Third-party key encryption

4. *CIA triad* is a frequently used term in the information security world. What does CIA stand for?

   a. Continuity, integrity, availability

   b. Confidentiality, integrity, availability

   c. Continuity, integrity, awareness

   d. Confidentiality, importance, availability

5. What are the two types of data masking?

   a. Ongoing

   b. Once in a while

   c. Static

   d. Dynamic

Answers

1. **Answer: c. RBAC.** Role-based access control (RBAC) is an established approach to data security whereby the system permits or restricts access based on an individual's role within the organization. Data consumers (that is, the users looking to access data) can only access the data that pertains to their specific job functions.

2. **Answer: a. PII, c. PHI.** A data use agreement (DUA) is a contractual agreement between a data user or requestor of access to information and the data provider or the organization or body offering the data. Protected data includes:

   ▶ Personally identifiable information (PII)

   ▶ Personal health information (PHI)

   ▶ Financial data

3. **Answer: c. Public key encryption.** This figure shows a public key encryption scheme, also known as asymmetric encryption.

4. **Answer: b. Confidentiality, integrity, availability.** The CIA triad is frequently leveraged to guide information security policies in an organization. Confidentiality enables organizations to deploy the right security measures (physical, technical, or administrative) to prevent sensitive information against unauthorized access attempts. Integrity enables organizations to ensure that the data is consistent and accurate over its entire life cycle and is not altered by an unauthorized entity. Availability implies that the data is always accessible in a consistent way for authorized users.

5. **Answer: c. Static, d. Dynamic.** Data masking can be static or dynamic. Whereas static data masking masks data at rest, dynamic data masking (also known as *on-the-fly data masking*) is focused on data in motion (also called data in transit). Data de-identification is a form of dynamic data masking.

Access Requirements

Organizations have to control data access in order to limit data exposure to only authorized users. In order to do that, they may leverage technical or administrative controls, as well as physical controls in some cases. There are also requirements around how data can be transferred and used between two organizations or the type of data that can be released based on the data being protected or unprotected data.

Role-Based and User Group–Based Access

The two major categories of data access requirements or data access control covered in this section are role-based access control and user group–based access control.

Role-Based Access Control

Role-based access control (RBAC) is an established approach to data security whereby the system permits or restricts access based on an individual's role within the organization. Data consumers (that is, the users looking to access data) can only access the data that pertains to their specific job functions. To contextualize this, let's look at an example.

Think of an organization where there are multiple departments, such as sales, services, marketing, HR, and finance. Say that you don't want HR to look at sales specifics and give data access from services department to finance, as these roles are not dependent on each other's data. The organization would create a role-based access control whereby any employee from HR doesn't have access to sales dataset(s) and, similarly, any employee from services doesn't have any access to finance dataset(s). This will ensure that anyone not entitled to data they're trying to access is shunted out; in addition, it will ensure that the right set of people have access to the right data to perform their job roles effectively.

> **Note**
>
> Role-based access control makes it possible to manage access to the database tables, columns, and fields/cells leveraging access control lists (ACLs).

An access management team/group enables RBAC by adding people to predetermined roles and determining the privileges associated with each role.

User Group–Based Access Control

The major difference between role-based and user group–based access control is that while in RBAC, a user can be assigned to one role explicitly, in user group–based access control, a user can be assigned to multiple groups, thereby gaining access to multiple datasets.

For example, consider a user from leadership who needs access to sales, finance, marketing, and HR datasets in order to compile a report on how each group did over the past 12 months. This user can be part of the executives group by definition of their role; however, to give cross-group privileges to this user, you can assign the user to a group called org_executives that has access to all organizational datasets they need access to. This assignment simplifies the problem of assigning one-to-one mapping on a user-to-role basis. Based on the user group assignment, this user would now have access to multiple datasets.

Data Use Agreements and Release Approvals

Now, let's look more closely at two data access requirements:

- ▶ Data use agreements
- ▶ Release approvals

A data use agreement (DUA) is brought into practice when moving protected data from one party to another. Specifically, a DUA is a contractual agreement between a data user or requester of access to information and the data provider or the organization or body offering the data. Protected data includes:

- ▶ Personally identifiable information (PII)
- ▶ Personal health information (PHI)
- ▶ Financial data

A DUA encompasses important topics such as right to use data (also called permitted use), liability arising from the use of data, privacy rights associated with the data, intellectual property rights, and obligations to use data properly. Some of the key aspects covered by a DUA are:

- ▶ Who has ownership of the data, and what are the terms of agreement?
- ▶ What type of data will be shared between the two parties (that is, the user and the provider)?
- ▶ What data will be shared outside of the two parties?

▶ What is the purpose for which the data will be used?

▶ Who is responsible for handling any violations of the agreement?

▶ What type of data security will be adopted?

Now that you understand DUAs, let's focus on data release approvals.

Any private and confidential data (that is, protected data) that is to be released must have certain approvals aligned to it. These approvals are based on policies of an organization—and are often in line with local legislation. If an organization collects data about your health, for example, it should ask for your consent to release it to another organization for processing or analysis; in addition, it must follow the requirements of state and other bodies that govern how such data can be released to the organization's wider network.

There are typically several requirements:

▶ The data must be managed as described in a data management plan.

▶ Any applications managing data and data flows must be well documented.

▶ Unique identifiers that identify an individual must be masked in transit/ storage.

▶ The data repository must be well documented and adhere to applicable standards.

> **Note**
>
> This list of release approvals is not comprehensive.

Security Requirements

Data security is an important topic for many reasons. The majority of organizations are aware that they handle data from different parts of the world and that a variety of different security requirements apply. For example, the European General Data Protection Regulation (GDPR) ensures consumer rights regarding the protection and privacy of their data. Following are some of the key aspects that GDPR protects:

▶ Basic identity information such as name, address, and ID numbers

▶ Health and genetic data

▶ Biometric data

▶ Racial or ethnic data

▶ Political opinions

▶ Sexual orientation

> **Note**
>
> There are many privacy and security requirements globally. Some of the most promi-nent ones in the United States are the California Consumer Privacy Act (CCPA), the Colorado Privacy Act, and the Virginia Consumer Data Privacy Act (Virginia CDPA).

Many data leaks and hacking attempts have left organizations with huge losses in terms of reputation and finances. Security of data in motion and at rest plays an important role, and we will discuss these aspects shortly.

Before we get into the nuts and bolts of data governance, however, it is impor-tant to understand a very basic construct called the *CIA triad* that guides all data security and governance principles. The CIA triad has three pillars:

▶ **Confidentiality:** Confidentiality enables organizations to deploy the right security measures (physical, technical, or administrative) to protect sensitive information from unauthorized access attempts.

▶ **Integrity:** Integrity enables organizations to ensure that data is consistent and accurate over its entire life cycle and is not altered by an unauthor-ized entity.

▶ **Availability:** Availability implies that the data is always accessible in a consistent way for authorized users.

The CIA triad is frequently used to guide information security policies in organizations.

Now that you know some of the basics of data security, you're ready to move on to the concept of data encryption—at rest and in transit.

Data Encryption

> **ExamAlert**
>
> Data security is a very popular topic, and you should expect to see questions on data security—and especially data encryption—on the CompTIA Data+ exam.

Simply put, *encryption* is the process of converting plaintext or readily readable information into ciphertext—scrambled randomized characters that cannot be interpreted easily by someone who is not supposed to have access to the information. Keys are used to encrypt and decrypt data, and only the appropriate users (that is, the users who should have access to the data/information) can use them.

> **Note**
>
> The study of cryptography covers topics such as data encryption and decryption.

Further, encryption can be broadly classified as symmetric and asymmetric. With symmetric encryption, the same key is used for encryption (scrambling) and decryption (unscrambling). In contrast, when using asymmetric encryption, the encrypting key is different from the decrypting key. Symmetric key encryption is also known as shared key encryption, and asymmetric encryption is also known as public key cryptography. Figure 15.2 shows the processes of symmetric and asymmetric encryption.

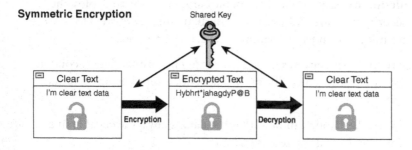

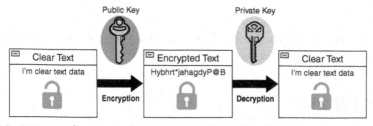

FIGURE 15.2 **Symmetric vs. Asymmetric Encryption Overview**

Symmetric and asymmetric encryption can be implemented by leveraging algorithms such as:

▶ **Blowfish:** Blowfish is a symmetric cipher that has a variable key length from 32 to 448 bits. Blowfish is a block cipher, which means it divides data into fixed blocks (of 64 bits each) when encrypting data.

▶ **Advanced Encryption Standard (AES):** AES, which was established by the U.S. government as a standard for encryption, is a symmetric key algorithm that uses block cipher methods. AES is available in 128-bit, 192-bit, and 256-bit forms, with increasing numbers of rounds of encryption (so that 256-bit AES is more secure than 128-bit and 192-bit AES).

▶ **RSA:** RSA is a public key algorithm, and RSA-based asymmetric encryption is used extensively throughout the Internet. For example, security protocols such as SSH, S/MIME, and SSL/TLS leverage RSA.

▶ **Elliptic Curve Cryptography (ECC):** ECC is an asymmetric cipher that offers better security than RSA, with significantly shorter key lengths.

Why is it important to encrypt data? It is important to keep customer and organizational data private and safe from misuse. Data is more accessible than ever before, and the attack surface (that is, the touchpoints that a hacker can misuse to access data) is ever increasing, thanks to ubiquitous connectivity and access mechanisms. Just storing data in a database that is accessible via username and password is not enough to protect it. Someone who's not supposed to get access to data may get it, but if the data is encrypted, the hacker will end up reading gibberish rather than what they came for. And without the right key, it's very difficult to decrypt the data. Encryption protects valuable data and also helps organizations comply with data-related regulations.

Data encryption can be used for data that is being stored (that is, data at rest) and for data as it is being transmitted (that is, data in motion). Keys are only provided to authorized users.

Data encryption at rest encrypts data when it resides on a storage device and is not actively being used or transferred. Compared to data in motion, data at rest is much less susceptible to attacks and data exfiltration. However, data at rest is not immune to hacking attempts. Encrypting data at rest improves the security posture by reducing accidental or malicious exposure of data due to stolen devices, ransomware attacks, privilege escalation, credential theft, and so on.

Data Transmission

Data is considered in transit or in motion when it is moving between devices or from one database, data warehouse, or data lake to another database, data warehouse, or data lake. This movement might be over an insecure medium such as the Internet or over a more secure medium, such as a virtual private network (VPN) or Multiprotocol Label Switching (MPLS). Sometimes data is even moved from personal or corporate devices, such as from a laptop to a USB drive or from a DVD to a laptop.

It is easy to see why data is at such great risk during transfer: It has to pass through potentially insecure media and may be exposed to an unintended audience. Sometimes, security concerns might be with the vulnerabilities of the transfer method (for example, an Internet session being hijacked).

Encrypting data during transfer (sometimes also referred to as *end-to-end encryption*) safeguards data that is being moved from source to destination through one or more media. There are various ways to protect data during transmission, including:

▶ **Encryption algorithms:** A longer encryption key length offers stronger protection. Hence, when you're selecting an encryption algorithm such as AES, consider going for AES-192 or AES-256.

▶ **Mobile device management (MDM):** It is pretty common today for organizations to allow employees to bring their own devices to work and to have corporate data such as emails or presentations on their personal devices. Data moving between corporate assets and these devices needs to be encrypted, and the security posture of such a device must be appropriate. This can be achieved by using a bring-your-own-device (BYOD) policy and MDM solutions.

▶ **Secure wireless access:** Almost everybody is on wireless networks at home or at an office, and wireless connectivity needs to be secure. Earlier wireless protocols such as Wired Equivalent Privacy (WEP) are considered to be very weak and are not recommended for use today. Wi-Fi Protected Access 2 (WPA2) and Wi-Fi Protected Access 3 (WPA3) are preferred protocols, and WPA2-AES and WPA3-AES offer maximum security for wireless clients. Further, rogue access points (APs) should not be allowed in a wireless network.

▶ **Secure wired access:** Servers are always hardwired, and sometimes you have to plug in a laptop to a corporate network. To secure the connectivity points (that is, switch ports) on these machines, you can deploy switch port security combined with Layer 2 and Layer 3 access control lists (ACLs), which allow only the relevant traffic to traverse.

▶ **Data loss prevention (DLP):** DLP can be used to ensure that any classified and protected data cannot be exfiltrated from the organization without proper approval. This helps ensure that any deliberate or unknown attempts to expose sensitive data are automatically thwarted.

Every organization should focus on encryption of both data at rest and data in motion as a baseline for good governance and ensuring that data integrity is maintained.

De-identifying Data/Data Masking

Many regulatory compliance requirements require data to be masked (or de-identified) before it can be transmitted or stored. Data de-identification/ masking is different from encryption, where data is changed from its original form. With data masking, some fields or parts of fields may be masked to hide explicit information. An organization's databases might contain personal and sensitive data, and one of the most effective ways to prevent exposure of the data is to mask it before it is used for analysis.

Data masking is important to satisfy multiple regulatory requirements, such as:

▶ **Payment Card Industry Data Security Standard (PCI–DSS):** Masking payment card data

▶ **Health Insurance Portability and Accountability Act (HIPAA):** Masking health data

▶ **General Data Protection Regulation (GDPR):** Masking personal data

▶ **Family Educational Rights and Privacy Act (FERPA):** Masking student data

▶ **Sarbanes-Oxley Act (SOX):** Masking U.S. public company and accounting firm data

Data masking can take two main forms: static data masking or dynamic data masking. Whereas static data masking masks data at rest, dynamic data masking is focused on data in motion (also known as *on-the-fly data masking*). Data de-identification is a form of dynamic data masking.

ExamAlert

Data masking is an important concept to know for the CompTIA Data+ exam, and you should know the difference between static and dynamic data masking.

Figure 15.3 shows an example of static data masking.

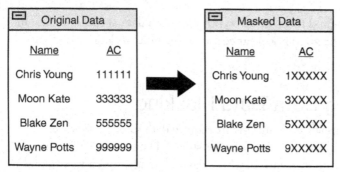

FIGURE 15.3 **Static Data Masking**

It should be apparent from Figure 15.3 that all data that is deemed sensitive (that is, the account numbers) is masked. Any user trying to access this information will see only the masked data, regardless of the user's role.

Static masking might not be useful when you have multiple users who should have different access to data based on their roles. For example, say that your organization wants to give full access to customer account information to sales and minimal access to IT. This can be achieved with dynamic data masking, illustrated in Figure 15.4.

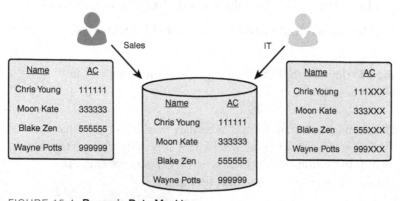

FIGURE 15.4 **Dynamic Data Masking**

As you can see in Figure 15.4, sales users have full access to customer data, whereas IT users only have access to customers' names and part of the account information.

You can use services such as AWS Lake Formation to provide access to data for users in your organization based on their roles/functions. AWS Athena can also anonymize datasets by masking specified fields.

Cram Quiz

Answer these questions. If you cannot answer these questions correctly, consider reading this section again until you can.

1. Organizations need which of the following before they can share the data of their consumers with partner organizations?

   a. Data updates

   b. Data checklist

   c. Data release approvals

   d. All of these answers are correct.

2. If you wanted to give a number of executives access to a consumer dataset, which of the following would be the most effective method?

   a. Email them the dataset every time it's updated.

   b. Give them group-based access for that dataset by placing them into one group.

   c. Put data in the cloud and enable the executives' role-based access.

   d. Enable automatic archival and send them reports.

3. Which encryption scheme is shown in the following figure?

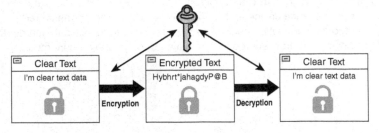

   a. Blowfish

   b. Symmetric key encryption

   c. Public key encryption

   d. Third-party key encryption

4. Which of the following security controls can be used to prevent data exfiltration?

   a. Packet filter

   b. Router

   c. Guards at gates

   d. DLP

5. You can encrypt data while it is _____. (Choose all that apply.)

   a. deleted

   b. printed

   c. in transit

   d. at rest

Cram Quiz Answers

1. **Answer: c. Data release approvals.** When an organization collects data—such as data about your health—it should ask for your consent to release it to another organization for processing or analysis. In addition, state and other bodies govern how such data can be released to the organization's wider network.

2. **Answer: b. Give them group-based access for that dataset by placing them into one group.** It would be most effective to create one group for all similar access requirements, add all individuals to this group, and enable group-based access. It would be far less efficient to give the executives access one by one by using RBAC.

3. **Answer: b. Symmetric key encryption.** This figure shows a shared key encryption scheme, also known as symmetric encryption.

4. **Answer: d. DLP.** Data loss prevention (DLP) can be used to ensure that any classified and protected data cannot be exfiltrated from the organization without proper approvals. This helps ensure that any deliberate or unknown attempts to expose sensitive data are automatically thwarted.

5. **Answer: c. in transit, d. at rest.** Encryption of data at rest encrypts data when it resides on a storage device and is not actively being used or transferred. Encryption of data in motion (that is, during transfer or in transit) safeguards data that is being moved from source to destination through one or more media.

Storage Environment Requirements

CramSaver

If you can correctly answer these questions before going through this section, save time by skimming the Exam Alerts in this section and then completing the Cram Quiz at the end of the section.

1. Which of the following are examples of cloud-based shared drives? (Choose all that apply.)

   a. OneDrive

   b. My Drive

   c. Our Drive

   d. Google Drive

2. The advantage of a cloud-based storage is that it offers which of the following? (Choose all that apply.)

   a. Access to user data from anywhere

   b. Reduction in costs for maintaining storage solutions

   c. Automatic cloud backups

   d. Ability to quickly restore from cloud-native backups

Answers

1. **Answer: a. OneDrive, d. Google Drive.** Modern collaboration workspaces such as Google Drive and Microsoft OneDrive enable users to collaborate and share documents.

2. **Answer: a. Access to user data from anywhere, b. Reduction in costs for maintaining storage solutions, c. Automatic cloud backups, d. Ability to quickly restore from cloud-native backups.** All of these are advantages of using cloud-based storage.

Data can be stored in multiple locations—from on-premises data stores or data lakes to cloud-based data lakes. Moreover, data sharing within and between organizations is required for many business transactions. This section covers data governance from the perspective of where data is stored.

Shared Drives

It is not unusual to see multiple copies of a dataset or a table when multiple users are trying to access data and generating reports or executing queries. Business problems such as redundant and multiple copies of datasets and piles of documents or images, in addition to ever-growing storage requirements, can be resolved by sharing datasets or documents via shared drives.

> **Note**
>
> Shared drives can be both on premises and in the cloud. Windows CIFS shares were the earliest shared drives. Modern collaboration workspaces such as Google Drive and Microsoft OneDrive enable users to collaborate and share documents.

Adopting a shared drive can enable an organization to simplify sharing of documents with intended recipients within and outside the organization. Shared drives can also help resolve storage space issues by reducing the number of duplicate copies of documents flying around in emails. However, it is important to understand that with a shared drive, document ownership gets shifted to the person who is sharing the document with others who have edit or copy rights, and the organizational security policy or governance may not provide appropriate protection. When a single person is the owner of data, they can deauthorize or authorize permissions for every user performing data transactions or edits on that dataset. Without appropriate security controls and data classification as well as user education, shared drives can become messy to manage from a data governance point of view.

On the other hand, shared drives are a boon if managed and deployed correctly. For example, Microsoft SharePoint automatically provides a history of changes and allows users to go back to a point in time and recover critical changes that may have been overwritten. In addition, most shared drives track changes to a document, making it clear who changed critical data and when.

> **ExamAlert**
>
> Shared and local storage are commonly used for data acquisition and post processing storage. These are an important topic for CompTIA Data+ exam.

Local Storage

Local storage refers to data stored on a drive (such as a hard disk drive, solid-state drive, zip drive) in a computer network on an organization's own premises. While it is easier to apply organizational security policies on local storage than in the cloud and to maintain any data egress from protected systems, an organization needs to continue investing in storage systems and must make the information available by performing backups. Table 15.1 covers the advantages and disadvantages of local storage.

TABLE 15.1 **Advantages and Disadvantages of Local Storage**

Advantages	Disadvantages
Local storage offers maximum security as document and file access as well as permissions are maintained by the internal IT staff.	If an end-user device (such as a laptop or phone) is stolen or server access is compromised, the data present on the local drive is compromised or lost.
The organization has physical possession of files and data.	If the systems are down, unless there is a good backup and restore strategy in place, users do not have access to data.
Data access is quick as data is stored locally.	Remote users may find that there is latency when accessing data as it is stored centrally.
The organization has full control of data assets and the way they are shared with external organizations.	Malware such as viruses may be able to destroy or steal data unless there are appropriate security controls and a good data protection/backup system in place.

Cloud-Based Storage

With cloud-based storage, users are able to store data in cloud provider storage (for example, AWS S3 or EBS, Azure Blobs, GCP Cloud Storage). Many cloud providers offer free storage up to a few gigabytes of data, and more storage space can be bought on a subscription basis so that you pay for what is used.

Again, unless there is governance around what type of data can be stored in cloud-based storage as well as how it is managed, it can be quite a task to keep track of documents flowing from cloud storage to external entities. Hence, it is a good idea to develop data classification and security policies, segregate sensitive and internal data, and take other measures to ensure that data quality and security are maintained.

Table 15.2 outlines the advantages and disadvantages of cloud-based storage.

TABLE 15.2 **Advantages and Disadvantages of Cloud-Based Storage**

Advantages	Disadvantages
Users can access data from any anywhere and from any device, which enables them to collaborate and work with data on the go.	Internet access is required to access the data and to update records.
Data loss can be minimized by using native cloud services, and any user or local server hardware crashes or stolen laptops do not impede data access.	Cloud-based data is an easy target for hackers, given the larger attack surface.

Advantages	Disadvantages
Hardware costs are reduced when you move from the up-front investment required for on-premises storage solutions to pay-as-you-go (PAYG) cloud storage solutions.	A data security and governance baseline must be established to ensure that data is accessible only by legitimate users.
Capacity can be extended easily to provide additional storage space when required.	Privacy and security of data stored in the cloud are special considerations.

Cram Quiz

Answer these questions. If you cannot answer these questions correctly, consider reading this section again until you can.

1. AWS S3 is an example of which of the following?

    ○ **a.** Local storage

    ○ **b.** Cloud storage

    ○ **c.** Cloud security

    ○ **d.** Storage encryption

2. Which of the following is an advantage of local storage solution?

    ○ **a.** An adequate backup strategy and plan are required.

    ○ **b.** If a system goes down, backups should be available to restore normal operations.

    ○ **c.** The organization has physical possession of files and data.

    ○ **d.** Stolen data cannot be recovered.

3. Your organization uses a shared drive to share documents with vendors. Which of the following is a disadvantage of using a shared drive?

    ○ **a.** Documents can be shared with vendors on the go.

    ○ **b.** It is easy to share a copy of a document with anyone.

    ○ **c.** Documents can be retrieved from internal and external networks.

    ○ **d.** Organization of documents is simpler, and it is easier to find relevant documents.

    ○ **e.** It is easy to lose sight of how documents are being shared, and implementation of proper governance requires time and effort.

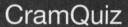

Cram Quiz Answers

1. **Answer: b. Cloud storage.** AWS S3 or EBS, Azure Blobs, and GCP Cloud Storage are examples of cloud storage options.

2. **Answer: c. The organization has physical possession of files and data.** The only real advantage in the context of this question is that the organization has physical possession of files and data and can be confident that it is not losing control of them as it would with a cloud-based storage solution.

3. **Answer: e. It is easy to lose sight of how documents are being shared, and implementation of proper governance requires time and effort.** With a shared drive, document ownership gets shifted to the person who is sharing the document with others who have edit or copy rights, and the organizational security policy or governance may not provide appropriate protection. Without appropriate security controls and data classification as well as user education, shared drives can become messy to manage from a data governance point of view.

Use and Entity Relationship Requirements

CramSaver

If you can correctly answer these questions before going through this section, save time by skimming the Exam Alerts in this section and then completing the Cram Quiz at the end of the section.

1. Which of the following are the main types of data deletion? (Choose two.)

   a. User-requested deletion

   b. Tactical deletion

   c. Regulation-enforced deletion

   d. Strategic deletion

2. Which of the following can you expect an acceptable use policy to address? (Choose all that apply.)

   a. Internet use

   b. Spam and email

   c. Clear desk

   d. Software use

   e. Break time

3. Which of the following are types of cardinality relationships? (Choose all that apply.)

   a. 1:1

   b. 1:N

   c. N:1

   d. N:N

   e. N:1:N

4. Which of these is a modern way to attach to data security restrictions that move with the data?

   a. Access controls

   b. Firewall

   c. Anti-malware

   d. DRM

Answers

1. **Answer: a. User-requested deletion, c. Regulation-enforced deletion.**
   Data deletion can be primarily of two types: user request based and regulation enforced.

2. **Answer: a. Internet use, b. Spam and email, c. Clear desk, d. Software use.** The following issues can be expected to be covered by an acceptable use policy:

   ▶ Internet use

   ▶ Spam and email

   ▶ Clear desk

   ▶ Mobile device use

   ▶ Software use

   ▶ Monitoring

   ▶ Passwords

3. **Answer: a. 1:1, b, 1:N, c. N:1, d. N:N.** All of these except for N:1:N are cardinality relationships.

4. **Answer: d. DRM.** Digital rights management (DRM) is a sophisticated way of ensuring that record linkage works properly and securely. DRM restrictions are attached to records and move wherever the records go or are linked.

Use Requirements

Data is a valuable resource; in fact, it is a lifeline for many organizations. When an organization collects user or consumer data, it must understand the implications of handling the data, from the data use policy to data processing to data deletion. This section starts by covering the basics of acceptable use policies and then discusses data processing, data deletion, and data retention.

Acceptable Use Policies

An organization wants its users to abide by security policies and other policies, such as data protection policies, when using organizational IT assets. An acceptable use policy (AUP) spells out what end users can and cannot do with the organization's assets and information. Organizations typically ask new organizational members and/or vendors as well as suppliers to sign an AUP before giving them permissions for the internal systems or information.

> **ExamAlert**
>
> AUPs are commonly used in enterprises, and you can expect to see questions around this topic on the CompTIA Data+ exam.

An AUP clearly defines the following:

▶ What end users can or cannot do with the corporate assets and information

▶ What happens when there is a breach of the AUP

▶ How to report any breach of the AUP

▶ Any compliance and other requirements associated with the AUP

The following are some of the aspects that can be expected to be covered in an AUP:

▶ Internet use

▶ Spam and email

▶ Clear desk

▶ Mobile device use

▶ Software use

▶ Monitoring

▶ Passwords

It is important for users to understand and accept the AUP before they are given access to organizational data and start leveraging it for analytics or reports. Their use of corporate data is based on their acceptance of the AUP.

Data Processing

Key aspects of data processing are related to data governance. For example, from data acquisition to data processing to data-driven insights, everything should be geared around leveraging data securely and respecting the privacy of personal and identifiable information. This applies to any data processing that is done either manually or using advanced algorithms, including artificial intelligence (AI). A good example of manual data processing would be processing data in multiple spreadsheets and creating pivot tables to reflect information in a primary sheet. A good example of AI-driven data processing would be to leverage metadata and process the most likely outcomes of a set of transactions (via predictive analysis).

Both data and the algorithms used to refine insights may change during their respective life cycles, and it is important for the personnel responsible for creating and using data and algorithms to be accountable. Moreover, as more and more data is collected by organizations, governments, and citizen charter services, the data will be processed by multiple entities using various algorithms. From a governance perspective, dependencies grow, and accountability may gradually be lost. Hence, it is crucial to set up a process in which any data processing mechanism has a clearly stated RACI matrix, which lists the following roles:

▶ Responsible

▶ Accountable

▶ Consulted

▶ Informed

This helps to dictate who owns which part of data processing and what security and privacy controls they should be using.

Data Deletion

Many privacy regulations require that when an organization collects personally identifiable data, the organization must have a good data deletion policy/ guideline in place. While on the business side, stakeholders may want to keep the data forever to drive decision making and prevent the need to collect the data again (which can be costly and time-consuming), on the security and privacy side, regulations limit data usage and retention.

> **Note**
>
> Data deletion can occur in a number of ways. A data deletion policy can specify how an organization deletes the data of users securely and ensure that this deletion is in line with local and international regulations.

Data deletion can be primarily of two types:

▶ **User request based:** Data deletion is usually mandatory when a user whose data was previously collected by the organization initiates a data deletion request. Such a request requires that certain types of data be deleted, such as user contact details or any transactional data. There may be some exceptions to data deletion requirements, including things like retaining data that is required for compliance and legal reasons.

▶ **Regulation enforced:** This type of data deletion, sometimes known as *data purging*, is commonly based on local or international privacy regulations. Data retention (covered in the next section) should be closely related to the organizational and regulatory requirements, and after the data retention cycle is over, data must be deleted/purged in accordance with compliance and/or regulatory requirements.

Cloud providers have formed user request–based deletion processes that are easy to understand and follow. For example, Google Cloud Platform (GCP) has clearly laid out a process for data deletion on Google Cloud (see https:// cloud.google.com/docs/security/deletion).

The four stages of a data deletion request in GCP are as follows:

▶ **Stage 1:** Request for deletion

▶ **Stage 2:** Soft deletion of data

▶ **Stage 3:** Logical deletion of data from active systems

▶ **Stage 4:** Expiration of data from backup systems

You can review the stages of Google Cloud's deletion pipeline at https:// cloud.google.com/docs/security/deletion.

The data deletion process can be very easy or very complex, depending on the organizational data use requirements as well as global or local requirements about safe disposal of customer data.

Data Retention

As briefly mentioned in the previous section, data retention guidelines define how long user/consumer data can be retained as well as how the data should be stored (for example, whether it needs encryption, who can access it and how). In other words, a data retention policy defines how long data can be kept by an organization before it can be securely disposed of or purged.

To simplify the process of data retention, an organization may create a data retention policy that provides directions for storing, holding, and deleting data. A data retention policy should be managed and owned by defined stakeholders within an organization and should meet both organizational needs and regulatory requirements.

Some of the key elements of a data retention policy are as follows:

▶ The time period for keeping each type of data

▶ The regulations that apply to the information collected

▶ Details of data acquisition, such as from whom, where, and why the data was collected

▶ Details on how the organization will store, secure, back up, and purge the information

▶ Directions on what should be done in the event of data breaches or policy violations

In the United States, there are a number of data retention regulations. For example, the Health Insurance Portability and Accountability Act of 1996 (HIPAA) protects individuals' health data, and the Gramm-Leach-Bliley (GLB) Act places a duty on financial service providers to explain to their customers how their information is shared.

Entity Relationship Requirements

This section details data governance as it pertains to entity relationship requirements, such as record link restrictions, data constraints, and cardinality.

Before we get into specifics of data governance pertinent to entity relationship (ER), let's first take a brief look at what entity relationships are and how they can be useful. An ER is a visual method of explaining the relationships among the various entities in a database. Essentially, if you already have a database and wish to derive relationships or are looking to create a relationship based on relationships between the entities, an ER is the ideal solution. Figure 15.5 shows an ER for a simple sales relationship between a seller, a product being sold, and a customer.

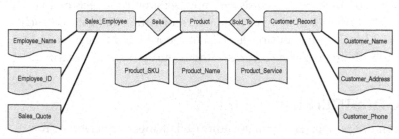

FIGURE 15.5   **ER Model for Product Sales**

In Figure 15.5, the entities are Sales_Employee, Product, and Customer_ Record, and the relationships are Sells and Sold_To. Every entity has certain attributes, and an ER uses them to make everything come together.

ER models give a data governance team a bird's-eye view into systems that contain data so they can more easily apply data classifications and provide valuable information to the teams that are required to protect and store the data.

Record Link Restrictions

Not all data is created equal, and organizations often need to combine data from various sources to get a better picture. In such cases, linking multiple datasets can help alleviate data quality issues. In many cases, linking multiple records can lead to better data quality as well as a better sample size (for statistical analysis). Record linking can be performed by identifying a unique identifier across datasets to be linked.

> **Note**
>
> Record linkage can be done using rule-based as well as probabilistic approaches.

From a governance point of view, it is important to note that records that might contain personally identifiable sensitive information should not be exposed to unauthorized personnel. Linkage from within the organization or from outside the organization (for example, with vendors or suppliers) should be controlled based on a need-to-access basis. Every record must have a security classification that determines who can access (or link to) the record. The most commonly used levels are public, private, and restricted, but an organization can set its own levels.

A more sophisticated way to ensure that record linkage works properly is to apply digital rights management (DRM) restrictions to the records. DRM restrictions can be attached to records and move wherever the records go or are linked. DRM solutions offer encryption of information and controls such as time-based deletion or automatic deletion of records, disabling of saving or printing, and inability to change records without the appropriate security level.

Data Constraints

It is important to protect data from unauthorized changes or deletions. You can use data constraints (that is, rules) to effectively enforce the type of data that can be inserted, updated, or deleted from a table or a column. Whereas table-level constraints apply to a whole table, column-level constraints apply to a specific column.

Why would you apply constraints instead of using access rights or data encryption? While the right level of access (based on the classification level) blocks unauthorized users and encryption keeps prying eyes off the data, neither of these solutions protects against human error or sabotage. Constraints prevent accidental and intentional change of data and offer a way to increase the accuracy and reliability of the data in a database.

> **Note**
>
> Constraints can be applied during creation of a database table or afterward.

The following constraints are typically used by database administrators:

▶ **Primary key:** Ensures that each record has unique values—and no null values.

▶ **Foreign key:** Enforces binding between two tables and verifies the existence of one table's data in the other table.

▶ **Uniqueness:** Ensures that columns have unique values.

▶ **Default value:** Assigns a default value to a column when there is no value provided.

▶ **Check:** Ensures valid entries for a given column by restricting the range of values, types of values, and format of values for the fields.

Cardinality

In the context of data modeling, *cardinality* (or *relationship cardinality*) refers to how one table relates to another table. For example, 1:1 implies that one row in Table 1 relates to one row in Table 2. In addition, there are other relationships, such as 1:N (that is, one-to-many), N:1 (that is, many-to-one), and N:N (that is, many-to-many).

> **ExamAlert**
>
> Cardinality refers to the maximum number of relationships, whereas ordinality refers to the minimum number of relationships.

Using our earlier example, Figure 15.6 shows the cardinality between the seller, the product, and the customer.

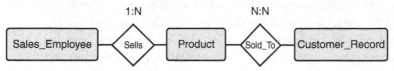

FIGURE 15.6 **Cardinality Overview**

Mapping relationships is great when it is done and leveraged by the intended audience; however, to properly implement governance around who can map what across databases, you should consider access-based and constraint-based controls. You want to ensure that only personnel with the proper level of access and ability to change constraints can amend data in a database and map it across other databases.

Cram Quiz

Answer these questions. If you cannot answer these questions correctly, consider reading this section again until you can.

1. A data retention policy outlines which of the following aspects?
   - ○ **a.** Details on how the organization stores, secures, backs up, and purges information.
   - ○ **b.** Details on what type of analyses are performed on the data.
   - ○ **c.** Details on how the data is linked to metadata.
   - ○ **d.** Details on where the data encryption keys are stored.

2. Which data deletion type is also called data purging?
   - ○ **a.** External deletion
   - ○ **b.** Normal deletion
   - ○ **c.** Regulation-enforced deletion
   - ○ **d.** Out-of-hours deletion

3. Data processing can be influenced in multiple ways, including by which of the following? (Choose two.)

   ○ **a.** Data collection

   ○ **b.** Data in transit

   ○ **c.** Manual processing

   ○ **d.** AI-based processing

4. Which of the following are valid data constraint types? (Choose all that apply.)

   ○ **a.** Primary key

   ○ **b.** Uniqueness

   ○ **c.** Validity

   ○ **d.** Foreign key

   ○ **e.** Integration

5. What is the opposite of cardinality?

   ○ **a.** Plausibility

   ○ **b.** Condity

   ○ **c.** Agility

   ○ **d.** Eagarlity

   ○ **e.** Ordinality

Cram Quiz Answers

1. **Answer: a. Details on how the organization stores, secures, backs up, and purges the information.** The key elements of a data retention policy include the following:

   ○ The time period for keeping each type of data

   ○ The regulations that apply to the information collected

   ○ Details of data acquisition, such as from whom, where, and why the data was collected

   ○ Details on how the organization will store, secure, back up, and purge the information

   ○ Directions on what should be done in the event of data breaches or policy violations

2. **Answer: c. Regulation-enforced deletion.** Regulation-enforced data deletion, also known as data purging, is mostly based on local or international privacy regulations.

3. **Answer: c. Manual processing, d. AI-based processing.** Any data processing that is done either manually or using advanced algorithms, including artificial intelligence (AI), can influence the way the data is processed as both data and the algorithms used change over the life cycle of the data.

4. **Answer: a. Primary key, b. Uniqueness, c. Validity, d. Foreign key.** These are valid data constraints.

5. **Answer: e. Ordinality.** Whereas cardinality specifies the maximum number of relationships across databases, ordinality specifies the minimum number of relationships across databases.

Data Classification, Jurisdiction Requirements, and Data Breach Reporting

CramSaver

If you can correctly answer these questions before going through this section, save time by skimming the Exam Alerts in this section and then completing the Cram Quiz at the end of the section.

1. Which of the following are basic classification levels that should be followed across any organization? (Choose all that apply.)

   a. Secret

   b. Restricted

   c. Private

   d. Public

2. HIPAA is a regulation on which of the following?

   a. PHI

   b. PII

   c. PCI

   d. PKI

3. Which of the following organizations jointly created the PCI-DSS standard? (Choose all that apply.)

   a. American Express

   b. MasterCard

   c. Visa

   d. Discover Financial Services

   e. JCB International

4. GDPR is applicable to which of the following?

   a. Organizations dealing with EU members in the EU only

   b. Organizations dealing with U.S. members in the EU only

   c. Organizations dealing with U.S. members in the United States only

   d. Organizations dealing with EU members anywhere in the world

5. Which term refers to the impact that local legislations of a country may have on data that is stored outside the country of origin?

   a. Data security

   b. Data usability

   c. Data control

   d. Data sovereignty

6. An organization should have which of the following to respond to a data breach?

   a. Data breach policy

   b. Security policy

   c. Risk and regulatory reports

   d. Compliance reports

7. Unauthorized exposure of which of the following would constitute a data breach? (Choose all that apply.)

   a. PII

   b. PHI

   c. PCI

   d. KPI

Answers

1. **Answer: b. Restricted, c. Private, d. Public.** Public, private, and restricted are the three basic classification levels or schemes that should be followed by any organization for classifying protected or non-protected data.

2. **Answer: a. PHI.** HIPAA helped establish baseline security controls and safeguards that administratively, technically, and physically uphold the CIA triad for personal health information (PHI).

3. **Answer: a. American Express, b. MasterCard, c. Visa, d. Discover Financial Services, e. JCB International.** PCI-DSS was created jointly by American Express, MasterCard, Visa, Discover Financial Services, and JCB International to protect cardholders against misuse of their personal and card information.

4. **Answer: d. Organizations dealing with EU members anywhere in the world.** Organizations that have businesses or transactions in the EU with EU members need to abide by the GDPR; in addition, all organizations worldwide need to consider their dealings with a person of EU origin in accordance with the GDPR.

5. **Answer: d. Data sovereignty.** Data sovereignty governs how data can be accessed if it is stored within the country of origin vs. if it is stored in a different country; different laws and governance may apply to the data use.

6. **Answer: a. Data breach policy.** This is a policy maintained by an organization and managed by a data breach management committee.

7. **Answer: a. PII, b. PHI, c. PCI.** All of these are examples of protected data, and any exposure of such data would constitute a data breach.

Data Classification

In an ideal world, all data resources would be available to all legitimate users, and any illegitimate users would be blocked from accessing a data resource. Data classification is a key step in helping ensure that the governance and protection of data from unauthorized access is executed as required and helping ensure that there is no unintentional alteration, disclosure, or damage to the data. There are industry standards that help indicate what information should be classified. The following are examples of common data classifications:

▶ Public

▶ Private

▶ Confidential

▶ Controlled

▶ Restricted

▶ Sensitive

▶ Internal use only

The typical data classification scheme that organizations use is a basic classification that includes three levels: public, private, and restricted (or confidential). Government classification tends to include many more levels, such as secret, top secret, controlled, and sensitive.

Personally Identifiable Information (PII)

It is important for an organization to choose a data classification methodology and use it to classify and categorize/prioritize software according to the kinds of data that the software handles. One of the ways to classify software based on the data it uses is to focus on personally identifiable information (PII).

> **ExamAlert**
>
> PII is a very key topic related to data governance, and the CompTIA Data+ exam will focus on this topic.

PII is regulated data that could possibly identify a specific individual. It includes the following:

▶ First and last names

▶ Physical addresses

▶ Personal and corporate email addresses

▶ Credit card numbers

▶ Birthdates

▶ Passport numbers

▶ Social Security number (SSNs)

▶ Driver's license and plate numbers

▶ Biometric data (such as fingerprints, voice prints)

▶ Medical records

PII can be classified as sensitive or non-sensitive. Sensitive PII is information that, upon disclosure to an unsanctioned person/entity, might result in maltreatment of the person whose data has been shared. On the other hand, the disclosure of non-sensitive PII is not likely to result in maltreatment of the person whose data has been shared.

In classifying PII data, at least the following data classifications would be required:

▶ **Private:** This classification includes data that a user or consumer does not wish to disclose. The disclosure of this data would result in a moderate level of risk to the individual. This data may include information such as home address and date of birth, and it would only be found in customer-specific databases, such as e-commerce records or survey records. This is the type of data that the organization would need to preserve and keep away from prying eyes (such as hackers). This classification requires security controls and access methods, including the ones discussed earlier—such as network security controls, access controls (for example, role-based access control), and masking—to ensure that only authorized individuals can access the data and that the data is not exchanged with another organization without prior approval of the user/consumer.

▶ **Public:** This classification refers to data that the user or consumer agrees can be used in the public domain or publicly. The disclosure of this data would result in minimal to no risk to the individual. Public data may include data such as a person's name, email address, and designation in an organization. This is data that can usually be found in public records, on social media, in telephone and/or business directories, and in blogs. Because this data is available publicly and anyone can access it, an organization must apply appropriate security access controls to prevent the unauthorized alteration or destruction of this user/consumer data.

▶ **Restricted:** This classification includes data that is strictly limited to use within the organization that collected it; under no circumstances should it be disclosed to anyone except people who should have access to it. The disclosure of this data would result in a very high level of risk to the individual. This data includes highly sensitive information such as SSNs, credit card numbers, medical data, and license details. A leak of data classified as restricted would disclose information that could easily identify an individual and allow hackers or other attackers to harm the individual by hacking their accounts or identity or by harming them physically or emotionally. This data requires the highest level of security to ensure that it is not even accessible by employees of the organization unless they have the right or need to access it.

Personal Health Information (PHI)

Personal health information (PHI) is protected by the Health Insurance Portability and Accountability Act of 1996 (HIPAA). HIPAA helped establish baseline security controls and safeguards to administratively, technically, and physically uphold the CIA triad for health and medical data.

Electronic protected health information (ePHI) is any PHI that is created, stored, received, and transmitted electronically, using electronic media such as computer disk drives, memory cards, optical discs, or health care networks.

> **Note**
>
> HIPAA requires organizations to ensure the integrity of PHI/ePHI by protecting it from being altered or destroyed in an unauthorized way.

PHI is very similar to PII in that PHI is any individually identifiable health information, such as the following:

- ▶ Patient's name
- ▶ Patient's physical address
- ▶ Patient's SSN
- ▶ Patient's general health history
- ▶ Patient's healthcare services
- ▶ Patient's mental health history
- ▶ Patient's medical record number
- ▶ Patient's health insurance beneficiary number
- ▶ Patient's license plate number
- ▶ Patient's biometric identifiers (fingerprints, voice prints, and so on)

> **Note**
>
> There is some overlap in the information considered PII and PHI because both focus on personally identifiable individual and health information.

PHI is typically classified using the same three classifications as PII: public, private, and restricted.

Payment Card Industry (PCI)

Much as PII and PHI focus on personally identifiable individual and health information, PCI focuses on an individual's payment card information, such as:

- ▶ Card numbers
- ▶ Card expiration dates
- ▶ Card verification value (CVV2) codes
- ▶ PINs

The Payment Card Industry Data Security Standard (PCI-DSS) applies to organizations that process, store, or transmit cardholder data, including:

▶ Merchants

▶ Card-issuing banks

▶ Payment processors

▶ Point-of-sale machine providers

> **Note**
>
> PCI-DSS was created jointly by American Express, MasterCard, Visa, Discover Financial Services, and JCB International to protect cardholders against misuse of their personal and card information.

At a minimum, the PCI-DSS security standard requires that an organization that processes, stores, or transmits cardholder data meet the following conditions:

▶ The organization secures and protects cardholder data.

▶ The organization maintains an information security policy.

▶ The organization builds and maintains a secure network.

▶ The organization maintains a vulnerability management program.

▶ The organization regularly monitors and tests networks for vulnerabilities.

▶ The organization implements strong access control measures.

PCI-DSS requires data classification to reduce the risks associated with unauthorized disclosure and access. PCI-DSS directs organizations to perform regular risk assessments and to review the security classification process. Cardholder data must be classified by type of data, the retention permissions, and the level of protection. The levels of classification are the same as those of PII and PHI:

▶ Public

▶ Private

▶ Restricted

Jurisdiction Requirements

Data is omnipresent, and keeping track of what is being stored where and who has access to it is becoming increasingly difficult. While industry verticals and governments are trying to regulate the way data is used across countries and states, data security and sovereignty are important issues for all organizations that leverage consumer data in any shape or form.

Impact of Industry and Government Regulations

It is important to understand that data can be stored just about anywhere, and where it is stored sometimes dictates how it can be used. *Data sovereignty* governs how data can be accessed if it is stored within the country of origin vs. if it is stored in a different country; different laws and governance may apply to the data use.

If an organization operating outside the United States hosts its data in a data center such as an AWS or Azure data center in the United States, the U.S. government has access to that data. Many organizations and their stakeholders may not even be aware of the fact that their data is hosted in another country, and they may be at risk of losing all access to their data or having their data used by the local government without their permission.

For example, according to the U.S. Patriot Act, the U.S. government has access to any data held within its borders as well as all data of companies that operate within the United States.

As another example, the General Data Protection Regulation (GDPR) has had a huge influence on those doing business with EU members as well as on EU members in other jurisdictions. Basically, any organization that has a business or handles transactions in the EU with EU members needs to abide by the GDPR; in addition, any other organization worldwide needs to consider its dealings with a person of EU origin in accordance with the GDPR. The GDPR is perhaps the single most significant regulation affecting businesses in the EU and the rest of the world.

Regulations have a big impact on businesses. The challenge that businesses face is that they do not have to deal with just a couple of simple local or international regulatory requirements that do not change over time; rather, they have to deal with multiple ever-changing and complex local and international regulations in multiple jurisdictions. This complication can impact the velocity with which businesses innovate and grow.

On the flip side, once customers realize that they are in control of how their data will be managed, they are often willing to share more and more data, knowing that it will benefit them as organizations work to make new solutions and offerings available to suit their needs. For example, Apple recently started giving users a choice about how apps can track their activity across other apps on iOS (see Figure 15.7). This is exactly what many consumers want—control over the way their information is used and shared. Such options instill confidence in consumers and allow them to share more information as they see fit.

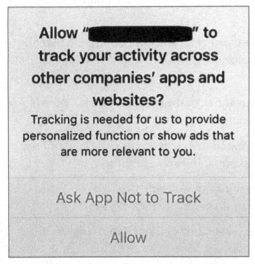

Allow "███████████" to track your activity across other companies' apps and websites?
Tracking is needed for us to provide personalized function or show ads that are more relevant to you.

Ask App Not to Track

Allow

FIGURE 15.7   **Permission to Track Activity on an iPhone**

While this isn't a direct regulation that Apple has enforced on all Apple Store apps, it is a way to show that the company cares about customers' privacy.

Data Breach Reporting

In a *data breach*, an individual's (or a set of individuals') information is unlawfully disclosed and, perhaps, leaked. A data breach may be caused by human error (for example, an appropriate security control not being applied) or may be due to hacking of targeted systems (where the hackers are after specific data).

Escalating to the Appropriate Authority

When a data breach occurs, it is crucial to be able to respond to it in a timely manner. An organization might have a data breach management committee, and the members of the committee should respond to a breach appropriately and make any regulatory bodies aware if the breach leads to the loss of sensitive, confidential, or restricted data. The following high-level steps should be taken in responding to a data breach:

1. **Try to contain the breach:** Sever the hacker's connections or take critical systems off the affected network segments.

2. **Evaluate the risks:** Ensure that the risk management plan helps identify the type of data that was lost.

3. **Start recovery:** Ensure that any critical systems are back online and are secured.

4. **Escalate to senior management and relevant bodies:** Ensure that all local bodies and organizational executives who should be informed are aware of the situation.

5. **Notify affected individuals:** Reach out to the individuals who were or could be affected by the data breach.

6. **Investigate the cause of the breach:** Try to determine the cause of the breach and how similar attempts can be thwarted in future.

It is crucial to contain a breach and to notify the appropriate local bodies so they can help with the remediation as well as manage the next steps.

In the United States, all 50 states have passed breach notification laws that require organizations to notify state residents of security breaches. These laws apply to sensitive categories of information, such as SSNs, credit card information, financial account numbers, health or medical information, birthdates, online account credentials, and digital signatures and/or biometrics. Moreover, U.S. federal laws require notification in the event of a breach of healthcare information, telecom usage information from service providers, information from financial institutions, and government agency information. Almost every aspect of sensitive, restricted, confidential, or higher tiers of classification requires some kind of reporting.

To contain data breaches, an organization may have a data breach policy that is managed by a data breach management committee. A data breach policy should include details about:

▶ Responding to a breach of data, including managing a data breach

▶ Notification of individuals whose privacy may be affected by a breach

▶ Documentation of a breach and the appropriate reporting (both internal and external)

▶ Organizational communications during and after a breach

Cram Quiz

Answer these questions. If you cannot answer these questions correctly, consider reading this section again until you can.

1. Which of the following information is protected by the PCI-DSS security standard? (Choose all that apply.)

   ○ **a.** Card number

   ○ **b.** Card expiration date

   ○ **c.** Card verification value (CVV2) code

   ○ **d.** PIN

2. Which of the following PHI data is protected by HIPAA? (Choose all that apply.)

   ○ **a.** Patient's name

   ○ **b.** Patient's physical address

   ○ **c.** Patient's SSN

   ○ **d.** Patient's general health history

   ○ **e.** Patient's habits

3. Are international and local regulations expected to slow down innovation?

   ○ **a.** Yes, because organizations have to spend more time on their initiatives

   ○ **b.** Yes, because these regulations prohibit data from being shared

   ○ **c.** No, because they increase trust between consumers and organizations, which leads to more data sharing and, thus, more innovation

   ○ **d.** No, because they allow free data exchange

4. Which of the following are important considerations when hosting data with cloud providers? (Choose all that apply.)

   ○ **a.** Location

   ○ **b.** Security

   ○ **c.** Availability

   ○ **d.** Recoverability

   ○ **e.** Cost

5. What is the first thing that an organization should do when it realizes its data systems have been breached or are under attack?

   ○ **a.** Contain the breach.

   ○ **b.** Talk to stakeholders.

   ○ **c.** Move data to the cloud.

   ○ **d.** Work on documentation.

6. Which of the following can help with lessons learned from a data breach?

    ○ **a.** Internal communication

    ○ **b.** External communication

    ○ **c.** Responding to the breach

    ○ **d.** Documentation

Cram Quiz Answers

1. **Answer: a. Card number, b. Card expiration date, c. Card verification value (CVV2) code, d. PIN.** All of this information is protected by the PCI-DSS security standard.

2. **Answer: a. Patient's name, b. Patient's physical address, c. Patient's SSN, d. Patient's general health history.** HIPAA protects all these things except for patient habits.

3. **Answer: c. No, because they increase the trust between consumers and organizations, which leads to more data sharing and, thus, more innovation.** While regulations do require organizations to spend more time and money making sure they are compliant, they also increase the trust between consumers and organizations, which leads to more data sharing and, thus, more innovation.

4. **Answer: a. Location, b. Security, c. Availability, d. Recoverability.** While cost is also important, it is not as important as other factors.

5. **Answer: a. Contain the breach.** Containing the breach is the first thing an organization should do to stop an attack in its tracks and safeguard data.

6. **Answer: d. Documentation.** Documenting lessons learned helps prevent further attacks.

What Next?

If you want more practice on this chapter's exam objective before you move on, remember that you can access all of the Cram Quiz questions on the Pearson Test Prep software online. You can also create a custom exam by objective with the Online Practice Test. Note any objective you struggle with and go to that objective's material in this chapter.

CHAPTER 16

Applying Data Quality Control

This chapter covers Objective 5.2 (Given a scenario, apply data quality control concepts) and includes the following topics:

▶ Circumstances to check for quality

▶ Automated validation

▶ Data quality dimensions

▶ Data quality rules and metrics

▶ Methods to validate quality

For more information on the official CompTIA Data+ exam topics, see the Introduction.

This chapter starts by examining data quality dimensions such as accuracy, coverage, consistency, timeliness, and completeness, as well as circumstances to check for quality, including data acquisition, data transformation, conversion, data manipulation, and final product. Next, this chapter focuses on automated validation, which depends on data type validation and number of data points. This chapter also discusses rules and metrics to be followed in data quality. Finally, this chapter looks at various methodologies for validating data quality, including cross-validation, data auditing, data profiling, spot checking, and ensuring reasonable expectations.

Data Quality Dimensions and Circumstances to Check for Quality

CramSaver

If you can correctly answer these questions before going through this section, save time by skimming the Exam Alerts in this section and then completing the Cram Quiz at the end of the section.

1. Which of the following are data quality dimensions? (Choose all that apply.)

   a. Data consistency

   b. Data accuracy

   c. Data completeness

   d. Data integrity

   e. Data sharing

2. Which of the following refers to describing real-world values correctly?

   a. Data consistency

   b. Continuous integration

   c. Data accuracy

   d. Continuous development

3. Which of the following refers to data correctness at the source?

   a. Data completeness

   b. Data attributes

   c. Data integrity

   d. Data validity

4. Which of the following is a way that data transformation can occur? (Choose all that apply.)

   a. Regular

   b. Sporadic

   c. Active

   d. Passive

Answers

1. **Answer: a. Data consistency, b. Data accuracy, c. Data completeness, d. Data integrity.** All these dimensions except for data sharing are data quality dimensions.

2. **Answer: c. Data accuracy.** Data accuracy refers to describing a real-world value correctly in the context of analytics.

3. **Answer: d. Data validity.** Data validity refers to the way data is entered in a system with the right inputs from end users in terms of data types and the format expected.

4. **Answer: c. Active, d. Passive.** Data transformations can be active or passive. In the active data transformation, the number of rows is modified, whereas in the passive data transformation, the data is changed at the row level, and the number of rows is not changed.

When you are making a business decision, it needs to be based on facts. If the facts are not right, the decision is not likely to be right either. This is why the quality of information to make an informed decision matters—and data quality is what this chapter is about.

To ensure that good-quality data is available for organizational stakeholders to make the right decisions at the right times, multiple factors need to be considered to ensure that the quality is acceptable. This focus on quality needs to begin when data is collected at the source, whether manually or automatically, and it needs to continue through transformation, manipulation, and display of data (as reports or dashboards, for example).

Data Quality

The quality of any dataset being leveraged for analysis and reporting can be measured across several key aspects:

▶ Data consistency

▶ Data accuracy

▶ Data completeness

▶ Data integrity and validity

▶ Data attribute limitations, including timing, retention, and range

Figure 16.1 illustrates these dimensions.

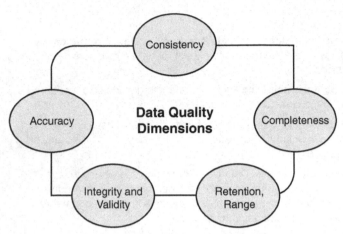

FIGURE 16.1   **Data Quality Dimensions Overview**

Let's explore these aspects in detail to better understand how they are relevant to data quality.

> **Note**
>
> Concepts related to data quality—including consistency, accuracy, completeness, integrity, and validity—are discussed in the following sections in the context of customer details in an organization's sales database.

Data Consistency

Data consistency refers to the ability to offer a consistent view of data across all users in an organization. Any transactions happening at any time need to be reflected across all the data views used by all consumers. For example, there can be multiple points of sale where customer information is captured and sellers are entering customer details across retail outlets. There are fields for name, sex, address, phone number, and email. While some of the fields are required, some are marked optional, and this may lead to the data being represented inconsistently, depending on the context. (See the section "Data Completeness," later in this chapter, for more insight.) Hence, to have consistency across datasets, it is best to either omit the optional fields or have fields set to required.

Another issue is that some sellers may be entering sex as male/female or man/woman or N/A, and this also leads to data possibly being inconsistent in the fields; in this case, the fields can be better defined to allow only a couple of options.

> **Note**
>
> A concept related to data consistency is data quality at the source, which is covered later in this chapter.

Data consistency can also be affected by database distribution. Distributed databases are not necessarily always in sync because latency may occur, and geographically separated instances may not always be available due to maintenance. Read and write locks as well as caching can help with these issues.

> **ExamAlert**
>
> Data quality is an important topic, and you need to understand the various dimensions described in this section for the CompTIA Data+ exam.

Data Accuracy

Data accuracy refers to information being correct at the time it is used for analytics. Data accuracy can also refer to a correct description of a real-world value in the context of analytics. Let's look at some examples to get a better idea of why accuracy is important.

When you go to a hospital, if your health records are inaccurate, the health analysis will not be accurate, and the doctor will not be able to prescribe the right medications for your ailment. As another example, if the sales numbers in a business are not accurate, the sales leaders will not be able to rely on past performance to gauge future performance.

Essentially, inaccurate data leads to inaccurate predictions or outcomes. In the world we live in, where data is an important currency, data accuracy is very important. So how do you ensure or improve data accuracy? Well, data accuracy can be improved by doing a number of checks, from the data acquisition phase to the transformation of data to reporting; data accuracy depends on the frequency of the checks.

Data Completeness

You learned about the various factors that can lead to data incompleteness and missing values in Chapter 6, "Cleansing and Profiling the Data." Getting a complete and comprehensive dataset for analysis is an important aspect of data quality. *Data completeness* refers to the expected wholeness or comprehensiveness of a dataset. In other words, in the dataset, values that are required for insights are not missing or incomplete.

Does this mean that every field needs to be filled—even if it is optional? Think about a dataset where a customer record has multiple fields, and the customer's first name and last name are required, but the middle name is optional. If this is a sales database outlining customer details, you can expect the middle name field to be filled only if a customer has one and provides it. In this context, the data is considered to be complete even if optional data is missing.

Data Integrity and Validity

Data integrity is a measure of the overall consistency, accuracy, and completeness of data stored in a database, data lake, or data warehouse over the life cycle of the data, from acquisition to insights. *Data validity* refers to the way the data is entered in the system to begin with—with the right inputs from the end users in terms of the data types and format expected.

For example, in a database that stores customer records, there should be a valid customer ID, with customer address, contact details (email address and phone number), and the products sold to the customer. When end users enter the right data in the right fields, the data is considered valid; if they don't enter the right data in the right fields, the data is invalid at the source. Data validity is also an issue with automatic data updates based on rules or queries.

Now, as the volume of data grows over time, splitting datasets across various databases might be required for better query performance and to make the table size manageable; this is where the integrity aspect becomes important. The customer details should be referenced across databases correctly, with the customer ID linked to the right address and other details.

There are a number of steps you can take to ensure data integrity. When segregating data across datasets and databases, all views should be referenced and show the same information. In addition, the keys and constraints should enforce data integrity across all databases.

Data Attribute Limitations

Data attribute limitations can be defined for a data point's retention and range, as well as the amount of time for which the data point remains usable. As you learned in Chapter 13, "Exploring the Different Types of Reports and Dashboards," there are two major types of data attributes: qualitative and quantitative. Certain limitations can be placed on these attributes in terms of number of characters and range, as well as when the data is received for analytics. Moreover, thinking about when data is considered good vs. stale gives a good idea about the quality of data being considered, and this quality is reflected in the insights produced using the dataset.

For example, a dataset might have multiple data attributes, such as numeric values, nominal data, and binary data about a certain subject. Within the dataset, there can only be as many characters or digits as you allow, and each data type needs to be well defined. On the other hand, this information may belong to a personally identifiable information (PII) category, such as name, address, and sex, and this information cannot be stored indefinitely. PII information should be removed from records upon request from the person from which it was collected or as per the organization's information retention policy.

> **Note**
>
> For more information on PII, refer to Chapter 15, "Data Governance Concepts: Ensuring a Baseline."

Another important aspect is the timeliness of data, which comes up in expectations of when certain data should be available and when data should be updated. All of these aspects impact the data quality and insights that can be made based on the data, which will certainly be affected by outdated or inaccessible data.

> **Note**
>
> Keep in mind that it is not just data that can be impacted by any attribute limitations; metadata can also be impacted by such limitations.

Besides understanding the dimensions (also sometimes known as *data quality metrics*) discussed here, you need to know that quality data should be available to those who need it in a timely manner. This metric, referred to as *data accessibility*, is related to the ease of retrieving data.

Circumstances to Check for Quality

As discussed in the previous section, data quality matters when making decisions, and the data quality it depends on multiple dimensions. There are ways to maintain data quality, and some of them can be deployed during data collection, whereas others are better used during the life cycle of data insights.

> **Note**
>
> A good-quality dataset can be more than just an asset; it can be used extensively to positively impact marketing campaigns, optimize operations, optimize business processes, and more. A data steward can help manage data quality by analyzing the data quality, optimizing data operations processes, and leveraging the right data toolsets.

Figure 16.2 shows an overview of the data quality life cycle.

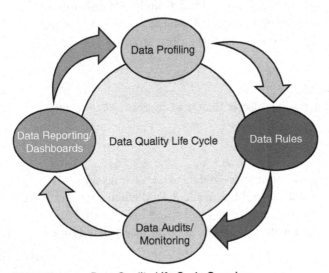

FIGURE 16.2 **Data Quality Life Cycle Overview**

> **Note**
>
> This figure shows only quality specifics and not details related to discovery, remediation, and other data life cycle processes.

Data Acquisition/Data Source

Most data dimensions can be maintained by leveraging data quality mechanisms at the source or where the data is being acquired. It is important to understand that a business problem or decision may require data from different sources to be used together, and the quality of data from these sources impacts the results. You can consider several factors to improve data quality at the source:

▶ **Ensuring data completeness:** If the data you need to make a business decision is not complete, it cannot be used for analysis. For example, to reach out to customers for an upcoming large sale, you would need their email and/or physical addresses. In a data source, while unnecessary data can be missing from a dataset and not impact the analysis (or query outcomes), if required data is missing, the data is considered incomplete and becomes unusable for analytics.

▶ **Ensuring data consistency:** Each source dataset needs to be logically consistent within itself and in line with its defined data model. Unless everyone interested in a dataset sees the same outputs, the data is not useful for decision making.

▶ **Maintaining data lineage:** It is always good for a data engineer to know where data has come from in terms of the source or acquisition as well as how it was transformed during the data life cycle, as the data transformations could potentially improve or reduce source data quality. (You'll learn more about this in the next section.)

> **Note**
>
> It is always better to ensure that data being sourced is of suitable quality than to implement correction mechanisms later.

Data Transformation/Intrahops

When you hear the word *transform*, it usually refers to altering something from its current state to a future state with a few or many changes. It is very common for business processes and technology implementations (including data) to undergo transformation. Data transformation essentially means standardizing the structure, format, and values of the source datasets and creating consistency between the datasets before allowing them to be leveraged by data engineers/ analysts for analysis. Transformation can be done by using extract, transform, and load (ETL) or extract, load, and transform (ELT) mechanisms, which are covered in Chapter 5, "Understanding Data Acquisition and Monetization."

Following are some the advantages of performing data transformation:

▶ Data transformation validates and formats data and therefore enhances the quality of the data by removing duplicates and incompatible formats.

▶ Data transformation enables compatibility between disparate systems and/or applications in terms of data types.

▶ Data transformation makes it possible to reduce duplication and store a current single version of data rather than multiple versions.

> **Note**
>
> Data transformation is performed by using rules or lookup tables or by combining the data with other data in ETL or ELT processes.

Data quality is important as organizations gather enterprise data from multiple sources and systems. After data goes through a transformation and cleansing process, it can be used for multidimensional analysis to provide insights. Quality data = quality insights!

Data transformation can be broadly categorized as pass-through or conversion. When data transformation happens, not all data needs to be transformed; in some cases, data from a source is in a usable format and can be copied from source columns to destination columns. This is referred to as *pass-through data*. When data is subjected to transformation from one data type/format to another while moving from a source column to a destination column, it is referred to as *conversion data*.

Data transformations can be active or passive. In an active transformation, the number of rows is modified, whereas in a passive transformation, the data is changed at the row level, and the number of rows is not changed. For example, data masking (discussed in Chapter 15) is a passive data transformation mechanism, and data filtering is an active data transformation mechanism. Whereas data masking will not alter the number of rows, during the transformation process, the filtering condition may drop rows. This means that any active or passive transformation process doesn't reduce the quality of datasets.

Data Manipulation

You learned about data reconciliation as well as data manipulation in Chapter 7, "Understanding and Executing Data Manipulation and Techniques." Recall that *data manipulation* refers to the process or methodology of organizing data to make it more structured.

Data manipulation is required to make it easier for organizations to organize and analyze data. With regard to quality, data manipulation has the following advantages:

▶ Data manipulation helps maintain consistency across data gathered from diverse sources, giving a unified view that helps organizations drive meaningful decision making.

▶ Data manipulation makes it possible to cleanse and organize data by focusing on important fields and data types, improving data completeness.

▶ Data manipulation helps remove unwanted data and keep information that matters, thereby improving data accuracy.

Final Product, Reports, and Dashboards

There's a very famous concept in computing—garbage in, garbage out (GIGO)—which means that the quality of output or information is determined by the quality of input or data. GIGO applies to data as well as other areas of computing: If the inputs are not meaningful, the reports and dashboards based on them are also not going to be very useful. It is important to maintain data quality throughout the data life cycle.

An organization can derive meaningful outcomes based on meaningful inputs, and maintaining and ensuring data quality leads to good reports and usable dashboards.

There is another dimension to look at when it comes to data quality dashboards. Some applications help ascertain data quality and can also help you focus on the various data quality dimensions. You can use tools such as Qlik Sense, Tableau, and Power BI with different business rules and KPIs to measure the data quality by checking for data completeness, data accuracy, data consistency, data integrity, and more. Figure 16.3 shows a sample data quality dashboard in Tableau (taken from https://tabsoft.co/3sTaYf0).

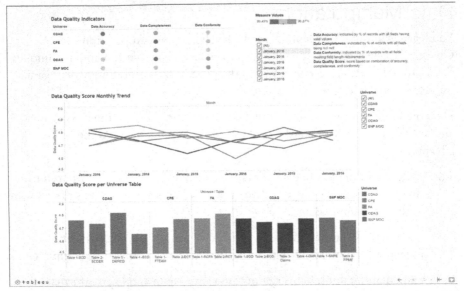

FIGURE 16.3   Data Quality Dashboard in Tableau

You don't have to guess about data quality because modern BI tools give analysts several opportunities to examine data for completeness. Some dashboard
graphs, for example, might show gaps where data is missing or incomplete.

> **Note**
>
> Data quality management is a recursive process and needs to be repeated again and
> again to ensure that quality data is available for usable insights.

Cram Quiz

Answer these questions. If you cannot answer these questions correctly, consider
reading this section again until you can.

1. Which of the following may happen during data transformation? (Choose all that
   apply.)

   ○ **a.** Standardizing the data structure

   ○ **b.** Standardizing the data format

   ○ **c.** Standardizing data values

   ○ **d.** Creating consistent data

   ○ **e.** Updating the file extension

2. Which of the following allows cleansing and organization of data by focusing on important fields and data types and improving data completeness?

 ○ **a.** Data collation

 ○ **b.** Data transformation

 ○ **c.** Data updates

 ○ **d.** Data governance

 ○ **e.** Data manipulation

3. Which of the following is a measure of overall consistency, accuracy, and completeness of data stored in a database?

 ○ **a.** Data manipulation

 ○ **b.** Data transformation

 ○ **c.** Data integrity

 ○ **d.** Data stewardship

4. Which of the following issues can be resolved by using data read and write locks?

 ○ **a.** Data updates

 ○ **b.** Data consistency

 ○ **c.** Data sourcing

 ○ **d.** Data timeliness

Cram Quiz Answers

1. **Answer: a. Standardizing the data structure, b. Standardizing the data format, c. Standardizing data values, d. Creating consistent data**. Data transformation essentially means standardizing the structure, format, and values of the source datasets and creating consistency between the datasets before allowing them to be leveraged by data engineers for analysis.

2. **Answer: e. Data manipulation.** Data manipulation allows cleansing and organization of data by focusing on important fields and data types and improving data completeness.

3. **Answer: c. Data integrity.** Data integrity is a measure of the overall consistency, accuracy, and completeness of data stored in a database.

4. **Answer: b. Data consistency.** Data consistency issues can be overcome by leveraging read and write locks as well as caching in some instances.

Data Quality Rules and Metrics, Methods to Validate Quality, and Automated Validation

CramSaver

If you can correctly answer these questions before going through this section, save time by skimming the Exam Alerts in this section and then completing the Cram Quiz at the end of the section.

1. Data quality rules can be categorized as which of the following? (Choose all that apply.)

   a. Data contextualization

   b. Data detection

   c. Data validation

   d. Data correction

2. Which of the following refers to conformance to data dimensions such as accuracy and completeness?

   a. Data velocity

   b. Data veracity

   c. Data validity

   d. Data climatization

3. Which of the following measures the alignment of data types and format with defined standards?

   a. Data accuracy

   b. Data completeness

   c. Data attributes

   d. Data conformity

4. What is shown in the following figure?

a. Data validation criteria

b. Data gathering criteria

c. Data updates criteria

d. Data metric criteria

Answers

1. **Answer: b. Data detection, c. Data validation, d. Data correction.** Data quality rules can be data detection, data validation, or data correction rules.
2. **Answer: b. Data veracity.** Data veracity refers to the quality of data, including conformance to data dimensions such as accuracy and completeness.
3. **Answer: d. Data conformity.** Data conformity measures the alignment of data types and format with defined standards.
4. **Answer: a. Data validation criteria.** This figure shows the data validation rules that can be created in Microsoft Excel.

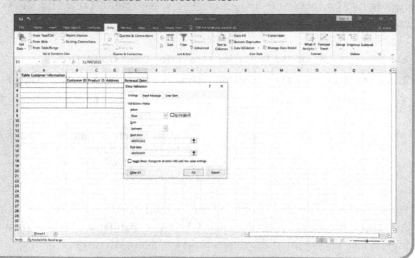

In this chapter we have already discussed the various data quality metrics and how they are important to ensuring the quality of data available for driving meaningful decisions. This section explores the various rules that can be used to check quality against these metrics and various methods for validating the quality of data being used for analytics.

Data Quality Rules and Metrics

Before we get into data quality rules, let's talk a little bit about data profiling. Data profiling can be leveraged for analysis and assessment of the quality of data values within a dataset. It also helps in finding relationships between datasets. Why is this important? It all starts with finding a baseline in one or more datasets in terms of data quality issues.

> **Note**
>
> Data profiling is based on algorithms, and performing data profiling can yield insights about various data rules associated with datasets.

By using data profiling, you can create data quality rules that are required to perform ongoing inspection of data values across datasets. Data quality rules are guides that allow data engineers and data analysts to determine whether the data being considered for analytics is fit for the desired purpose. These rules specify what is considered good in data quality. Data quality rules can focus on data detection, data validation, or data correction. These rules can be broadly classified as business rules and physical data store rules. Table 16.1 shows some examples of business rules.

TABLE 16.1 Business Rules for Customer Data Collection

Business Rule	Quality Dimension	Rule	Data Field
Email Format	Accuracy	Check for the email format \<name@email.domain\>	Email_ID
Phone Number	Completeness	Check for the phone number format \<country code\> \<area code\>\<number\>	Phone_Number

Validation rules, on the other hand can be used to validate values, data ranges, and data types as well as to distinguish between mandatory and optional fields. Figure 16.4 shows the validation rules available in Microsoft Excel.

FIGURE 16.4 **Excel Data Validation Rules**

The following sections cover several topics related to data validation: conformity, non-conformity, rows passed, and rows failed.

Conformity and Non-conformity

Data conformity measures the alignment of data types and format with defined standards. These might be industry standards or internal standards set by an organization. In simpler terms, data conformity refers to the amount of data stored in a standard format in an organization.

> **ExamAlert**
>
> Data conformity is a key topic and CompTIA Data+ exam may test you on this topic.

Let's consider an example. At a product sales organization, the customer records are maintained and updated regularly by various departments. These departments may use different data stores, and the formatting and data types across these records may therefore be different. Table 6-2 and Table 6-3 show the different records and the conformity across these records.

TABLE 16.2 **Marketing Dataset**

Customer ID	Customer Name	Customer Address	Product Renewal Date	Product Value	Marketing Email Subscription
C101	Marteen Huges	67 Brooklyn St, Brooklyn	MAY/10/27	$1300	Yes
C103	Cheryl Vantage	85 Kites St, Kites	SEP/30/27	$1900	Yes

TABLE 16.3 **Sales Dataset**

Customer ID	Customer Name	Customer Address	Product Renewal Date	Product Value	Potential New Leads
C101	Marteen Huges	67 Brooklyn St, Brooklyn	05/10/2027	USD 1,300.00	Yes
C103	Cheryl Vantage	85 Kites St, Kites	09/30/2027	USD 1,900.00	Yes

If you compare the sales table (Table 16.3) to the marketing table (Table 16.2), you can see that the formatting of renewal dates is different, and so are the data types used for the product value field. To ensure conformity across these tables for these specific fields, you could develop business rules and validation rules such that the renewal date is set to the format MM/DD/YYYY, and the product value is a numeric value.

What about non-conformity? *Non-conforming data* refers to dataset elements where values are missing, inconsistent, or incomplete compared to values in related or comparable datasets.

For example, a non-conforming product that fails to meet one or many requirements such as specified requirements, customer expectations, or usage requirements would not be fit for its intended purpose. Similarly, any data that is non-conforming to expectations would be less than useful for analytics. Again, leveraging Tables 16.2 and 16.3, if the customer names have not been captured properly or if their contact details are not complete, the marketing team would not be able to personalize a marketing message, and sales could not follow up regarding an existing or new requirement. Now you can see the effect of data non-conformity in the context of real-world applications.

Before we jump into the next section, there's a term that you should be aware of: data veracity. *Data veracity* refers to the quality of data in terms of conformity to data dimensions such as accuracy and completeness.

Rows Passed and Rows Failed

As you learned in the previous section, data conformity can be achieved by accessing data being entered via validation rules. (You'll learn more details about validation in the next section.) As you have already seen, you can validate data being entered in databases by using record validation rules or field validation rules. Whereas a field validation rule focuses on a specific field within a dataset, a record validation rule checks for all relevant fields, depending on the query, in a table. The query can be set up to check for specific values, data type, data length, duplicate information, and referential integrity across rows in a database. A validation rule can also count the number of rows across the datasets, based on source or target-based row count. Thus validation rules lead to conformity of data.

Another key aspect to consider when looking at conformity of data is the way data quality rules operate. These rules may be based on metrics such as:

▶ Greater than or less than

▶ Equals or not equals

▶ Within range or outside range

▶ Null or contains

▶ Starts with or ends with

▶ Valid

▶ Unique

▶ Match

Columns and/or rows can be matched based on the field content (such as ranges or values). Based on a rule, a row may be declared fit for insertion in the target data store and use in analytics.

Let's consider an example in which a number of rules are applied to transformed data to ensure that the data that will be used for analytics will be validated for errors. Say that an organization has a customer database that is extracted as an Excel sheet and put through an ETL tool. As shown in Figure 16.5, there are 200 rows and 20 columns; all the rows are being validated for missing email addresses, missing customer IDs, and products with quantities less than 1. In this case, metrics such as "is null" can be used for email and customer ID, and "less than" can be used for number of products.

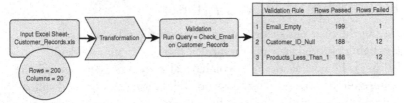

	Validation Rule	Rows Passed	Rows Failed
1	Email_Empty	199	1
2	Customer_ID_Null	188	12
3	Products_Less_Than_1	188	12

Input Excel Sheet-
Customer_Records.xls → Transformation → Validation
Run Query = Check_Email
on Customer_Records

Rows = 200
Columns = 20

FIGURE 16.5   **Validation Rules for Data Across Rows in a Customer Dataset**

Based on how many rows passed vs. failed, the database administrator or a data engineer can fix the rows with missing data before the information is processed.

Methods to Validate Data Quality and Automated Validation

As important as it is to have the right data for analytics in order to come out with the right results, it is equally important to ensure that the data is validated before it is used for insights. Data validation is significant as it ensures that data is clean and complete and, therefore, meaningful.

If, for example, there are hundreds of sources of live events or static data, it would not make sense to cleanse data after processing without validation just before running any analysis. It would, however, make sense to validate the data by leveraging the various methods or algorithms nearest to the source and only process intelligible data before you try to run any analysis. This section discusses these methods.

Data Profiling

We started to talk about data profiling earlier in this chapter. Let's now take a deeper dive.

> **Note**
>
> Think of data profiling as a prescribed method of examining datasets to determine if there are any quality issues in the metadata and/or data being used.

The key purpose of data profiling is to discover any discrepancies, imprecisions, and missing data so that the data engineers can correct the data before it leads to incorrect outcomes. Data profiling enables data engineers to get a representation of the structure of the data, any validation rules that may apply to the data, data types, data field lengths, cross-file and cross-column data relationships, and more.

Data profiling provides a better understanding of the quality of datasets in terms of structure and interrelationships, and it leads to the creation of data quality rules pertinent to the business outcomes and insights required.

> **Note**
>
> Remember that business requirements drive the metrics that are required for quality data.

Let's consider an example. Say that there are two major divisions in your organization that drive sales activities: sales and marketing. Following are the business objectives for these divisions:

1. **Marketing:** The business objective of the marketing division is advertising new products/services. The following data is required:

   ▶ Customer name

   ▶ Profile/title

   ▶ Company name

   ▶ Email address

   ▶ Mailing address

   ▶ Phone/mobile number

   ▶ Past products or services sold

   Insights include:

   ▶ Subscription to marketing updates

   ▶ Possibility of event attendance

2. **Sales:** The business objectives of the sales division are finding new leads and identifying new opportunities. The following data is required:

   ▶ Customer name

   ▶ Profile/title

   ▶ Company name

   ▶ Email address

- ▶ Mailing address
- ▶ Phone/mobile number
- ▶ Past products or services sold
- ▶ Annual revenue
- ▶ Industry
- ▶ Number of employees
- ▶ Lead/opportunity source
- ▶ Next steps

Insights include:

- ▶ Possibility of closure of product or service sales
- ▶ Possibility of cross-selling/upselling

This list qualifies the business requirements and the objectives as well as the insights. To move ahead, you would need to qualify the data quality metrics (for example, completeness, accuracy, consistency, validity, timeliness). To do so, you create data rules (both business and validation rules) to ensure that you get the complete datasets needed for analysis and ensure that the data profiling is performed based on these rules.

At a high level, it is good to understand that data profiling can be broadly categorized as relationship discovery (that is, exploring relationships between datasets) and structure discovery (that is, ensuring the formatting, data types, and fields across datasets).

Cross-Validation

Cross-validation is a popular validation method pertinent to training machine learning models. Cross-validation is based on splitting data into training and test sets. The whole idea is to partition a given dataset into several subsets. While one of them acts as a test set, the others are training sets. Whereas a training set is data used to construct a model, a test set is data used for validation of the model being created.

> **Note**
>
> Data engineers use a K designation for each split (for example, K1, K2, K3, K4) also in a form of validation known as *K-fold cross-validation* (see Figure 16.6).

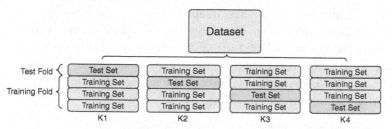

FIGURE 16.6   **Cross-Validation Data Split Across Multiple Sets**

Now, with the splits across K1 through K4, you can train the data model on the first fold starting with K1, and then you can proceed to the second fold and so on. Each iteration yields an accuracy score, so in this case, you would be getting four accuracy scores.

Sample/Spot Check

Data validation need not be always structured. You can in some cases just pick a random sample and check it for any errors. For example, you might pick up a dataset and run a null validation against rows 110 through 130.

> **Fun Fact**
>
> At schools, teachers may ask toddlers to show their hands and check whether the students' fingernails are overgrown. Data samples/spot checks are not very different.

Sampling or spot checking does not guarantee an error-free outcome as it does not involve checking against all queries and all data fields. However, you can use these methods on data that has high confidence in terms of the data quality—that is, when other validation methods have already been used on the data. In addition, if you cannot check everything due to time or other constraints, then spot checking can be a good option. In fact, it is possible to leverage BI solutions as shown in Figure 16.3 to perform sample checks on data.

Data Audits and Reasonable Expectations

The term *audit* can mean different things to different people. IT folks might think of IT asset management audits, compliance teams might think of compliance audits, and data people might think of data quality audits. A data quality audit is a process of ensuring that the data quality is above an established baseline and meets an acceptable standard. Ongoing data quality audits help maintain the data quality standards and also ensure that more time-consuming corrections are not performed; for example, these audits ensure that data metrics such as data completeness, accuracy, and consistency are maintained by deploying the right tools during the ETL or ELT processes.

A data quality audit includes a number of checks, including:

▶ Data source verification

▶ Data formatting checks

▶ Data type checks

▶ Data profiling rule checks

▶ Data report/dashboard checks

The outcomes from data audits are reports that highlight the non-conformities across various metrics/dimensions.

Data quality expectations can be qualified when working with data stewards as well as business stakeholders. These expectations guide what should be measured and indicate the impact of these measurements on decisions. For example, data quality expectations may be very high for sales stakeholders as they are driving front-end sales with customers—and any unusable insights may be quite frustrating for them. A customer's incomplete details for the last orders placed can be very challenging for a salesperson as he cannot go to the customer and ask what products they have; the customer would expect the salesperson to know this. This example shows again that data completeness and accuracy matter.

Now let's consider the data quality expectations of a marketing team. Unusable insights might not prevent the marketing team from operating successfully as it uses different KPIs and outcomes than the sales team. Even without information on what products a customer has, marketing can still engage the customer for an upcoming marketing event where a new product is being promoted.

So again, expectations for data quality depend on the person or group using the data. Particular expectations can be reasonably fulfilled by leveraging business rules to validate the data, as shown in Figure 16.7. Based on the rules, the variation from expectation can be measured by using a report or dashboard.

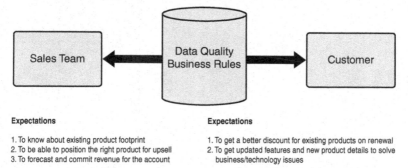

Expectations

1. To know about existing product footprint
2. To be able to position the right product for upsell
3. To forecast and commit revenue for the account

Expectations

1. To get a better discount for existing products on renewal
2. To get updated features and new product details to solve business/technology issues

FIGURE 16.7 **Expectations from Sales and Marketing for Customer Data**

Automated Validation

We all love automation; you probably use some form of home automation, car automation, or coffee machine automation. Automation aims to make life simpler by taking care of repeatable tasks. Data quality validation automation can automate the task of running rules against datasets. With automated data quality validation, it becomes easier to automatically detect changes and thereby improve data quality over time.

There are two basic automated data validation types: data field-to-data type validation and number of data points validation. Data field-to-data type validation confirms that the data entered in a data field has the correct data type. For example, a birthday data field is designed to accept only numeric characters, and thus, the system should reject any data containing other characters such as letters or special symbols. Figure 16.8 shows how a simple rule can be created in Microsoft Excel to validate a data field as a date data type and to ensure that it cannot be left empty or contain any special symbols.

Microsoft Excel offers validation for several data types to restrict data fields or cells as needed:

- ► Whole number
- ► Decimal
- ► List
- ► Date
- ► Time
- ► Text length
- ► Custom

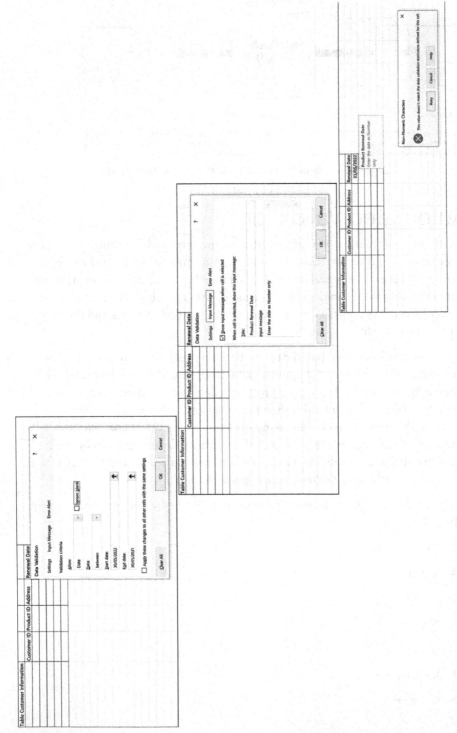

FIGURE 16.8   Data field-to-data type Validation in Excel

You can make and automate additional rules by using Excel macros and other tools. For data stores, SQL-based rules can be run on a regular schedule to ensure that the data being entered in the database or taken from an existing data source is validated in terms of the data types expected for various data fields.

You can consider data points to be measurements across a certain population. For example, when doing a study on volcanos, you might need to have data points for volcanic activity, temperature, and lava quantity. Unless you have multiple data points, you cannot make useful comparisons. However, you can have too many data points; you might not need more than a few data points to arrive at a statistical conclusion. Automated validation of the number of data points can be provisioned when the ideal number of data points for a certain activity is known and anything less than or more than the approximate ideal number would be considered unfit for analysis. In such a case, you might use rules including greater-than or less-than metrics.

Cram Quiz

Answer these questions. If you cannot answer these questions correctly, consider reading this section again until you can.

1. What is shown in the following figure?

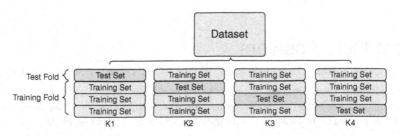

   - a. Ongoing updates
   - b. Security of data folds
   - c. Data conformity
   - d. Data refinement
   - e. Data cross-validation

2. Which of the following offers a better understanding about quality of data pertinent to the structure and interrelationships in datasets?

○ **a.** Cross-validation

○ **b.** Outcome validation

○ **c.** Data profiling

○ **d.** Documentation

3. Who would be the likely stakeholders to consult when discussing data quality expectations? (Choose all that apply.)

○ **a.** Data owners

○ **b.** Consultants

○ **c.** Business heads

○ **d.** Data stewards

4. Which of the following parameters should be the focus of a data quality audit? (Choose all that apply.)

○ **a.** Data source verification

○ **b.** Data formatting checks

○ **c.** Data type checks

○ **d.** Data profiling rule checks

○ **e.** Data upload checks

Cram Quiz Answers

1. **Answer: e. Data cross-validation.** This figure shows data cross-validation.

2. **Answer: c. Data profiling.** Data profiling provides a better understanding of the quality of datasets in terms of structure and interrelationships, and it leads to the creation of data quality rules pertinent to the business outcomes and insights required.

3. **Answer: c. Business heads, d. Data stewards.** Data quality expectations can be qualified when working with data stewards as well as business stakeholders. These expectations guide what should be measured and indicate the impact of these measurements on decisions.

4. **Answer: a. Data source verification, b. Data formatting checks, c. Data type checks, d. Data profiling rule checks.** For a data quality audit, you should consider a few points:

○ Data source verification

○ Data formatting checks

○ Data type checks

○ Data profiling rule checks

○ Data report/dashboard checks

What Next?

If you want more practice on this chapter's exam objective before you move on, remember that you can access all of the Cram Quiz questions on the Pearson Test Prep software online. You can also create a custom exam by objective with the Online Practice Test. Note any objective you struggle with and go to that objective's material in this chapter.

Understanding Master Data Management (MDM) Concepts

> ## This chapter covers Objective 5.3 (Explain master data management [MDM] concepts) of the CompTIA Data+ exam and includes the following topics:
>
> ▶ Processes
>
> ▶ Circumstances for MDM
>
> For more information on the official CompTIA Data+ exam topics, see the Introduction.

This chapter focuses on master data management (MDM) concepts. Think of master data as the single source of truth across an organization. Everything depends on how it is managed—from data quality to time-bound decision making to everything else that depends on data. This chapter covers specifics related to MDM from a process perspective and explores where it makes sense for an organization to invest time and effort into MDM.

> ### Note
>
> Use of the terms *master* and *slave* is ONLY in association with the official terminology used in industry specifications and standards and in no way diminishes Pearson's commitment to promoting diversity, equity, and inclusion and challenging, countering, and/or combating bias and stereotyping in the global population of the learners we serve.

Processes

CramSaver

If you can correctly answer these questions before going through this section, save time by skimming the Exam Alerts in this section and then completing the Cram Quiz at the end of the section.

1. Which of the following solutions enables management, organization, categorization, synchronization, and localization of all organizational data?

   a. MDM

   b. Data owning

   c. IAM

   d. Data reporting

2. Which of the following does an MDM platform leverage when consolidating data?

   a. Semi-structured data stores

   b. Continuous integration

   c. Tub

   d. Hub

3. Which of the following are characteristics of data standardization? (Choose all that apply.)

   a. Creating a single organizationwide view of all data fields

   b. Enhancing productivity and reducing costs due to data overlapping or errors

   c. Enabling an organization to maintain a clean and trusted master database that can be governed

   d. Enabling the same data to be leveraged across the organization

Answers

1. **Answer: a. MDM.** Master data management (MDM) enables management, organization, categorization, synchronization, and localization of all organizational data. It provides a single master database to drive insight-based decision making.

2. **Answer: d. Hub.** During the consolidation process, MDM leverages a central repository known as a hub (or consolidation hub). A hub is a single source of truth where all the master data from multiple data sources is consolidated.

> 3. **Answer: a. Creating a single organizationwide view of all data fields, b. Enhancing productivity and reducing costs due to data overlapping or errors, c. Enabling an organization to maintain a clean and trusted master database that can be governed, d. Enabling the same data to be leveraged across the organization.** All of these are characteristics of data standardization.

Master data is a dependable set of identifiers that are core to the business operations of an organization. These identifiers describe business data such as:

▶ Customer details

▶ Addresses

▶ Email addresses

▶ Phone numbers

▶ Site or location details

Say that an organization is trying to interact with its customers but has incorrect information about who's in charge of purchasing; imagine the sort of impression that would leave with a customer. If the organization were to keep the master data updated, all other dependent information and records would be updated, and the organization will come across as a very well-informed and customer-focused entity. This is an example of the real power and benefit of keeping master data updated; the way to do this is through master data management (MDM).

ExamAlert

MDM is an important topic, and you should expect a number of questions related directly or indirectly to it on the CompTIA Data+ exam.

There are many ways to look at what MDM does and how it does it. Basically, MDM enables management, organization, categorization, synchronization, and localization of all organizational data. It enables informed, effective, and efficient decision making for various business units, functional areas, and business processes.

Of course, MDM cannot be built in a bubble. A set of processes, technologies, and supporting functions is needed for consistency, quality, precision, and timely decision-making capability for the data being leveraged across multiple organizational applications and databases.

> **Note**
>
> MDM is most effective in organizing and categorizing information so that stakeholders know where the data is when they need it and know that it is being stored and managed in the most efficient fashion.

Figure 17.1 summarizes how MDM encompasses master data and requires interaction across business supporting processes, technology (IT), people, and governance in order to function properly. Further, Figure 17.1 illustrates how MDM impacts various business functions, such as sales, customer service, operations, and marketing.

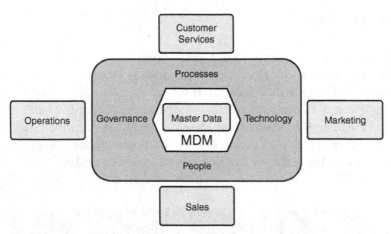

FIGURE 17.1 **MDM Interaction Setup with Business Functions**

Let's consider an example to highlight the importance of MDM and why it makes sense for organizations to invest in it. Figure 17.2 shows three different records from three business units in one organization, all showing information on one customer.

Sales	SFDC ID	FName	MName	LName	Address	Email	Phone	Product
	C760	Adam	Lamel	Nathan	33 Winstone St, NY	adam.nathan@winstone.ny	5551110000	Web Server, Anti Virus

Marketing	CustID	FName	MName	LName	Address	Email	Phone	Product
	M130	Adam	N/A	Nathan	33 Winstone St, NY	adam.nathan@winstone.ny	5551110000	Multi

Customer Service	ServiceID	FName	MName	LName	Address	Email	Phone	Product
	WS743	Adam	N/A	Nathan	N/A, NY	contract@winstone.ny	5551110000	Web Server

FIGURE 17.2 **Different Aspects of the Same Customer Across Different Records**

If we go across the customer records from the three databases, we can infer that:

▶ The customer is being identified differently depending on the department (that is, by SFDC ID, customer ID, and service ID).

▶ The first, middle, and last name fields are similar, although they are not exactly the same across the three databases. The middle name is missing in the marketing and customer service databases.

▶ The address field is incomplete in the customer service database.

▶ The email address in the customer service database is different from the email address in the other databases.

▶ The products are different across the three databases with the marketing database showing products clubbed together as multiple (multi) products and the customer service database showing no entitlement for supporting antivirus.

Based on the same customer records being referenced in different ways, a number of business-focused questions need to be answered:

▶ Which of these records should be the single source of truth?

▶ What decisions can be driven by the variety of data available to engage the customer further?

▶ What type of marketing campaigns would be of interest to this customer?

▶ What services or product upsell would appeal to the customer?

▶ Which records should be updated if the address or any other information changes?

Wouldn't it be nice if a customer could contact your support or sales department and get a representative who knows all there is to know about that customer's history with the organization at a glance and without looking at multiple systems? MDM makes this scenario possible.

Now, a million $ question—Does every organization require MDM? Well, not really. Setting up and maintaining MDM involves time, effort, and costs. An MDM may cost a couple hundred thousand dollars. The size and complexity of an organization as well as the amount of data the organization consumes might make MDM essential. However, if it is not required or outlined by the data interactions in an organization, MDM isn't really necessary. Think about an organization that has more than 100,000 employees and serves a number of customers; in this case, MDM would be much more beneficial than it would be for an organization with around 100 employees and a handful of customers.

MDMs can be deployed on-premises or can be cloud based and can use a pay-as-you-go (PAYG) structure.

Consolidation of Multiple Data Fields

MDM can help eliminate duplicate records by merging them together into a single, consolidated record. This would be great for the scenario shown in Figure 17.2 as the customer records across the three different databases could potentially be consolidated into one database that contains true information about the customer and the relationship of the organization with that customer.

During the consolidation process, MDM leverages a central repository known as a *hub* (or *consolidation hub*). A hub is a single source of truth where all the master data from multiple data sources is consolidated. Once the data is in a hub, MDM leverages algorithms for cleansing, matching, and merging to come up with a complete single record—the golden record—that is stored in the hub. After this consolidation, all systems and applications will leverage the golden record instead of pulling master data from various systems.

Building on our example of customer records across multiple databases, Figure 17.3 shows how data is consolidated in MDM (into the hub) and what the golden record looks like.

All systems and applications will now leverage the golden record instead of pulling master data from various systems. The golden records may be used for analytics, report generation, or customer interaction.

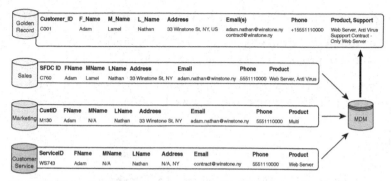

FIGURE 17.3 Golden Record Creation in an MDM Hub

> **Note**
>
> Various MDM suites, such as Oracle, Informatica, TIBCO, and SAP, all have some sort of MDM consolidation hub.

Data stewards play an important role in MDM as they can further optimize the output from the algorithms and ensure that the golden records are optimized. (Data stewards were introduced in Chapter 15, "Data Governance Concepts: Ensuring a Baseline.") Data stewards ensure that proper governance is adhered to when it comes to golden records and look after aspects of life cycle management.

Now, you might ask—how does the field matching and merging process work? The matching process leverages matching rules (or matching groups) to identify similar records across columns and shortlists them for merging. Matching processes might use exact matching or fuzzy matching with similar or nearly similar values. The merging of data fields is driven by the MDM post-matching process, which tags fields with identical data so that values can be merged to arrive at golden records.

At a high level, MDM data consolidation occurs in the following stages:

1. **Data loading and initial check:** In this stage, the data is loaded from the master database, and the data is checked against a set of predefined rules to ensure that it is clean.

2. **Data matching:** This stage involves matching the data based on matching rules or matching groups to find duplicates.

3. **Finding best records:** Best records are created based on matching rules or matching groups.

4. **Merging:** Data is merged based on matched field values.

5. **Validation and promotion:** Once the newly created records are validated, they are promoted to become golden records.

Finally, after golden records are created, as mentioned earlier, they are used for analysis and business intelligence reporting. Figure 17.4 illustrates this process.

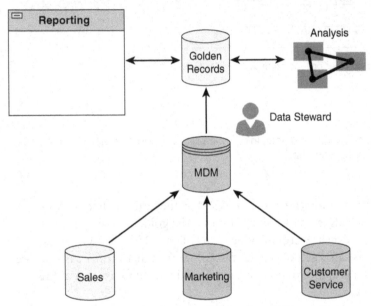

FIGURE 17.4   **Consolidation Process: Golden Record Generation**

Standardization of Data Field Names

Organizations typically have standards in place to manage things (including data) in a certain way. An organization that is standardizing data is trying to achieve a consistent and well-defined data format across all business functions. Converting multiple datasets into a common data format helps everyone understand and transact in the same way; however, in the real world, this doesn't often happen, and many types of data formats coexist. For example, one software vendor might structure its datasets in a unique way; as another example, the fields that different datasets cover may vary.

> **Note**
>
> Data standardization is an ideal state that every organization should strive to achieve. Realistically, however, it takes a lot of time and effort to go through the iterations and set up the process to ensure that all data being used is homogenous and standardized.

Let's consider an example of how data standardization can bring harmony to the way data is managed in an organization. Consider a sales customer database that captures customer details such as:

▶ Name

▶ Address

▶ Email

▶ Phone

▶ Unique identifier

▶ Dates when transactions happened or will happen (new sale, renewal, and so on)

These fields are visually depicted in Figure 17.5.

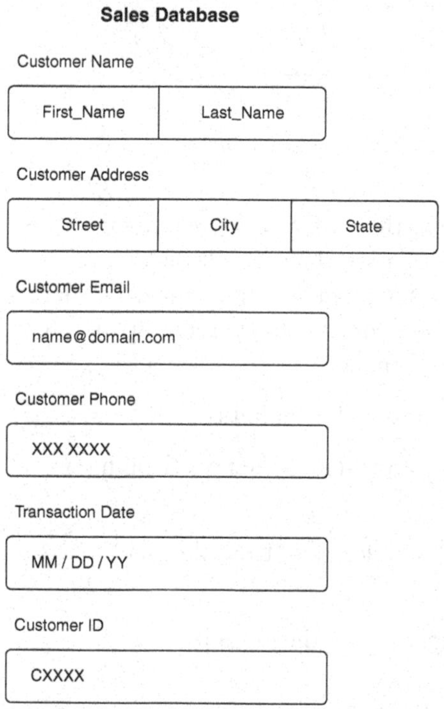

Sales Database

Customer Name

First_Name	Last_Name

Customer Address

Street	City	State

Customer Email

name@domain.com

Customer Phone

XXX XXXX

Transaction Date

MM / DD / YY

Customer ID

CXXXX

FIGURE 17.5 **Sales Customer Database Fields and Format**

The organization's marketing business unit has the database fields and formats shown in Figure 17.6 (which compares the marketing data fields and formats with the sales data fields and formats).

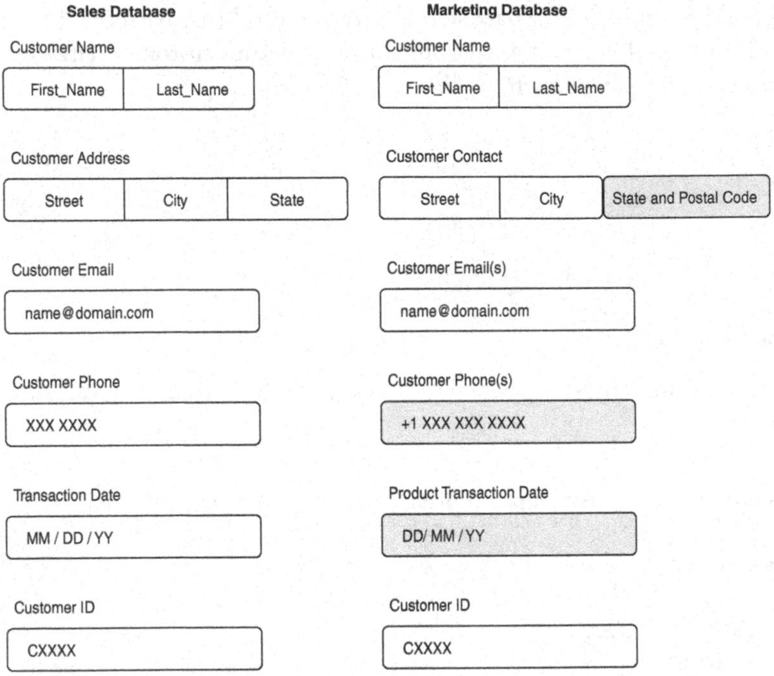

FIGURE 17.6   **Sales vs. Marketing Customer Database Fields and Formats**

As you can see, the two databases have fields that differ not only in their names but also in their formats and expected information. This is a classic case of an organization maintaining multiple databases without any uniformity. This lack of uniformity leads to formatting issues and errors due to overlapping or absent data. Data standardization has a number of benefits:

▶ Creating a single organizationwide view of all data fields

▶ Enhancing productivity and reducing costs due to data overlapping or errors

▶ Enabling the organization to maintain a clean and trusted master database that can be governed

▶ Enabling the same data to be leveraged across the organization

Data standardization is commonly done when onboarding datasets from internal or external databases that are based on varying definitions for fields and/or formats and transforming them into a trustworthy central dataset with common fields and a common data format.

Data standardization can be performed based on predefined business standards using rules or by leveraging third-party tools. While some data standardization might be trivial (such as capitalization of all characters, removing punctuation, or reordering date or time units), some datasets might require creation of rules or algorithms offered by third-party solutions, such as DataLadder, Datamation, and Experian.

Data Dictionary

A *data dictionary* is a centralized store for metadata (which, you'll recall, is data about the data). It is not unusual to have very complex database structures and multiple fields across these databases. In such cases, the data dictionary is important because it can explain and expand on information such as the following:

▶ The names of fields in the databases

▶ The data types that are stored in those fields

▶ The roles that have access to the data in these databases

▶ The relationships between fields across the databases

▶ The security constraints that are applicable

Hence, data dictionaries can make it simpler to navigate through the tons of data that get processed from multiple sources in MDM.

Figure 17.7 shows a data dictionary developed for sales, marketing, and other sales-focused databases in an organization that sells products and associated services.

Field Name	Data Type	Field Size	Description	Required Field
First Name	String	25	Customer First Name	Yes
Middle Name	String	25	Customer Middle Name	No
Last Name	String	25	Customer Last Name	Yes
Address	String	45	Contact Address	Yes
Phone Number	Numbers	10	Primary Phone Number	Yes
Email	String	20	Primary Email Address	Yes
Products	String	40	Products Bought	Yes
Services	String	40	Service Subscribed	Yes
Marketing Subscription	String	25	Subscribed to Marketing Email	No

FIGURE 17.7 **Data Dictionary Overview**

Figure 17.8 shows a database that is built leveraging this data dictionary.

First Name	Middle Name	Last Name	Address	Email	Phone
Adam		Jones	111 Kitts St, IN, 46063	adam.jones@kitts.com	463 565 5050
Akash		Trivedi	222 Mills St, CA, 94118	akash.trived@mills.com	418 676 8776

FIGURE 17.8   **Database Built Leveraging Data Dictionary**

ExamAlert

Data dictionaries are an important topic. You should expect to see a few questions related to them on the CompTIA Data+ exam.

There are two ways to build data dictionaries, and each method builds a different type of data dictionary:

▶ **Active data dictionary:** A data dictionary can be built automatically by a database (or databases) such that the data dictionary and the database(s) remain in sync. This is a major advantage as there is no need to keep the data dictionary updated manually.

▶ **Passive data dictionary:** A passive data dictionary is manually built and maintained. It is not referenced to any specific database and contains only reference information across one or more databases. Compared to an active data dictionary, a passive data dictionary requires more maintenance.

Note

Data dictionaries are not directly used by end users; rather, they are used by database administrators.

The key advantages of developing and maintaining data dictionaries are as follows:

▶ An expanded data dictionary allows for enhanced decision making based on analysis of better-understood information.

▶ A data dictionary promotes standardization of data and consistency across multiple domains in an organization.

▶ A data dictionary provides better documentation about data aspects (metadata).

Cram Quiz

Answer these questions. If you cannot answer these questions correctly, consider reading this section again until you can.

1. Which of the following are types of data dictionaries that can be built? (Choose two.)

   ○ **a.** Ongoing

   ○ **b.** Backtracking

   ○ **c.** Active

   ○ **d.** Passive

2. Which of the following does an organization use in order to achieve a consistent and well-defined data format across all business functions?

   ○ **a.** Common data

   ○ **b.** Original data

   ○ **c.** Data governance

   ○ **d.** Data standardization

3. Which of the following is leveraged to match similar records across datasets when performing data consolidation?

   ○ **a.** Match making

   ○ **b.** Matching lines

   ○ **c.** Matching groups

   ○ **d.** Matching aspects

Cram Quiz Answers

1. **Answer: c. Active, d. Passive.** Data dictionaries can be built as active or passive.

2. **Answer: d. Data standardization.** An organization that is standardizing data is trying to achieve a consistent and well-defined data format across all business functions.

3. **Answer: c. Matching groups.** The matching process leverages matching rules (or matching groups) to identify similar records across columns and shortlists them for merging.

Circumstances for MDM

In the previous section you learned the basics of MDM and multiple aspects of how MDM helps collate information in an organization—working with data coming from multiple sources, working across multiple domains, and benefitting multiple business functions. This section focuses on some of the key scenarios and use cases where MDM deployment can make data management much more effective.

Mergers and Acquisitions

This section sheds light on the topic of mergers and acquisitions and how MDM helps with governance of data and bringing together disparate data sources.

Organizations aim to grow their business reach and their customer base, and this growth can be organic growth (that is, growth via innovation or developing new products or services) or can occur via mergers and acquisitions (M&A), which pertains to merging with or acquiring another organization that can complement the product or service capabilities and therefore help increase the market size. In the case of M&A, an organization may have the right processes to ensure that there's still a single source of truth after M&A is complete, or it may have to go through the rather painstaking process of finding the right datasets.

ExamAlert

Mergers and acquisitions are very common in real world and data collection and processing can be cumbersome if not managed properly. Be sure to read and understand this topic thoroughly.

For example, consider an example. Say that Organization A develops CRM software and has a good market share. Customers are now expecting new features and an integrated analytics functions, so Organization A looks at acquiring a well-known analytics platform provider, Organization B. This acquisition will give Organization A access to a new client base—and that's huge. However, after the acquisition, Organization A struggles to formulate a strategy to combine the customer data from Organization B and loses steam.

In this example, MDM would mitigate the problem by integrating with new data sources and creating a single master source that provides a single source of truth for all enterprise-related data, resulting in minimal errors and minimal redundancy in business processes and giving the outcomes expected. The key aspects from an M&A perspective are *timely integration* and *utilization of data*. In our example, if Organization A deployed and prepared the MDM solution before the acquisition, it would take a much shorter time for Organization A to realize the benefits and reach the outcomes.

MDM helps integrate data with varying attributes and formats from disparate sources of data; it offers a single unified representation of all information rather than leaving the information in silos. This integration can be achieved by merging data from multiple systems and managing the master data via MDM to improve not just the data usability but also data governance and streamlined data access, as discussed in the following sections.

Compliance with Policies and Regulations

MDM provides unification of data, which directly relates to how an organization can direct its people, processes, and technology to comply with organization policies as well as local and other regulations—with ease. The key aspect is that properly managed and unified data is reliable and trustworthy; therefore, the compliance with regulations is more seamless.

Where there is a unified view of all the organization's information, regulated data can be viewed the same way across the whole organization. Thanks to MDM, the organization can more easily determine which data can or cannot be disclosed, which data requires extra security, which data needs access restrictions, and which data can or cannot be shared with any external parties.

Further, MDM platforms make it easier to adhere to regulation frameworks (for example, HIPAA), which means an organization doesn't have to work it out on its own and go about doing many tasks to secure data. For example, a financial organization could leverage MDM to record, store, and submit know your customer (KYC) data to regulators as required.

Streamline Data Access

MDM brings master data to the right audience by streamlining data access. It streamlines access to data insights from MDM golden records as well as access to compliance data for regulators.

Following are some of the key ways that MDM impacts customer interactions:

▶ MDM offers a cohesive view of customers across the organization, which enables sales, services, marketing, and so on to approach customers effectively.

▶ MDM improves customer engagement as everyone has the same level of visibility into customer accounts.

▶ MDM reduces costs for reengaging with customers as a single campaign covers the desired customers without wasting money on duplicate efforts.

▶ MDM offers access to information across applications and enables automation for repetitive processes.

▶ MDM offers compliance insights, which would be difficult to obtain on a system-by-system basis.

▶ MDM improves decision making as updated data is available to drive insights.

Cram Quiz

Answer these questions. If you cannot answer these questions correctly, consider reading this section again until you can.

1. Which of the following are key aspects of MDM in streamlining data access? (Choose all that apply.)

   ○ **a.** Reduces costs for reengaging with customers as a single campaign covers the desired customers without wasting money on duplicate efforts

   ○ **b.** Offers access to information across applications and enables automation for repetitive processes

   ○ **c.** Improves decision making as updated data is available to drive insights

   ○ **d.** Offers a cohesive view of customers across the organization, which enables sales, services, marketing, and so on to approach customers effectively

2. Which of the following can MDM help with?

   ○ **a.** Improving internal communication

   ○ **b.** Breaking information silos

   ○ **c.** Responding to data leaks

   ○ **d.** Masking information

Cram Quiz Answers

1. **Answer: a. Reduces costs for reengaging with customers as a single campaign covers the desired customers without wasting money on duplicate efforts, b. Offers access to information across applications and enables automation for repetitive processes, c. Improves decision making as updated data is available to drive insights, d. Offers a cohesive view of customers across the organization, which enables sales, services, marketing, and so on to approach customers effectively.** All of these are key aspects of how MDM helps streamline data access for all stakeholders.

2. **Answer: b. Break information silos.** MDM can be used to break information silos.

What Next?

If you want more practice on this chapter's exam objective before you move on, remember that you can access all of the Cram Quiz questions on the Pearson Test Prep software online. You can also create a custom exam by objective with the Online Practice Test. Note any objective you struggle with and go to that objective's material in this chapter.

Getting Ready for the CompTIA Data+ Exam

This chapter provides some additional tools and information to help you succeed in preparing for and taking the CompTIA Data+ exam. It covers the following topics:

▶ Getting ready for the CompTIA Data+ exam

▶ Tips for taking the real exam

▶ Beyond the CompTIA Data+ certification

ExamAlert

Don't skip this chapter! It is intended to impart some of the most vital things you need to know about taking the CompTIA Data+ exam.

Getting Ready for the CompTIA Data+ Exam

The CompTIA Data+ certification exam can be taken by anyone, and there are no prerequisites. However, CompTIA recommends that you have 18 to 24 months of experience in a reporting or business analyst job role, exposure to databases and analytical tools, a basic understanding of statistics, and data visualization experience. For more information on CompTIA Data+ certification, visit https://www.comptia.org/certifications/data.

To obtain the Data+ certification, you need to pass the online exam that is administered by Pearson VUE, and you need to register with Pearson VUE to take the exam (see https://home.pearsonvue.com/comptia).

The CompTIA Data+ exam consists of two types of questions:

▶ **Multiple choice:** This type of question asks you to select the correct answer (or answers) from a group of four or more choices. These questions are quite similar to the questions you've seen throughout this book.

▶ **Performance based:** This type of question asks you to answer a question, complete a configuration, or solve a problem in a hands-on fashion. The questions might ask you to drag and drop information to the correct location or complete a simulation in an emulated or virtual system.

To become proficient at both types of questions, you need to have a deep understanding of the theory, and you also need hands-on skills. This is, of course, imperative for the Data+ exam, but it is even more important for the real world. The more you work with databases, data warehouses, data lakes, and visualization tools, the better prepared you will be for job interviews and whatever comes your way once you have acquired a data-focused profile within an organization.

An Important Note Regarding Exam Questions

This book does not offer the exact questions that are on the exam. There are two reasons for this:

▶ CompTIA reserves the right to change the questions at any time. Any changes, however, will still reflect the content within the current Data+ objectives.

▶ The contents of the CompTIA Data+ exam are protected by a nondisclosure agreement (NDA); anyone who sits for this exam has to agree to the NDA before beginning a test. The NDA states that the questions within the exams are not to be discussed with anyone.

Hence, this book cannot tell you exactly what is on the exam, but it attempts to cover all of the objectives in order to give you the best possible chance of passing the exam.

A great way to study and to remember key points is to compile and use a "cheat sheet"—a *key facts* document that contains things that you want to memorize or that you have a hard time memorizing, such as acronyms, procedures, merits of one system over another, different tools, and so on. Include whatever you feel would help you best.

Table 18.1 provides an example of a cheat sheet that you can create to aid in your studies. Fill in the appropriate information in the right column. Then you can study the cheat sheet to focus on just the information that is most important for the exam.

TABLE 18.1 **Sample Cheat Sheet**

Concept	Key Information
Data warehouse vs. data lake	
List of commonly used databases on-premises and in the cloud	
The ETL and ELT processes	
Types of data analysis	
Star schema characteristics	
Why standardize field names?	
Which chart is best for showing continuous data?	

> **Note**
>
> Feel free to print Table 18.1 on paper. The key is to write down various technologies, processes, step-by-step procedures, and so on and commit them to memory.

Tips for Taking the Real Exam

You may be new to online certification exams, and if so, this section is for you. Being new to online exams or certifications is absolutely okay. All of us do many things for the first time.

> **Note**
>
> If you have taken online certification exams before, feel free to skip this section or use it as a review.

CompTIA exams are conducted on a computer and are composed of multiple-choice and performance-based questions. You have the option to skip questions. If you do so, be sure to mark, or "flag," them for review before moving on. Feel free to also mark questions that you have answered but that you are not completely sure about.

When you get to the end of the exam, you will see an item review section that shows you any questions that you did not answer and any that you flagged for review. Be sure to answer any questions that have not yet been not completed.

> **ExamAlert**
>
> Leaving a question unanswered means you get no points for that question. Since the exam does not penalize you for wrong answers, if you don't know what the right answer is, take your best guess and mark that answer.

If you finish early, rather than leaving the exam early, use the time allotted to you to review your answers. Make sure that everything you have marked has a proper answer that makes sense to you. At the same time, try not to overthink and don't change an answer if you were confident that it was the right answer! You don't want to second-guess yourself!

This section includes tips and tricks that the authors have developed over the years. We have taken at least 20 certification exams over the past two decades, and these points have served us well.

Here's a simple study plan from the point at which you finish reading through Chapter 17 until you take the CompTIA Data+ exam. Certainly, you can ignore this plan, use it as is, or just take suggestions from it. The plan involves several steps:

Step 1. Review the Cram Saver questions from the beginning of each major section in each chapter as they can be helpful for review.

Step 2. Review the Cram Quiz questions at the end of each section in the chapter to identify areas where you need more study.

Step 3. Review the Exam Alerts throughout the chapters to ensure that you have a good understanding of these sections.

Here are some general leading practices to help you with your exam preparation and ensure that you ace the exam:

▶ **Practice exams:** Consider taking practice exams and going through the practice questions available at https://www.comptia.org/training/certmaster-practice/data and third-party sites such as Udemy to ensure that you get a better understanding of the types of questions you can expect. You have the option to buy the Exam Prep Bundle or eLearning Bundle from CompTIA (see https://www.comptia.org/certifications/data#buyoptions), as shown in Figure 18.1.

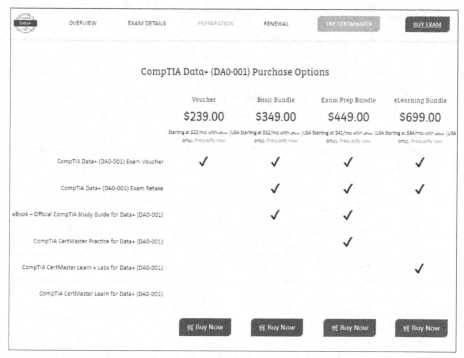

FIGURE 18.1   **CompTIA Data+ Exam Bundle Options**

Remember: It is very important that you *not schedule the exam until you are ready to take it*. It is a good idea to set a target date for taking the exam. However, before you actually schedule it, you should be confident that you can pass it. Keep in mind that CompTIA exams can be rescheduled or canceled as long as you give at least 24 hours' notice. However, it is recommended to check the time frame for rescheduling or canceling the exam when registering (see https://help.comptia.org/hc/en-us/ articles/115005195146-How-to-Reschedule-Your-Exam).

▶ **Registering for the exam:** You have an option to take the exam at a test center or take it online. It is your choice to pick one of these two proctored exam options. While you have to travel to take the exam at a test center, you can take the online exam at home or in an office. Schedule a time that works well for you, when you don't have to worry about anything else, such as work or family commitments. Evenings or weekends might be best, depending on your schedule. See the following links for more information:

  ▶ Scheduling your CompTIA exam: https://help.comptia.org/hc/en-us/ articles/115005195066-Scheduling-your-CompTIA-exam

▶ Pearson Vue CompTIA exam scheduling site:
https://home.pearsonvue.com/comptia/onvue

▶ Taking an exam online and what to expect:
https://www.comptia.org/testing/testing-options/take-online-exam

▶ **Relax and don't overstress the day before the exam:** Some people like
to study hard the day before, and others may relax by watching a movie or
going for a walk. The recommendation is to not overstress and to leverage the cheat sheet you created. Get a good night's sleep the night before
you take the exam to get your mind refreshed and ready for exam.

▶ **Get in early:** If you are driving to a test center, ensure that you leave
early enough to reach the center well before the start time to go through
the check-in process. If you are taking the exam online, log in 30 to
45 minutes prior to the exam time and test your PC with the testing
application. For both test center and online exams, you need to present
a photo ID, so ensure that you have your driver's license and/or passport
with you.

▶ **Exam questions and duration:** For the CompTIA Data+ exam, you
have to answer about 90 questions while staring at a screen for an hour
or more. The time allocated is typically 90 minutes, so that's about
a minute per question. (See https://www.comptia.org/certifications/
data#examdetails for updated information.) It's a good idea to take some
brief breaks from staring at the screen and to do some deep breathing to
refocus.

▶ **Acing your exam:** When you have done everything you need to do in
order to prep for the exam—studied hard, gone through the Cram Saver
and Cram Quiz questions, taken practice exams, created a cheat sheet—
you should have confidence and be able to ace the exam. Focus on each
question and think about how you would respond to it in a real-world
situation. For example, doing a fancy visualization for an executive makes
more sense than doing it for an IT manager; the IT manager needs more
detailed insights than the executive needs.

▶ **Use the process of elimination and use logical analysis:** If you are not
sure about an answer, first eliminate any answers that are definitely incorrect. You might be surprised how often this helps you get down to two
remaining answers. The most difficult questions are the ones where two
answers appear to be correct. Sometimes you need to slow down, think
logically, and compare the two possible correct answers. The more you

can visualize the scenario, the more easily you can figure out which of the two answers is the best one. When you have gone through all the other techniques mentioned, make an educated, logical guess. Try to imagine why the test would bring up this topic, as vague or as strange as it might appear. However, remember that the more you study, the less you will have to guess.

Beyond the CompTIA Data+ Certification

After you pass the CompTIA Data+ exam, it's time to really think about your technical future. Keeping your current technical skills sharp is important, and so is technical growth. Consider expanding your technical horizons by learning different technologies.

Getting more hands-on exposure to data-focused technologies that are commonly being adopted by organizations gives you a better chance to clear an interview and get the job you're after.

Practice installing, configuring, testing, securing, maintaining, and trouble-shooting databases and explore the various business intelligence (BI) tools. Tableau, for example, offers a free trial, as does Power BI.

Check out streaming video tech channels on the Internet. Attend technology events in person and online to enrich yourself and to network.

Remember that you are limited only by your desire. Whatever the field, learn as much as you can about that field and its vendors to stay ahead.

We wish you the best of luck on your CompTIA Data+ exam and in your IT career endeavors.

Sincerely,

Akhil Behl

Siva G. Subramanian

Index

Symbols

A

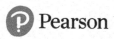

To receive your 10% off
Exam Voucher, register
your product at:

www.pearsonitcertification.com/register

and follow the instructions.